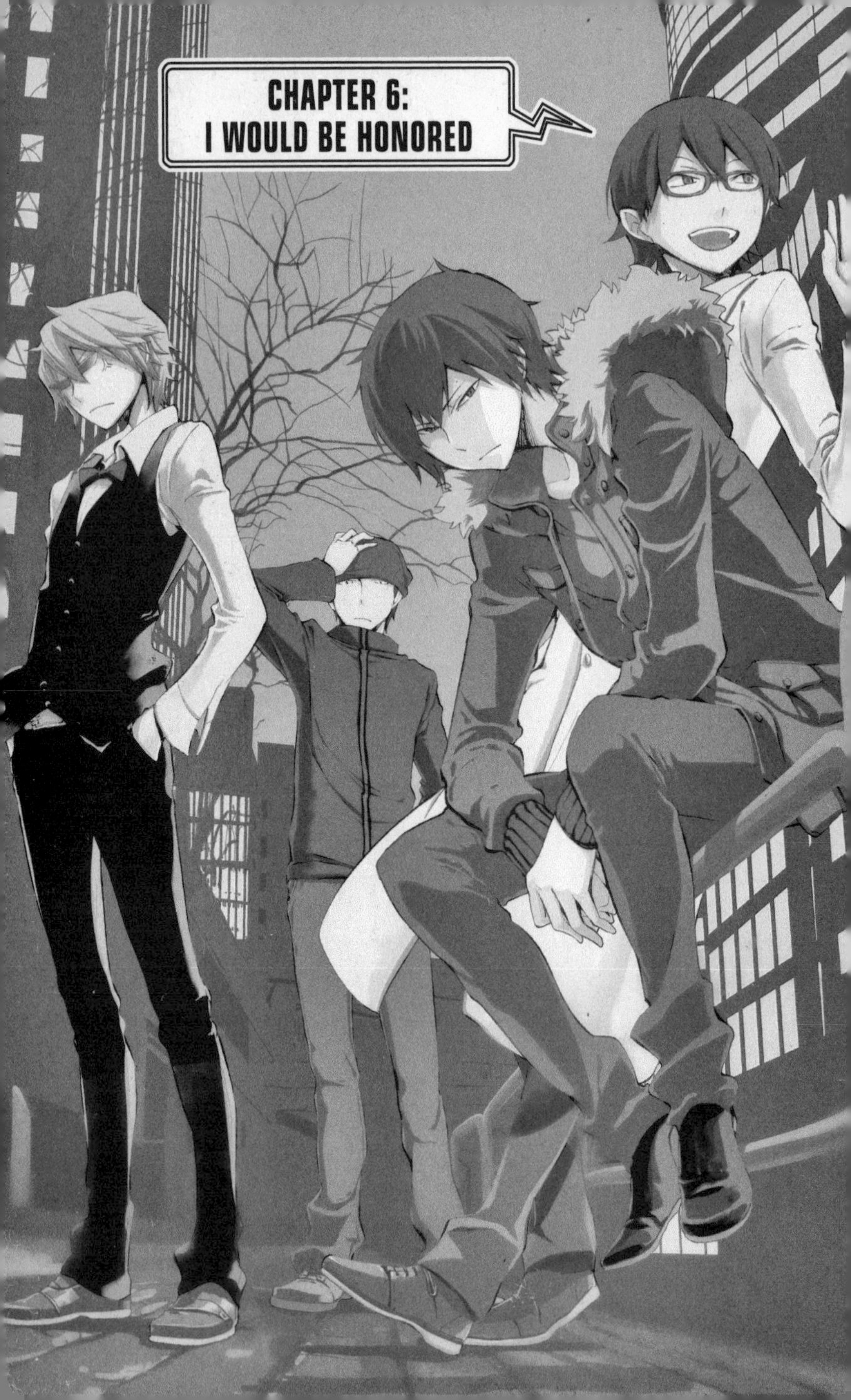
CHAPTER 6:
I WOULD BE HONORED

DRRR!!

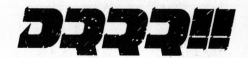

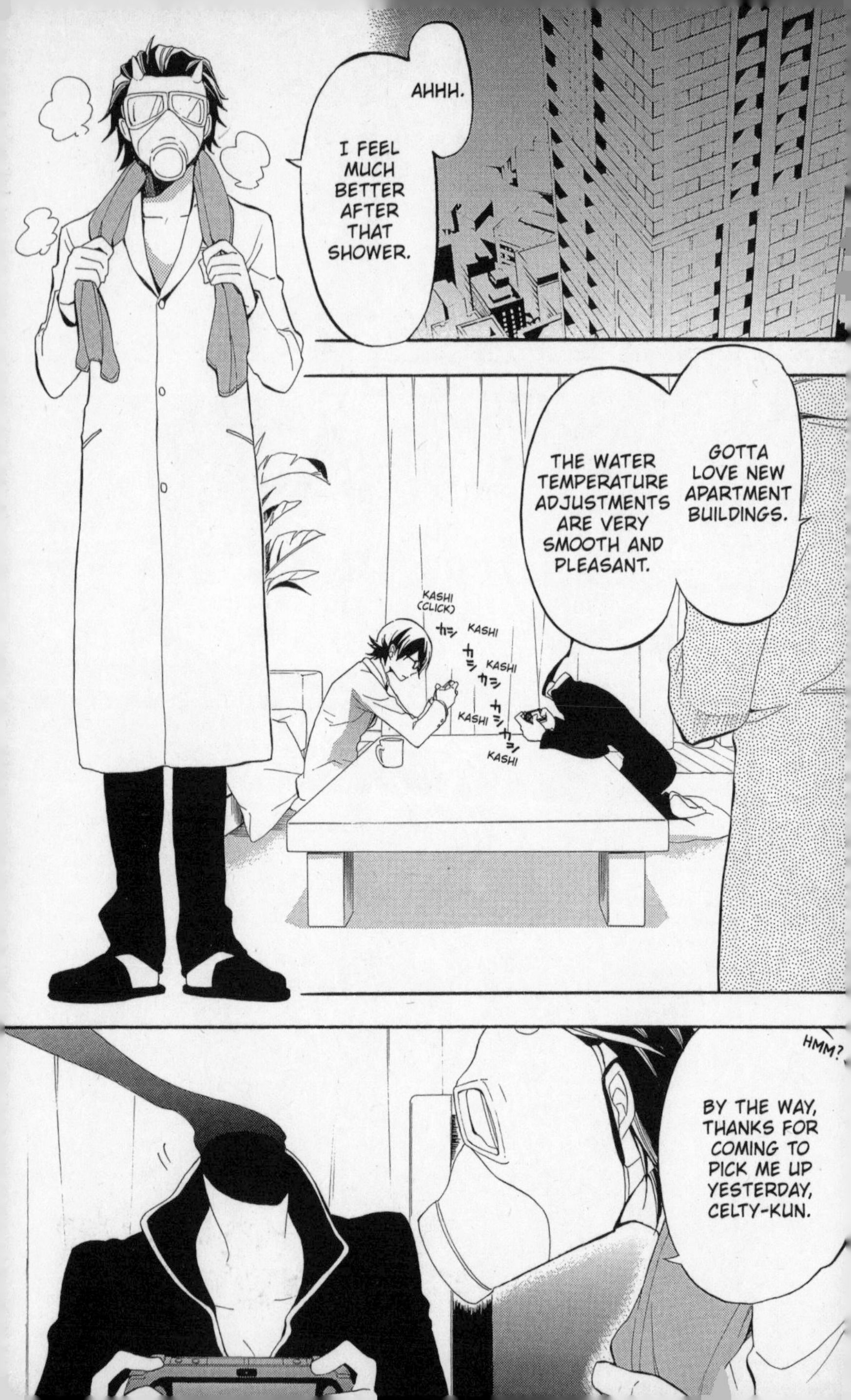
AHHH.
I FEEL MUCH BETTER AFTER THAT SHOWER.
GOTTA LOVE NEW APARTMENT BUILDINGS.
THE WATER TEMPERATURE ADJUSTMENTS ARE VERY SMOOTH AND PLEASANT.
KASHI (CLICK)
KASHI
KASHI
KASHI
KASHI
HMM?
BY THE WAY, THANKS FOR COMING TO PICK ME UP YESTERDAY, CELTY-KUN.

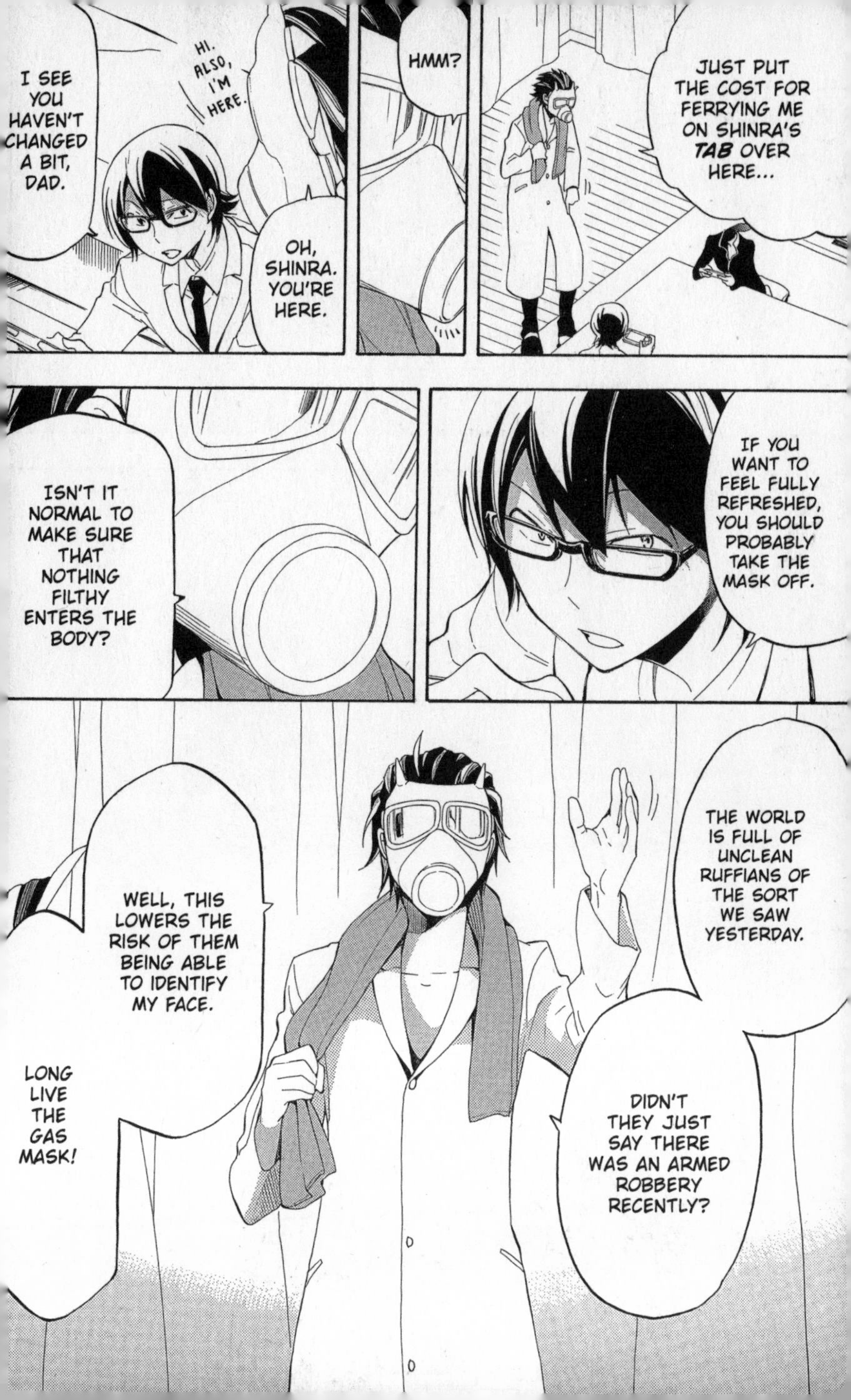
JUST PUT THE COST FOR FERRYING ME ON SHINRA'S *TAB* OVER HERE...
HMM?
OH, SHINRA. YOU'RE HERE.
HI. ALSO, I'M HERE.
I SEE YOU HAVEN'T CHANGED A BIT, DAD.
IF YOU WANT TO FEEL FULLY REFRESHED, YOU SHOULD PROBABLY TAKE THE MASK OFF.
ISN'T IT NORMAL TO MAKE SURE THAT NOTHING FILTHY ENTERS THE BODY?
THE WORLD IS FULL OF UNCLEAN RUFFIANS OF THE SORT WE SAW YESTERDAY.
WELL, THIS LOWERS THE RISK OF THEM BEING ABLE TO IDENTIFY MY FACE.
LONG LIVE THE GAS MASK!
DIDN'T THEY JUST SAY THERE WAS AN ARMED ROBBERY RECENTLY?

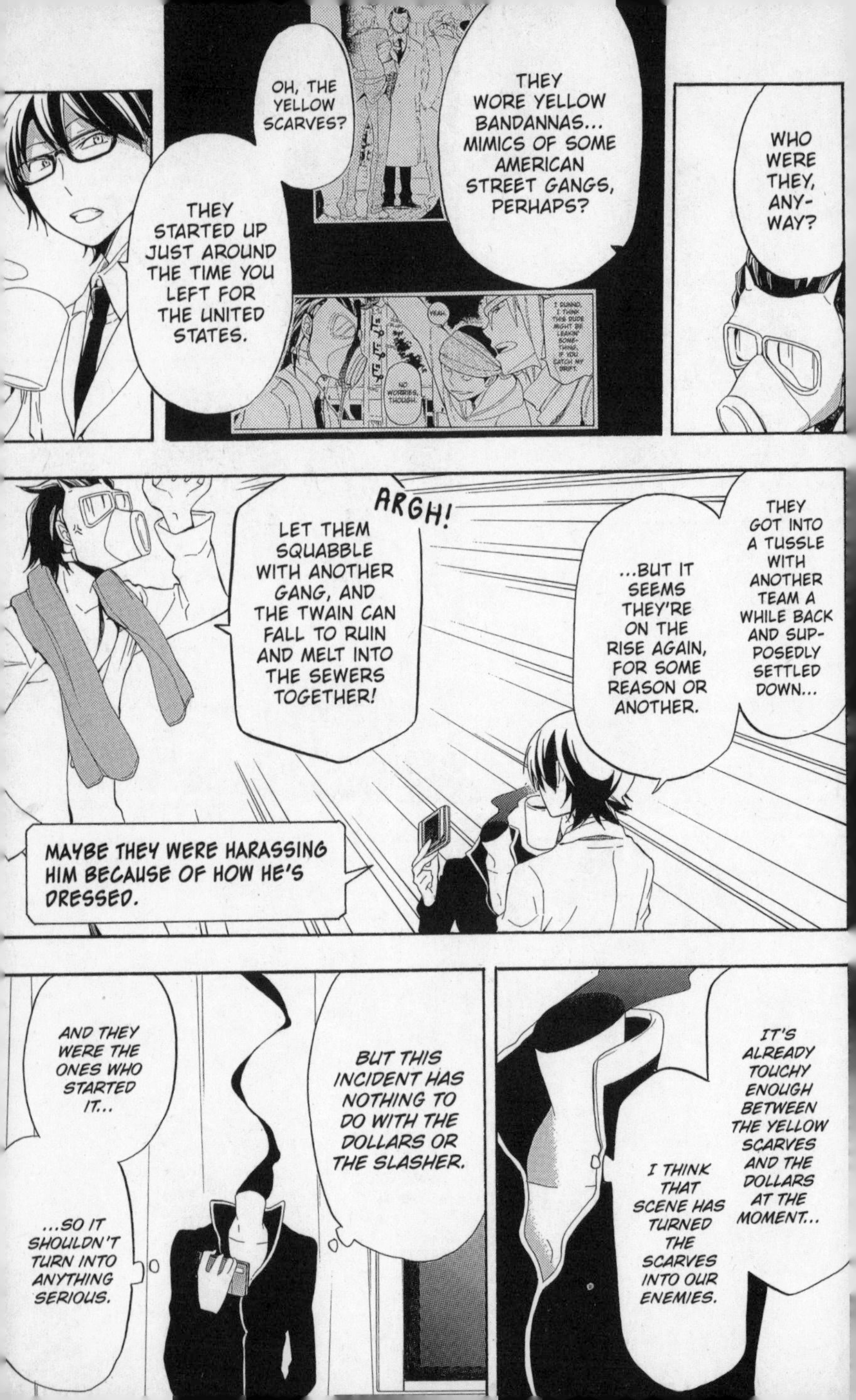
WHO WERE THEY, ANYWAY?
THEY WORE YELLOW BANDANNAS... MIMICS OF SOME AMERICAN STREET GANGS, PERHAPS?
OH, THE YELLOW SCARVES?
I DUNNO. I THINK THIS DUDE MIGHT BE LEAKIN' SOMETHING, IF YOU CATCH MY DRIFT.
YEAH.
NO WORRIES, THOUGH.
THEY STARTED UP JUST AROUND THE TIME YOU LEFT FOR THE UNITED STATES.
THEY GOT INTO A TUSSLE WITH ANOTHER TEAM A WHILE BACK AND SUPPOSEDLY SETTLED DOWN...
...BUT IT SEEMS THEY'RE ON THE RISE AGAIN, FOR SOME REASON OR ANOTHER.
ARGH!
LET THEM SQUABBLE WITH ANOTHER GANG, AND THE TWAIN CAN FALL TO RUIN AND MELT INTO THE SEWERS TOGETHER!
MAYBE THEY WERE HARASSING HIM BECAUSE OF HOW HE'S DRESSED.
IT'S ALREADY TOUCHY ENOUGH BETWEEN THE YELLOW SCARVES AND THE DOLLARS AT THE MOMENT...
I THINK THAT SCENE HAS TURNED THE SCARVES INTO OUR ENEMIES.
BUT THIS INCIDENT HAS NOTHING TO DO WITH THE DOLLARS OR THE SLASHER.
AND THEY WERE THE ONES WHO STARTED IT...
...SO IT SHOULDN'T TURN INTO ANYTHING SERIOUS.

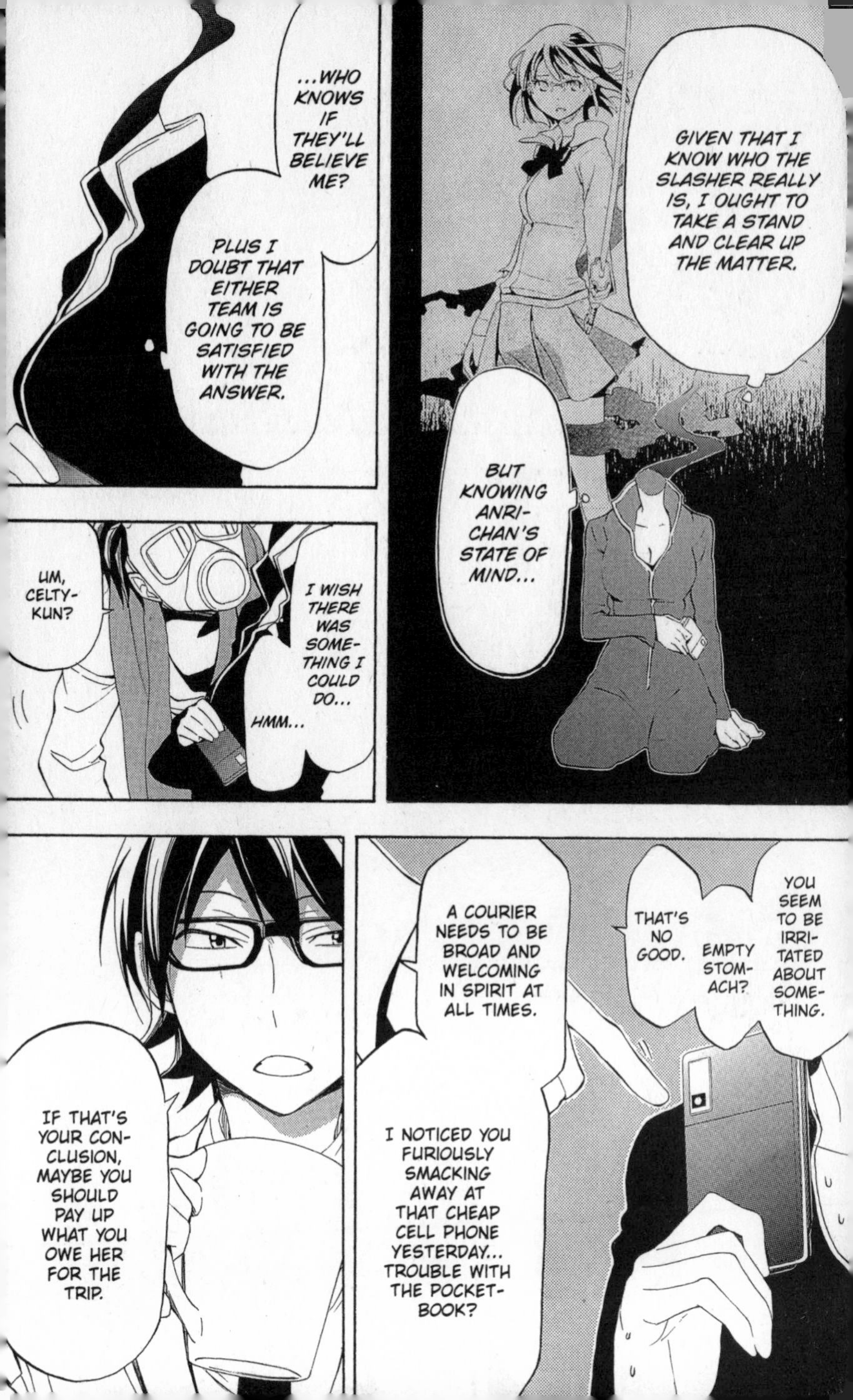
GIVEN THAT I KNOW WHO THE SLASHER REALLY IS, I OUGHT TO TAKE A STAND AND CLEAR UP THE MATTER.
BUT KNOWING ANRI-CHAN'S STATE OF MIND...
...WHO KNOWS IF THEY'LL BELIEVE ME?
PLUS I DOUBT THAT EITHER TEAM IS GOING TO BE SATISFIED WITH THE ANSWER.
I WISH THERE WAS SOMETHING I COULD DO...
HMM...
UM, CELTY-KUN?
YOU SEEM TO BE IRRITATED ABOUT SOMETHING.
EMPTY STOMACH?
THAT'S NO GOOD.
A COURIER NEEDS TO BE BROAD AND WELCOMING IN SPIRIT AT ALL TIMES.
I NOTICED YOU FURIOUSLY SMACKING AWAY AT THAT CHEAP CELL PHONE YESTERDAY... TROUBLE WITH THE POCKETBOOK?
IF THAT'S YOUR CONCLUSION, MAYBE YOU SHOULD PAY UP WHAT YOU OWE HER FOR THE TRIP.

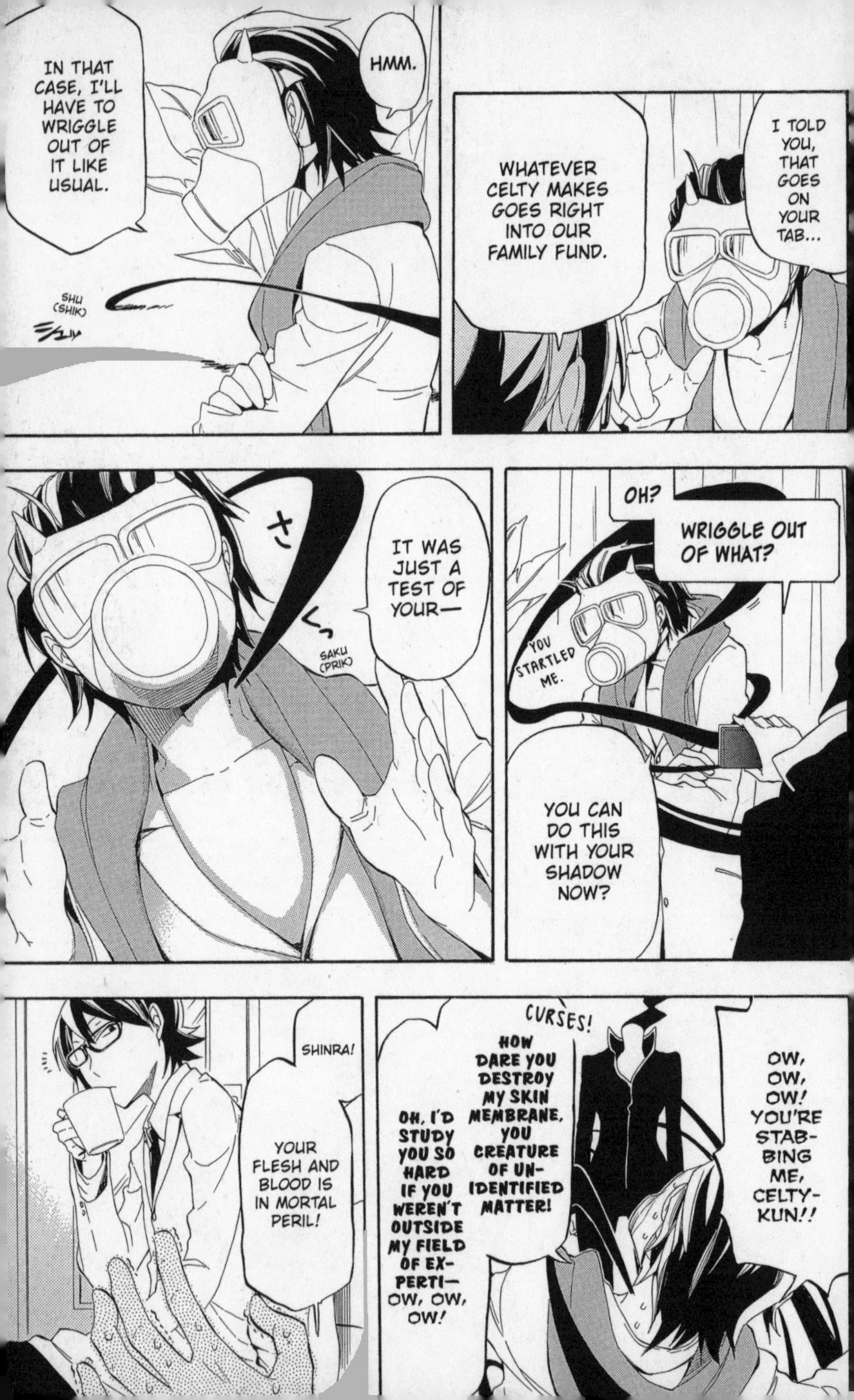
I TOLD YOU, THAT GOES ON YOUR TAB...
WHATEVER CELTY MAKES GOES RIGHT INTO OUR FAMILY FUND.
HMM.
IN THAT CASE, I'LL HAVE TO WRIGGLE OUT OF IT LIKE USUAL.
SHU (SHIK)
OH?
WRIGGLE OUT OF WHAT?
YOU STARTLED ME.
YOU CAN DO THIS WITH YOUR SHADOW NOW?
IT WAS JUST A TEST OF YOUR—
SAKU (PRIK)
OW, OW, OW! YOU'RE STAB-BING ME, CELTY-KUN!!
CURSES!
HOW DARE YOU DESTROY MY SKIN MEMBRANE, YOU CREATURE OF UN-IDENTIFIED MATTER!
OH, I'D STUDY YOU SO HARD IF YOU WEREN'T OUTSIDE MY FIELD OF EX-PERTI— OW, OW, OW!
SHINRA!
YOUR FLESH AND BLOOD IS IN MORTAL PERIL!

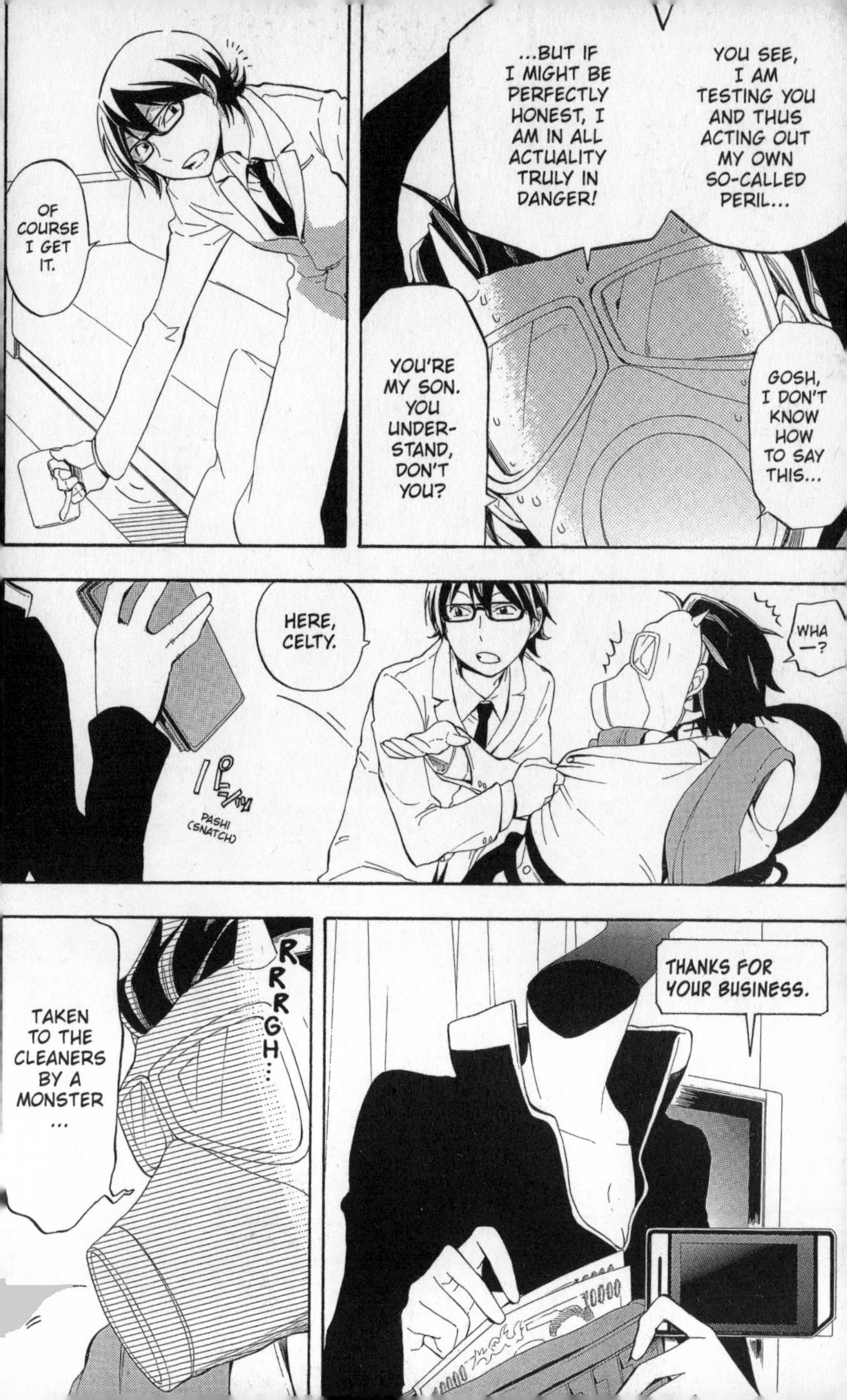
YOU SEE, I AM TESTING YOU AND THUS ACTING OUT MY OWN SO-CALLED PERIL...
...BUT IF I MIGHT BE PERFECTLY HONEST, I AM IN ALL ACTUALITY TRULY IN DANGER!
GOSH, I DON'T KNOW HOW TO SAY THIS...
YOU'RE MY SON. YOU UNDER-STAND, DON'T YOU?
OF COURSE I GET IT.
WHA—?
HERE, CELTY.
PASHI (SNATCH)
THANKS FOR YOUR BUSINESS.
RRRGH...
TAKEN TO THE CLEANERS BY A MONSTER...

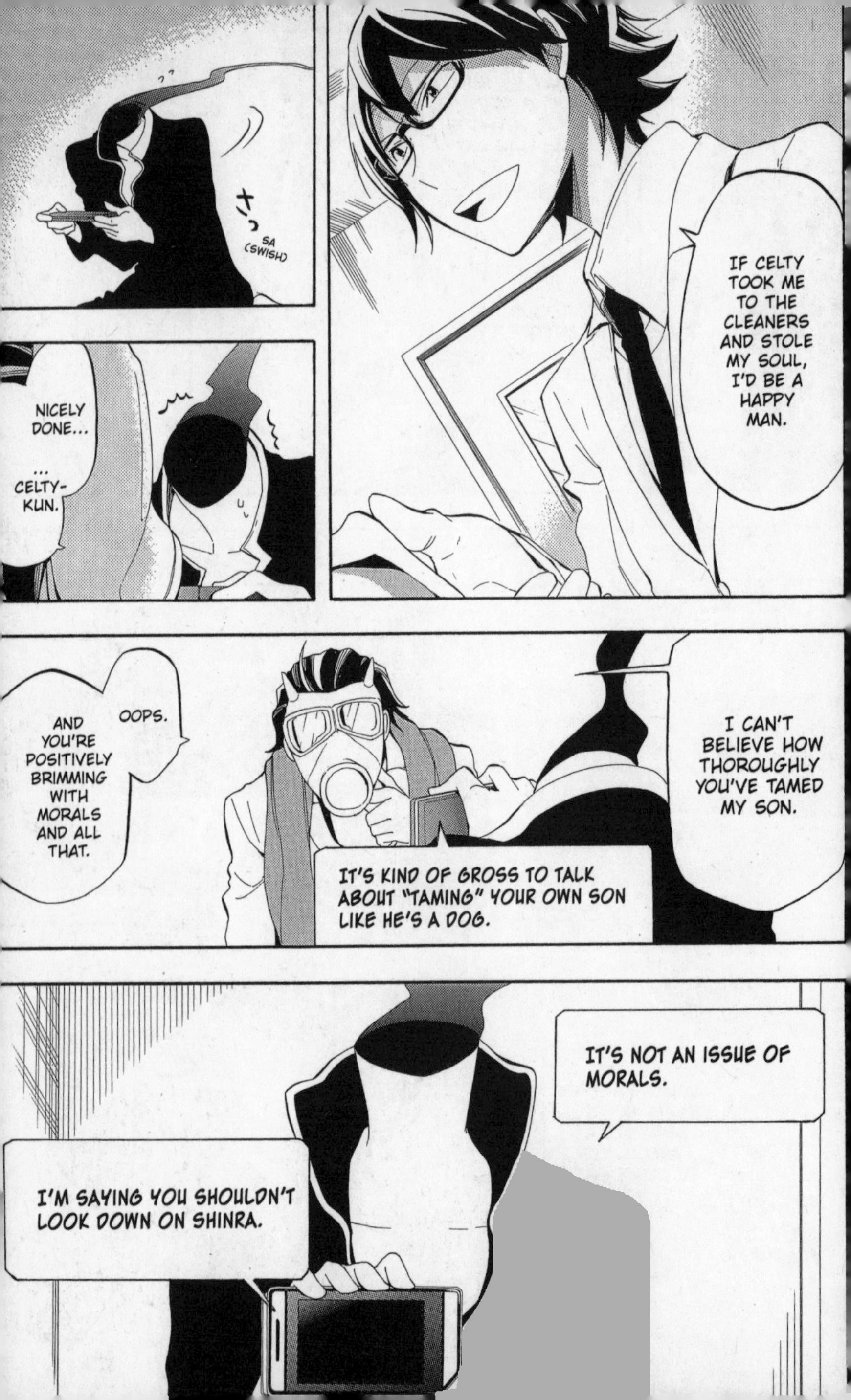

IF CELTY TOOK ME TO THE CLEANERS AND STOLE MY SOUL, I'D BE A HAPPY MAN.
さっ
SA (SWISH)
NICELY DONE... ... CELTY-KUN.
I CAN'T BELIEVE HOW THOROUGHLY YOU'VE TAMED MY SON.
IT'S KIND OF GROSS TO TALK ABOUT "TAMING" YOUR OWN SON LIKE HE'S A DOG.
OOPS.
AND YOU'RE POSITIVELY BRIMMING WITH MORALS AND ALL THAT.
IT'S NOT AN ISSUE OF MORALS.
I'M SAYING YOU SHOULDN'T LOOK DOWN ON SHINRA.

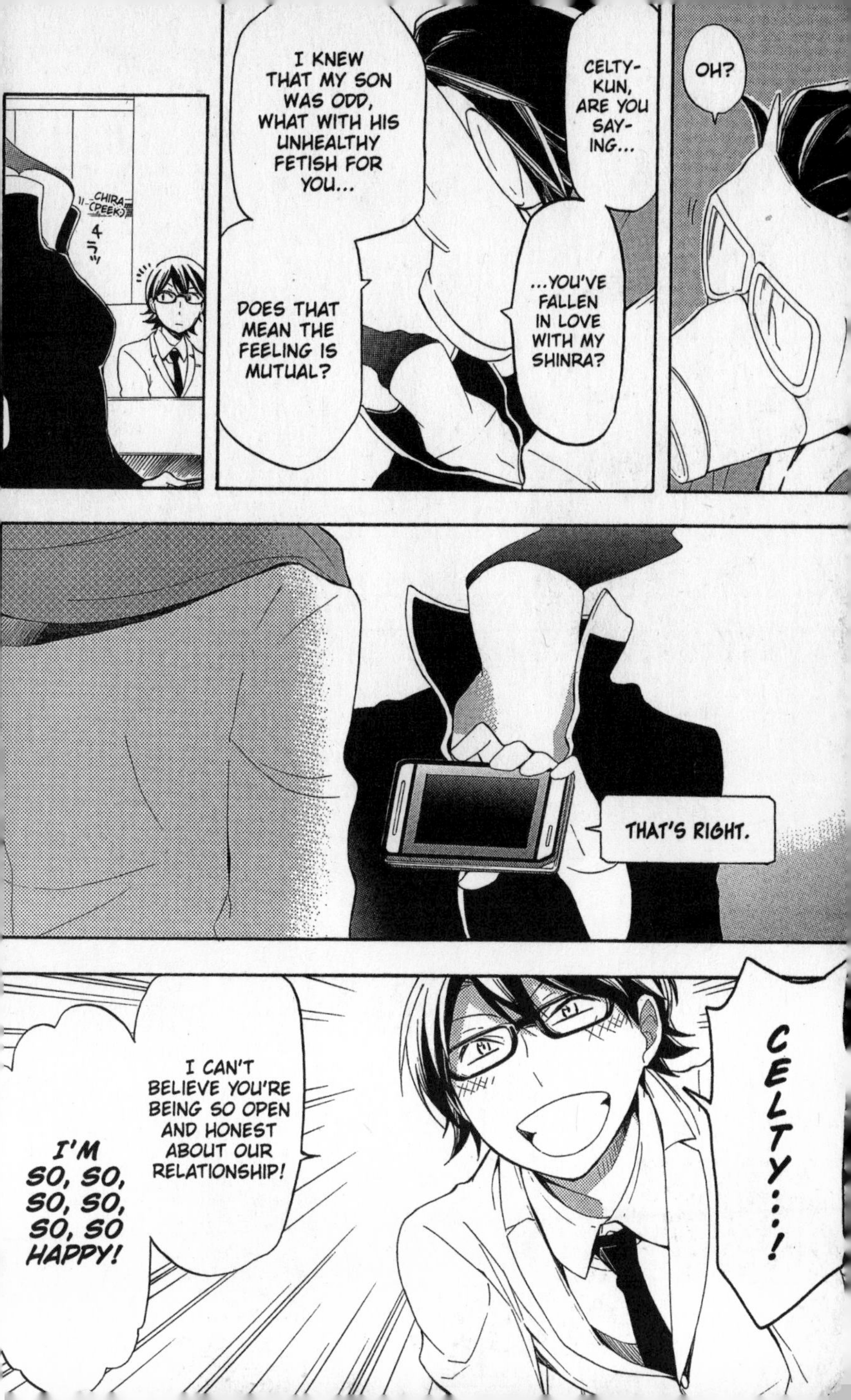
OH?
CELTY-KUN, ARE YOU SAYING...
...YOU'VE FALLEN IN LOVE WITH MY SHINRA?
I KNEW THAT MY SON WAS ODD, WHAT WITH HIS UNHEALTHY FETISH FOR YOU...
DOES THAT MEAN THE FEELING IS MUTUAL?
CHIRA (PEEK)
THAT'S RIGHT.
CELTY...!
I CAN'T BELIEVE YOU'RE BEING SO OPEN AND HONEST ABOUT OUR RELATIONSHIP!
I'M SO, SO, SO, SO, SO, SO HAPPY!

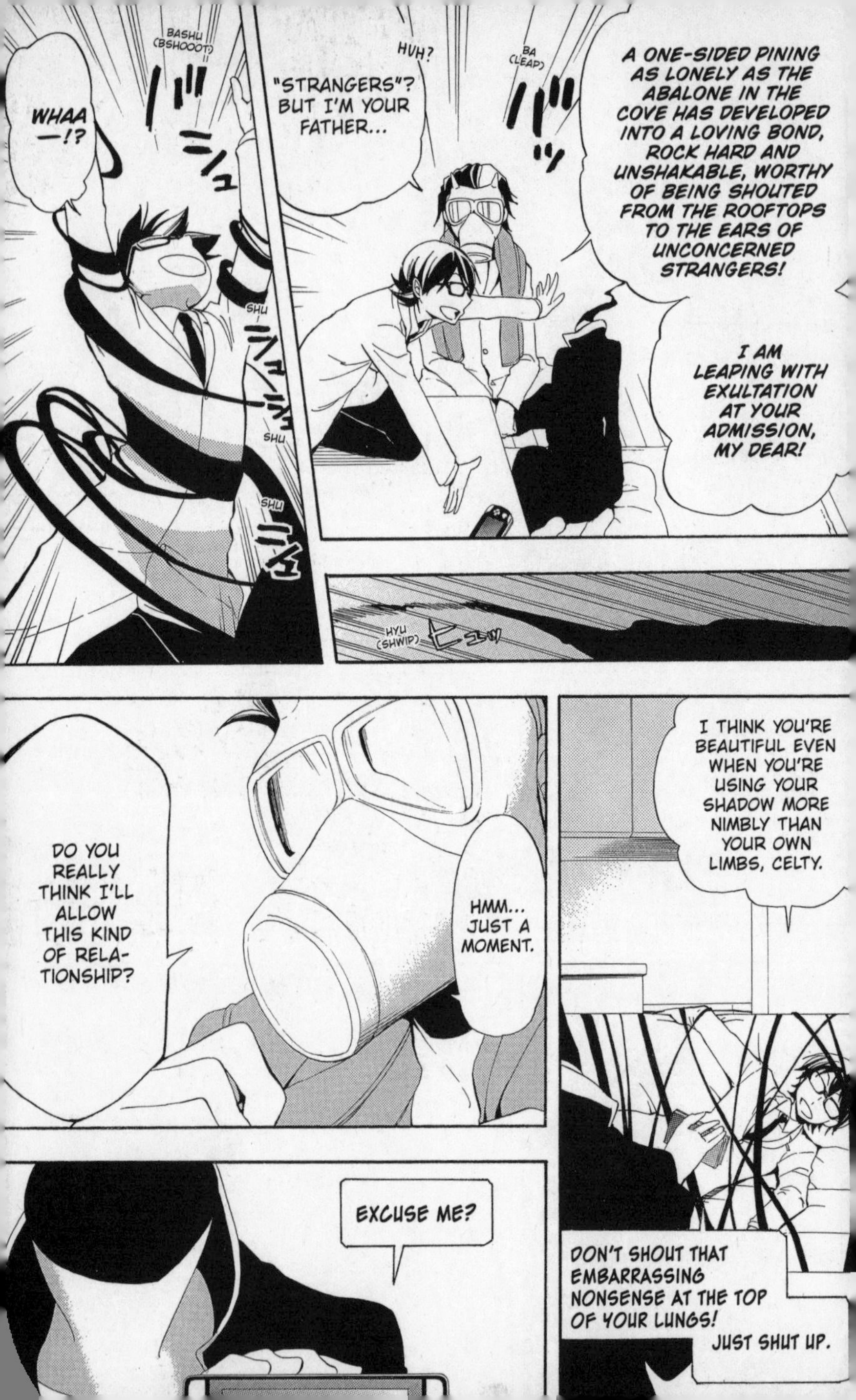
BA (LEAP)
A ONE-SIDED PINING AS LONELY AS THE ABALONE IN THE COVE HAS DEVELOPED INTO A LOVING BOND, ROCK HARD AND UNSHAKABLE, WORTHY OF BEING SHOUTED FROM THE ROOFTOPS TO THE EARS OF UNCONCERNED STRANGERS!
I AM LEAPING WITH EXULTATION AT YOUR ADMISSION, MY DEAR!
HUH?
"STRANGERS"? BUT I'M YOUR FATHER...
BASHU (BSHOOOT)
WHAA—!?
SHU
SHU
SHU
HYU (SHWIP)
I THINK YOU'RE BEAUTIFUL EVEN WHEN YOU'RE USING YOUR SHADOW MORE NIMBLY THAN YOUR OWN LIMBS, CELTY.
HMM... JUST A MOMENT.
DO YOU REALLY THINK I'LL ALLOW THIS KIND OF RELA-TIONSHIP?
DON'T SHOUT THAT EMBARRASSING NONSENSE AT THE TOP OF YOUR LUNGS!
JUST SHUT UP.
EXCUSE ME?

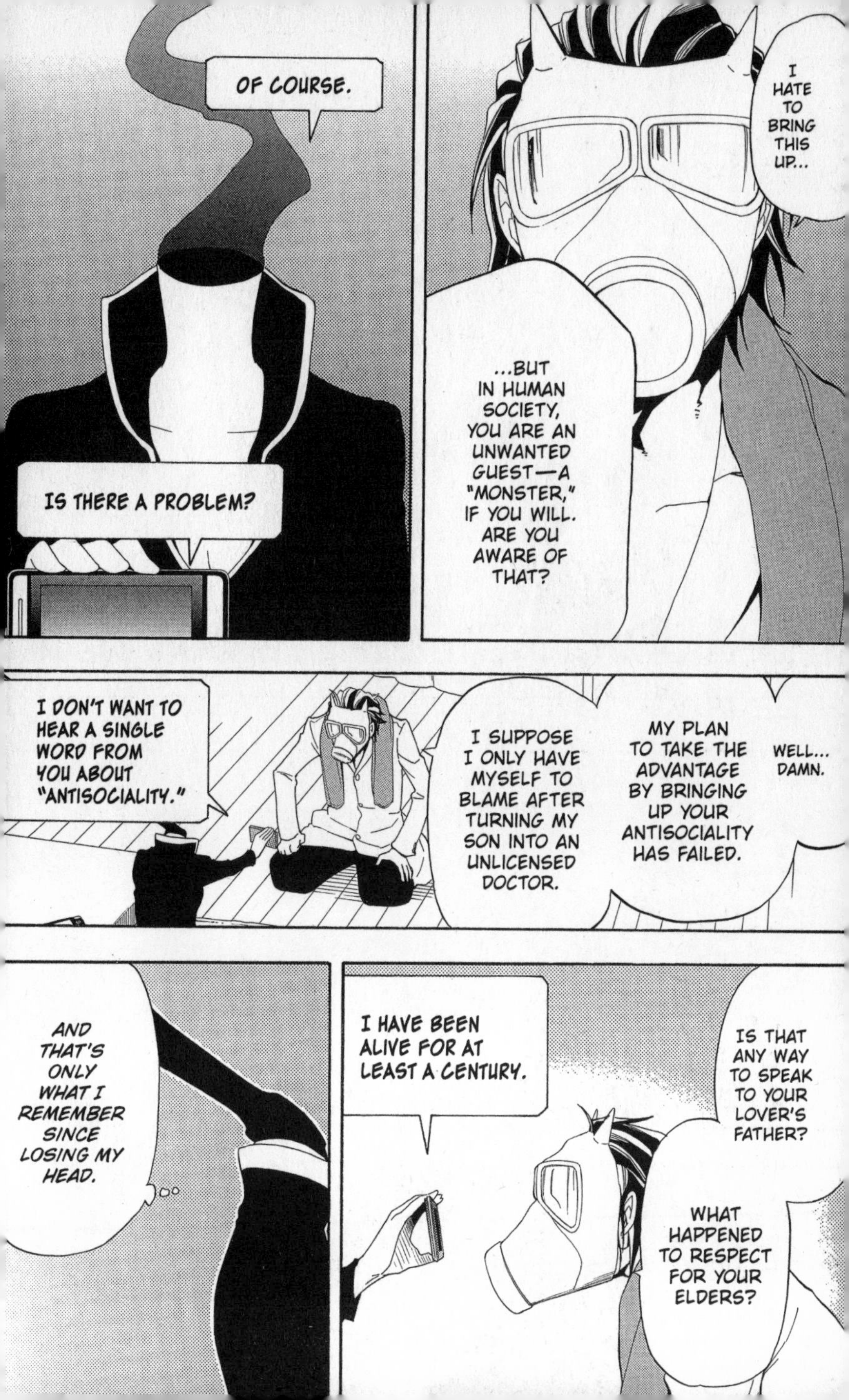
I HATE TO BRING THIS UP...
...BUT IN HUMAN SOCIETY, YOU ARE AN UNWANTED GUEST—A "MONSTER," IF YOU WILL. ARE YOU AWARE OF THAT?
OF COURSE.
IS THERE A PROBLEM?
WELL... DAMN.
MY PLAN TO TAKE THE ADVANTAGE BY BRINGING UP YOUR ANTISOCIALITY HAS FAILED.
I SUPPOSE I ONLY HAVE MYSELF TO BLAME AFTER TURNING MY SON INTO AN UNLICENSED DOCTOR.
I DON'T WANT TO HEAR A SINGLE WORD FROM YOU ABOUT "ANTISOCIALITY."
IS THAT ANY WAY TO SPEAK TO YOUR LOVER'S FATHER?
WHAT HAPPENED TO RESPECT FOR YOUR ELDERS?
I HAVE BEEN ALIVE FOR AT LEAST A CENTURY.
AND THAT'S ONLY WHAT I REMEMBER SINCE LOSING MY HEAD.

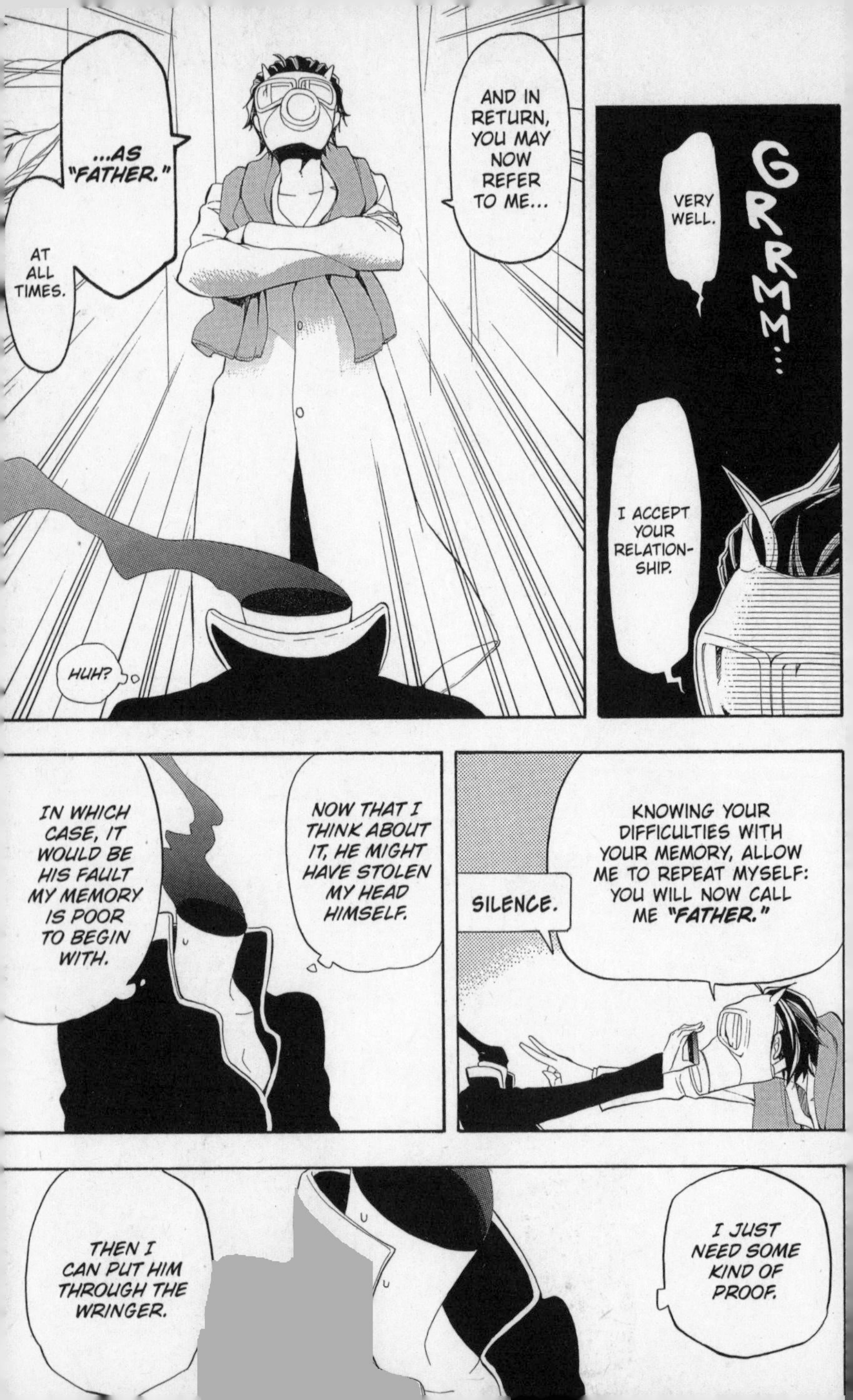
GRRMM...
VERY WELL.
I ACCEPT YOUR RELATIONSHIP.
AND IN RETURN, YOU MAY NOW REFER TO ME...
...AS "FATHER."
AT ALL TIMES.
HUH?
KNOWING YOUR DIFFICULTIES WITH YOUR MEMORY, ALLOW ME TO REPEAT MYSELF: YOU WILL NOW CALL ME "FATHER."
SILENCE.
NOW THAT I THINK ABOUT IT, HE MIGHT HAVE STOLEN MY HEAD HIMSELF.
IN WHICH CASE, IT WOULD BE HIS FAULT MY MEMORY IS POOR TO BEGIN WITH.
I JUST NEED SOME KIND OF PROOF.
THEN I CAN PUT HIM THROUGH THE WRINGER.

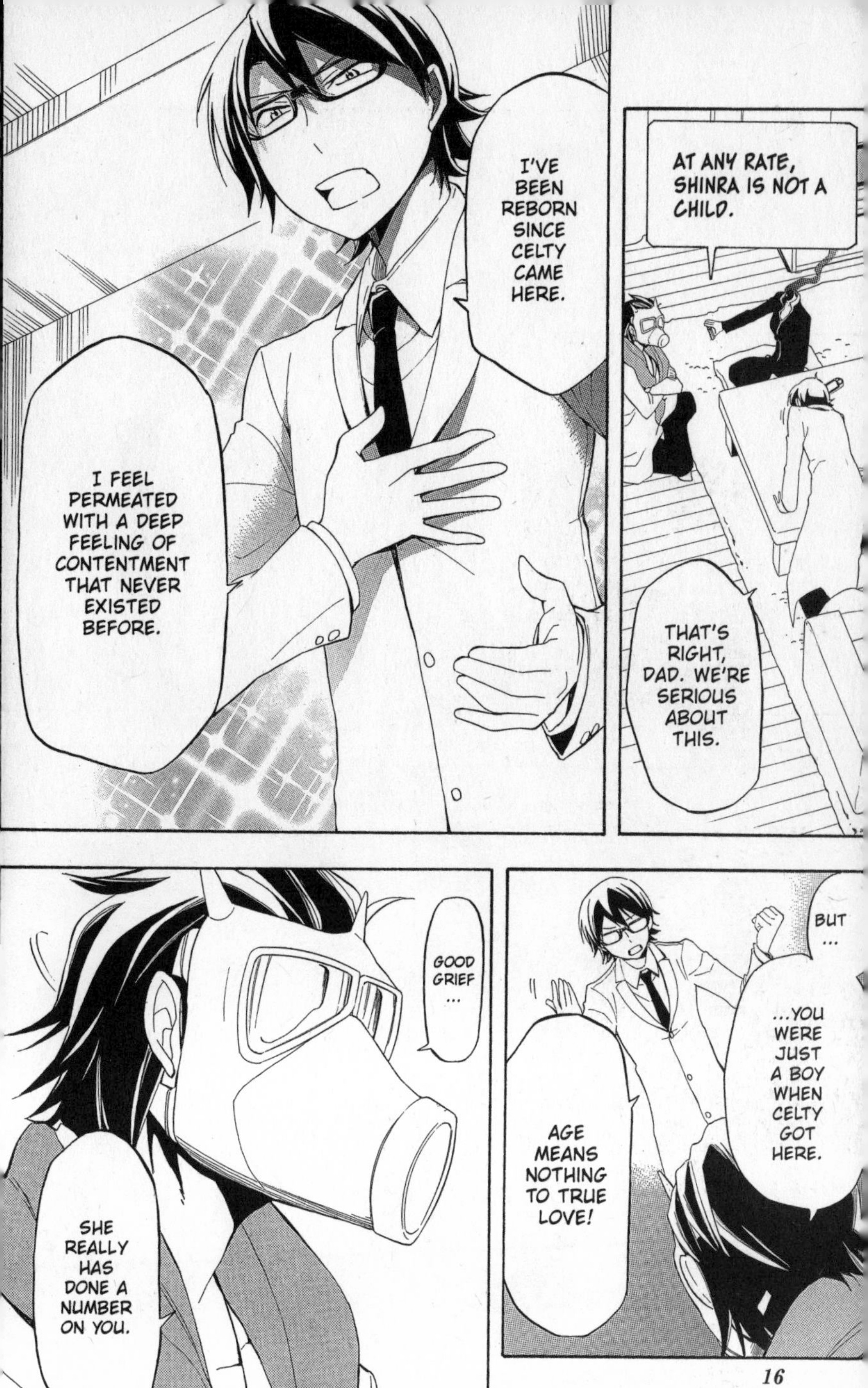
AT ANY RATE, SHINRA IS NOT A CHILD.
THAT'S RIGHT, DAD. WE'RE SERIOUS ABOUT THIS.
I'VE BEEN REBORN SINCE CELTY CAME HERE.
I FEEL PERMEATED WITH A DEEP FEELING OF CONTENTMENT THAT NEVER EXISTED BEFORE.
BUT...
...YOU WERE JUST A BOY WHEN CELTY GOT HERE.
AGE MEANS NOTHING TO TRUE LOVE!
GOOD GRIEF...
SHE REALLY HAS DONE A NUMBER ON YOU.

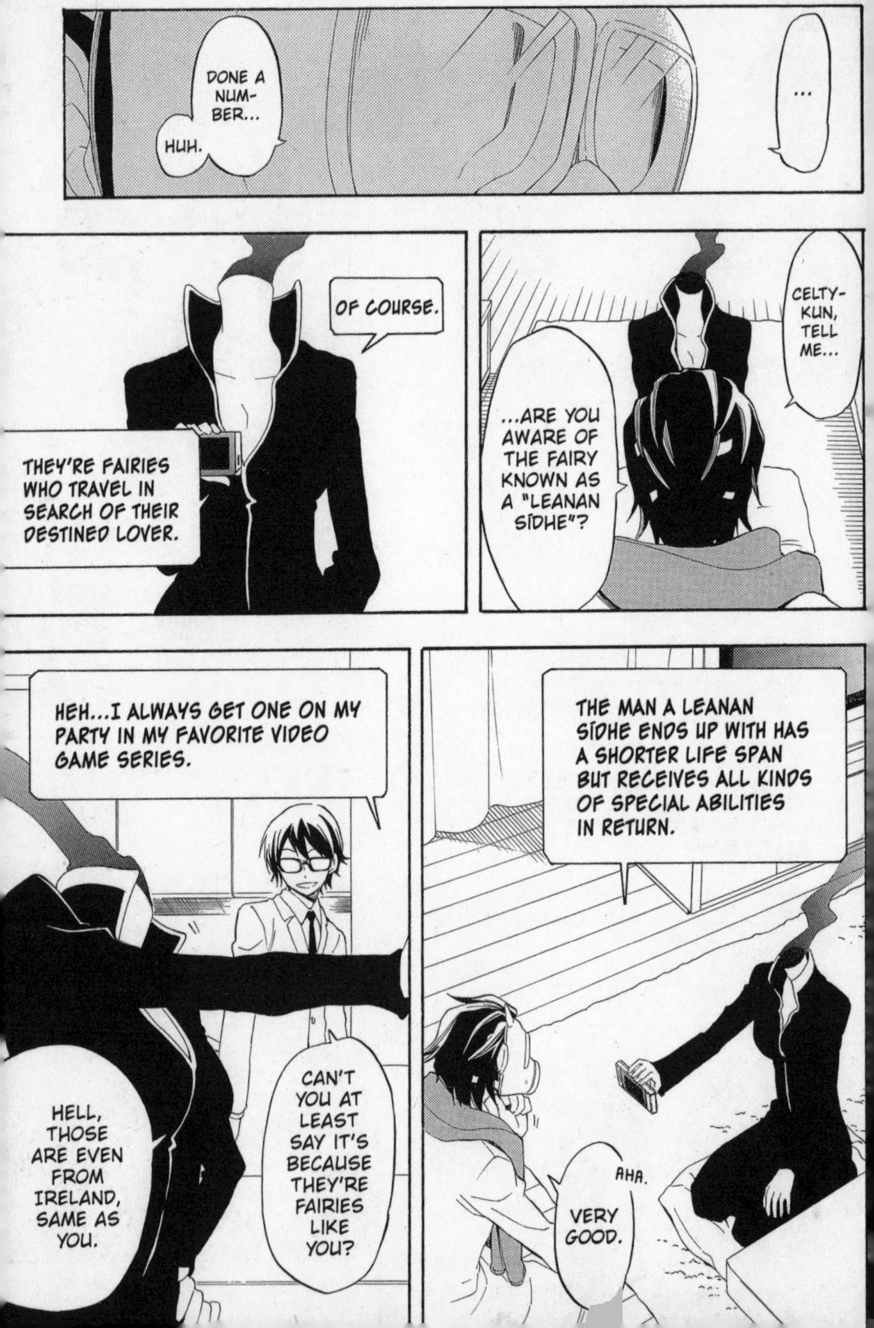
...
DONE A NUMBER... HUH.
CELTY-KUN, TELL ME...
...ARE YOU AWARE OF THE FAIRY KNOWN AS A "LEANAN SÍDHE"?
OF COURSE.
THEY'RE FAIRIES WHO TRAVEL IN SEARCH OF THEIR DESTINED LOVER.
THE MAN A LEANAN SÍDHE ENDS UP WITH HAS A SHORTER LIFE SPAN BUT RECEIVES ALL KINDS OF SPECIAL ABILITIES IN RETURN.
AHA.
VERY GOOD.
HEH...I ALWAYS GET ONE ON MY PARTY IN MY FAVORITE VIDEO GAME SERIES.
CAN'T YOU AT LEAST SAY IT'S BECAUSE THEY'RE FAIRIES LIKE YOU?
HELL, THOSE ARE EVEN FROM IRELAND, SAME AS YOU.

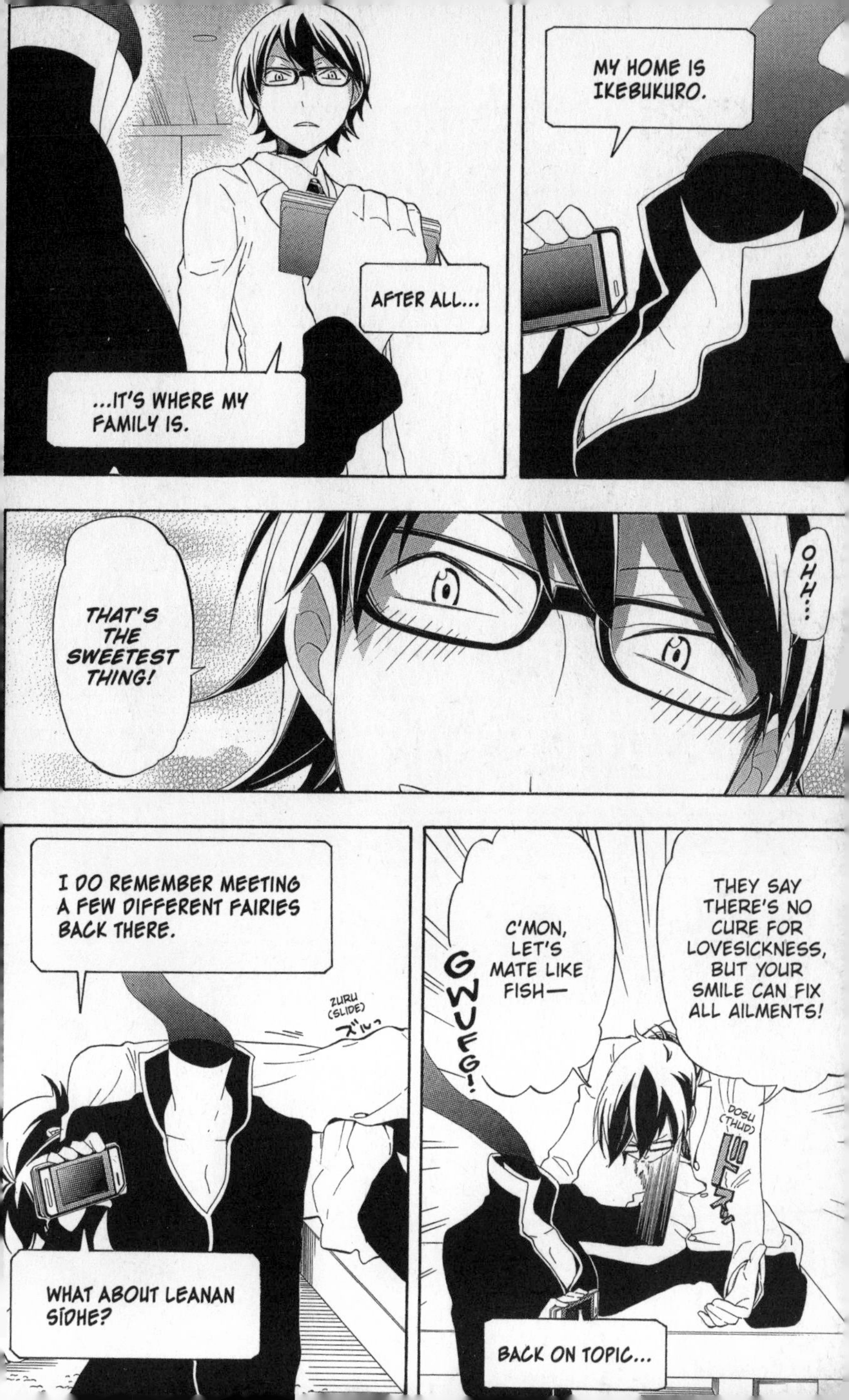
MY HOME IS IKEBUKURO.
AFTER ALL...
...IT'S WHERE MY FAMILY IS.
OHH...
THAT'S THE SWEETEST THING!
THEY SAY THERE'S NO CURE FOR LOVESICKNESS, BUT YOUR SMILE CAN FIX ALL AILMENTS!
C'MON, LET'S MATE LIKE FISH—
GWUFG!
DOSU (THUD)
BACK ON TOPIC...
I DO REMEMBER MEETING A FEW DIFFERENT FAIRIES BACK THERE.
ZURU (SLIDE)
WHAT ABOUT LEANAN SIDHE?

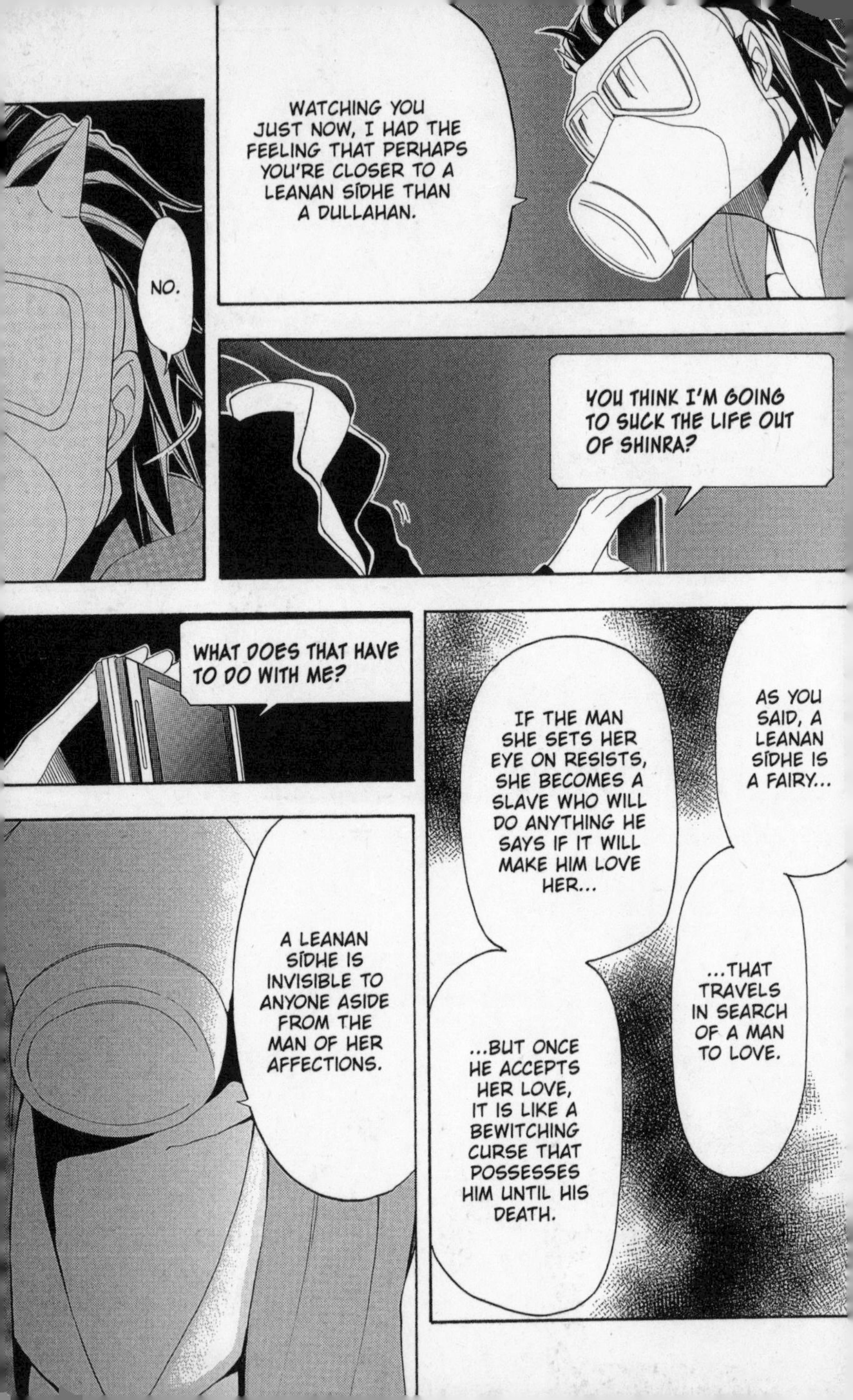
WATCHING YOU JUST NOW, I HAD THE FEELING THAT PERHAPS YOU'RE CLOSER TO A LEANAN SÍDHE THAN A DULLAHAN.
YOU THINK I'M GOING TO SUCK THE LIFE OUT OF SHINRA?
NO.
AS YOU SAID, A LEANAN SÍDHE IS A FAIRY...
...THAT TRAVELS IN SEARCH OF A MAN TO LOVE.
IF THE MAN SHE SETS HER EYE ON RESISTS, SHE BECOMES A SLAVE WHO WILL DO ANYTHING HE SAYS IF IT WILL MAKE HIM LOVE HER...
...BUT ONCE HE ACCEPTS HER LOVE, IT IS LIKE A BEWITCHING CURSE THAT POSSESSES HIM UNTIL HIS DEATH.
WHAT DOES THAT HAVE TO DO WITH ME?
A LEANAN SÍDHE IS INVISIBLE TO ANYONE ASIDE FROM THE MAN OF HER AFFECTIONS.

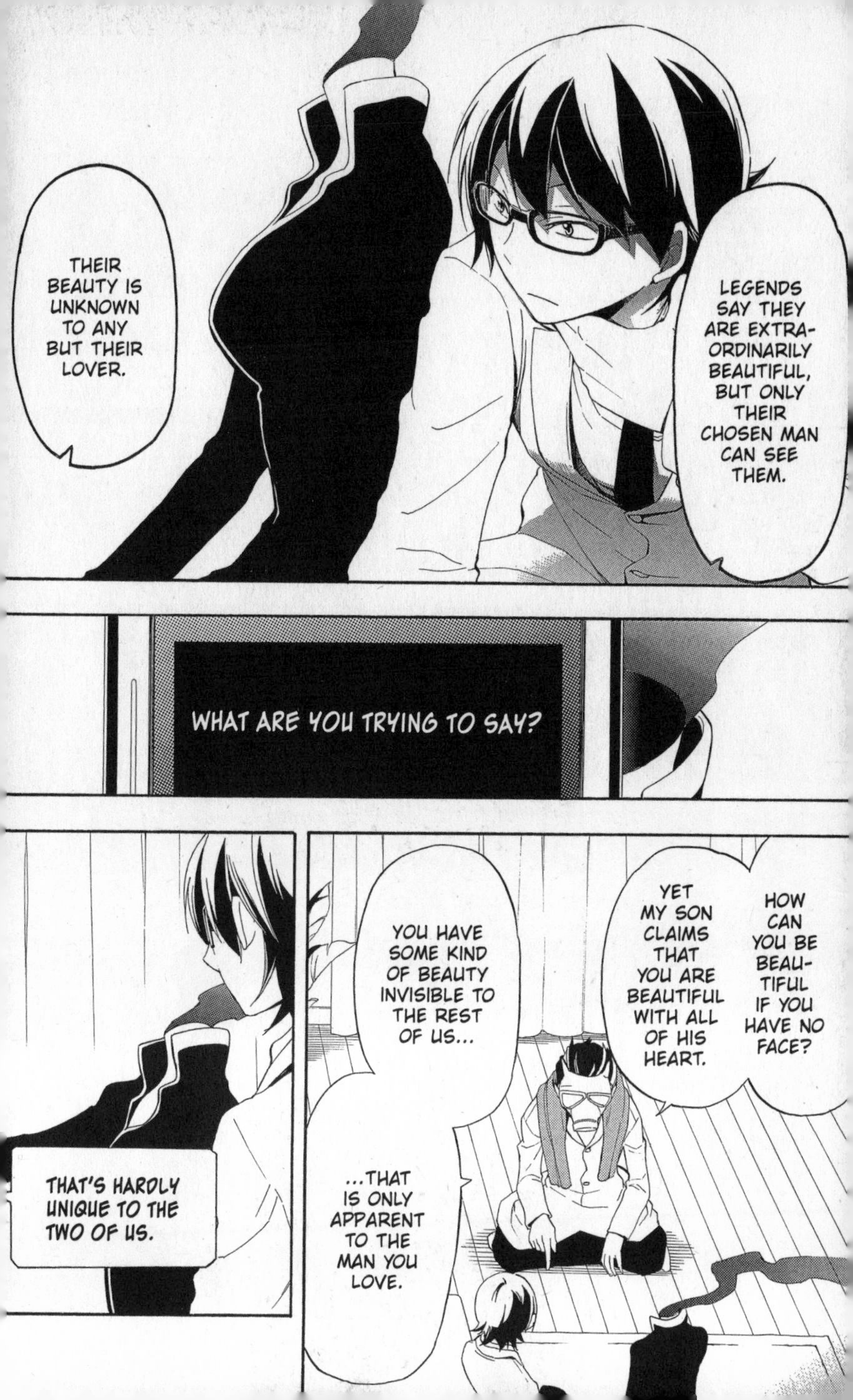
LEGENDS SAY THEY ARE EXTRA-ORDINARILY BEAUTIFUL, BUT ONLY THEIR CHOSEN MAN CAN SEE THEM.
THEIR BEAUTY IS UNKNOWN TO ANY BUT THEIR LOVER.
WHAT ARE YOU TRYING TO SAY?
HOW CAN YOU BE BEAU-TIFUL IF YOU HAVE NO FACE?
YET MY SON CLAIMS THAT YOU ARE BEAUTIFUL WITH ALL OF HIS HEART.
YOU HAVE SOME KIND OF BEAUTY INVISIBLE TO THE REST OF US...
...THAT IS ONLY APPARENT TO THE MAN YOU LOVE.
THAT'S HARDLY UNIQUE TO THE TWO OF US.

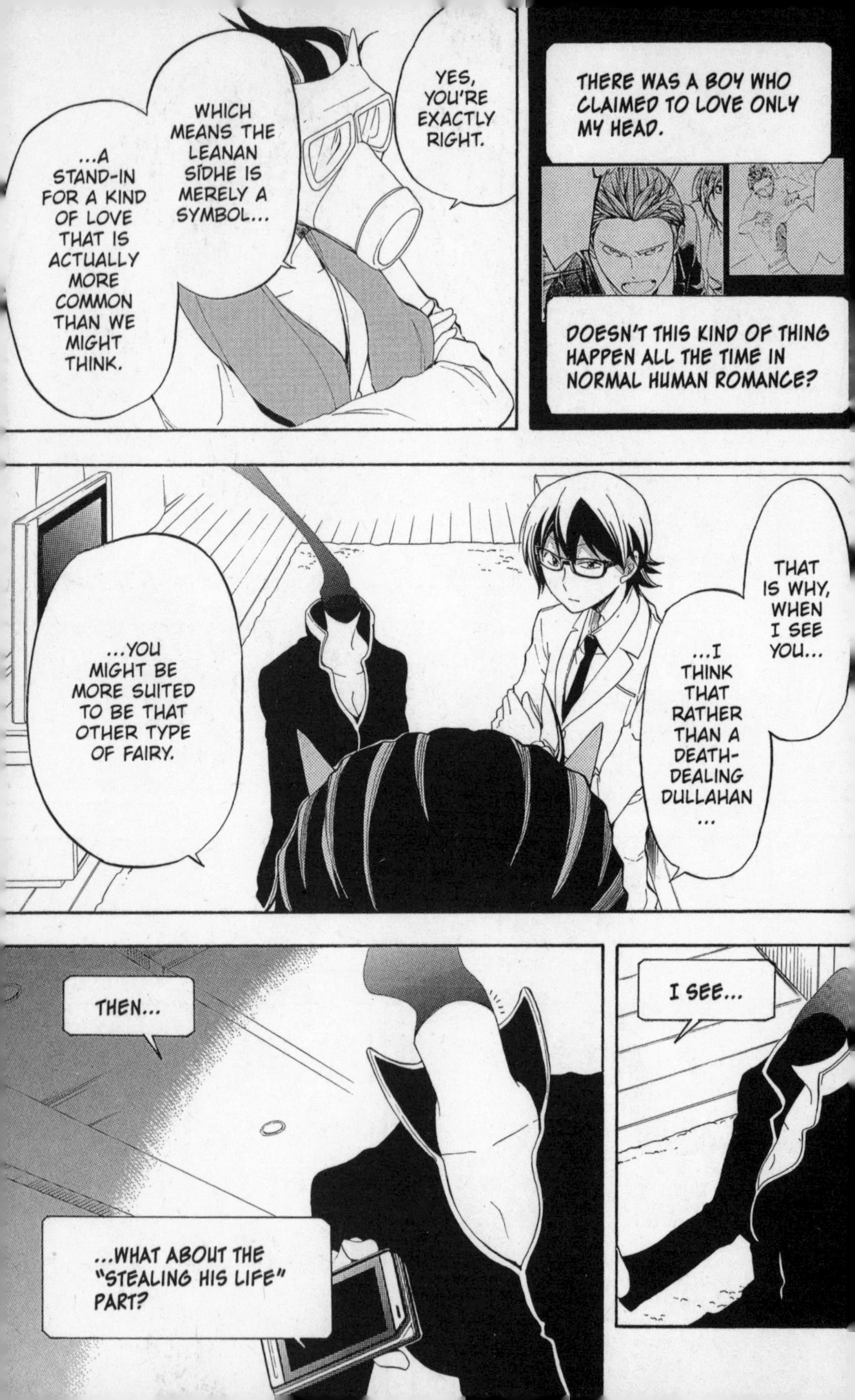
THERE WAS A BOY WHO CLAIMED TO LOVE ONLY MY HEAD.
DOESN'T THIS KIND OF THING HAPPEN ALL THE TIME IN NORMAL HUMAN ROMANCE?
YES, YOU'RE EXACTLY RIGHT.
WHICH MEANS THE LEANAN SÍDHE IS MERELY A SYMBOL...
...A STAND-IN FOR A KIND OF LOVE THAT IS ACTUALLY MORE COMMON THAN WE MIGHT THINK.
THAT IS WHY, WHEN I SEE YOU...
...I THINK THAT RATHER THAN A DEATH-DEALING DULLAHAN...
...YOU MIGHT BE MORE SUITED TO BE THAT OTHER TYPE OF FAIRY.
I SEE...
THEN...
...WHAT ABOUT THE "STEALING HIS LIFE" PART?

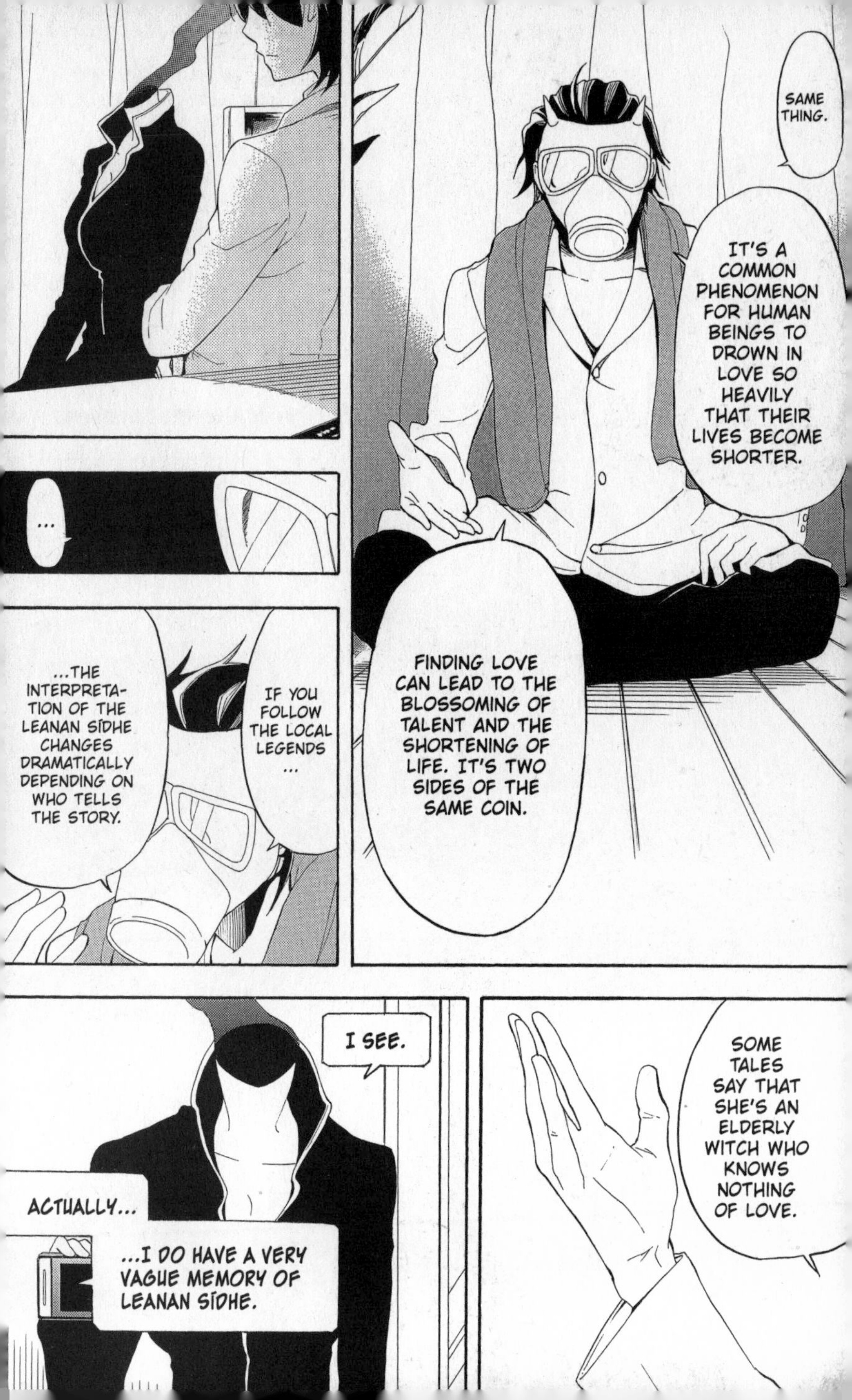
SAME THING.
IT'S A COMMON PHENOMENON FOR HUMAN BEINGS TO DROWN IN LOVE SO HEAVILY THAT THEIR LIVES BECOME SHORTER.
FINDING LOVE CAN LEAD TO THE BLOSSOMING OF TALENT AND THE SHORTENING OF LIFE. IT'S TWO SIDES OF THE SAME COIN.
...
IF YOU FOLLOW THE LOCAL LEGENDS ...
...THE INTERPRETATION OF THE LEANAN SÍDHE CHANGES DRAMATICALLY DEPENDING ON WHO TELLS THE STORY.
SOME TALES SAY THAT SHE'S AN ELDERLY WITCH WHO KNOWS NOTHING OF LOVE.
I SEE.
ACTUALLY...
...I DO HAVE A VERY VAGUE MEMORY OF LEANAN SÍDHE.

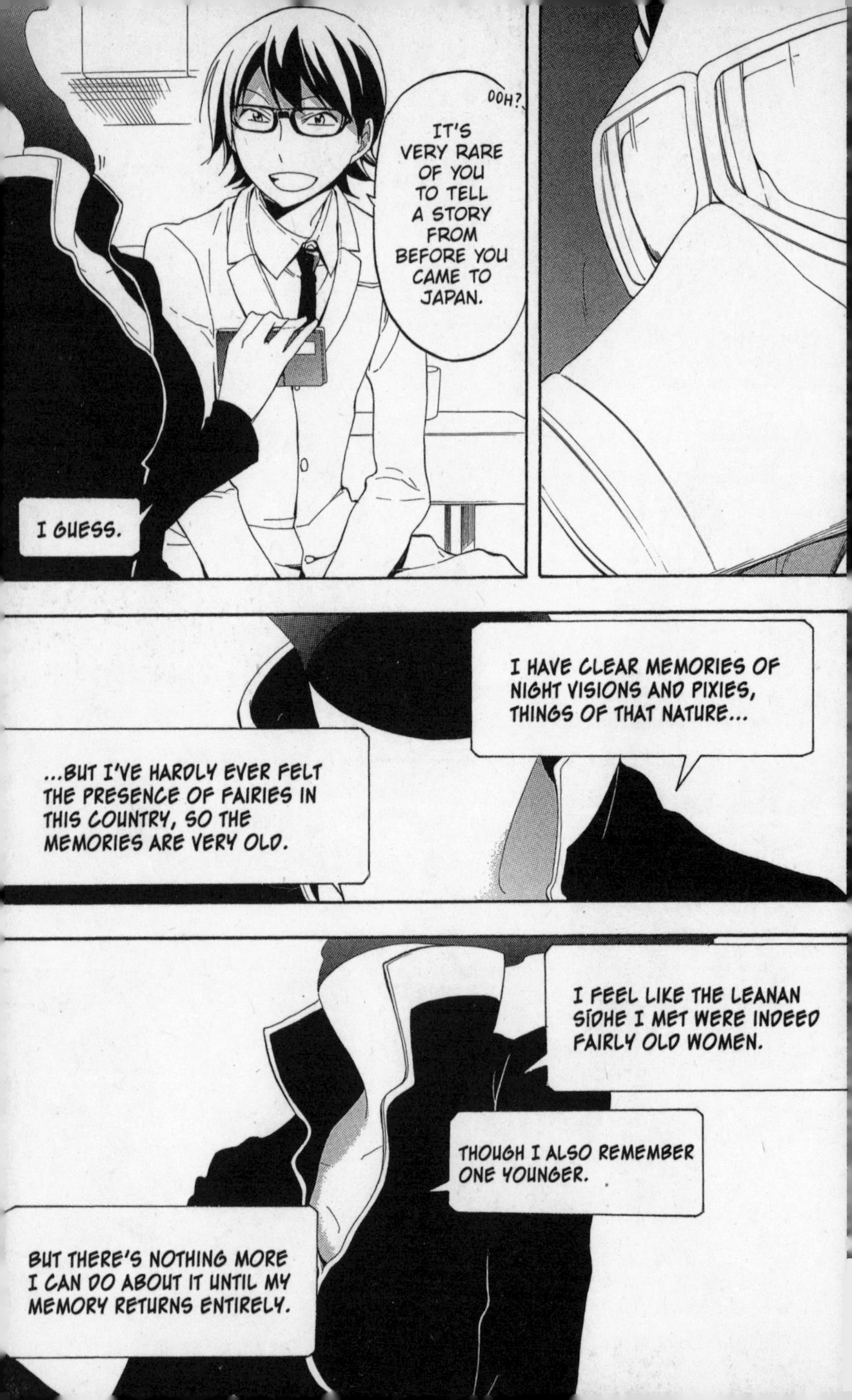
OOH?
IT'S VERY RARE OF YOU TO TELL A STORY FROM BEFORE YOU CAME TO JAPAN.
I GUESS.
I HAVE CLEAR MEMORIES OF NIGHT VISIONS AND PIXIES, THINGS OF THAT NATURE...
...BUT I'VE HARDLY EVER FELT THE PRESENCE OF FAIRIES IN THIS COUNTRY, SO THE MEMORIES ARE VERY OLD.
I FEEL LIKE THE LEANAN SÍDHE I MET WERE INDEED FAIRLY OLD WOMEN.
THOUGH I ALSO REMEMBER ONE YOUNGER.
BUT THERE'S NOTHING MORE I CAN DO ABOUT IT UNTIL MY MEMORY RETURNS ENTIRELY.

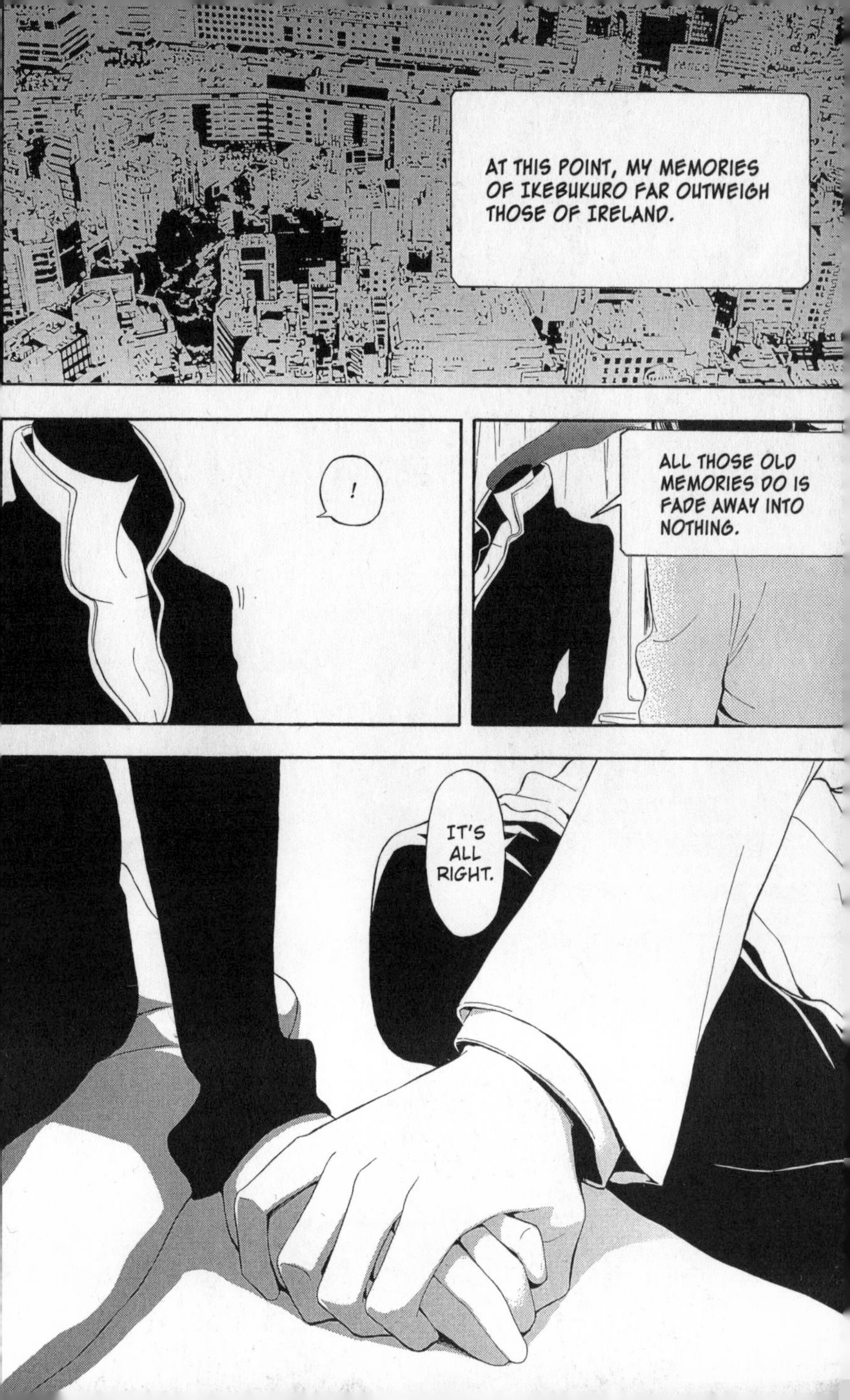
AT THIS POINT, MY MEMORIES OF IKEBUKURO FAR OUTWEIGH THOSE OF IRELAND.
ALL THOSE OLD MEMORIES DO IS FADE AWAY INTO NOTHING.
!
IT'S ALL RIGHT.

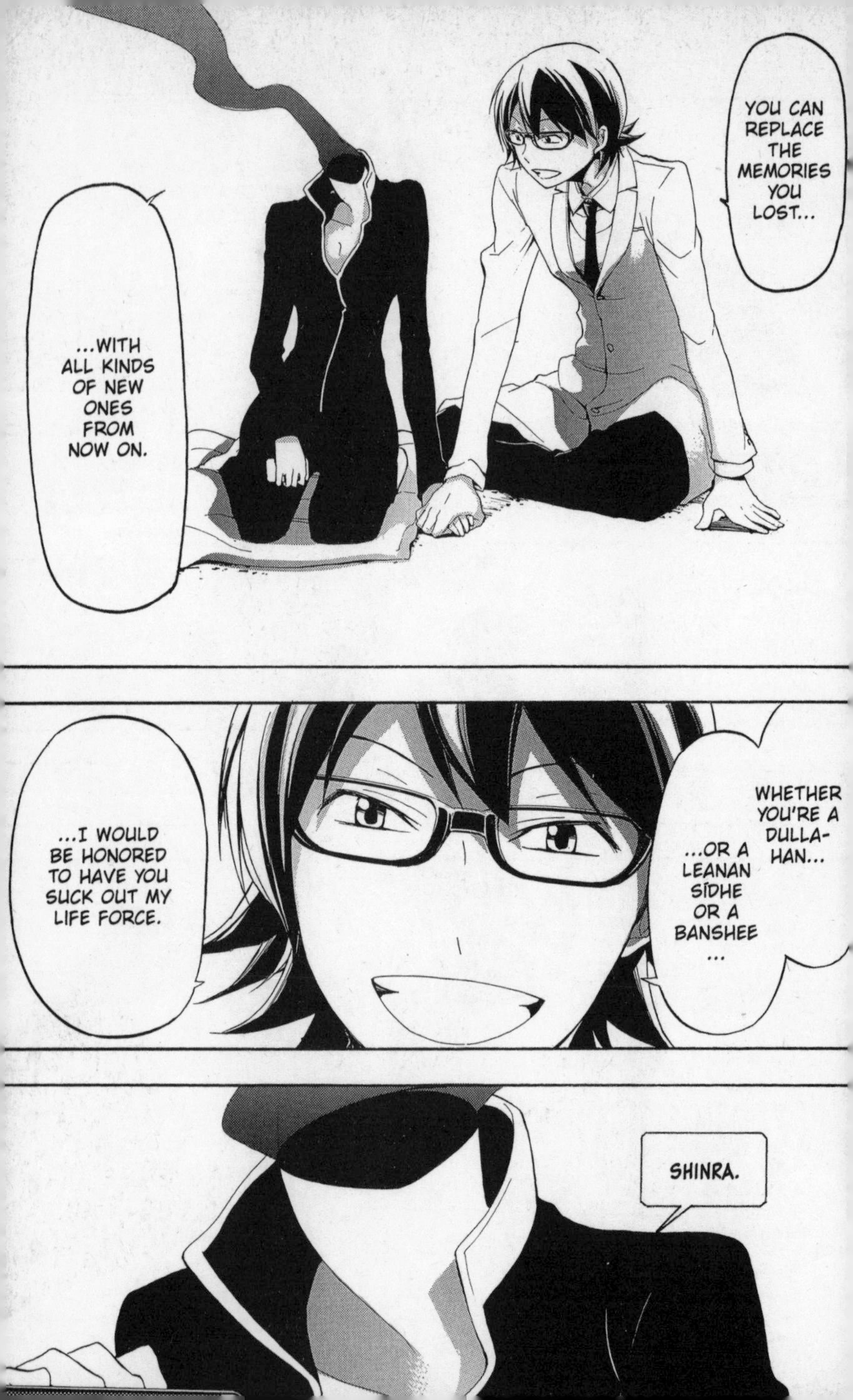
YOU CAN REPLACE THE MEMORIES YOU LOST...
...WITH ALL KINDS OF NEW ONES FROM NOW ON.
WHETHER YOU'RE A DULLA-HAN...
...OR A LEANAN SÍDHE OR A BANSHEE ...
...I WOULD BE HONORED TO HAVE YOU SUCK OUT MY LIFE FORCE.
SHINRA.

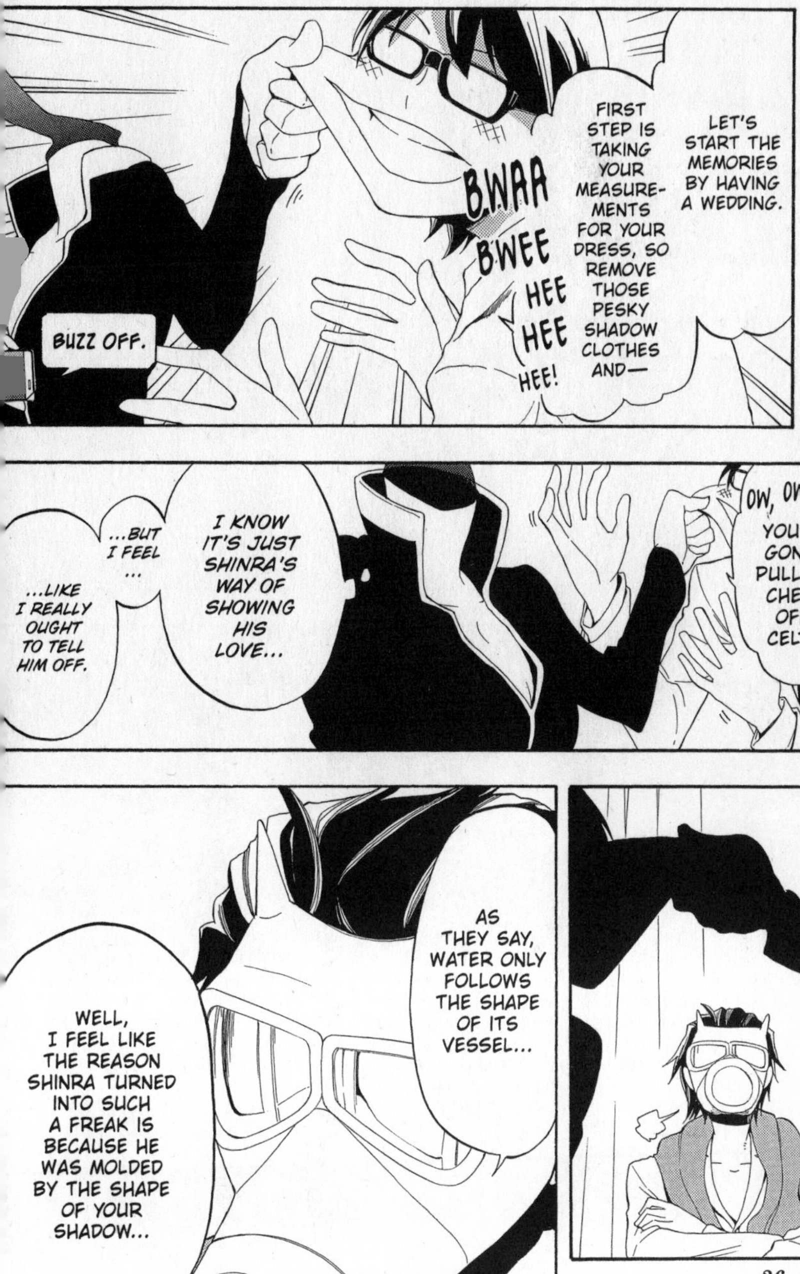

LET'S START THE MEMORIES BY HAVING A WEDDING.
FIRST STEP IS TAKING YOUR MEASURE-MENTS FOR YOUR DRESS, SO REMOVE THOSE PESKY SHADOW CLOTHES AND—
BWAA BWEE HEE HEE HEE!
BUZZ OFF.
OW, OW, OW!
YOU'RE GONNA PULL MY CHEEK OFF, CELTY.
I KNOW IT'S JUST SHINRA'S WAY OF SHOWING HIS LOVE...
...BUT I FEEL ...
...LIKE I REALLY OUGHT TO TELL HIM OFF.
AS THEY SAY, WATER ONLY FOLLOWS THE SHAPE OF ITS VESSEL...
WELL, I FEEL LIKE THE REASON SHINRA TURNED INTO SUCH A FREAK IS BECAUSE HE WAS MOLDED BY THE SHAPE OF YOUR SHADOW...

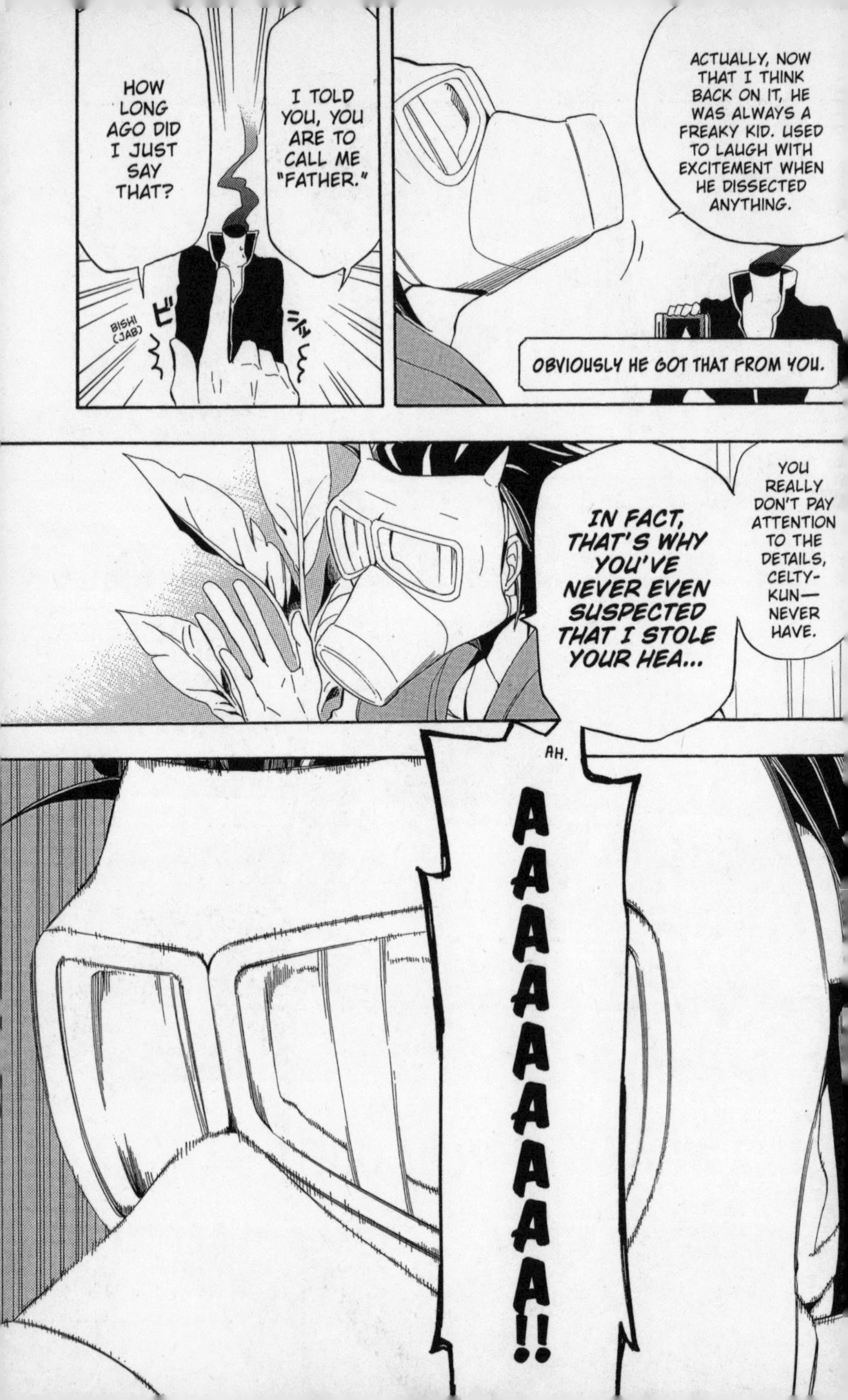
ACTUALLY, NOW THAT I THINK BACK ON IT, HE WAS ALWAYS A FREAKY KID. USED TO LAUGH WITH EXCITEMENT WHEN HE DISSECTED ANYTHING.
OBVIOUSLY HE GOT THAT FROM YOU.
I TOLD YOU, YOU ARE TO CALL ME "FATHER."
HOW LONG AGO DID I JUST SAY THAT?
BISHI (JAB)
YOU REALLY DON'T PAY ATTENTION TO THE DETAILS, CELTY-KUN— NEVER HAVE.
IN FACT, THAT'S WHY YOU'VE NEVER EVEN SUSPECTED THAT I STOLE YOUR HEA...
AH.
AAAAAAAAAA!!

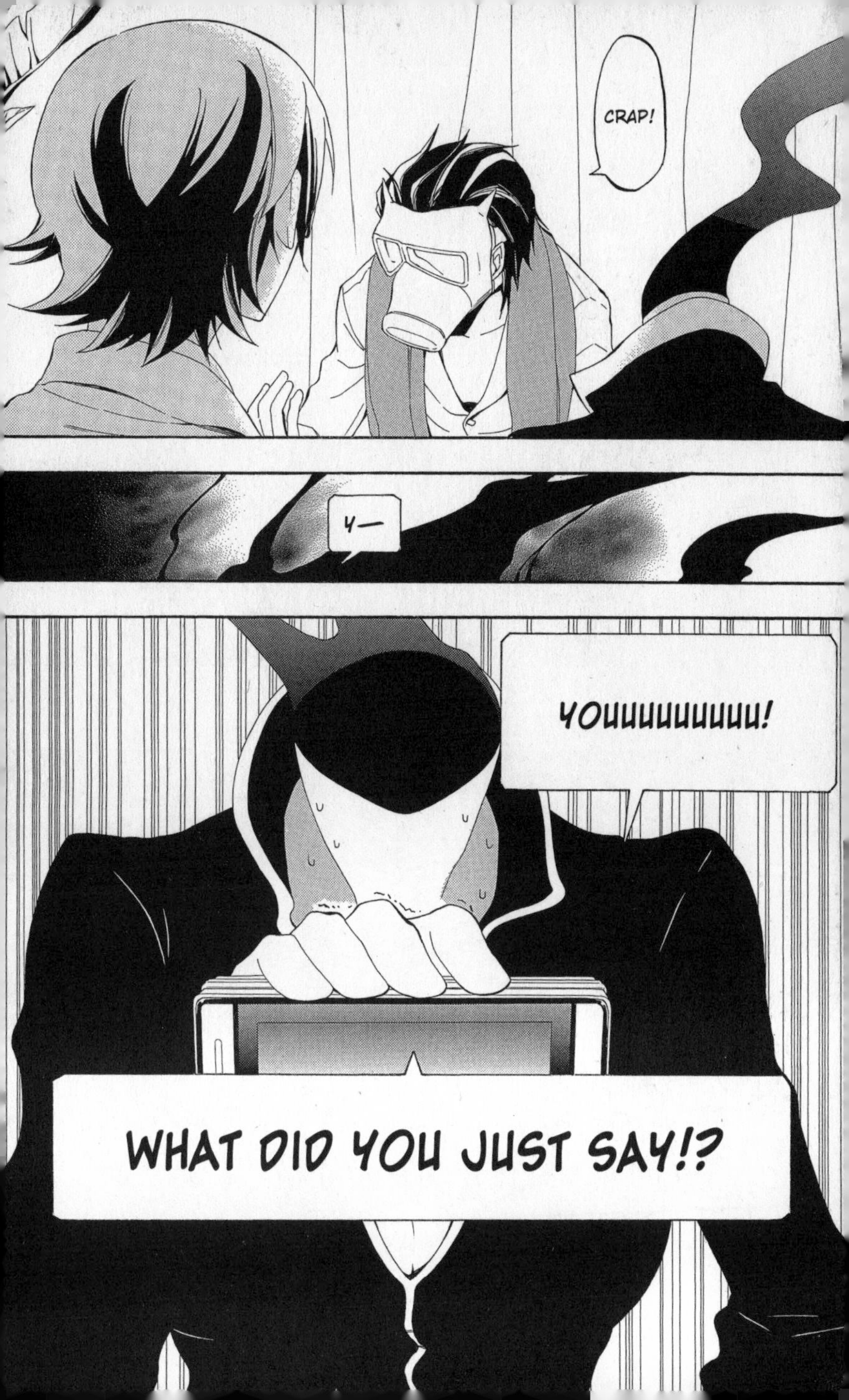
CRAP!
Y—
YOUUUUUUUUUU!
WHAT DID YOU JUST SAY!?

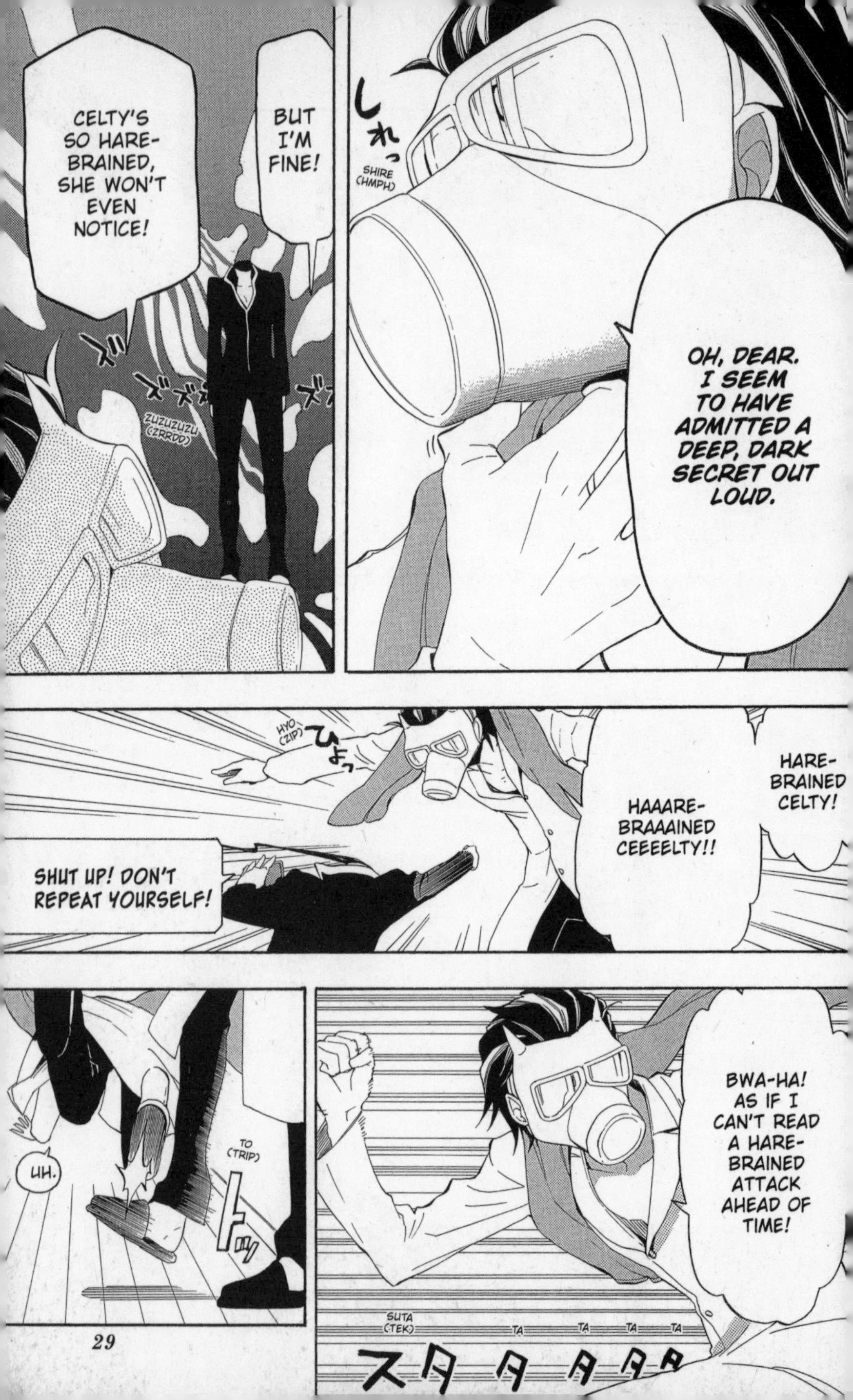
しれっ
SHIRE (HMPH)
OH, DEAR. I SEEM TO HAVE ADMITTED A DEEP, DARK SECRET OUT LOUD.
BUT I'M FINE!
CELTY'S SO HARE-BRAINED, SHE WON'T EVEN NOTICE!
ズズズズ
ZUZUZUZU (ZRRDD)
HARE-BRAINED CELTY!
HAAARE-BRAAAINED CEEEELTY!!
ひょっ
HYO (ZIP)
SHUT UP! DON'T REPEAT YOURSELF!
BWA-HA! AS IF I CAN'T READ A HARE-BRAINED ATTACK AHEAD OF TIME!
SUTA (TEK)
TA
TA
TA
TA
スタタタタタ
TO (TRIP)
トッ
UH.

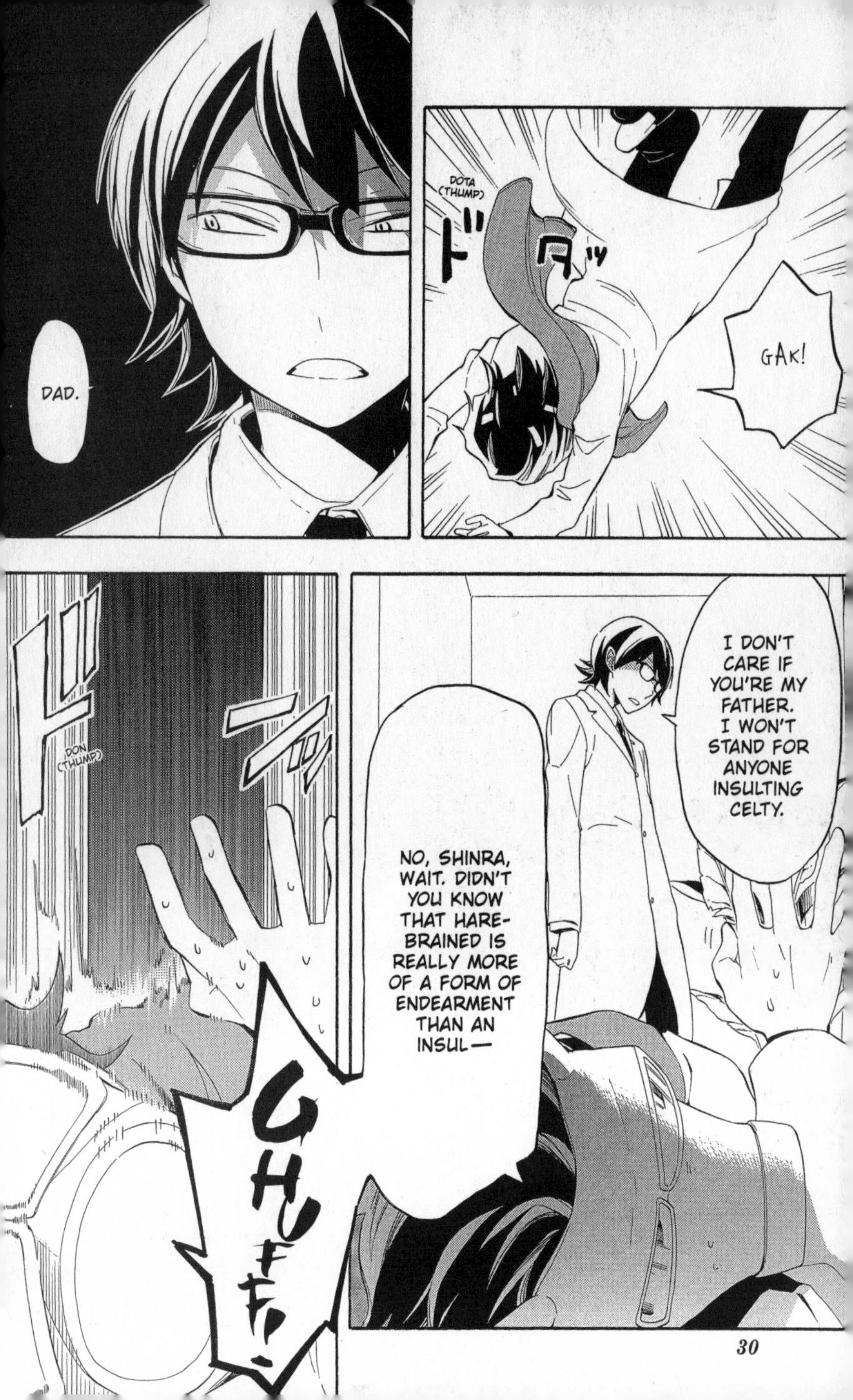
DOTA (THUMP)
GAK!
DAD.
I DON'T CARE IF YOU'RE MY FATHER. I WON'T STAND FOR ANYONE INSULTING CELTY.
NO, SHINRA, WAIT. DIDN'T YOU KNOW THAT HARE-BRAINED IS REALLY MORE OF A FORM OF ENDEARMENT THAN AN INSUL—
DON (THUMP)
CHUFF!

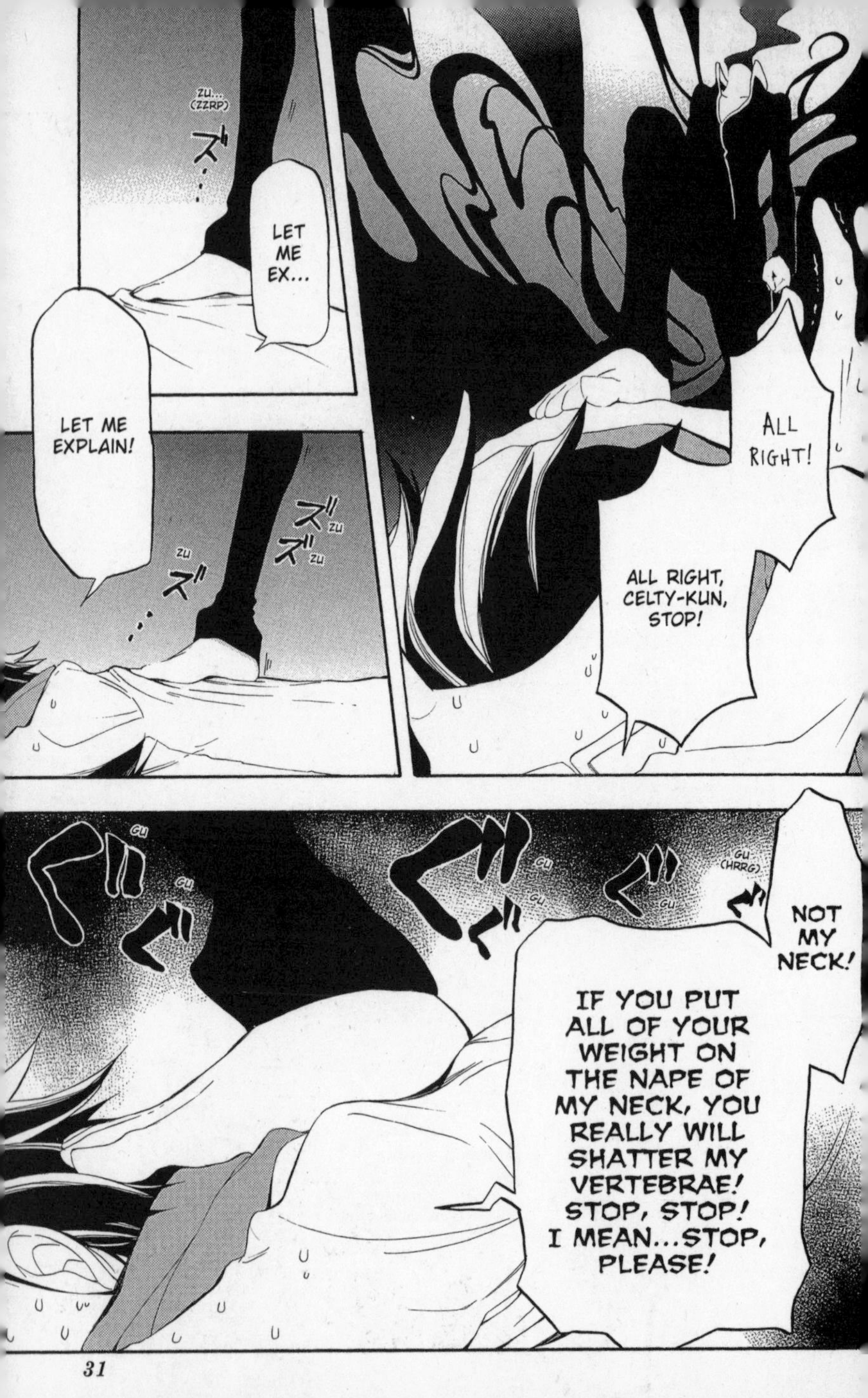

ALL RIGHT!
ALL RIGHT, CELTY-KUN, STOP!
ZU... (ZZRP)
LET ME EX...
LET ME EXPLAIN!
ZU
ZU
ZU
NOT MY NECK!
GU (HRRG)
GU
GU
GU
GU
GU
IF YOU PUT ALL OF YOUR WEIGHT ON THE NAPE OF MY NECK, YOU REALLY WILL SHATTER MY VERTEBRAE! STOP, STOP! I MEAN...STOP, PLEASE!

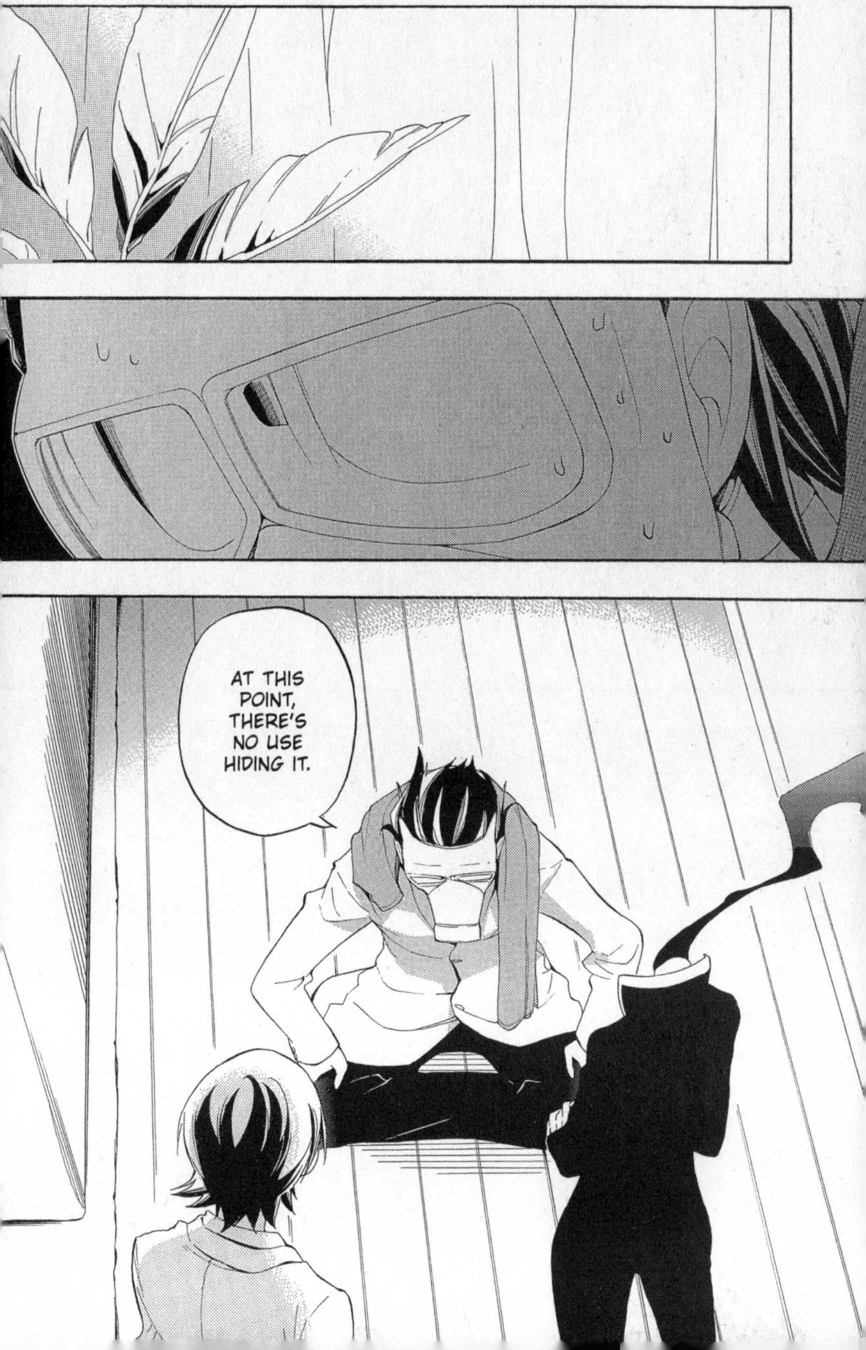
AT THIS POINT, THERE'S NO USE HIDING IT.

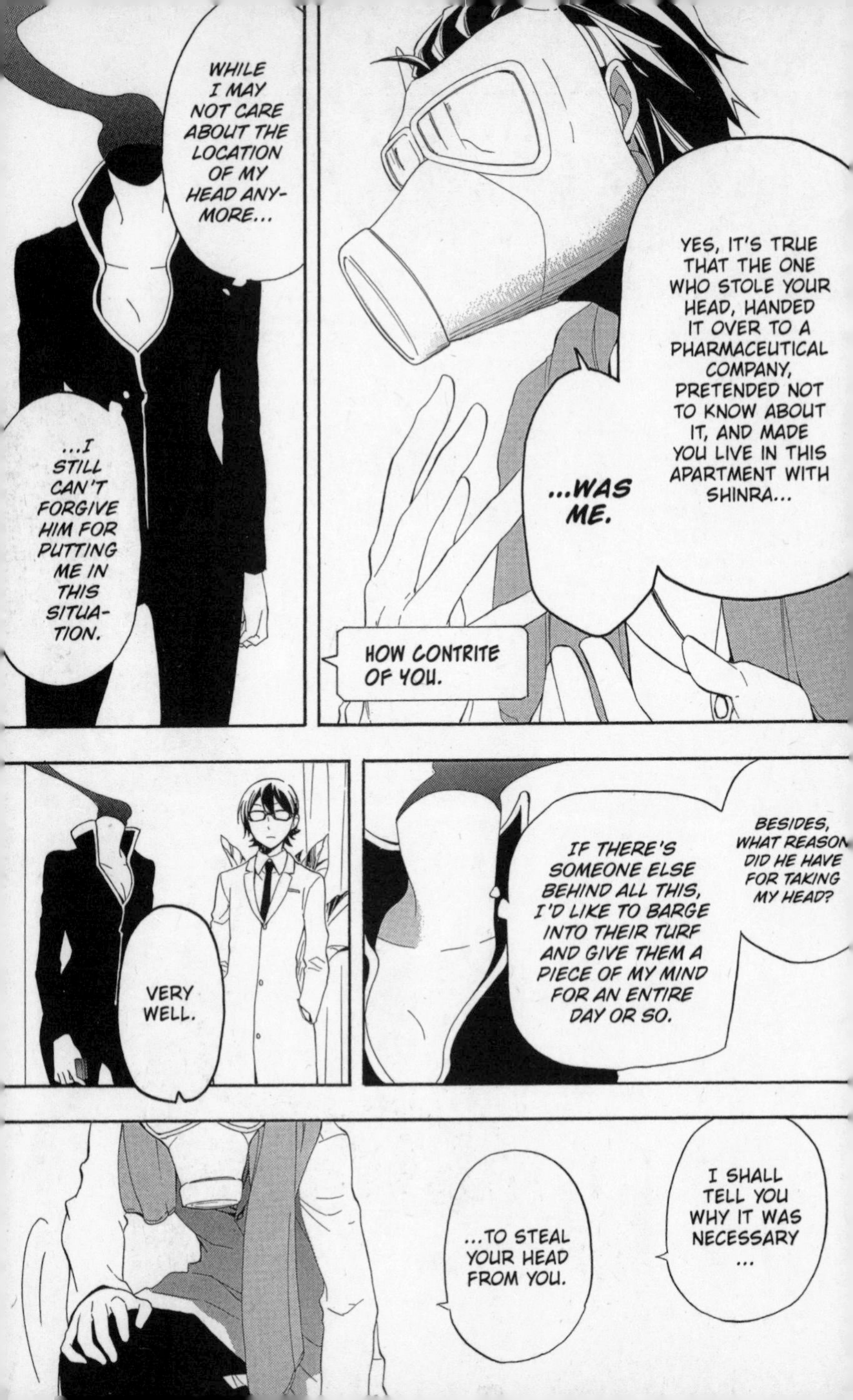
YES, IT'S TRUE THAT THE ONE WHO STOLE YOUR HEAD, HANDED IT OVER TO A PHARMACEUTICAL COMPANY, PRETENDED NOT TO KNOW ABOUT IT, AND MADE YOU LIVE IN THIS APARTMENT WITH SHINRA...
...WAS ME.
HOW CONTRITE OF YOU.
WHILE I MAY NOT CARE ABOUT THE LOCATION OF MY HEAD ANY-MORE...
...I STILL CAN'T FORGIVE HIM FOR PUTTING ME IN THIS SITUA-TION.
BESIDES, WHAT REASON DID HE HAVE FOR TAKING MY HEAD?
IF THERE'S SOMEONE ELSE BEHIND ALL THIS, I'D LIKE TO BARGE INTO THEIR TURF AND GIVE THEM A PIECE OF MY MIND FOR AN ENTIRE DAY OR SO.
VERY WELL.
I SHALL TELL YOU WHY IT WAS NECESSARY...
...TO STEAL YOUR HEAD FROM YOU.

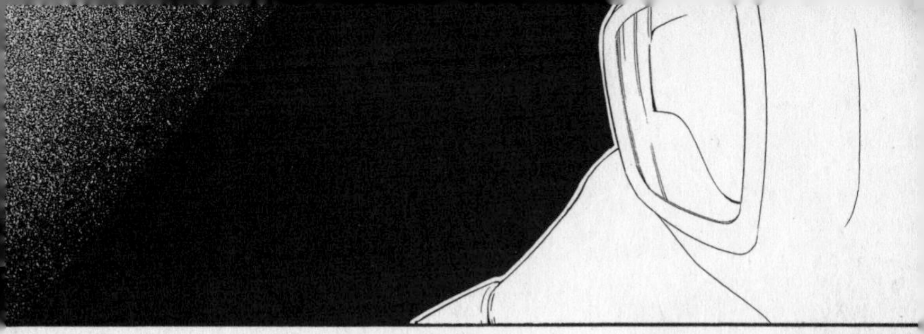
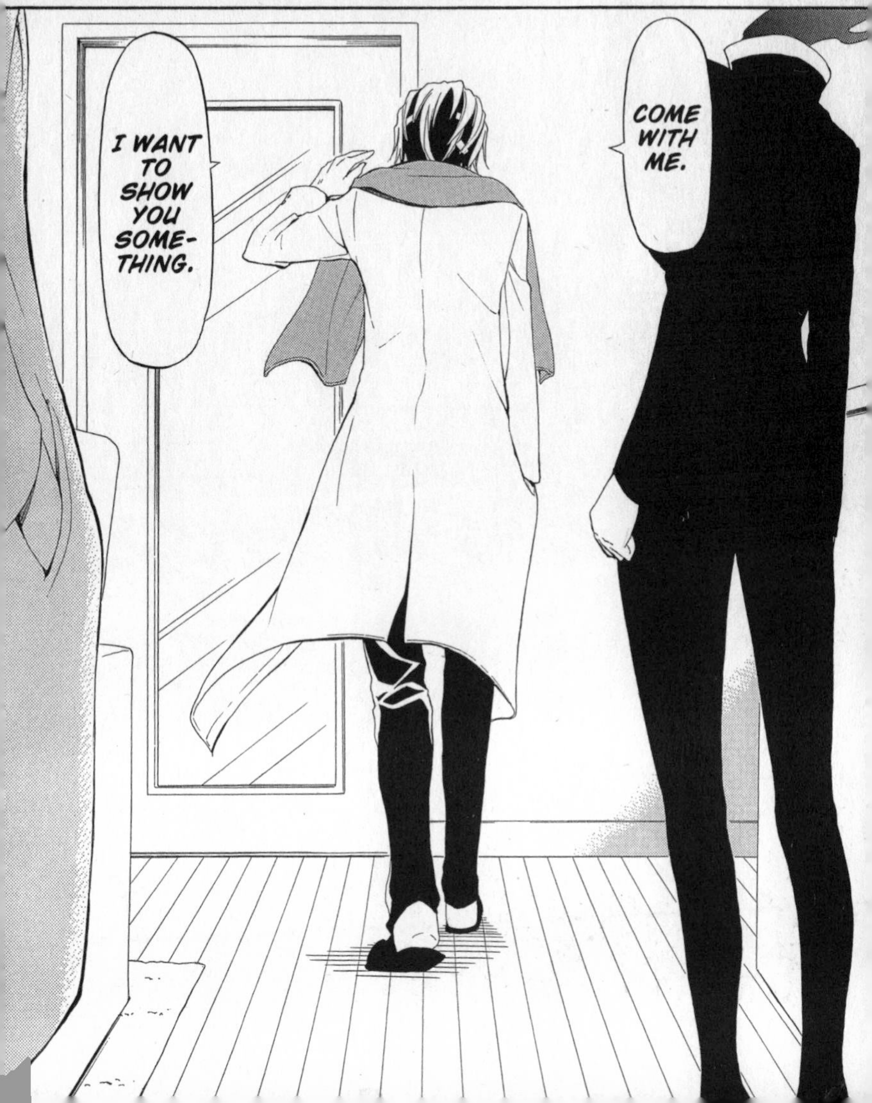
COME WITH ME.
I WANT TO SHOW YOU SOME-THING.

DURARARA!!

ORRR!!

DRRR!!

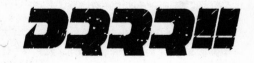

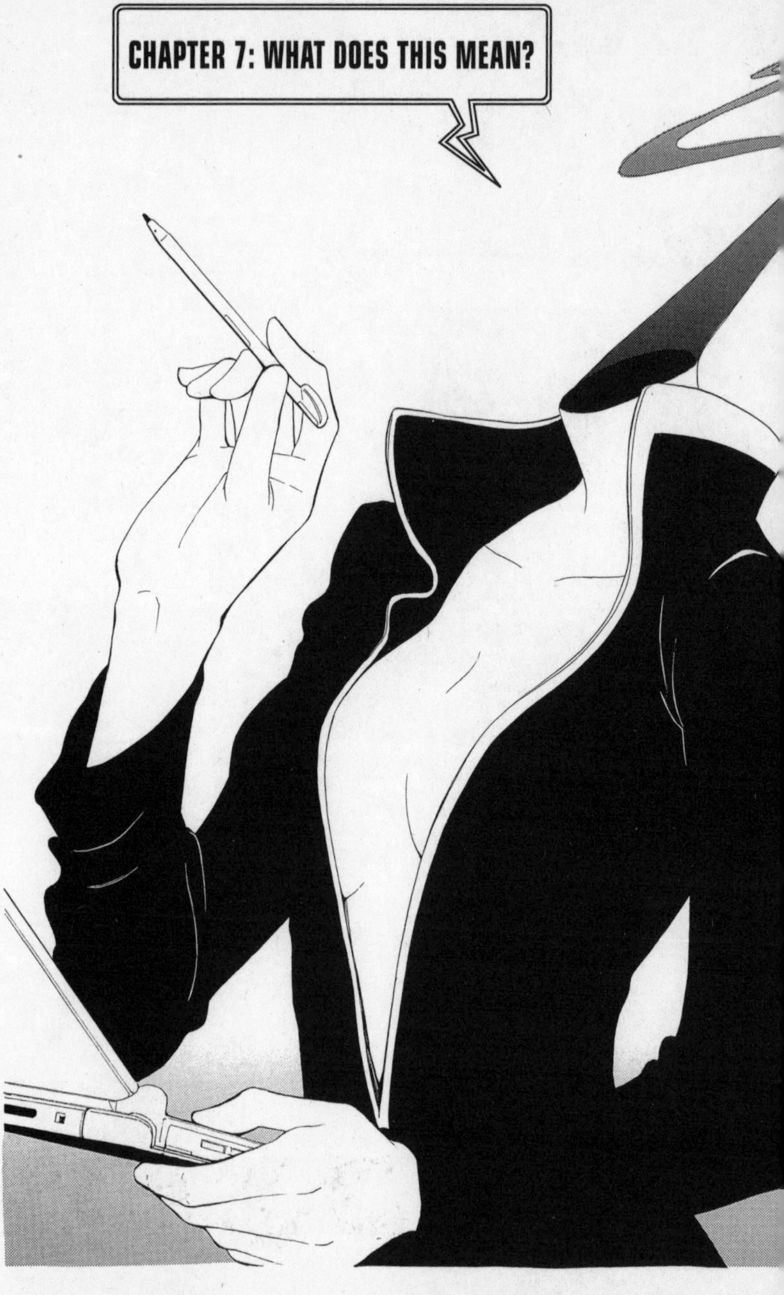
CHAPTER 7: WHAT DOES THIS MEAN?

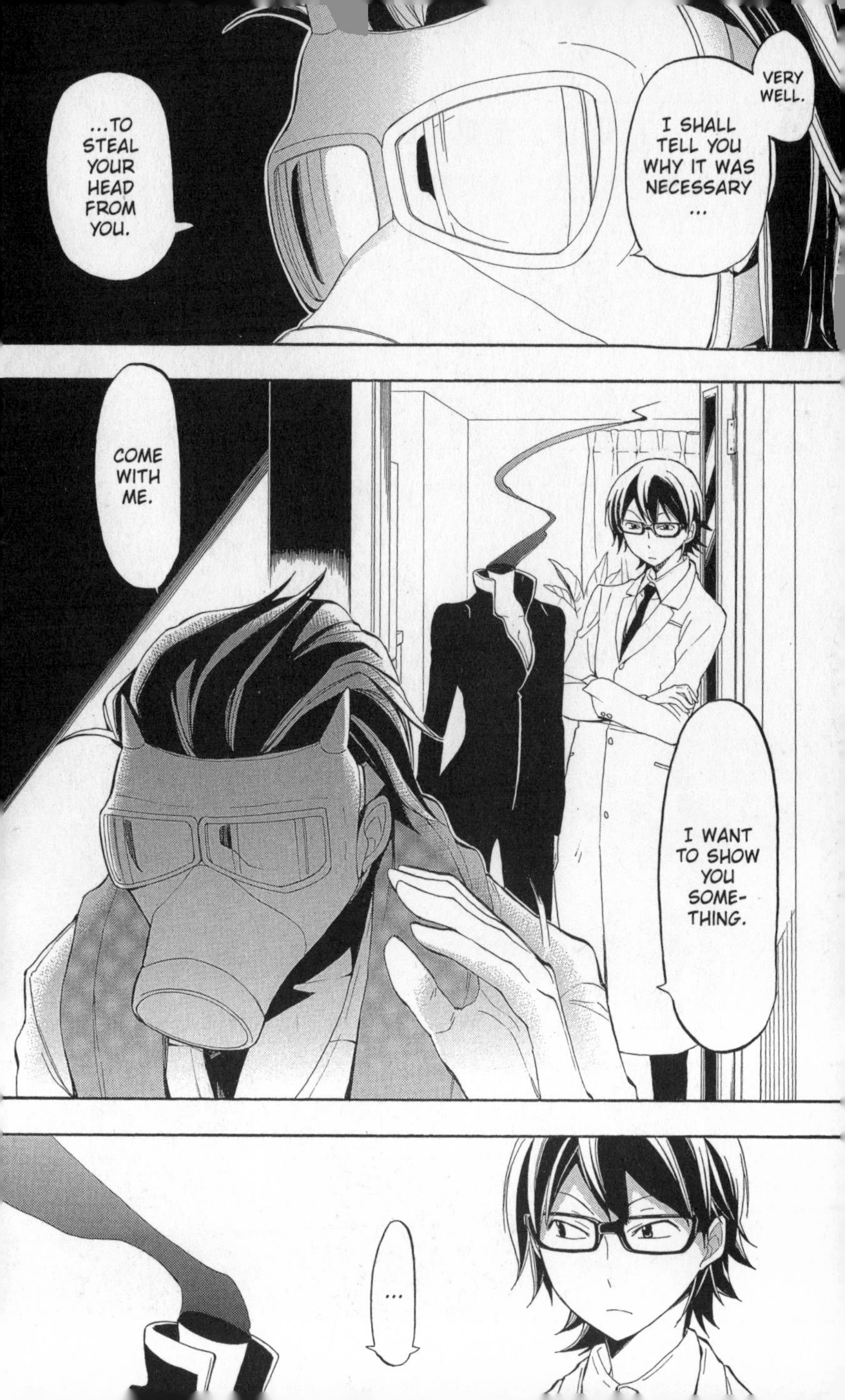
VERY WELL.
I SHALL TELL YOU WHY IT WAS NECESSARY...
...TO STEAL YOUR HEAD FROM YOU.
I WANT TO SHOW YOU SOMETHING.
COME WITH ME.
...

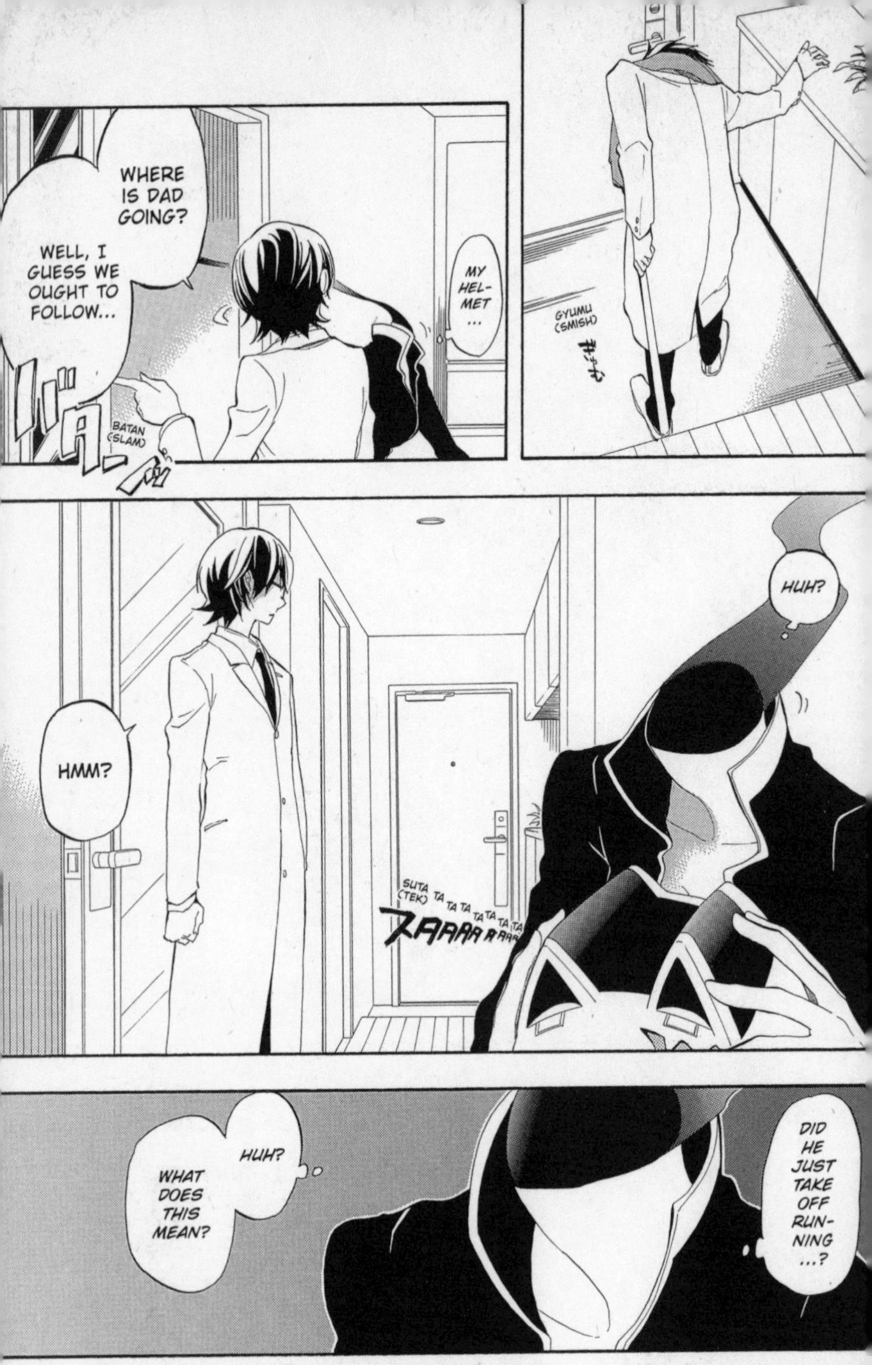
GYUMU (SMISH)
MY HEL-MET ...
WHERE IS DAD GOING?
WELL, I GUESS WE OUGHT TO FOLLOW...
BATAN (SLAM)
HUH?
SUTA (TEK) TA TA TA TA TA TA TA
HMM?
DID HE JUST TAKE OFF RUN-NING ...?
HUH?
WHAT DOES THIS MEAN?

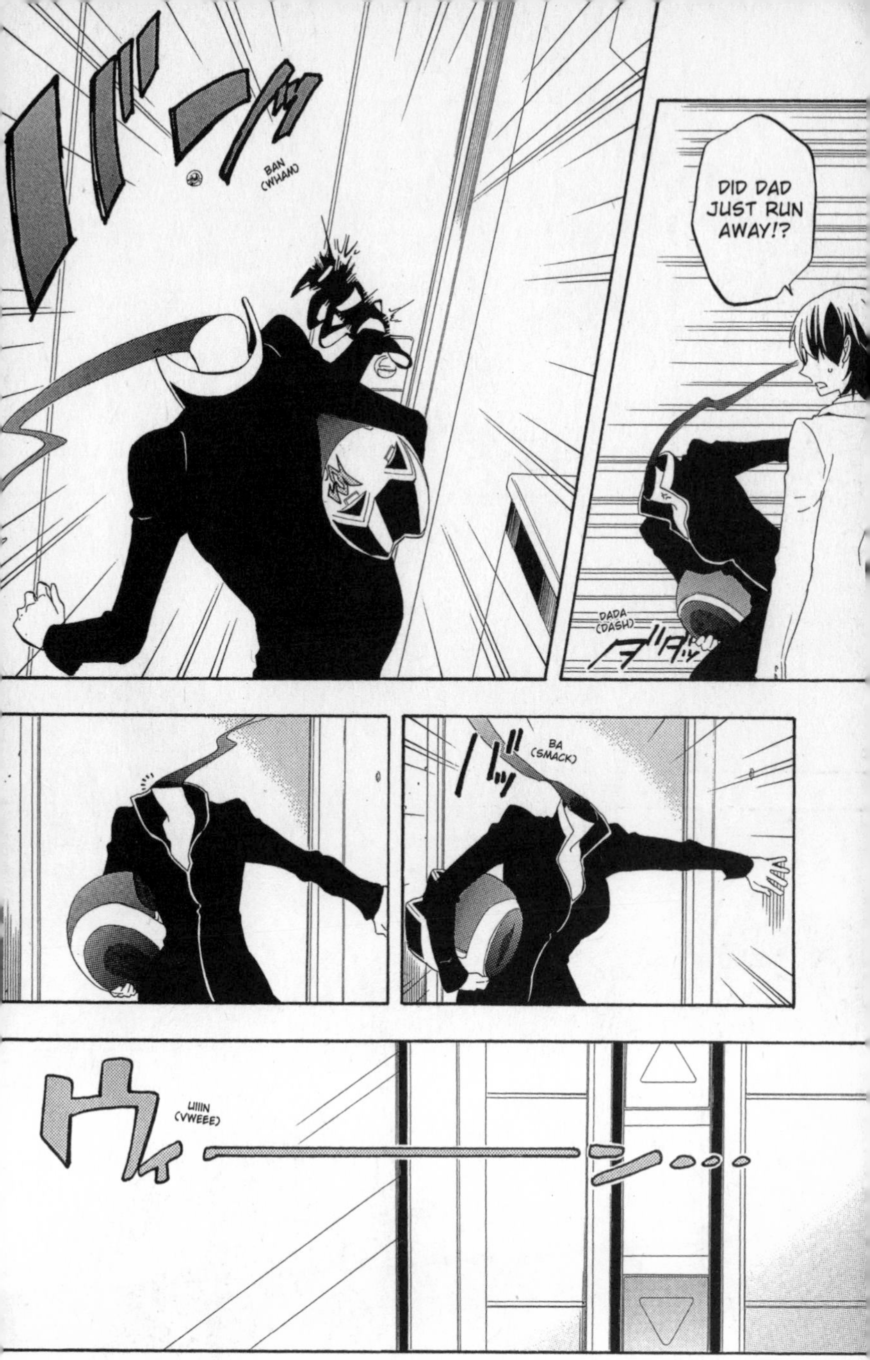
DID DAD JUST RUN AWAY!?
BAN (WHAM)
DADA (DASH)
BA (SMACK)
UIIIN (VWEEE)

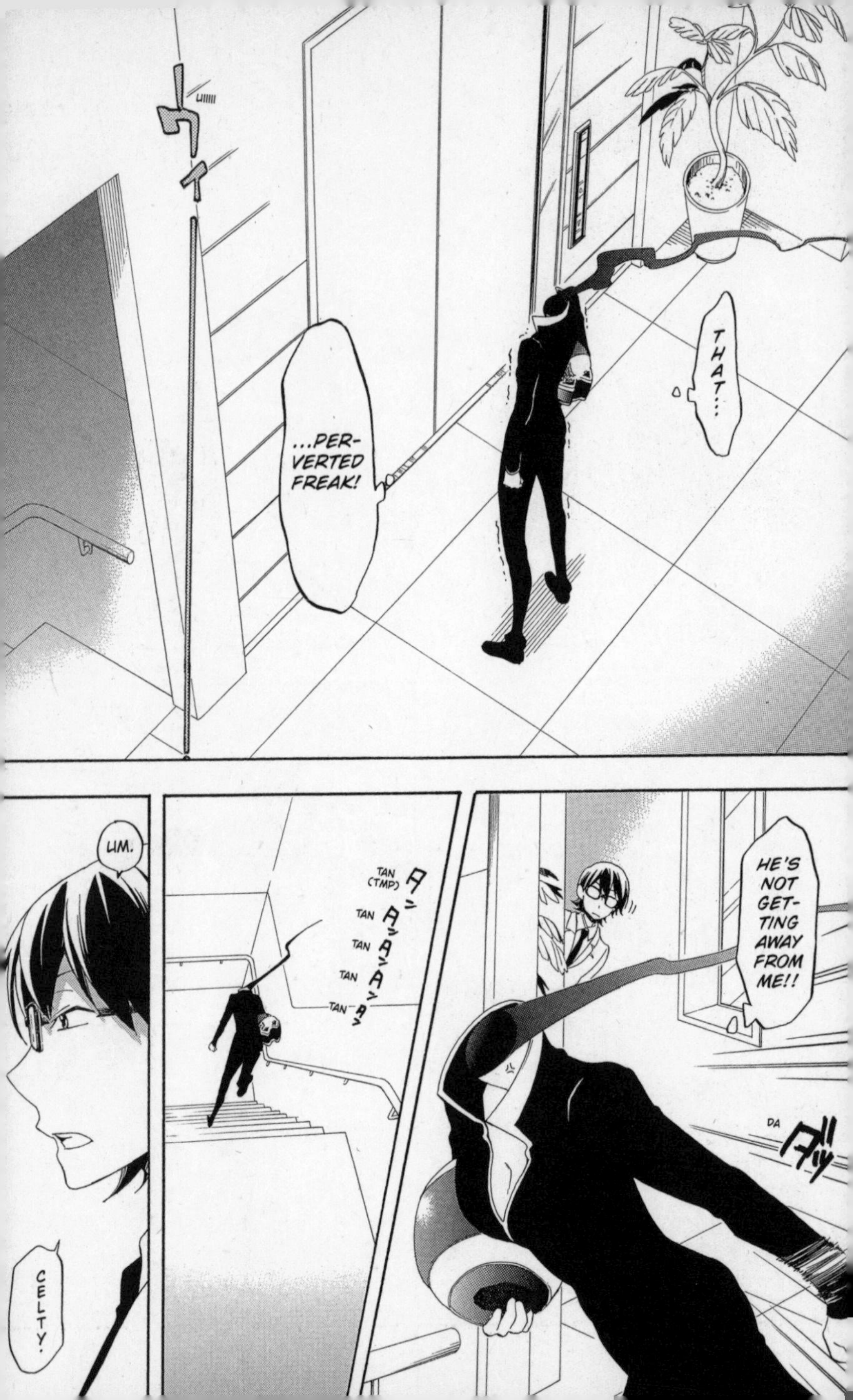
THAT...
...PERVERTED FREAK!
UIIIII
HE'S NOT GETTING AWAY FROM ME!!
DA
TAN (TMP)
TAN
TAN
TAN
TAN
UM.
CELTY.

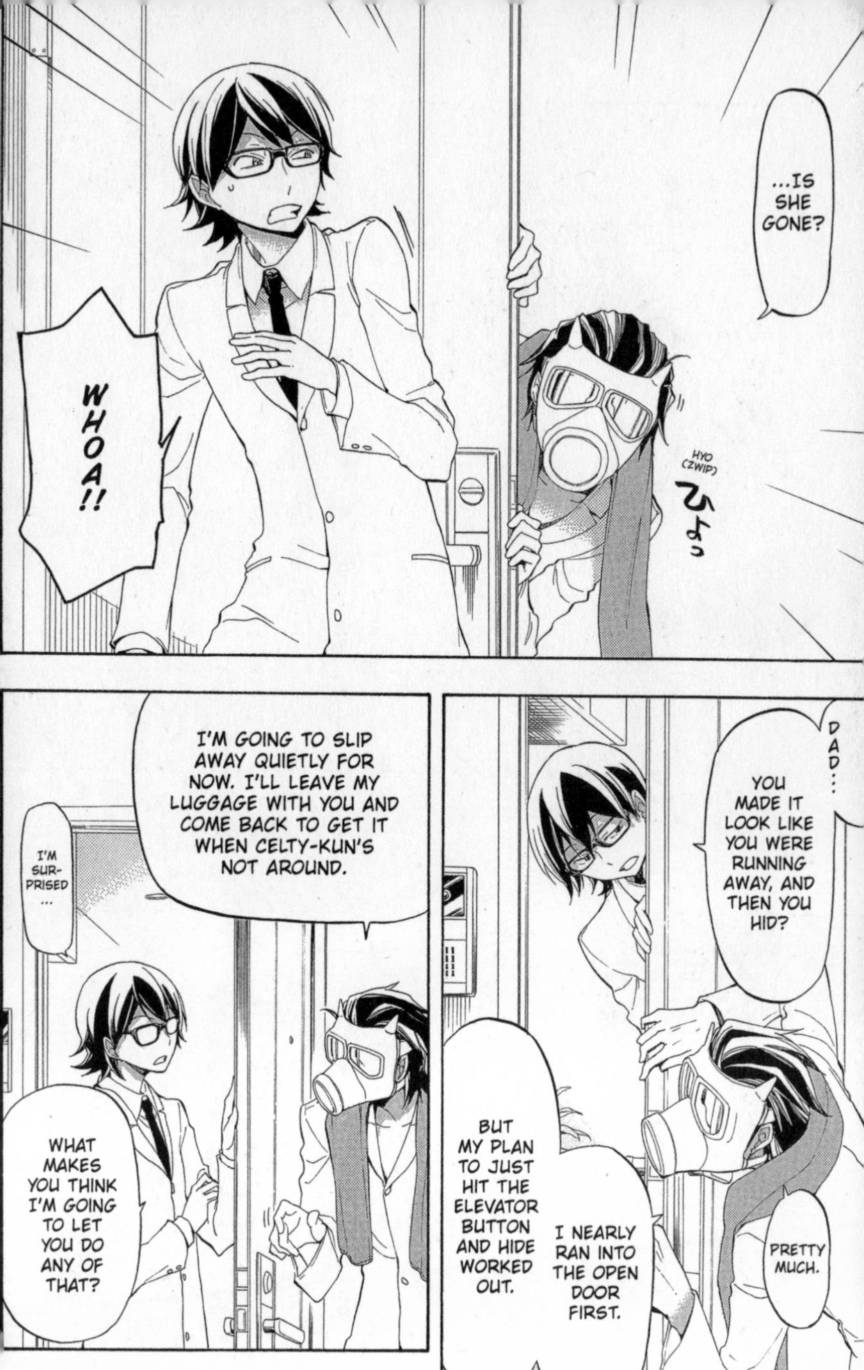
...IS SHE GONE?
HYO (ZWIP)
ひょっ
WHOA!!
DAD...
YOU MADE IT LOOK LIKE YOU WERE RUNNING AWAY, AND THEN YOU HID?
PRETTY MUCH.
I NEARLY RAN INTO THE OPEN DOOR FIRST.
BUT MY PLAN TO JUST HIT THE ELEVATOR BUTTON AND HIDE WORKED OUT.
I'M GOING TO SLIP AWAY QUIETLY FOR NOW. I'LL LEAVE MY LUGGAGE WITH YOU AND COME BACK TO GET IT WHEN CELTY-KUN'S NOT AROUND.
I'M SURPRISED...
WHAT MAKES YOU THINK I'M GOING TO LET YOU DO ANY OF THAT?

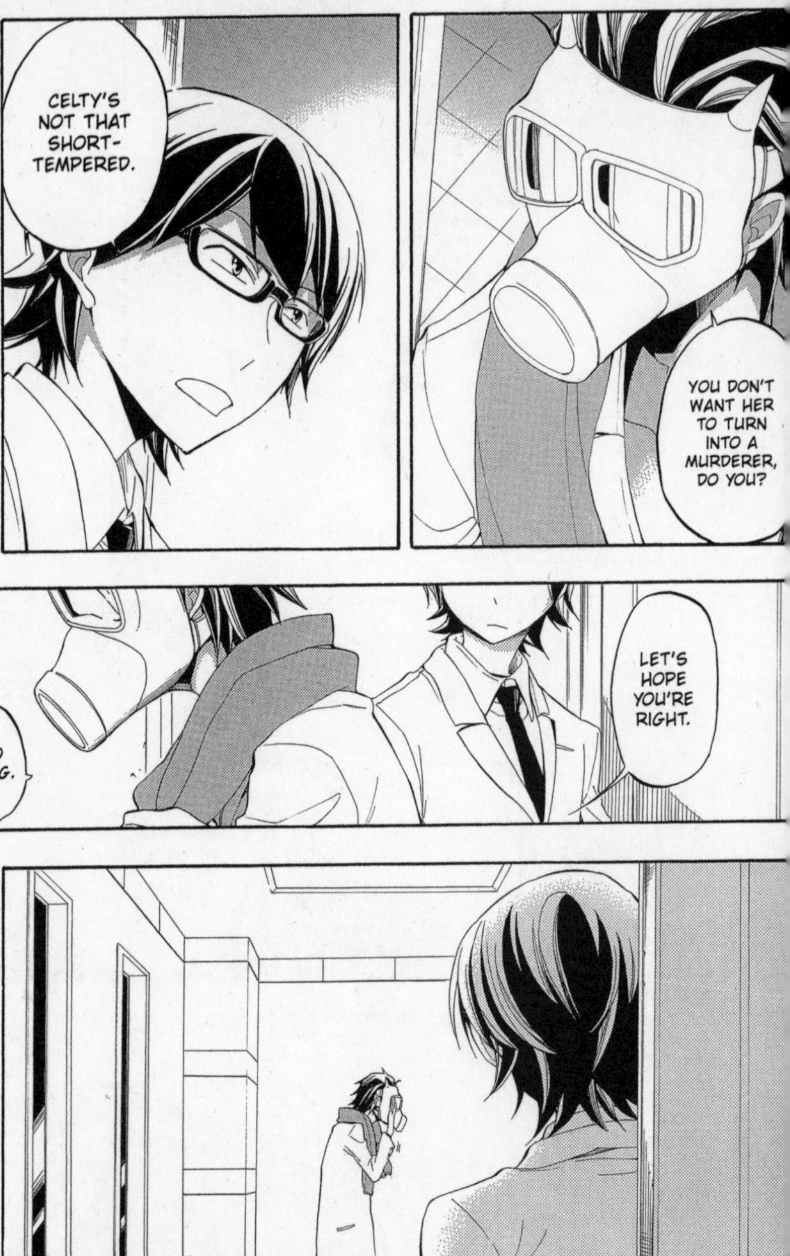
YOU DON'T WANT HER TO TURN INTO A MURDERER, DO YOU?
CELTY'S NOT THAT SHORT-TEMPERED.
LET'S HOPE YOU'RE RIGHT.
SO LONG.

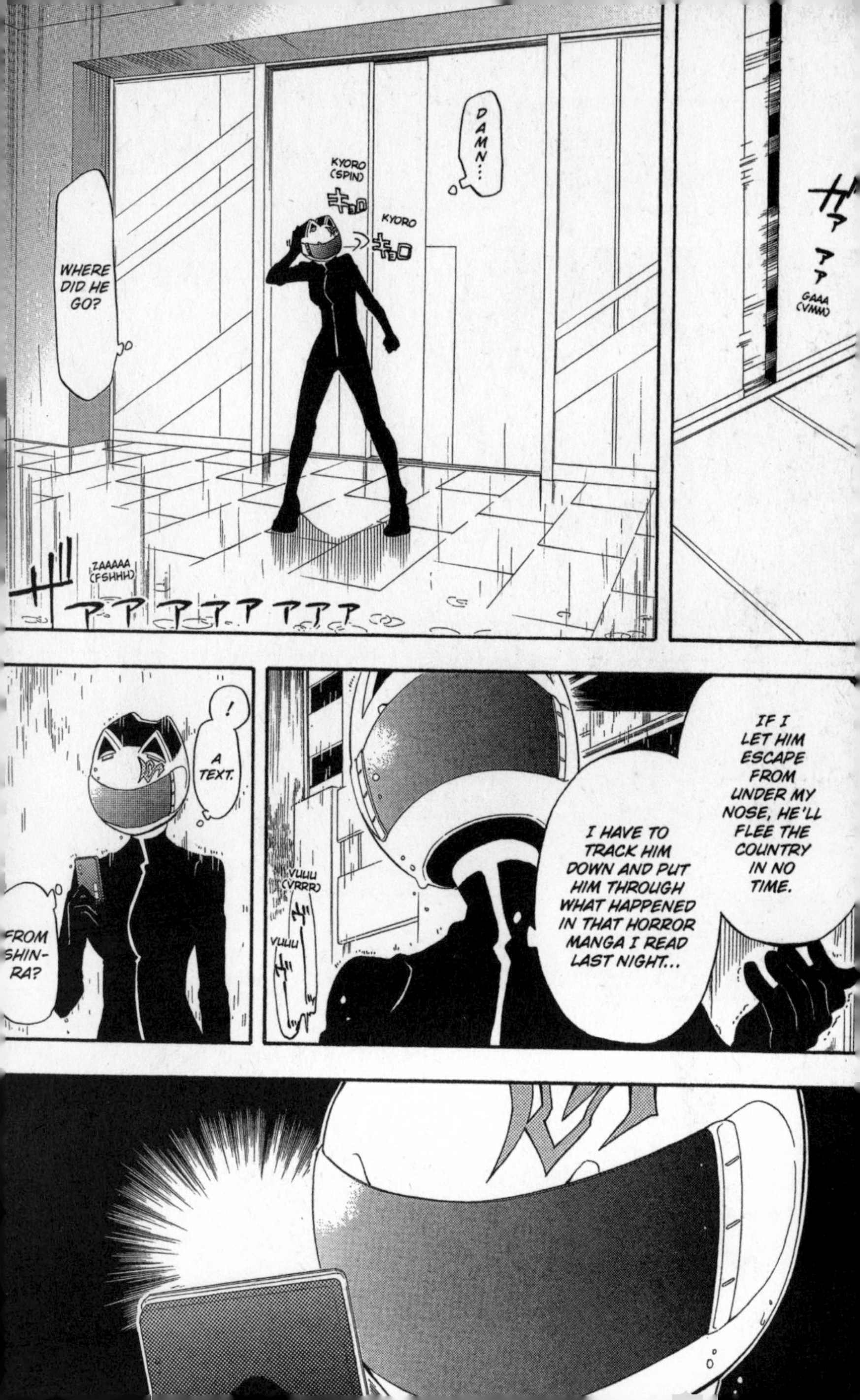
GAAA (VMM)
DAMN...
KYORO (SPIN)
KYORO
WHERE DID HE GO?
ZAAAAA (FSHHH)
IF I LET HIM ESCAPE FROM UNDER MY NOSE, HE'LL FLEE THE COUNTRY IN NO TIME.
I HAVE TO TRACK HIM DOWN AND PUT HIM THROUGH WHAT HAPPENED IN THAT HORROR MANGA I READ LAST NIGHT...
VUUU (VRRR)
VUUU
!
A TEXT.
FROM SHIN-RA?

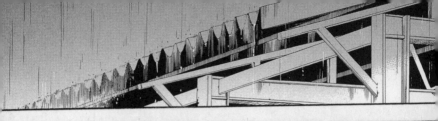

HUFF...

HUFF...

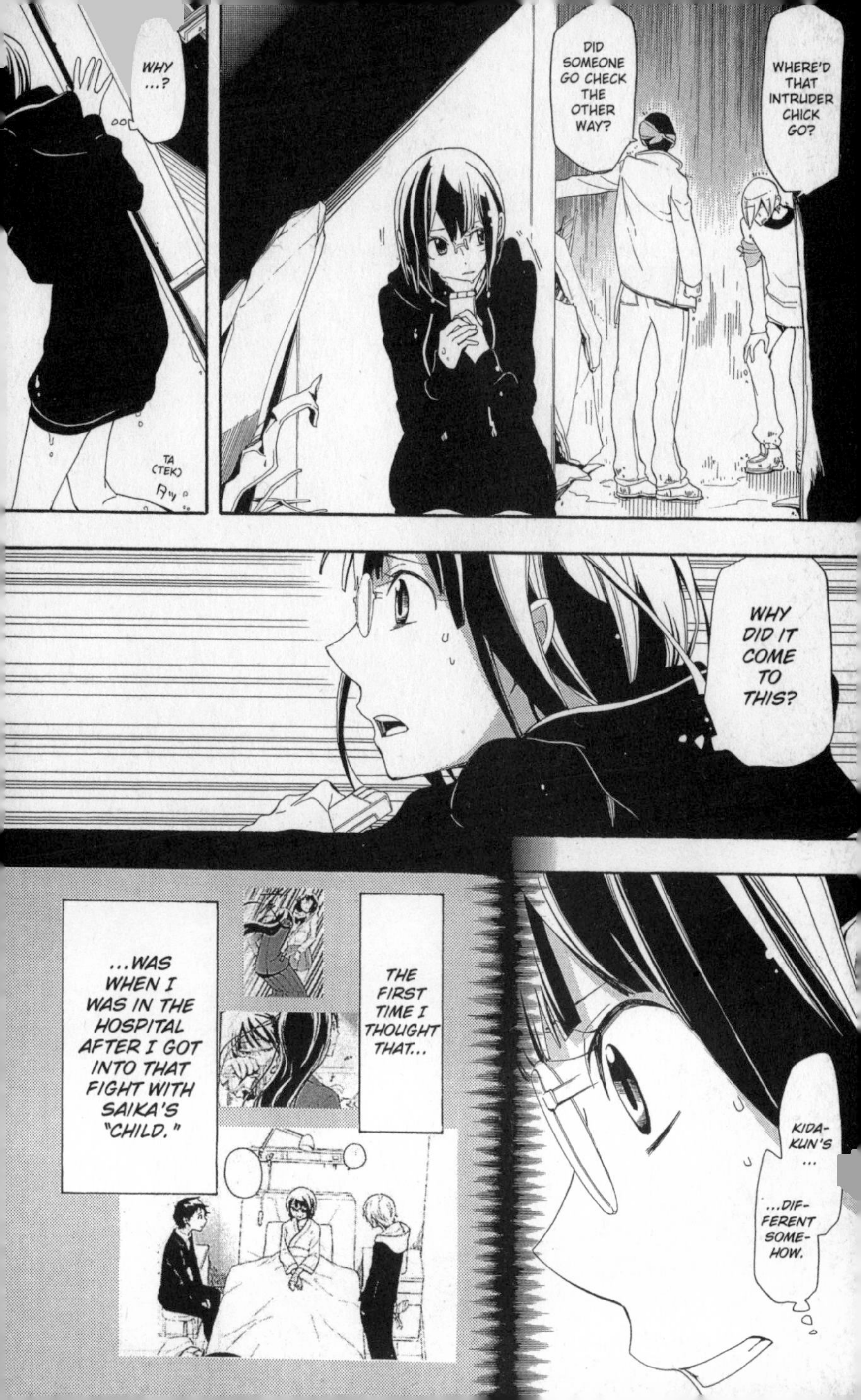
WHERE'D THAT INTRUDER CHICK GO?
DID SOMEONE GO CHECK THE OTHER WAY?
WHY ...?
TA (TEK)
WHY DID IT COME TO THIS?
KIDA-KUN'S ...
...DIF-FERENT SOME-HOW.
THE FIRST TIME I THOUGHT THAT...
...WAS WHEN I WAS IN THE HOSPITAL AFTER I GOT INTO THAT FIGHT WITH SAIKA'S "CHILD."

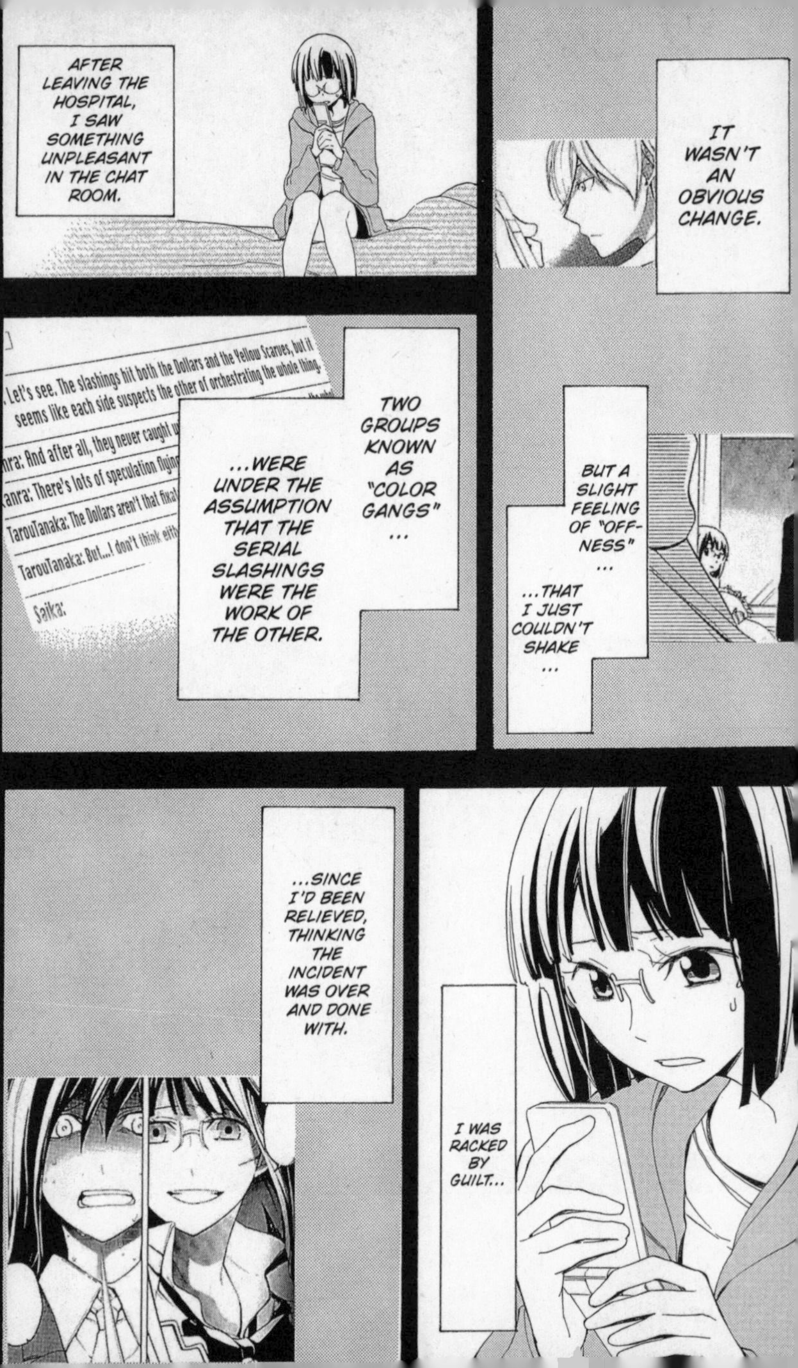
IT WASN'T AN OBVIOUS CHANGE.
BUT A SLIGHT FEELING OF "OFF-NESS"...
...THAT I JUST COULDN'T SHAKE...
AFTER LEAVING THE HOSPITAL, I SAW SOMETHING UNPLEASANT IN THE CHAT ROOM.
Let's see. The slashings hit both the Dollars and the Yellow Scarves, but it seems like each side suspects the other of orchestrating the whole thing.
nra: And after all, they never caught
anra: There's lots of speculation flying
TarouTanaka: The Dollars aren't that
TarouTanaka: But...I don't think
Saika:
TWO GROUPS KNOWN AS "COLOR GANGS"...
...WERE UNDER THE ASSUMPTION THAT THE SERIAL SLASHINGS WERE THE WORK OF THE OTHER.
I WAS RACKED BY GUILT...
...SINCE I'D BEEN RELIEVED, THINKING THE INCIDENT WAS OVER AND DONE WITH.

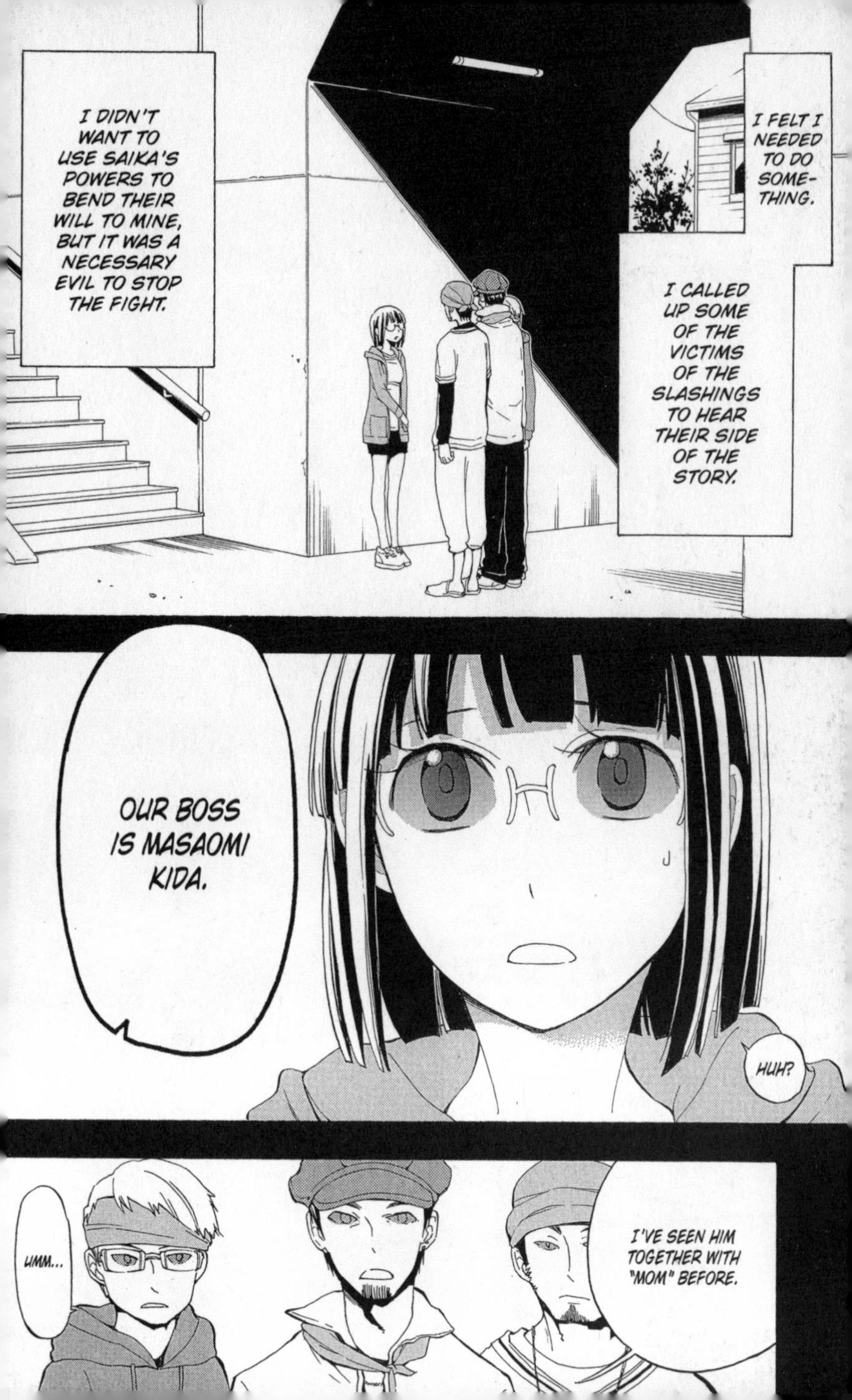
I FELT I NEEDED TO DO SOME-THING.
I CALLED UP SOME OF THE VICTIMS OF THE SLASHINGS TO HEAR THEIR SIDE OF THE STORY.
I DIDN'T WANT TO USE SAIKA'S POWERS TO BEND THEIR WILL TO MINE, BUT IT WAS A NECESSARY EVIL TO STOP THE FIGHT.
OUR BOSS IS MASAOMI KIDA.
HUH?
I'VE SEEN HIM TOGETHER WITH "MOM" BEFORE.
UMM...

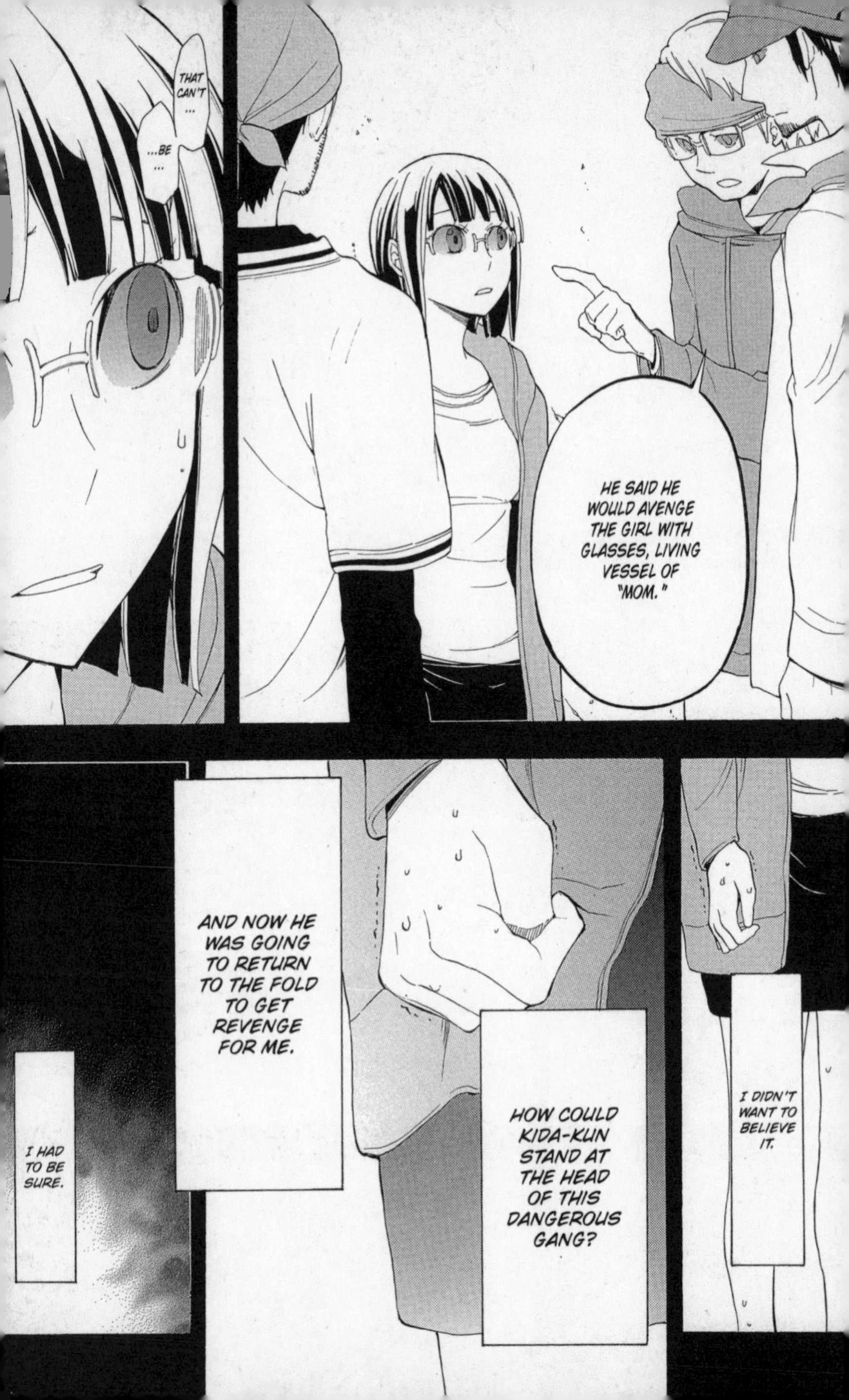
HE SAID HE WOULD AVENGE THE GIRL WITH GLASSES, LIVING VESSEL OF "MOM."
THAT CAN'T ...
...BE ...
I DIDN'T WANT TO BELIEVE IT.
AND NOW HE WAS GOING TO RETURN TO THE FOLD TO GET REVENGE FOR ME.
HOW COULD KIDA-KUN STAND AT THE HEAD OF THIS DANGEROUS GANG?
I HAD TO BE SURE.

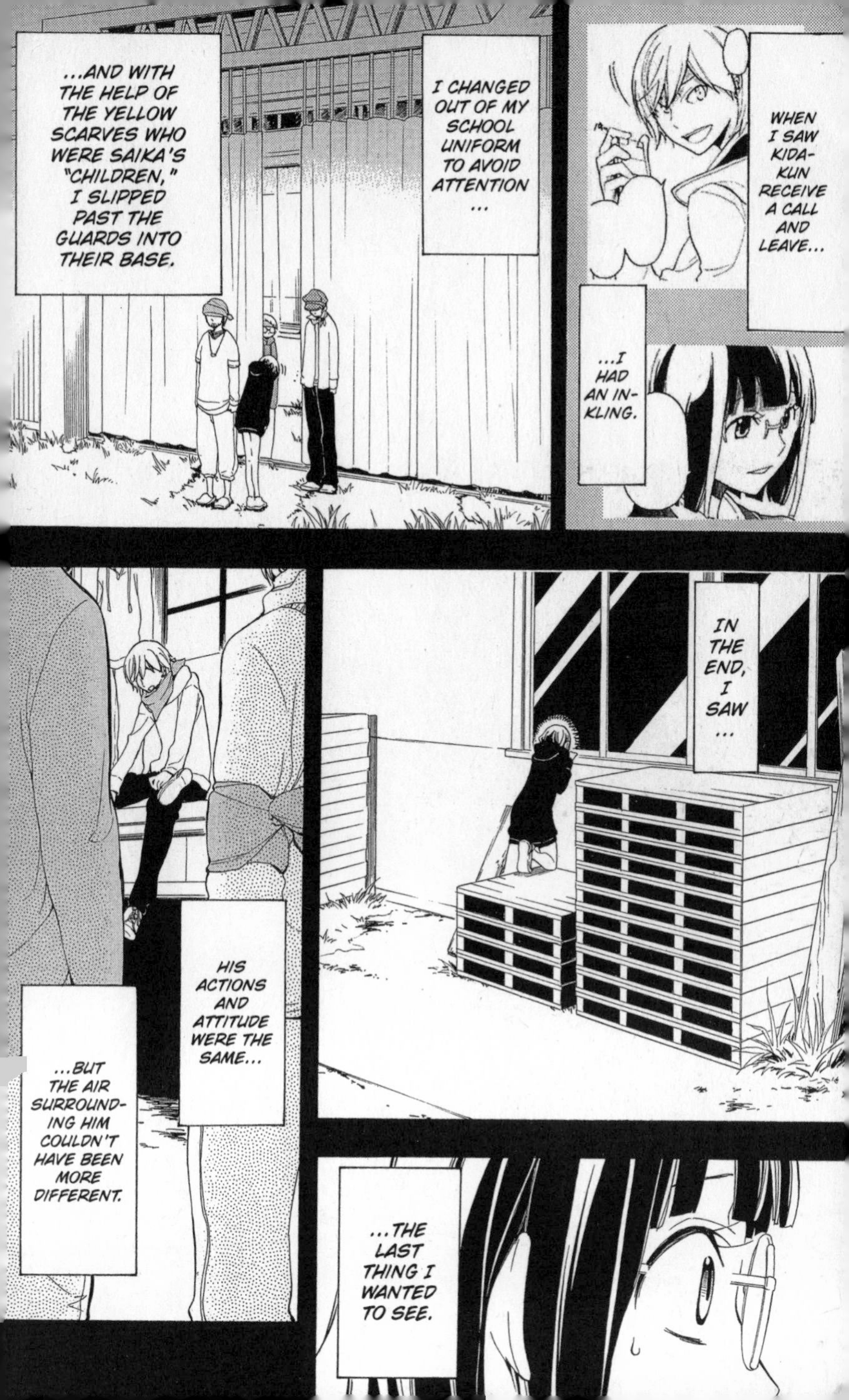
WHEN I SAW KIDA-KUN RECEIVE A CALL AND LEAVE...
...I HAD AN INKLING.
...AND WITH THE HELP OF THE YELLOW SCARVES WHO WERE SAIKA'S "CHILDREN," I SLIPPED PAST THE GUARDS INTO THEIR BASE.
I CHANGED OUT OF MY SCHOOL UNIFORM TO AVOID ATTENTION...
IN THE END, I SAW...
...THE LAST THING I WANTED TO SEE.
HIS ACTIONS AND ATTITUDE WERE THE SAME...
...BUT THE AIR SURROUNDING HIM COULDN'T HAVE BEEN MORE DIFFERENT.

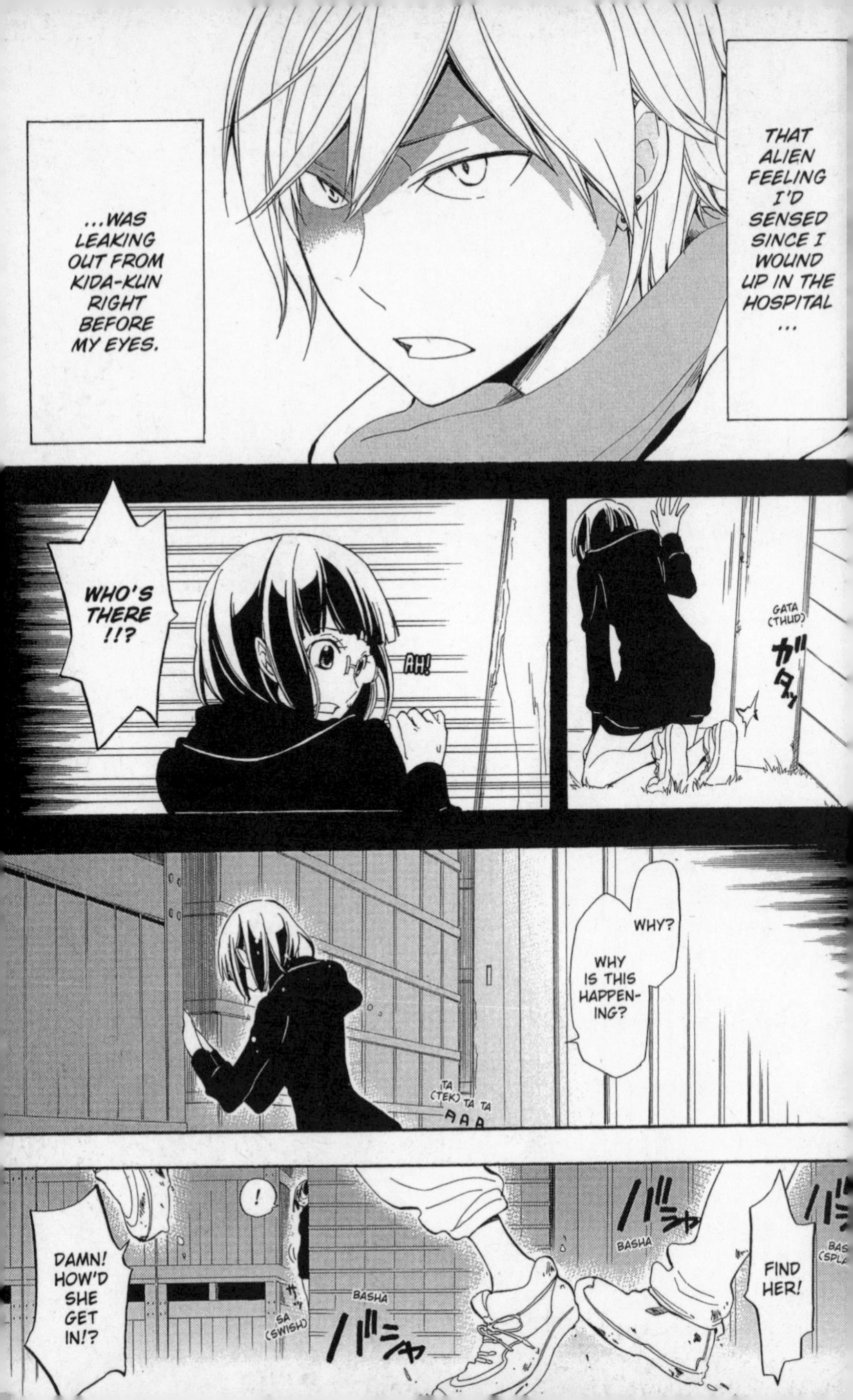
THAT ALIEN FEELING I'D SENSED SINCE I WOUND UP IN THE HOSPITAL...
...WAS LEAKING OUT FROM KIDA-KUN RIGHT BEFORE MY EYES.
GATA (THUD)
WHO'S THERE!!?
AH!
WHY?
WHY IS THIS HAPPENING?
TA (TEK) TA TA
BAS (SPLA
FIND HER!
BASHA
!
DAMN! HOW'D SHE GET IN!?
SA (SWISH)
BASHA

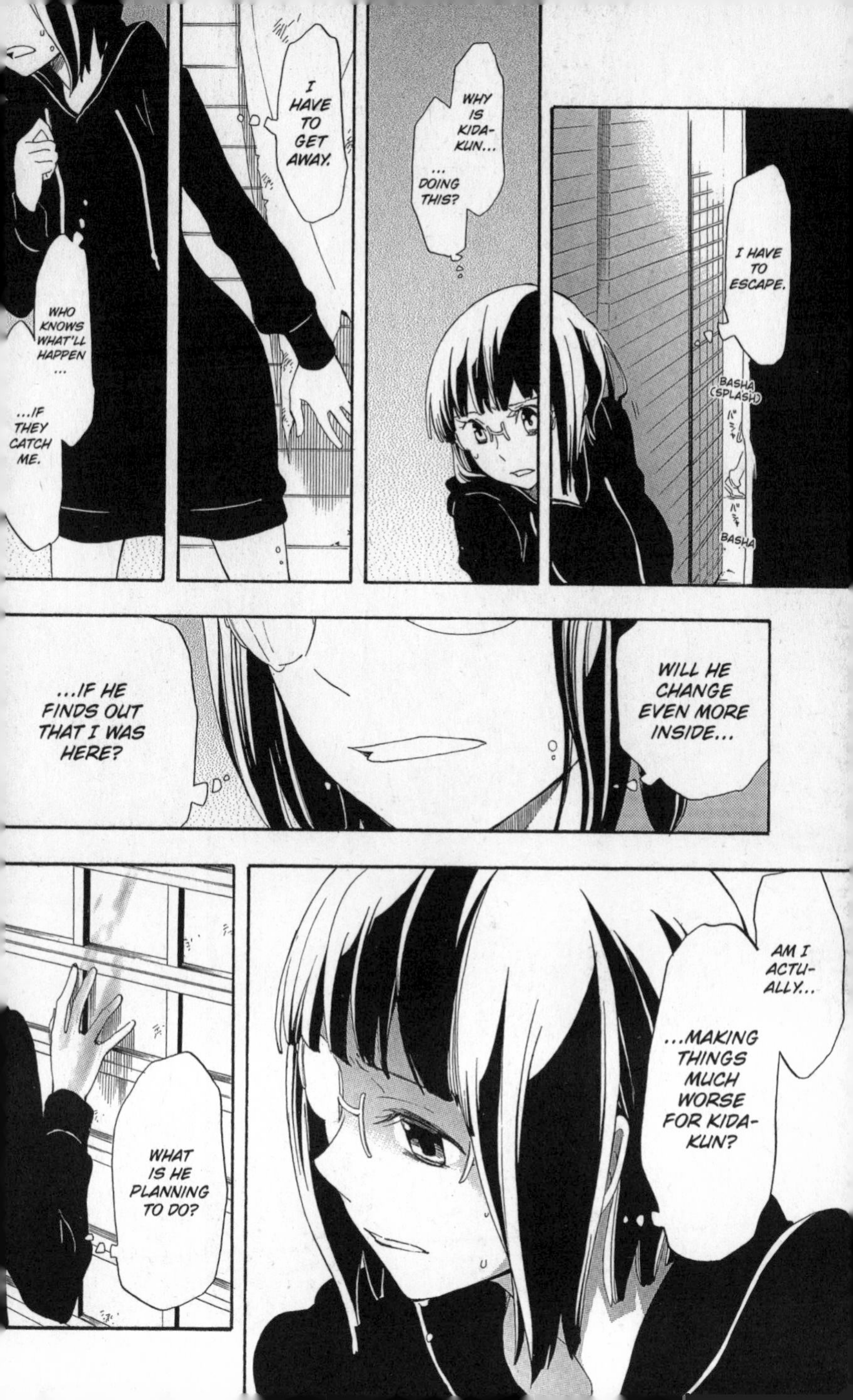
I HAVE TO ESCAPE.
BASHA (SPLASH)
BASHA
WHY IS KIDA-KUN...
...DOING THIS?
I HAVE TO GET AWAY.
WHO KNOWS WHAT'LL HAPPEN...
...IF THEY CATCH ME.
WILL HE CHANGE EVEN MORE INSIDE...
...IF HE FINDS OUT THAT I WAS HERE?
AM I ACTUALLY...
...MAKING THINGS MUCH WORSE FOR KIDA-KUN?
WHAT IS HE PLANNING TO DO?

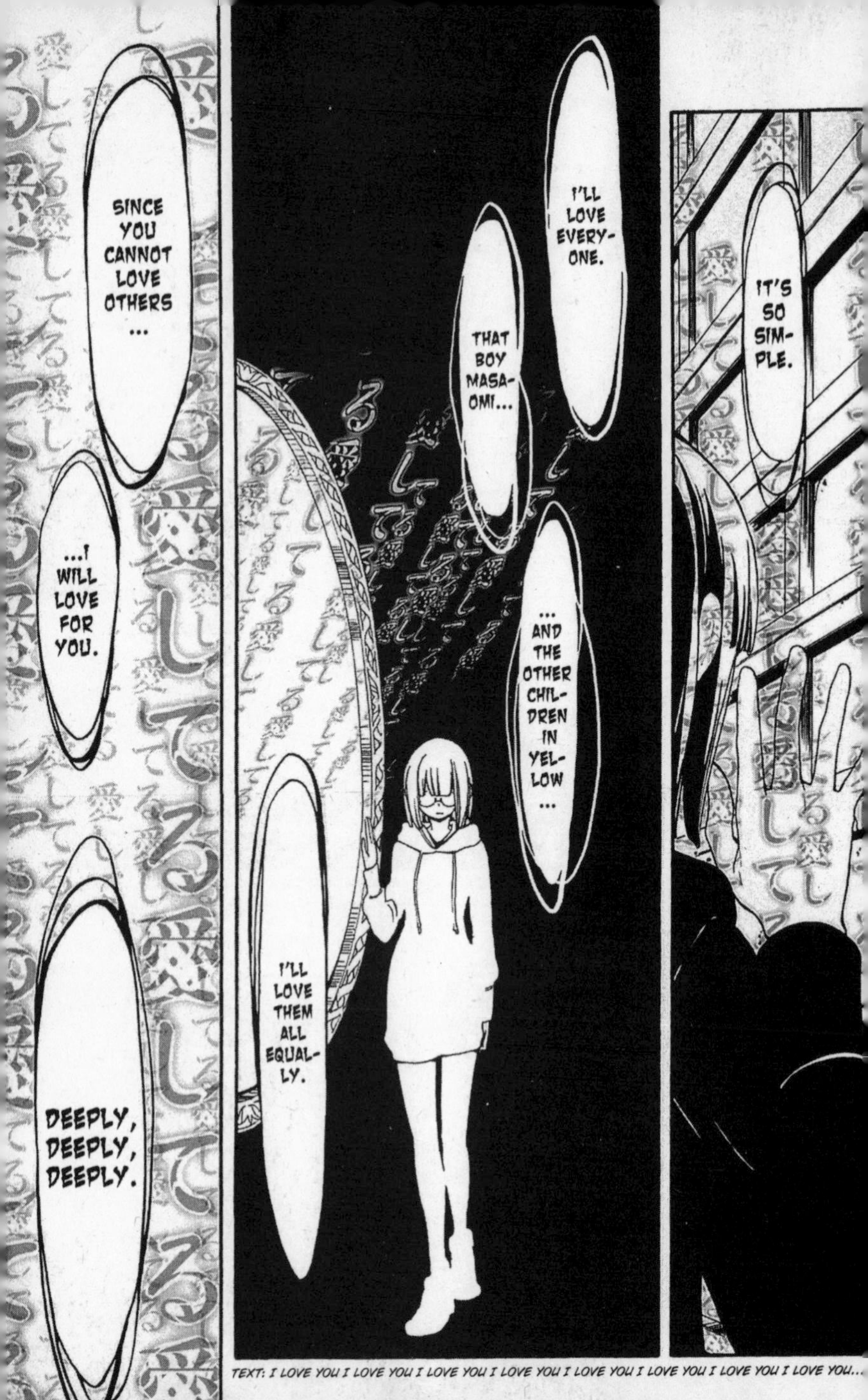
IT'S SO SIMPLE.
I'LL LOVE EVERYONE.
THAT BOY MASAOMI...
...AND THE OTHER CHILDREN IN YELLOW...
I'LL LOVE THEM ALL EQUALLY.
SINCE YOU CANNOT LOVE OTHERS...
...I WILL LOVE FOR YOU.
DEEPLY, DEEPLY, DEEPLY.

TEXT: I LOVE YOU I LOVE YOU I LOVE YOU I LOVE YOU I LOVE YOU I LOVE YOU I LOVE YOU I LOVE YOU...

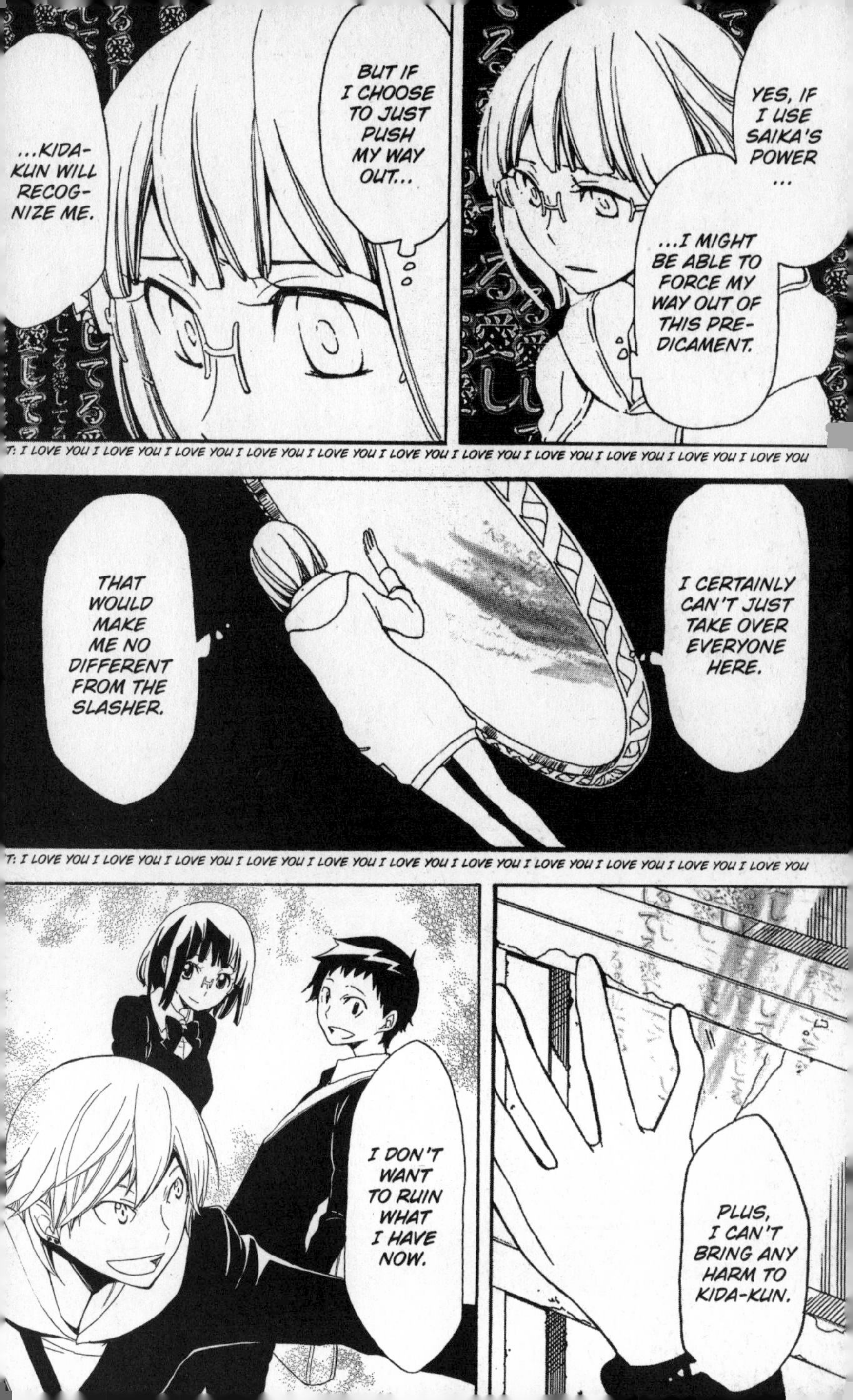
YES, IF I USE SAIKA'S POWER...
...I MIGHT BE ABLE TO FORCE MY WAY OUT OF THIS PRE-DICAMENT.
BUT IF I CHOOSE TO JUST PUSH MY WAY OUT...
...KIDA-KUN WILL RECOG-NIZE ME.
T: I LOVE YOU I LOVE YOU I LOVE YOU I LOVE YOU I LOVE YOU I LOVE YOU I LOVE YOU I LOVE YOU I LOVE YOU I LOVE YOU I LOVE YOU
I CERTAINLY CAN'T JUST TAKE OVER EVERYONE HERE.
THAT WOULD MAKE ME NO DIFFERENT FROM THE SLASHER.
T: I LOVE YOU I LOVE YOU I LOVE YOU I LOVE YOU I LOVE YOU I LOVE YOU I LOVE YOU I LOVE YOU I LOVE YOU I LOVE YOU I LOVE YOU
PLUS, I CAN'T BRING ANY HARM TO KIDA-KUN.
I DON'T WANT TO RUIN WHAT I HAVE NOW.

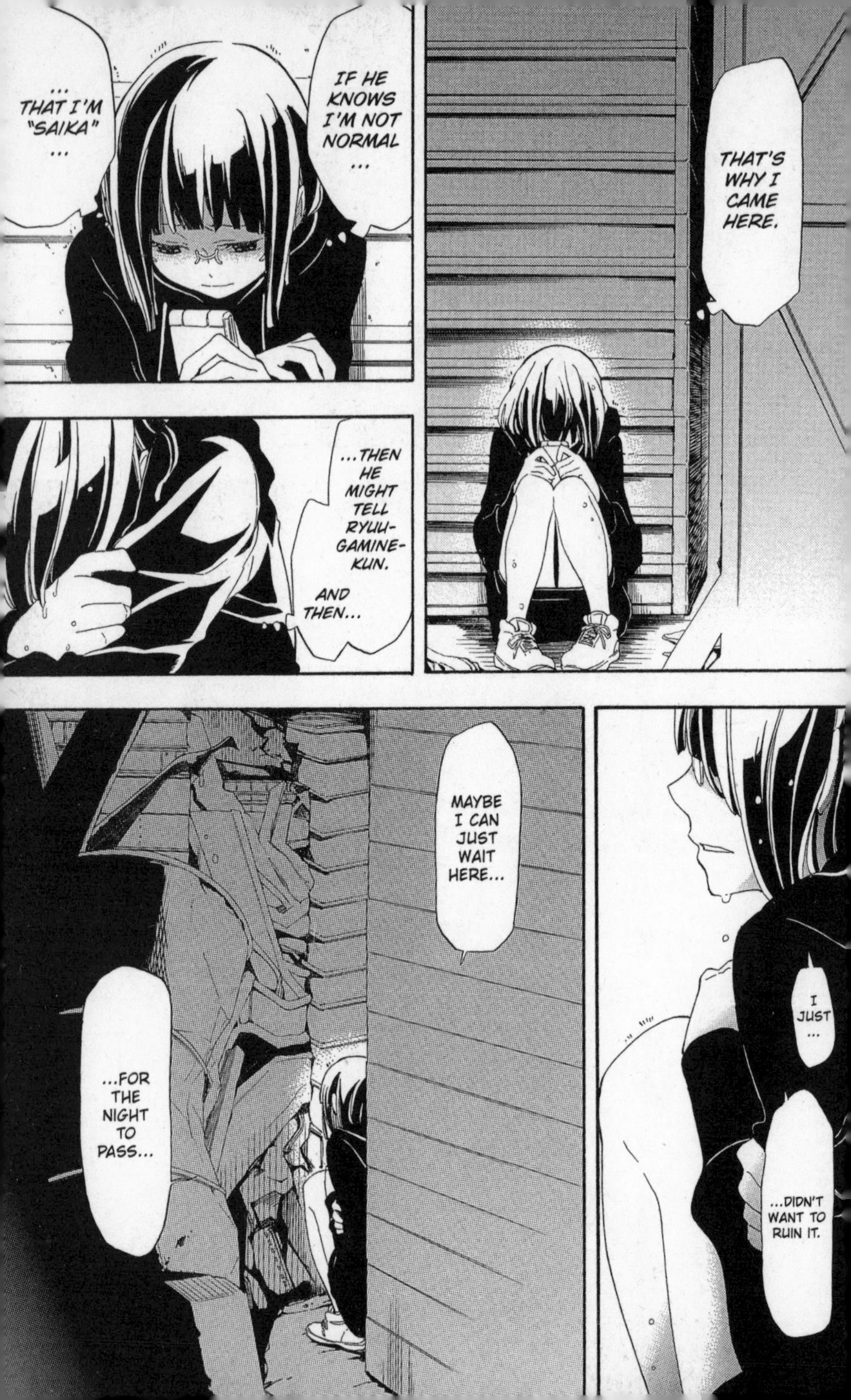
THAT'S WHY I CAME HERE.
IF HE KNOWS I'M NOT NORMAL...
...THAT I'M "SAIKA"...
...THEN HE MIGHT TELL RYUU-GAMINE-KUN.
AND THEN...
I JUST...
...DIDN'T WANT TO RUIN IT.
MAYBE I CAN JUST WAIT HERE...
...FOR THE NIGHT TO PASS...

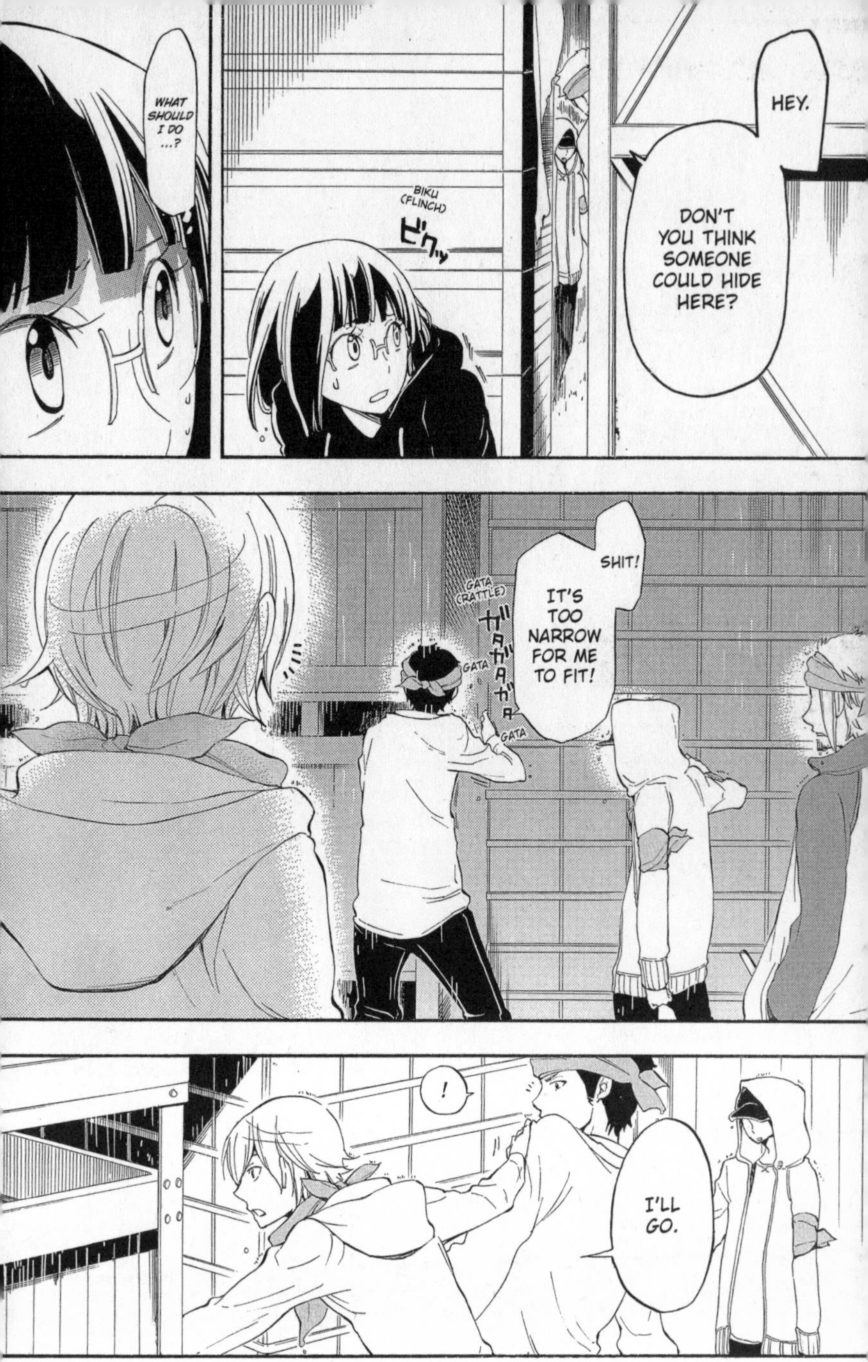
HEY.
DON'T YOU THINK SOMEONE COULD HIDE HERE?
BIKU (FLINCH)
ビクッ
WHAT SHOULD I DO ...?
SHIT!
IT'S TOO NARROW FOR ME TO FIT!
GATA (RATTLE)
ガタガタガタ
GATA
GATA
I'LL GO.
!

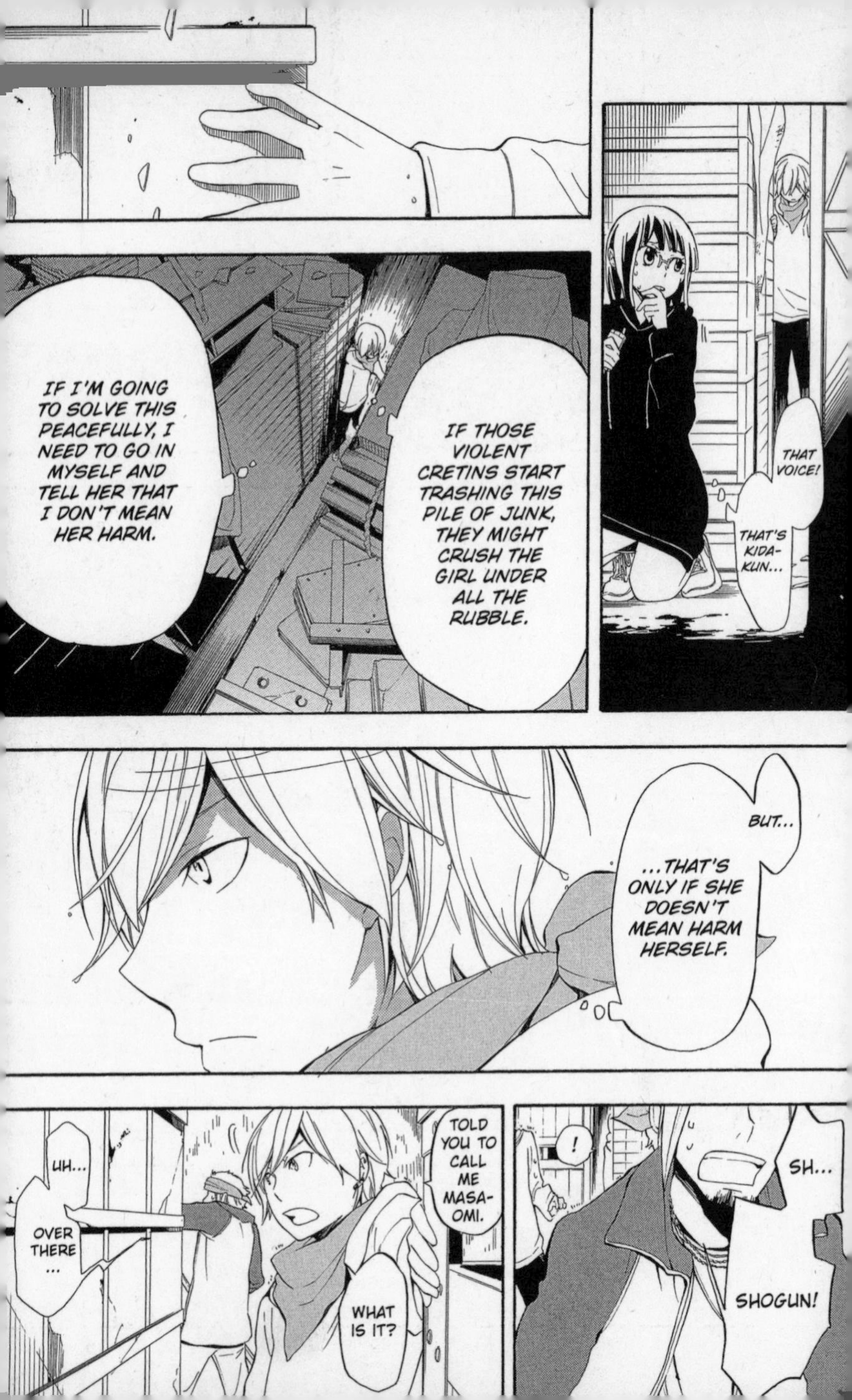
THAT VOICE!
THAT'S KIDA-KUN...
IF THOSE VIOLENT CRETINS START TRASHING THIS PILE OF JUNK, THEY MIGHT CRUSH THE GIRL UNDER ALL THE RUBBLE.
IF I'M GOING TO SOLVE THIS PEACEFULLY, I NEED TO GO IN MYSELF AND TELL HER THAT I DON'T MEAN HER HARM.
BUT...
...THAT'S ONLY IF SHE DOESN'T MEAN HARM HERSELF.
SH...
SHOGUN!
!
TOLD YOU TO CALL ME MASA-OMI.
WHAT IS IT?
UH...
OVER THERE...

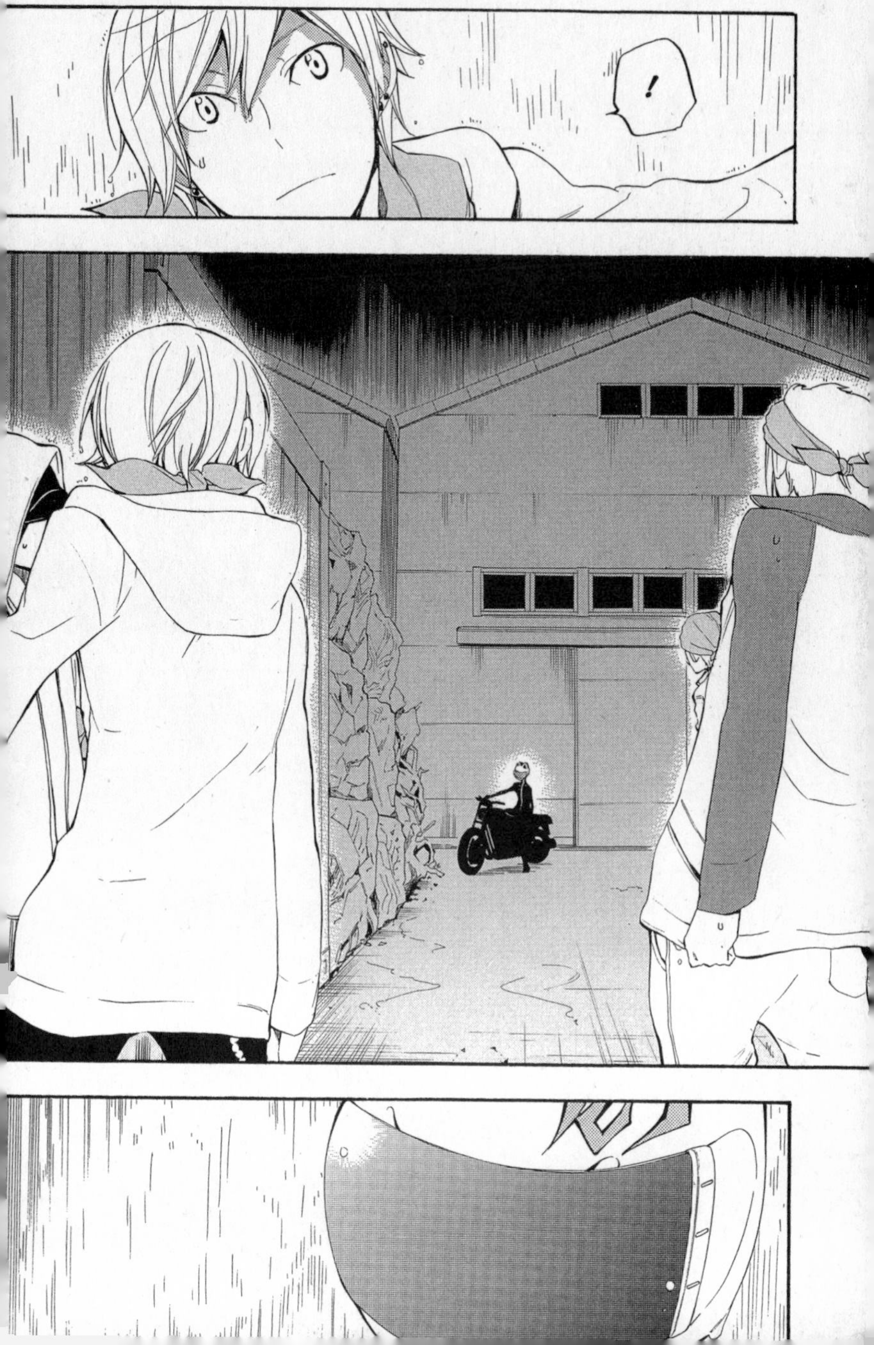
!

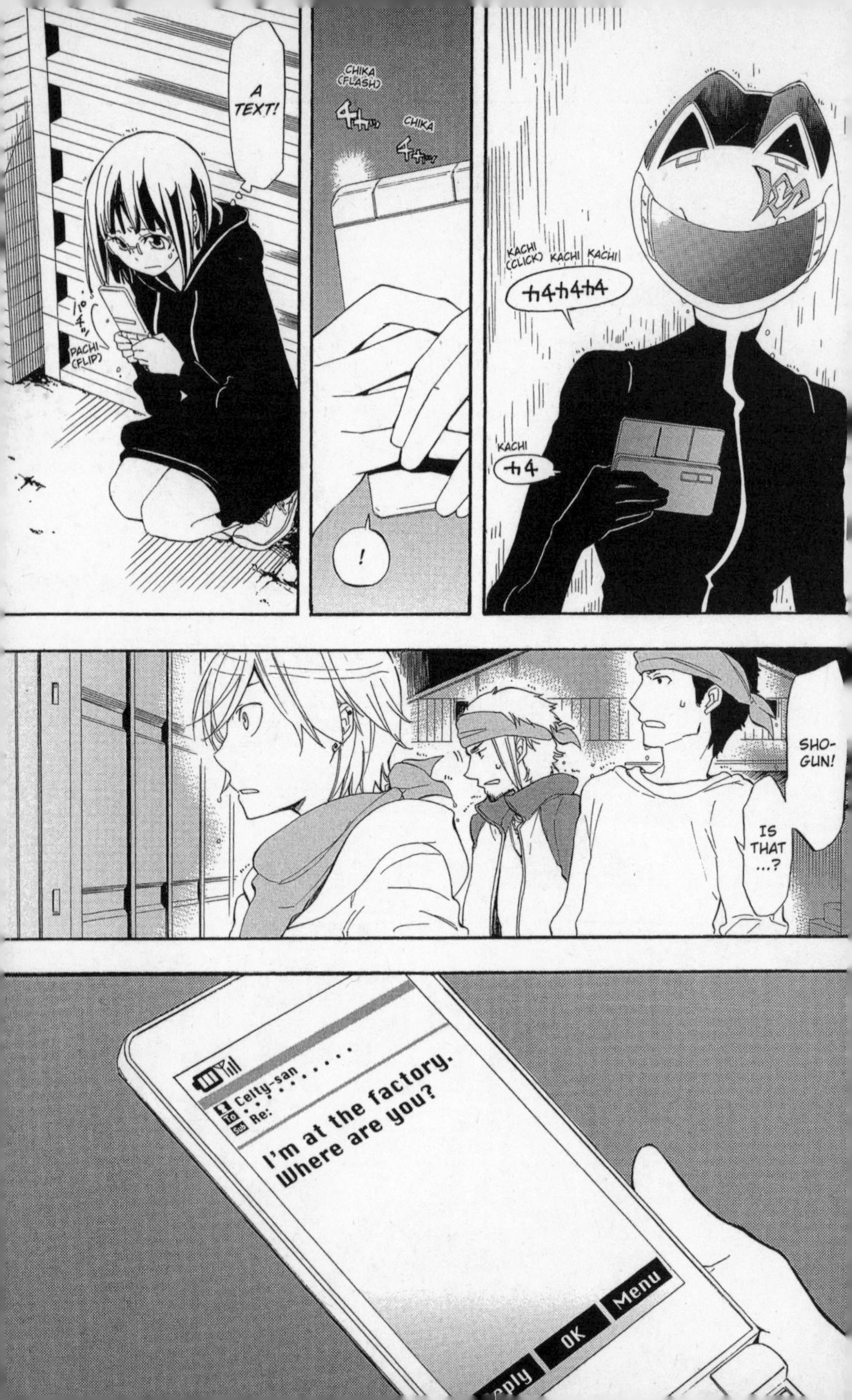
KACHI (CLICK) KACHI KACHI
カチカチカチ
KACHI
カチ
CHIKA (FLASH)
チカッ
CHIKA
チカッ
!
A TEXT!
PACHI (FLIP)
パチッ
SHO-GUN!
IS THAT ...?
Celty-san
Re:
I'm at the factory. Where are you?
Menu
OK

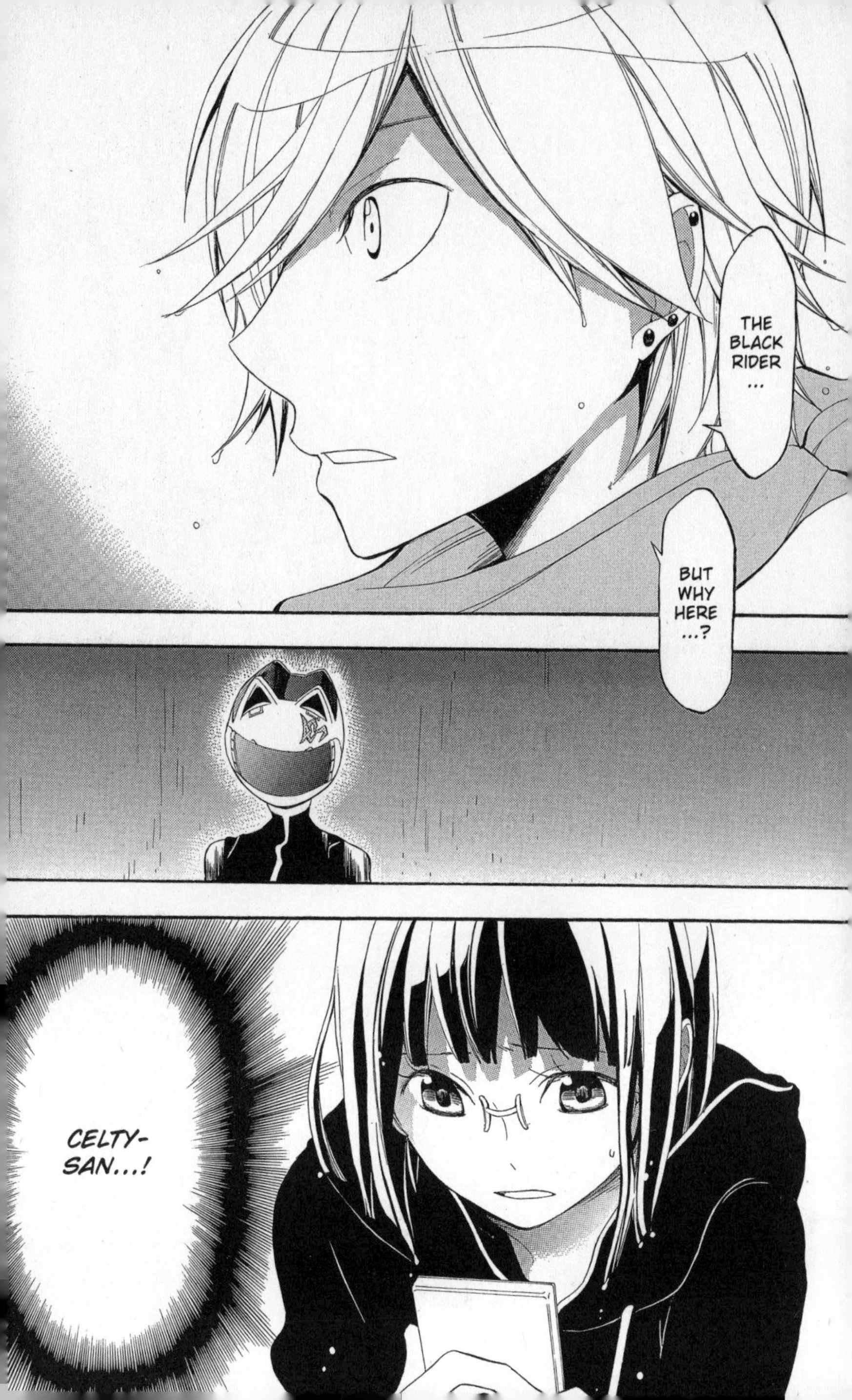
THE BLACK RIDER ...
BUT WHY HERE ...?
CELTY-SAN...!

DURARARA!!

ORRR!!

DRRR!!

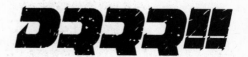

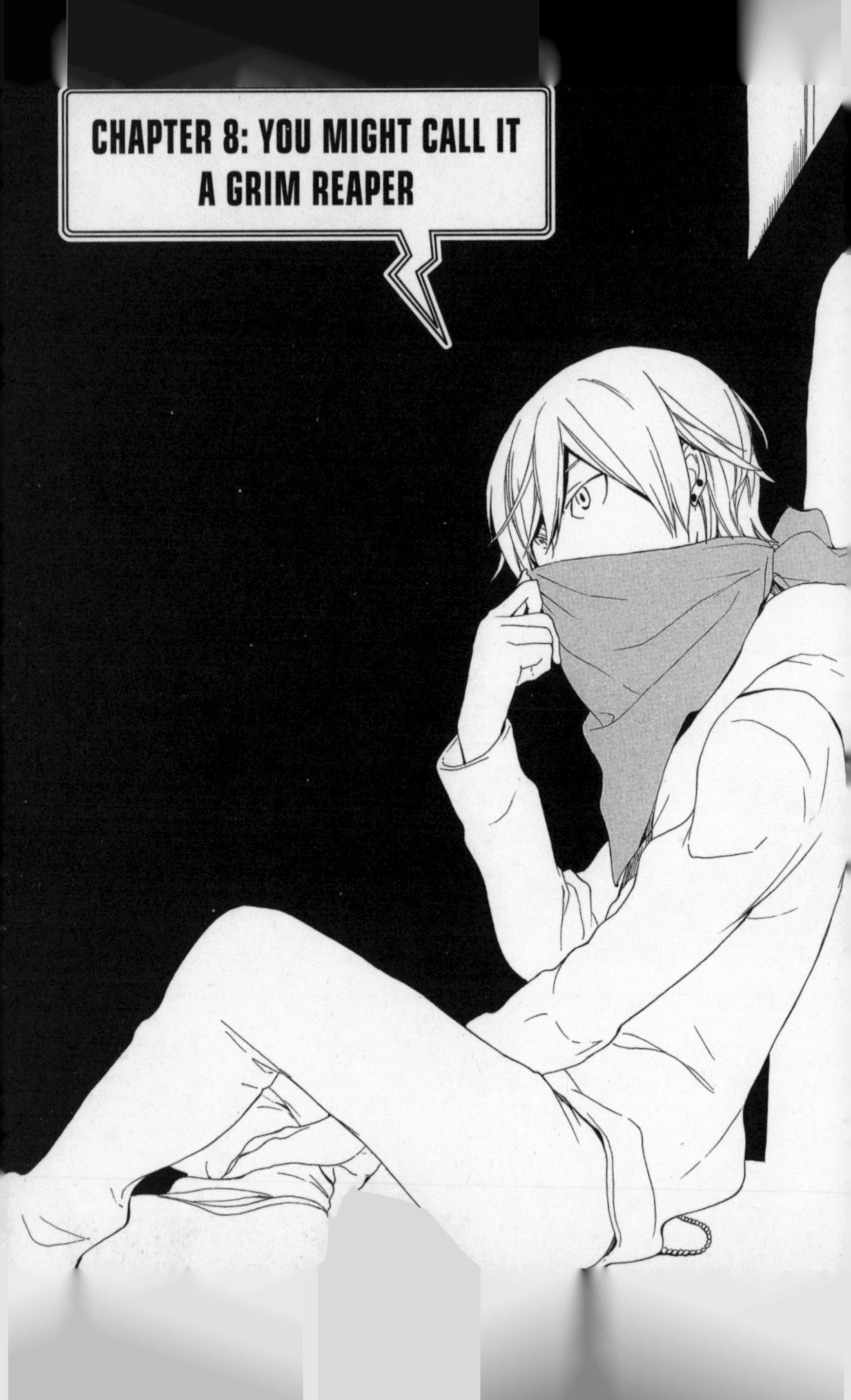
CHAPTER 8: YOU MIGHT CALL IT A GRIM REAPER

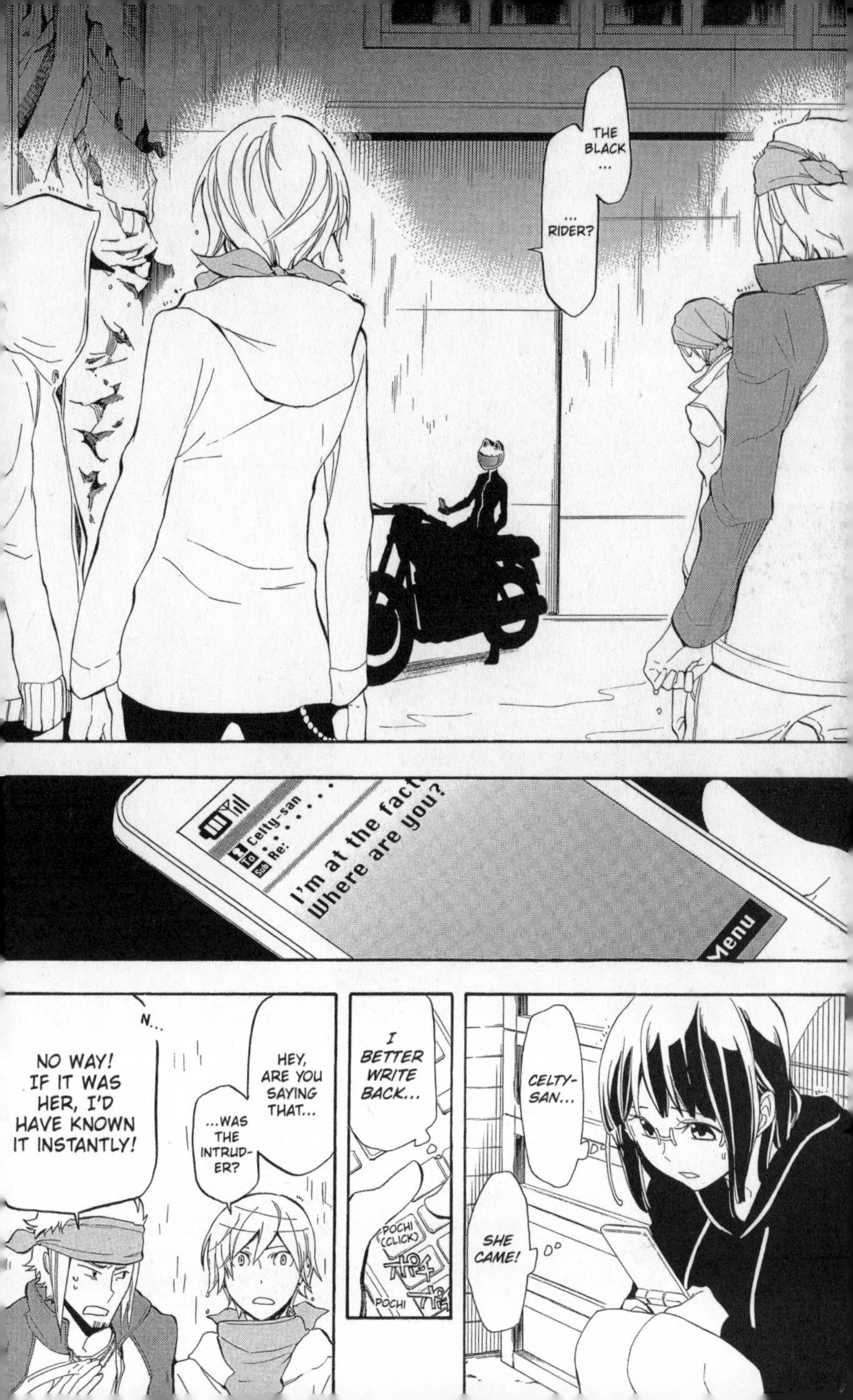
THE BLACK ...
... RIDER?
Celty-san
Re:
I'm at the fact
Where are you?
Menu
CELTY-SAN...
SHE CAME!
I BETTER WRITE BACK...
POCHI (CLICK)
POCHI
N...
HEY, ARE YOU SAYING THAT...
...WAS THE INTRUD-ER?
NO WAY! IF IT WAS HER, I'D HAVE KNOWN IT INSTANTLY!

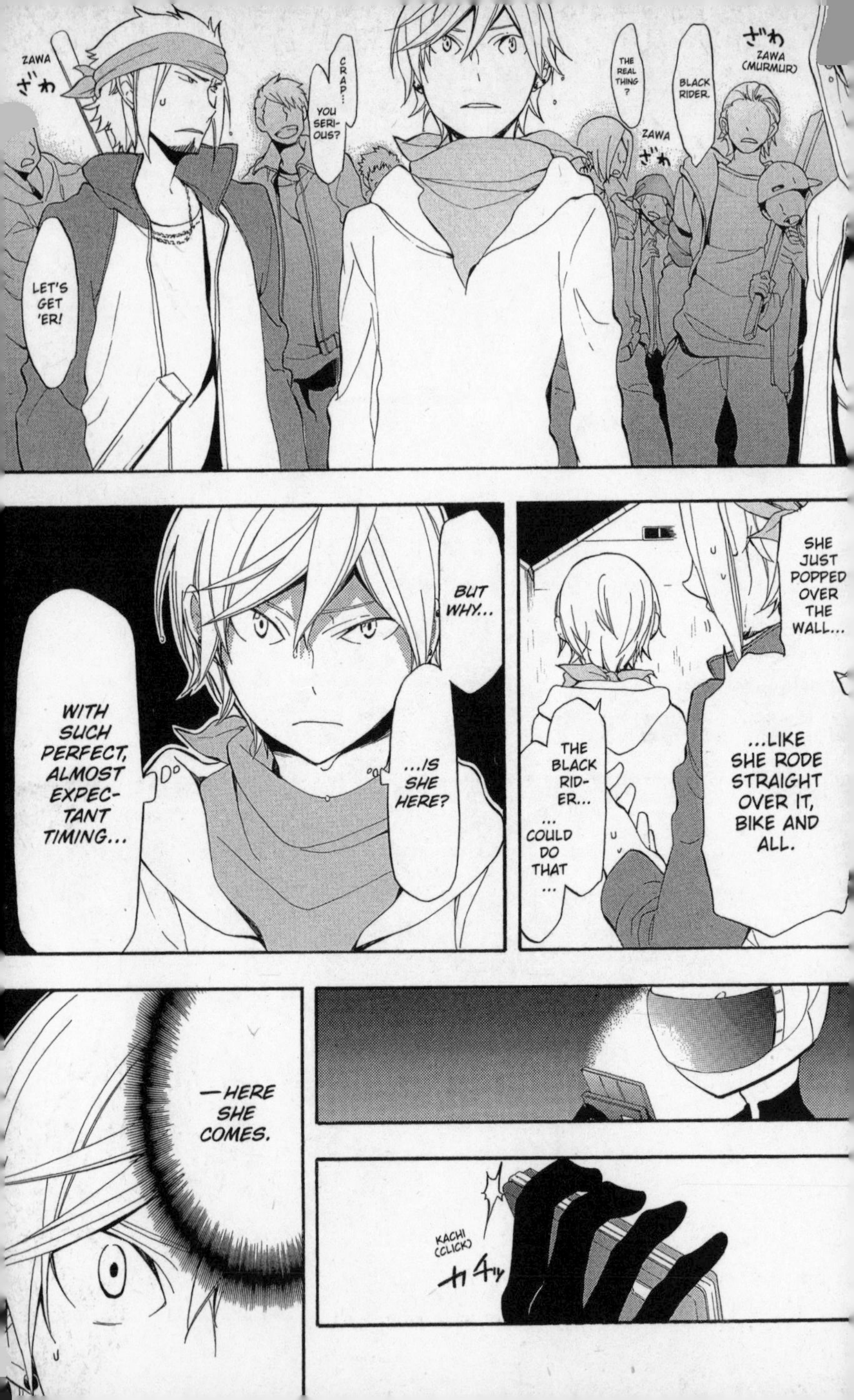
ざわ
ZAWA (MURMUR)
BLACK RIDER.
THE REAL THING?
ZAWA
ざわ
CRAP... YOU SERIOUS?
ZAWA
ざわ
LET'S GET 'ER!
SHE JUST POPPED OVER THE WALL...
...LIKE SHE RODE STRAIGHT OVER IT, BIKE AND ALL.
THE BLACK RIDER... ...COULD DO THAT...
BUT WHY...
...IS SHE HERE?
WITH SUCH PERFECT, ALMOST EXPECTANT TIMING...
KACHI (CLICK)
カチッ
—HERE SHE COMES.

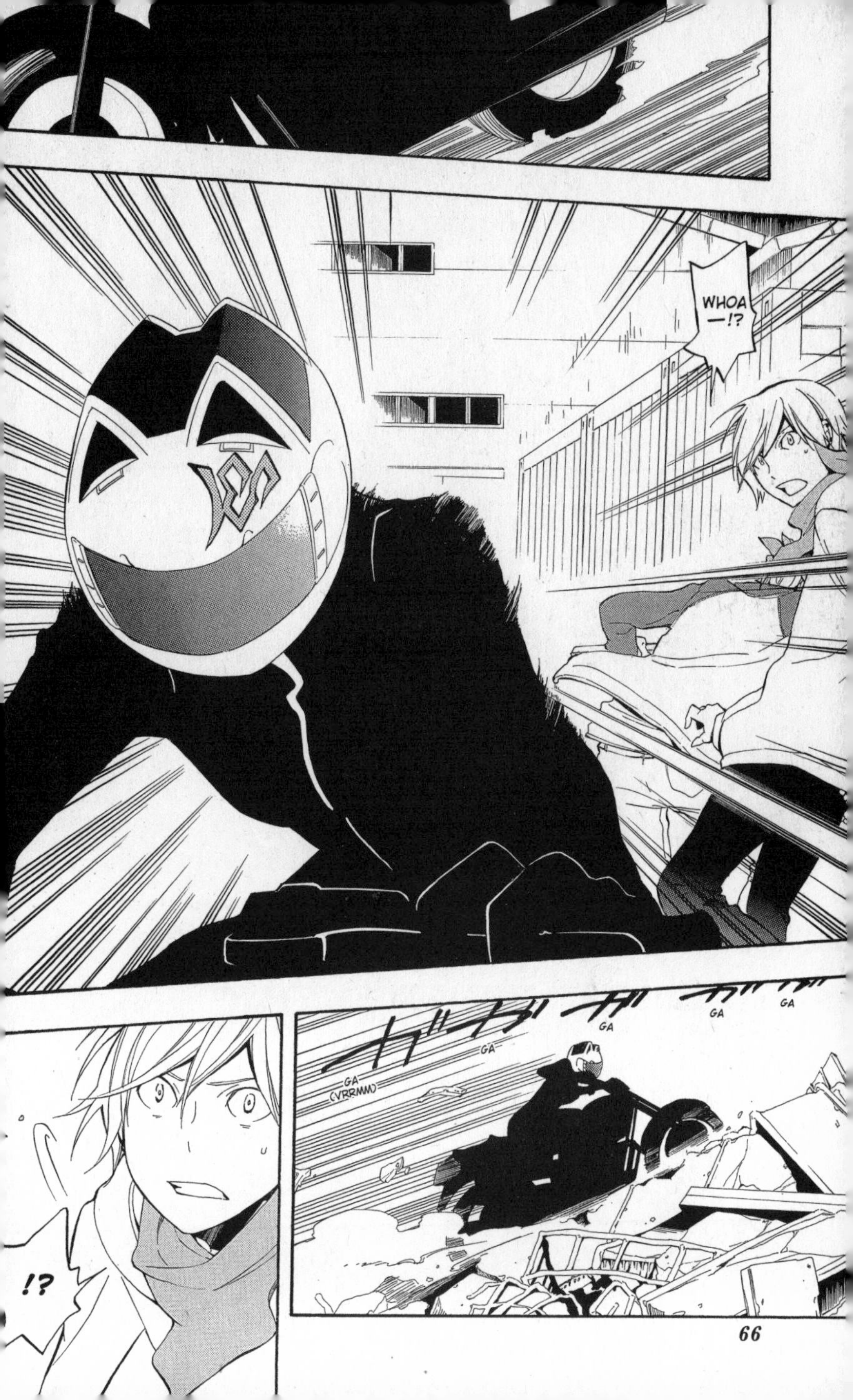
WHOA—!?
GA
GA
GA
GA
GA
(VRRMM)
!?

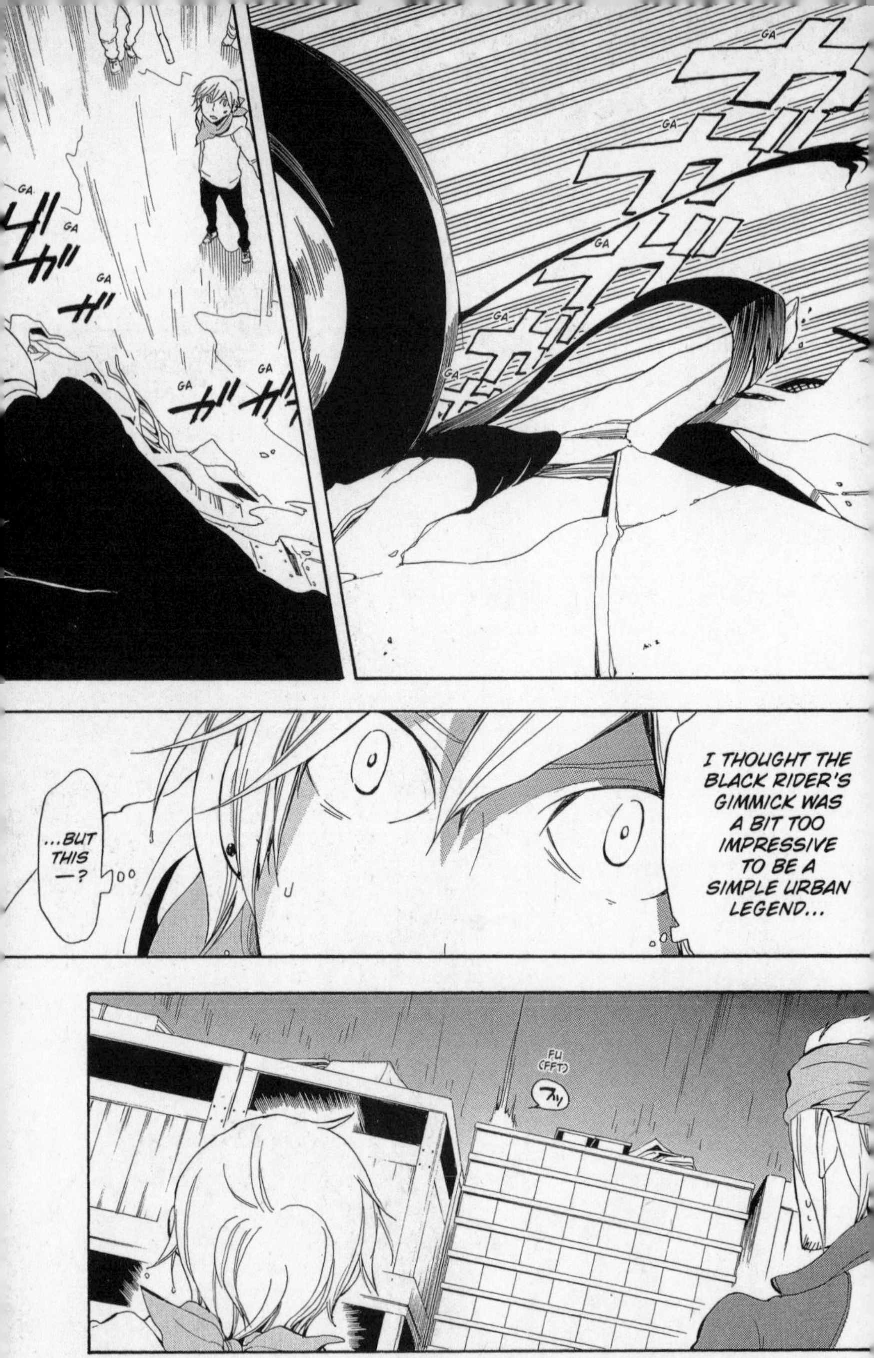
GA
GA
GA
GA
GA
GA
GA
GA
GA
GA
I THOUGHT THE BLACK RIDER'S GIMMICK WAS A BIT TOO IMPRESSIVE TO BE A SIMPLE URBAN LEGEND...
...BUT THIS—?
FU (FFT)

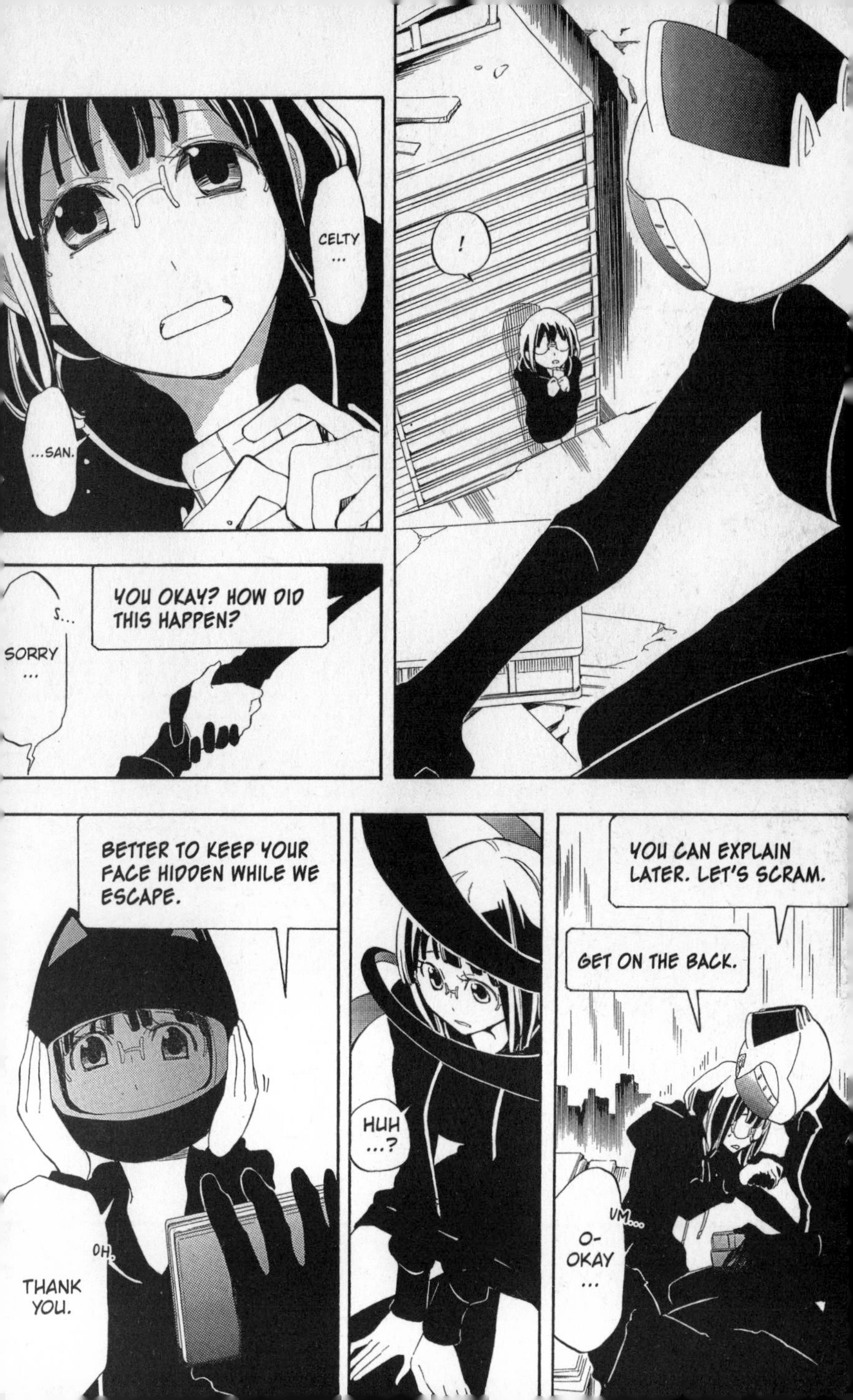
!
CELTY ...
...SAN.
YOU OKAY? HOW DID THIS HAPPEN?
S... SORRY ...
YOU CAN EXPLAIN LATER. LET'S SCRAM.
GET ON THE BACK.
UM...
O-OKAY ...
HUH ...?
BETTER TO KEEP YOUR FACE HIDDEN WHILE WE ESCAPE.
OH,
THANK YOU.

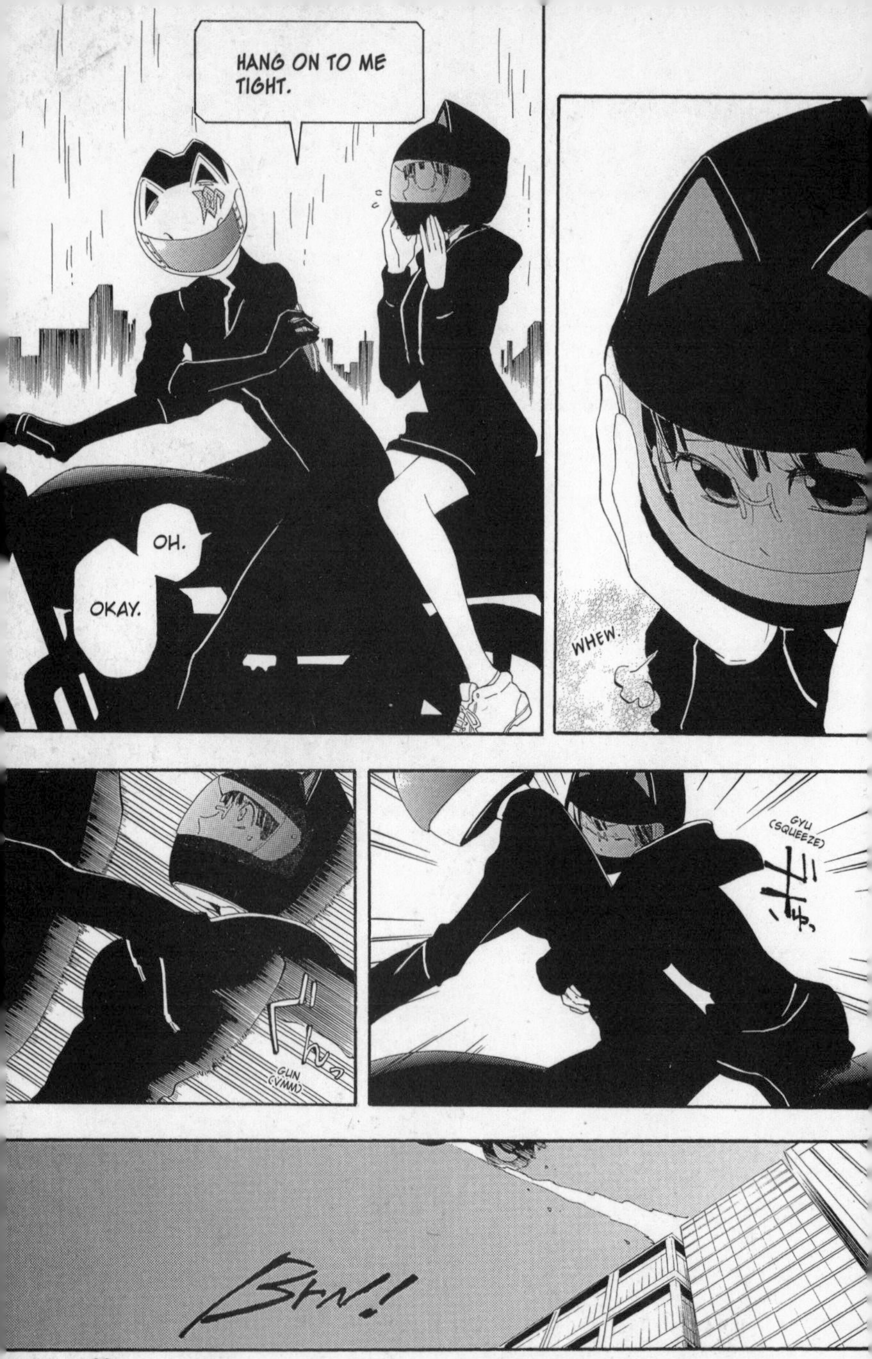
WHEW.
HANG ON TO ME TIGHT.
OH.
OKAY.
GYU (SQUEEZE)
GUN (VMM)

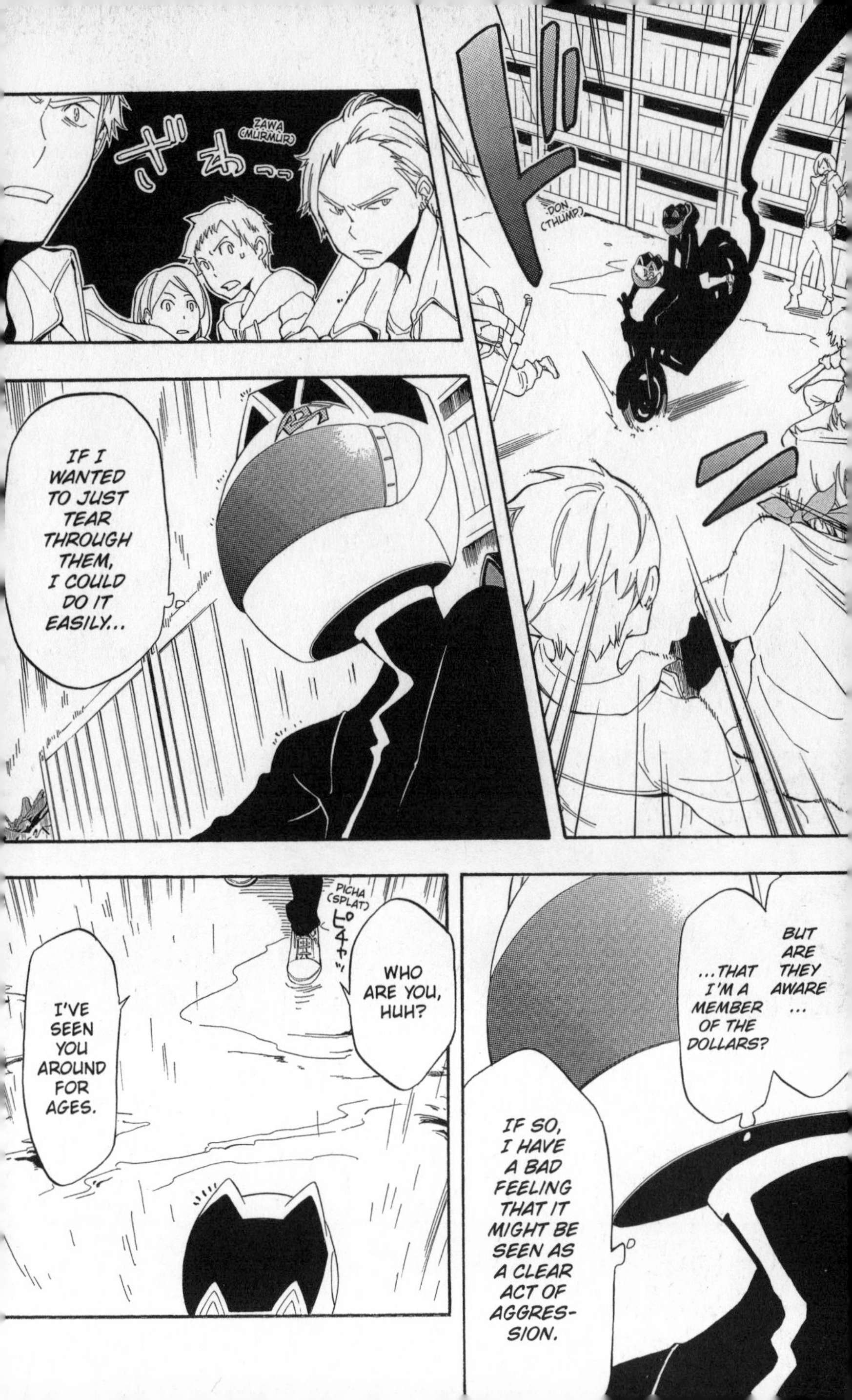
DON (THUMP)
ZAWA (MURMUR)
IF I WANTED TO JUST TEAR THROUGH THEM, I COULD DO IT EASILY...
BUT ARE THEY AWARE...
...THAT I'M A MEMBER OF THE DOLLARS?
IF SO, I HAVE A BAD FEELING THAT IT MIGHT BE SEEN AS A CLEAR ACT OF AGGRES-SION.
PICHA (SPLAT)
WHO ARE YOU, HUH?
I'VE SEEN YOU AROUND FOR AGES.

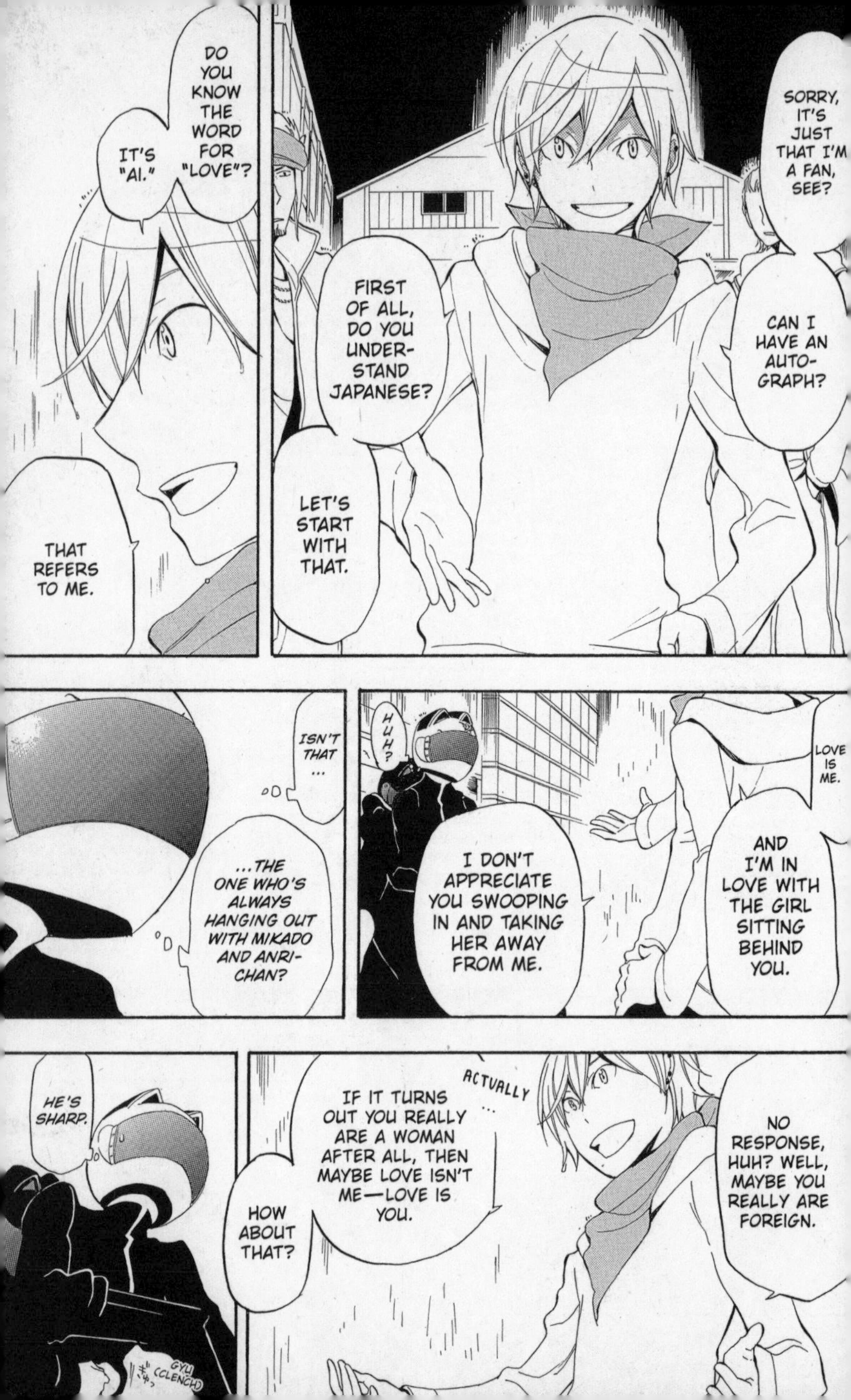
SORRY, IT'S JUST THAT I'M A FAN, SEE?
CAN I HAVE AN AUTO-GRAPH?
FIRST OF ALL, DO YOU UNDER-STAND JAPANESE?
LET'S START WITH THAT.
DO YOU KNOW THE WORD FOR "LOVE"?
IT'S "AI."
THAT REFERS TO ME.
LOVE IS ME.
AND I'M IN LOVE WITH THE GIRL SITTING BEHIND YOU.
I DON'T APPRECIATE YOU SWOOPING IN AND TAKING HER AWAY FROM ME.
HUH?
ISN'T THAT...
...THE ONE WHO'S ALWAYS HANGING OUT WITH MIKADO AND ANRI-CHAN?
NO RESPONSE, HUH? WELL, MAYBE YOU REALLY ARE FOREIGN.
ACTUALLY...
IF IT TURNS OUT YOU REALLY ARE A WOMAN AFTER ALL, THEN MAYBE LOVE ISN'T ME—LOVE IS YOU.
HOW ABOUT THAT?
HE'S SHARP.
GYU (CLENCH)

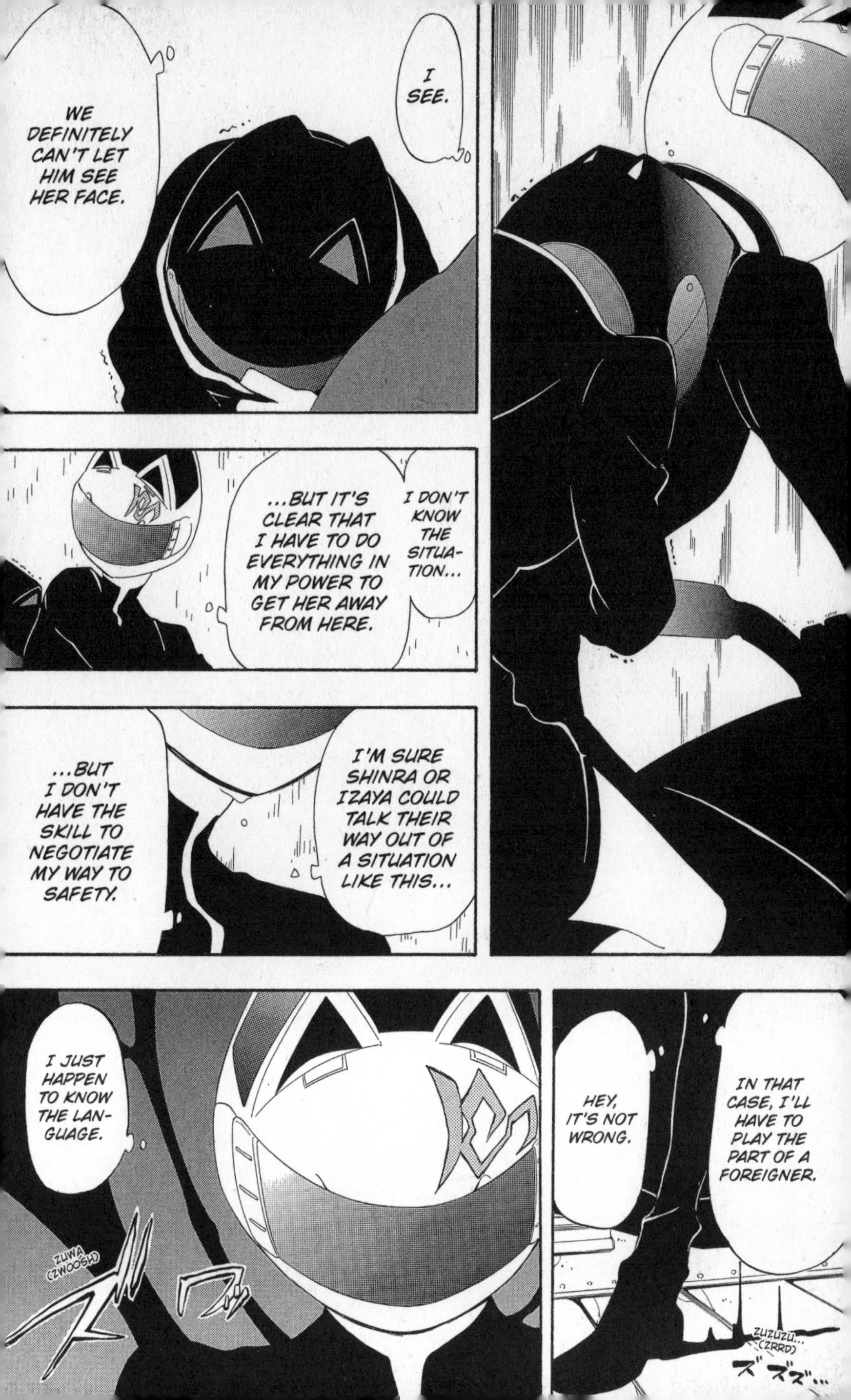
I SEE.
WE DEFINITELY CAN'T LET HIM SEE HER FACE.
I DON'T KNOW THE SITUA-TION...
...BUT IT'S CLEAR THAT I HAVE TO DO EVERYTHING IN MY POWER TO GET HER AWAY FROM HERE.
I'M SURE SHINRA OR IZAYA COULD TALK THEIR WAY OUT OF A SITUATION LIKE THIS...
...BUT I DON'T HAVE THE SKILL TO NEGOTIATE MY WAY TO SAFETY.
IN THAT CASE, I'LL HAVE TO PLAY THE PART OF A FOREIGNER.
HEY, IT'S NOT WRONG.
ZUZUZU... (ZRRD)
I JUST HAPPEN TO KNOW THE LAN-GUAGE.
ZUWA (ZWOOSH)

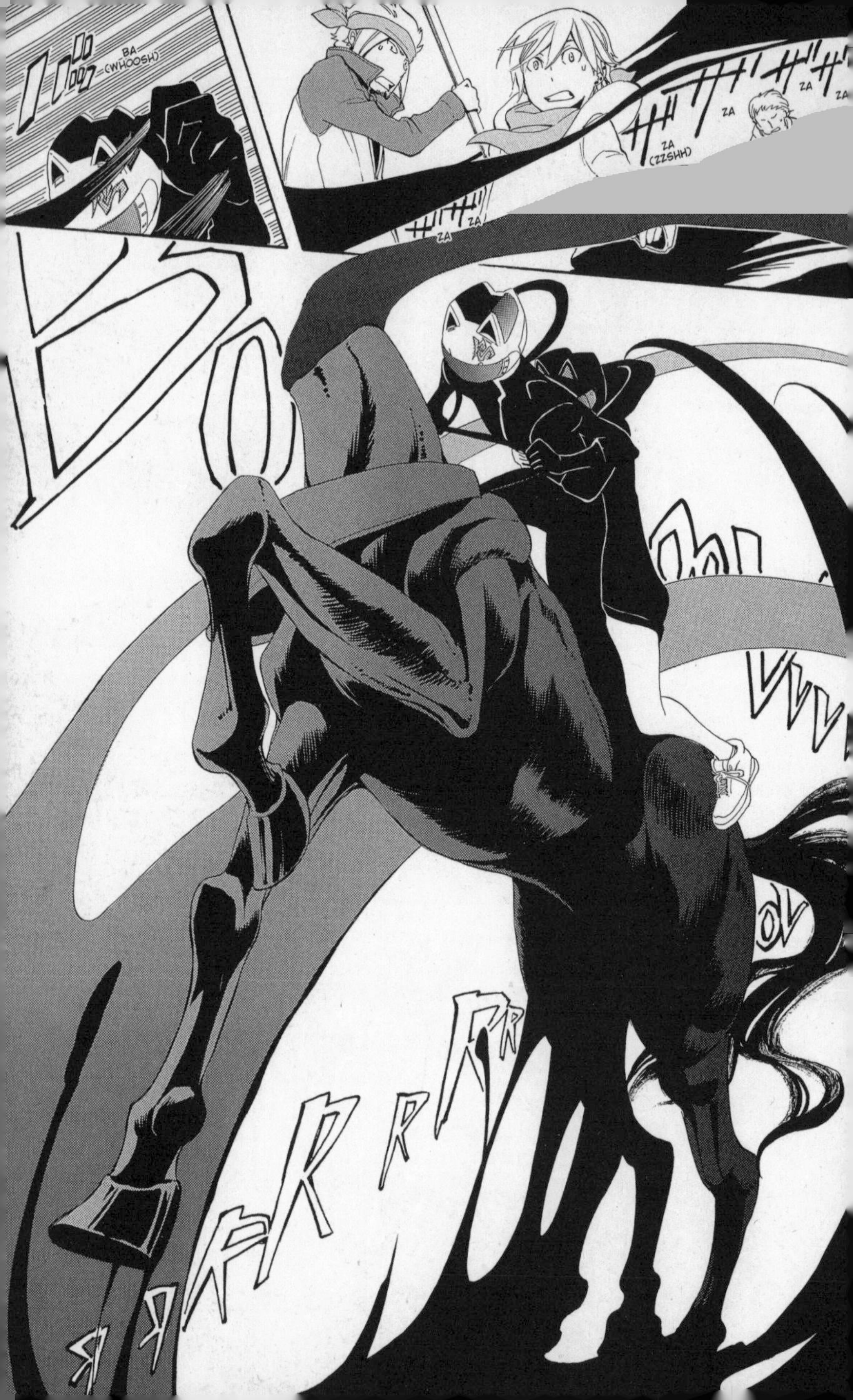

ZA
ZA
ZA (ZZSHH)
ZA
ZA
BA (WHOOSH)

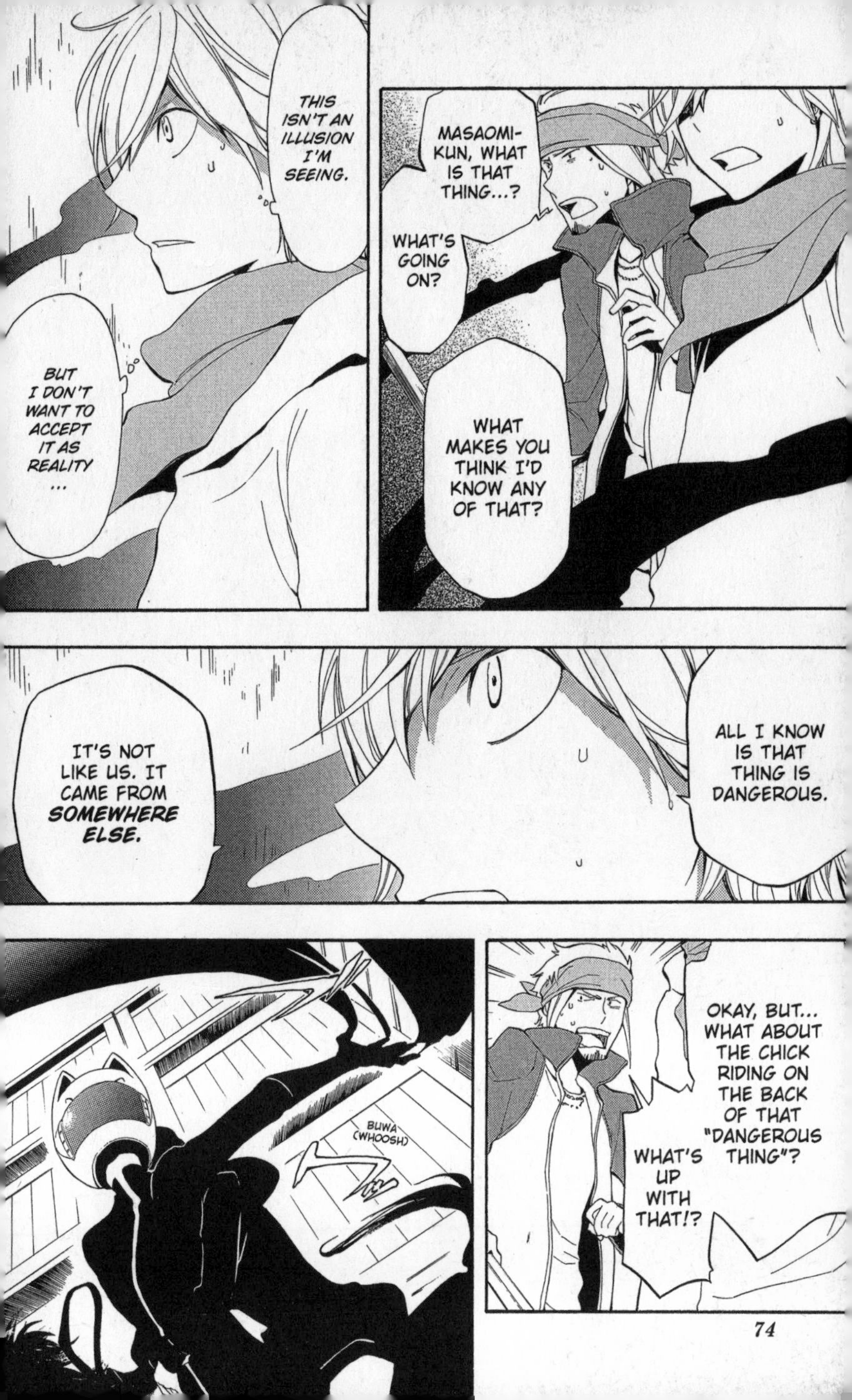
MASAOMI-KUN, WHAT IS THAT THING...?
WHAT'S GOING ON?
WHAT MAKES YOU THINK I'D KNOW ANY OF THAT?
THIS ISN'T AN ILLUSION I'M SEEING.
BUT I DON'T WANT TO ACCEPT IT AS REALITY ...
ALL I KNOW IS THAT THING IS DANGEROUS.
IT'S NOT LIKE US. IT CAME FROM **SOMEWHERE ELSE.**
OKAY, BUT... WHAT ABOUT THE CHICK RIDING ON THE BACK OF THAT "DANGEROUS THING"?
WHAT'S UP WITH THAT!?
BUWA (WHOOSH)

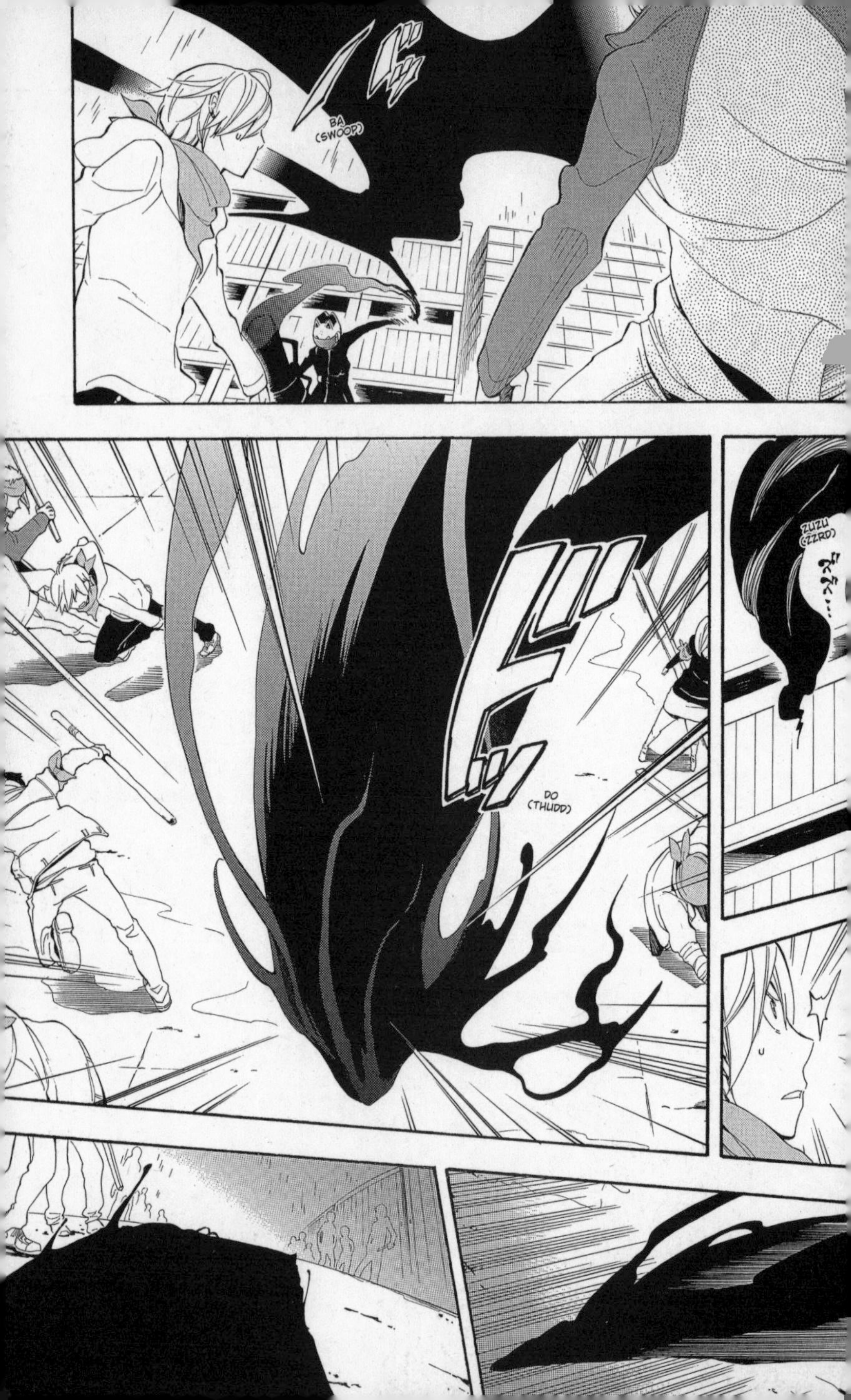
BA (SWOOP)
ZUZU (ZZRD)
DO (THUDD)

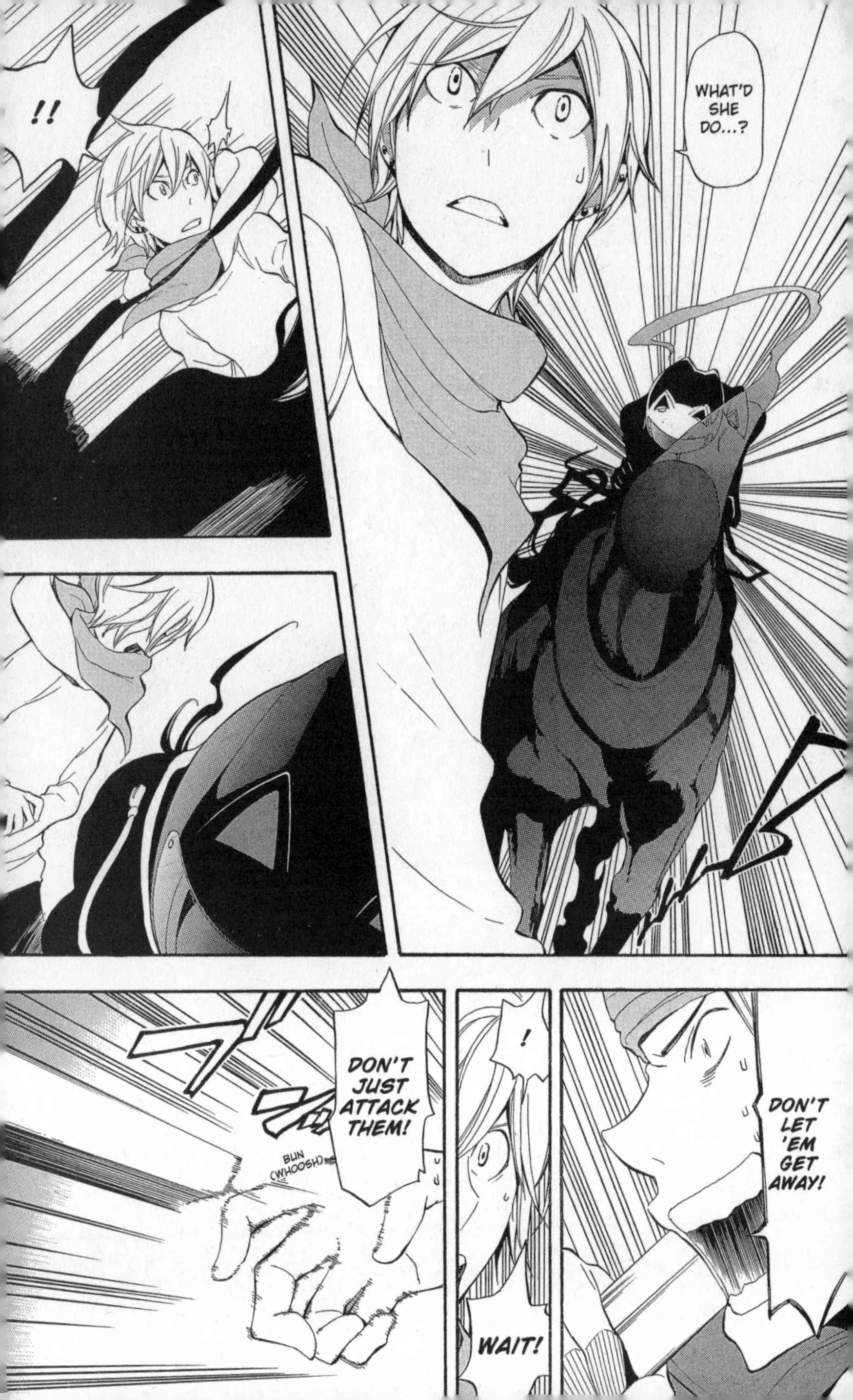
WHAT'D SHE DO...?
!!
DON'T LET 'EM GET AWAY!
!
WAIT!
DON'T JUST ATTACK THEM!
BUN (WHOOSH)

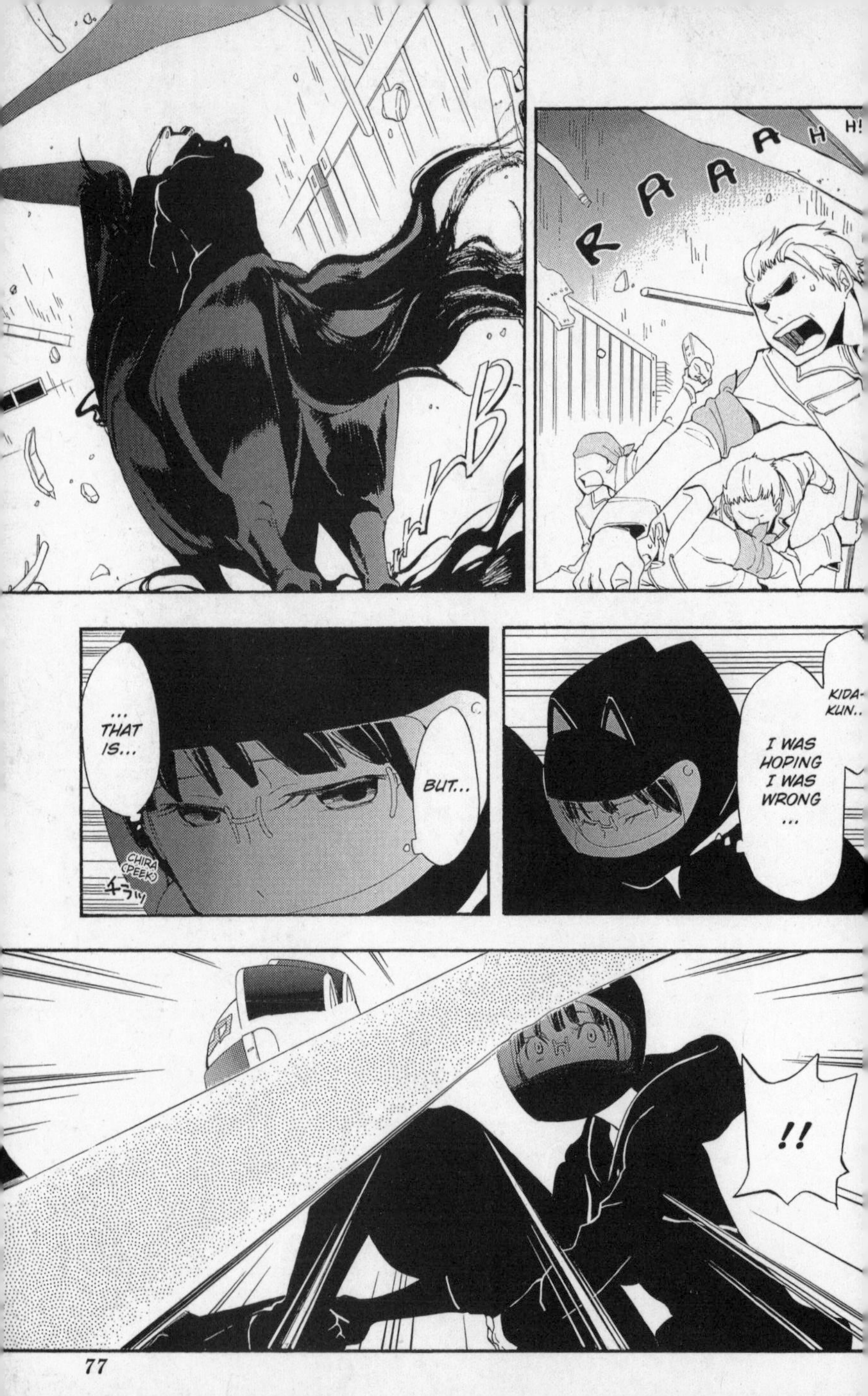
RRAAAAH!
KIDA-KUN..
I WAS HOPING I WAS WRONG ...
BUT...
... THAT IS...
CHIRA (PEEK)
チラッ
!!

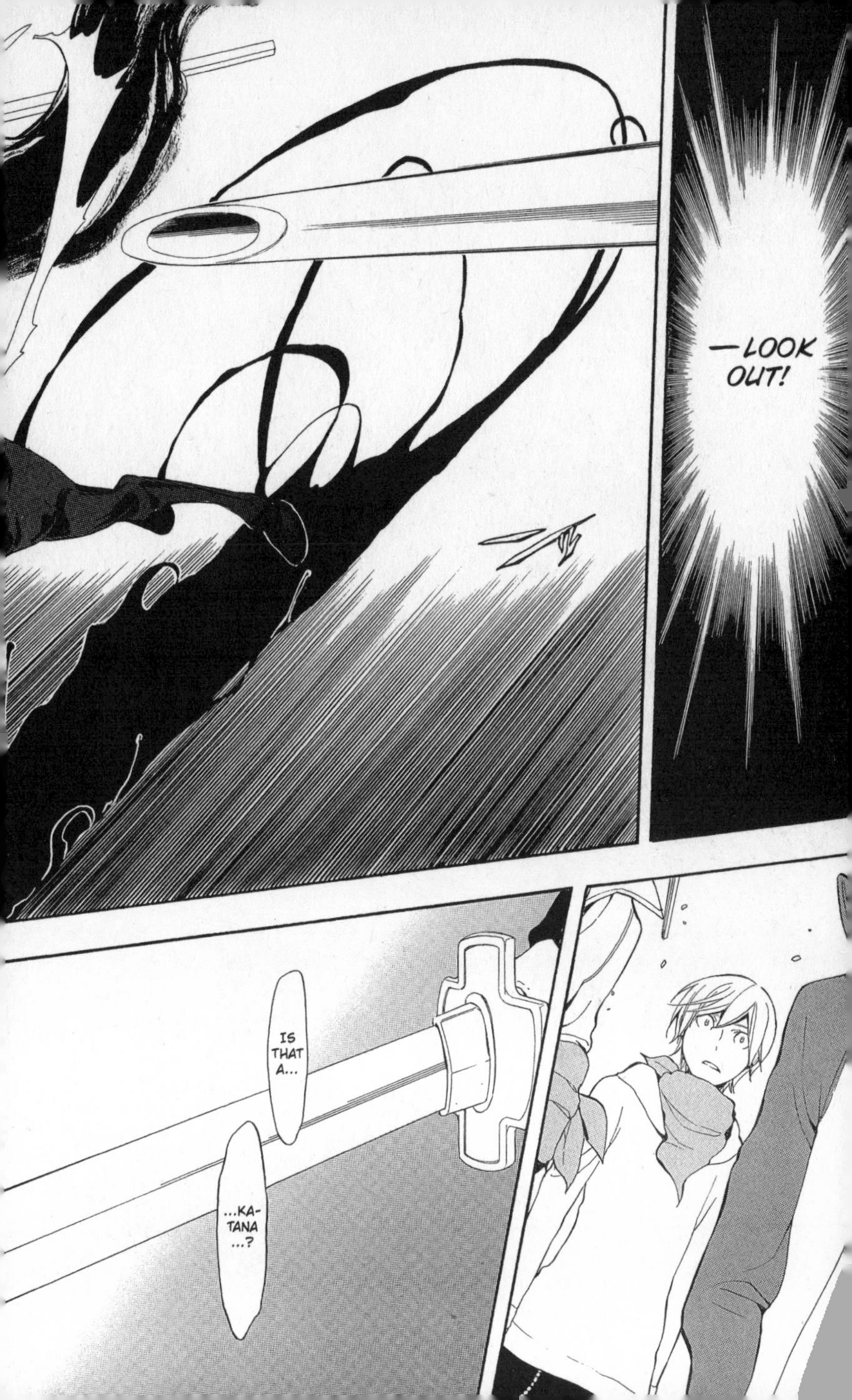
—LOOK OUT!
IS THAT A...
...KA-TANA ...?

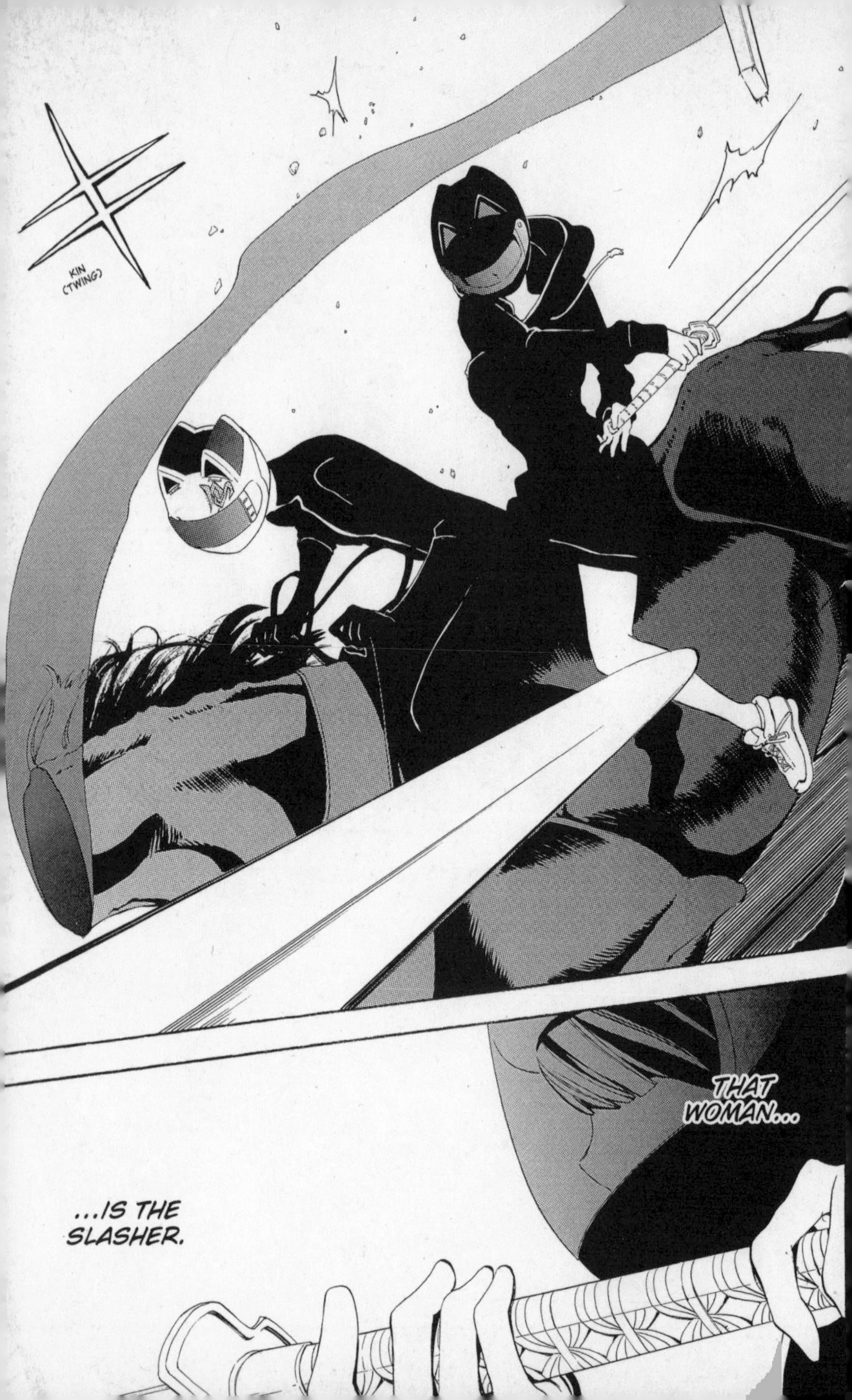
KIN (TWING)
THAT WOMAN...
...IS THE SLASHER.

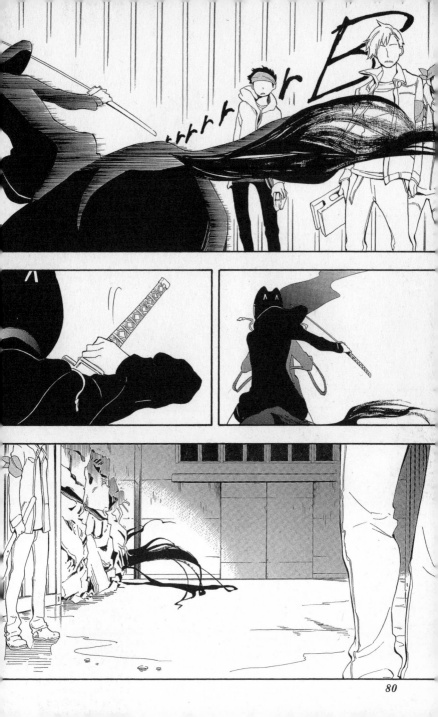

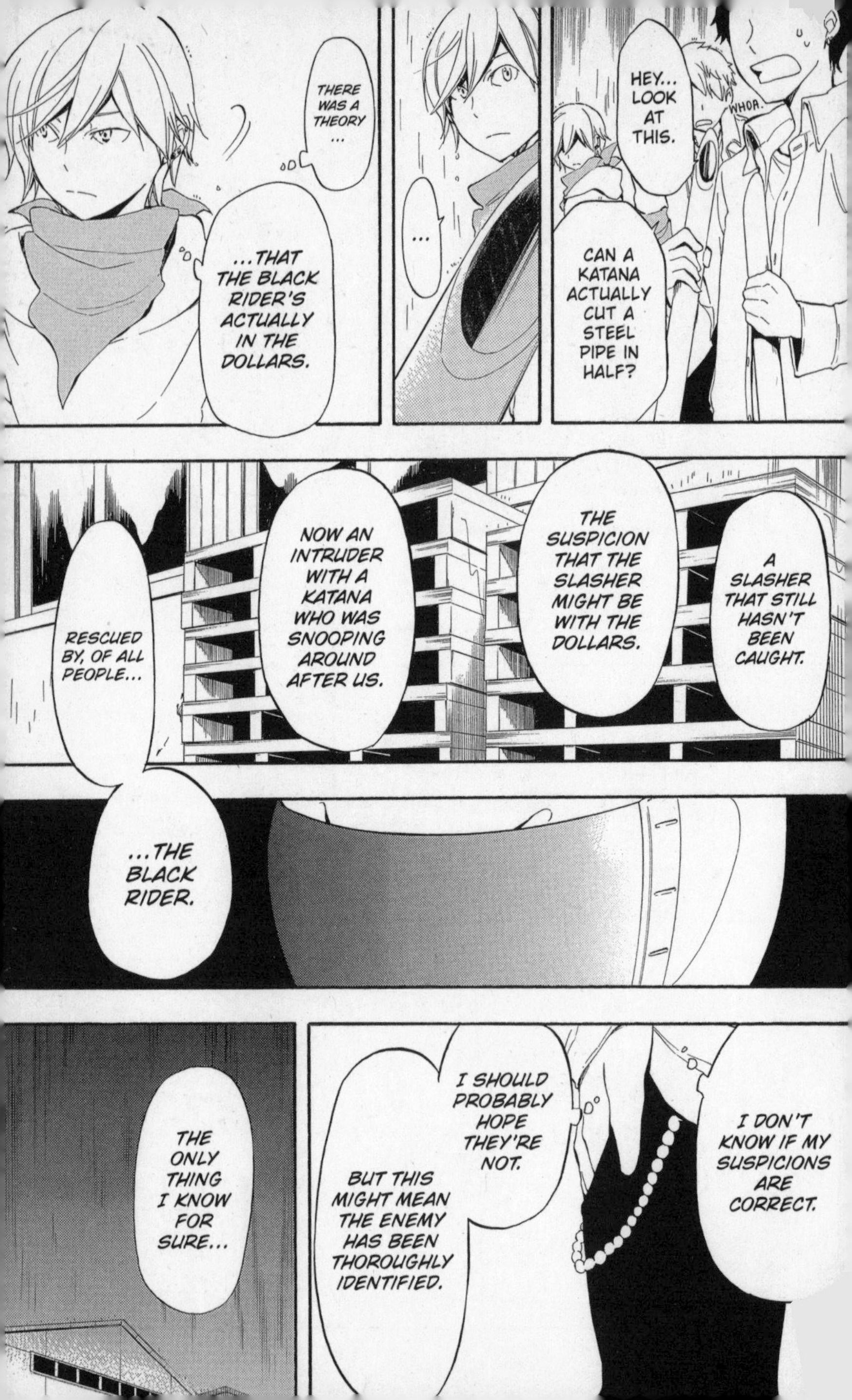
HEY... LOOK AT THIS.
WHOA.
CAN A KATANA ACTUALLY CUT A STEEL PIPE IN HALF?
...
THERE WAS A THEORY...
...THAT THE BLACK RIDER'S ACTUALLY IN THE DOLLARS.
A SLASHER THAT STILL HASN'T BEEN CAUGHT.
THE SUSPICION THAT THE SLASHER MIGHT BE WITH THE DOLLARS.
NOW AN INTRUDER WITH A KATANA WHO WAS SNOOPING AROUND AFTER US.
RESCUED BY, OF ALL PEOPLE...
...THE BLACK RIDER.
I DON'T KNOW IF MY SUSPICIONS ARE CORRECT.
I SHOULD PROBABLY HOPE THEY'RE NOT.
BUT THIS MIGHT MEAN THE ENEMY HAS BEEN THOROUGHLY IDENTIFIED.
THE ONLY THING I KNOW FOR SURE...

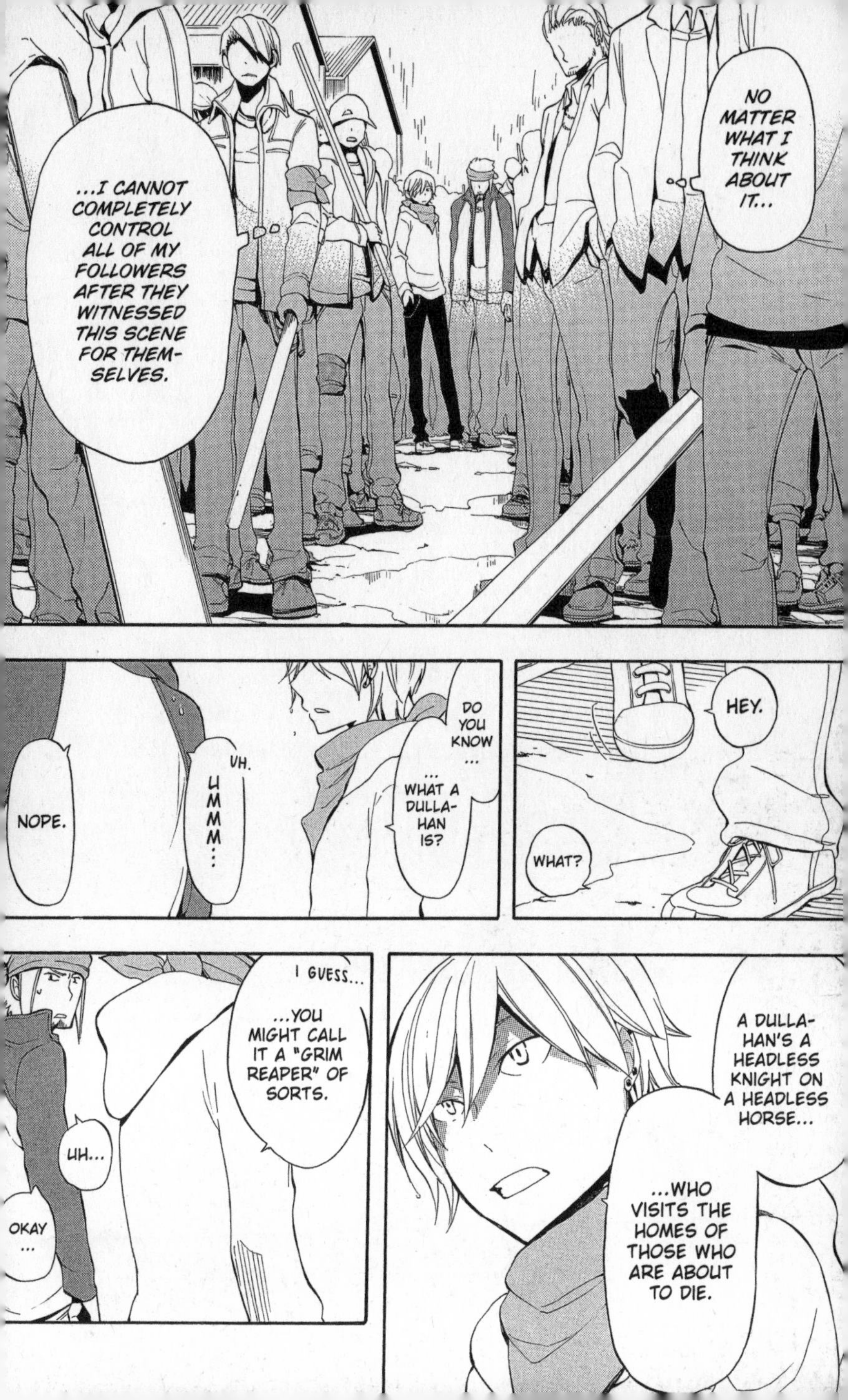
NO MATTER WHAT I THINK ABOUT IT...
...I CANNOT COMPLETELY CONTROL ALL OF MY FOLLOWERS AFTER THEY WITNESSED THIS SCENE FOR THEMSELVES.
HEY.
WHAT?
DO YOU KNOW ...
...WHAT A DULLA-HAN IS?
UH.
UMMM...
NOPE.
A DULLA-HAN'S A HEADLESS KNIGHT ON A HEADLESS HORSE...
...WHO VISITS THE HOMES OF THOSE WHO ARE ABOUT TO DIE.
I GUESS...
...YOU MIGHT CALL IT A "GRIM REAPER" OF SORTS.
UH...
OKAY ...

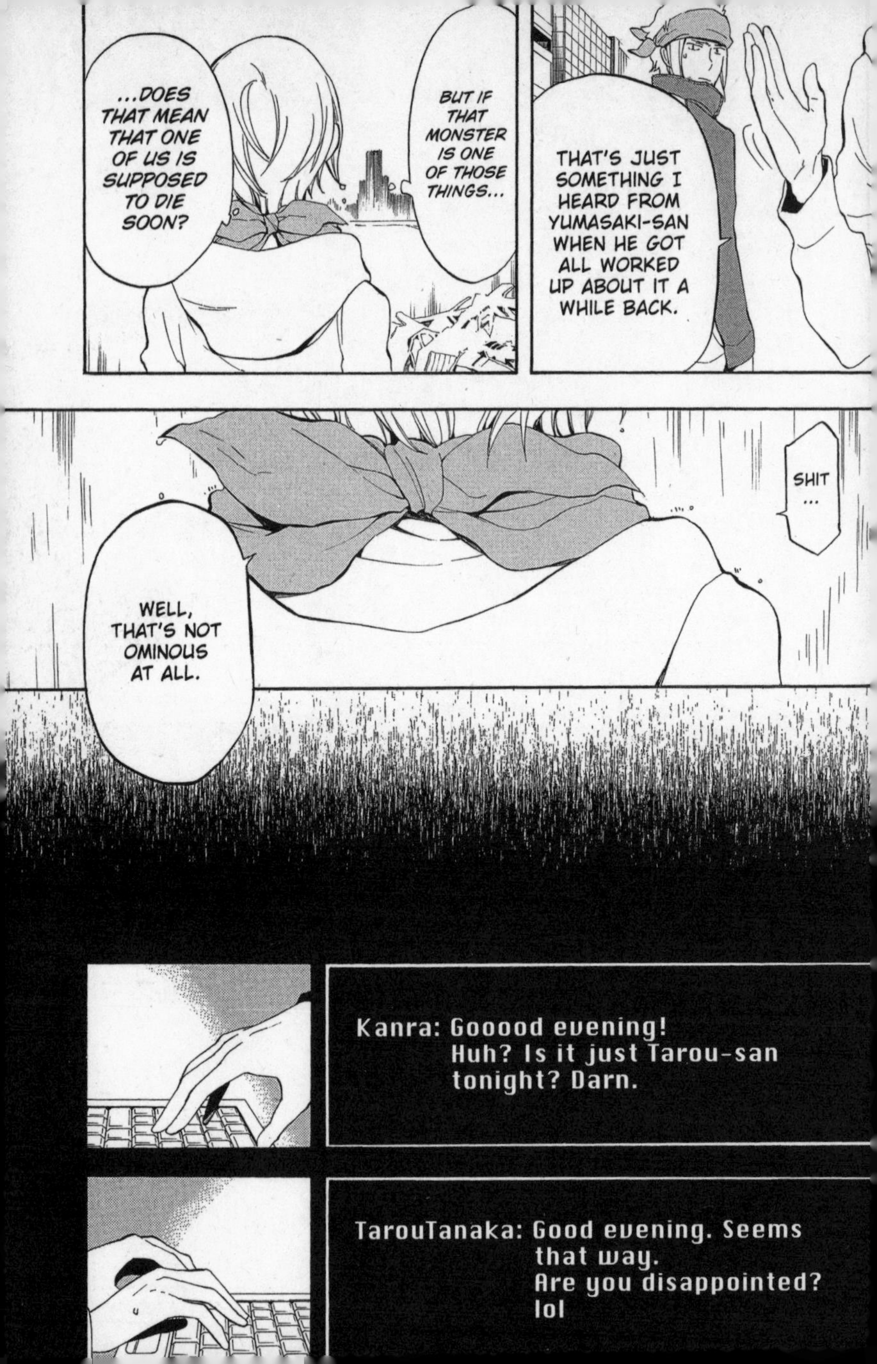
THAT'S JUST SOMETHING I HEARD FROM YUMASAKI-SAN WHEN HE GOT ALL WORKED UP ABOUT IT A WHILE BACK.
BUT IF THAT MONSTER IS ONE OF THOSE THINGS...
...DOES THAT MEAN THAT ONE OF US IS SUPPOSED TO DIE SOON?
SHIT...
WELL, THAT'S NOT OMINOUS AT ALL.
Kanra: Gooood evening!
Huh? Is it just Tarou-san tonight? Darn.
TarouTanaka: Good evening. Seems that way.
Are you disappointed? lol

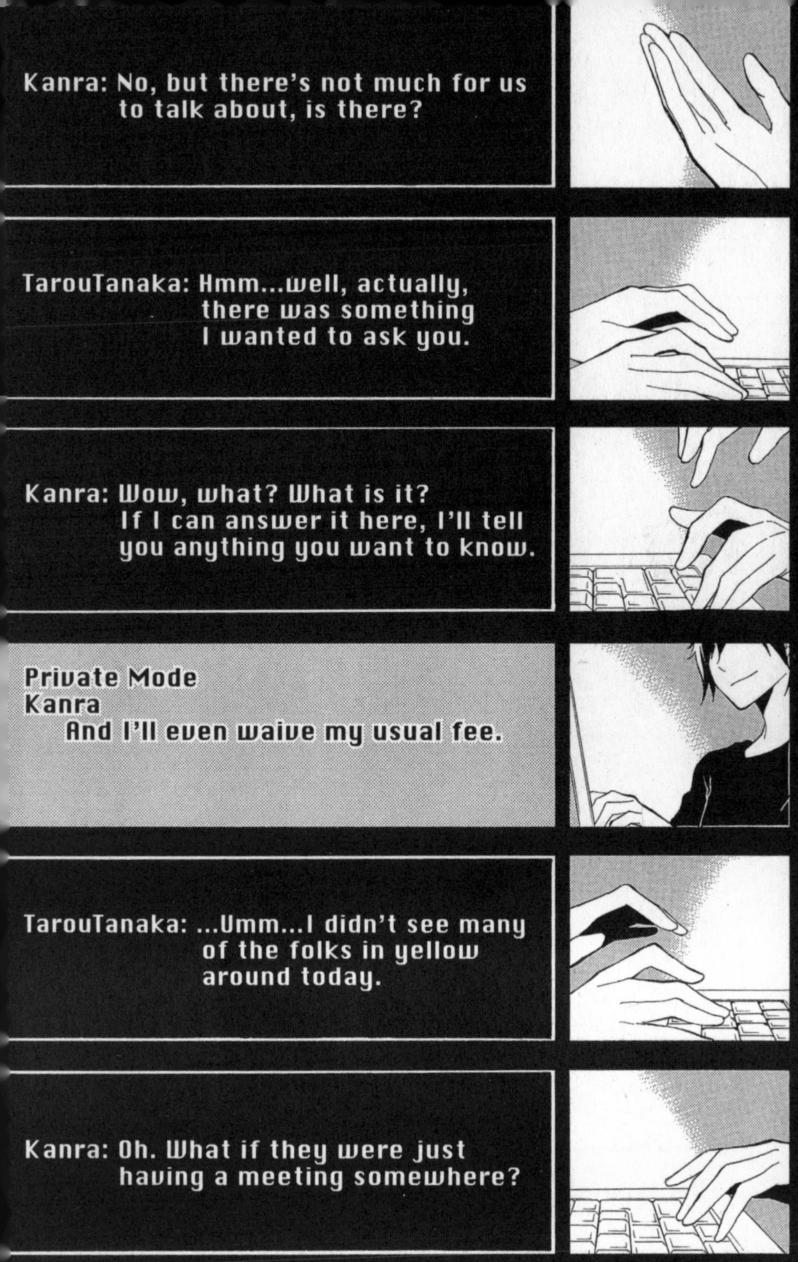
Kanra: No, but there's not much for us to talk about, is there?
TarouTanaka: Hmm...well, actually, there was something I wanted to ask you.
Kanra: Wow, what? What is it? If I can answer it here, I'll tell you anything you want to know.
Private Mode
Kanra
And I'll even waive my usual fee.
TarouTanaka: ...Umm...I didn't see many of the folks in yellow around today.
Kanra: Oh. What if they were just having a meeting somewhere?

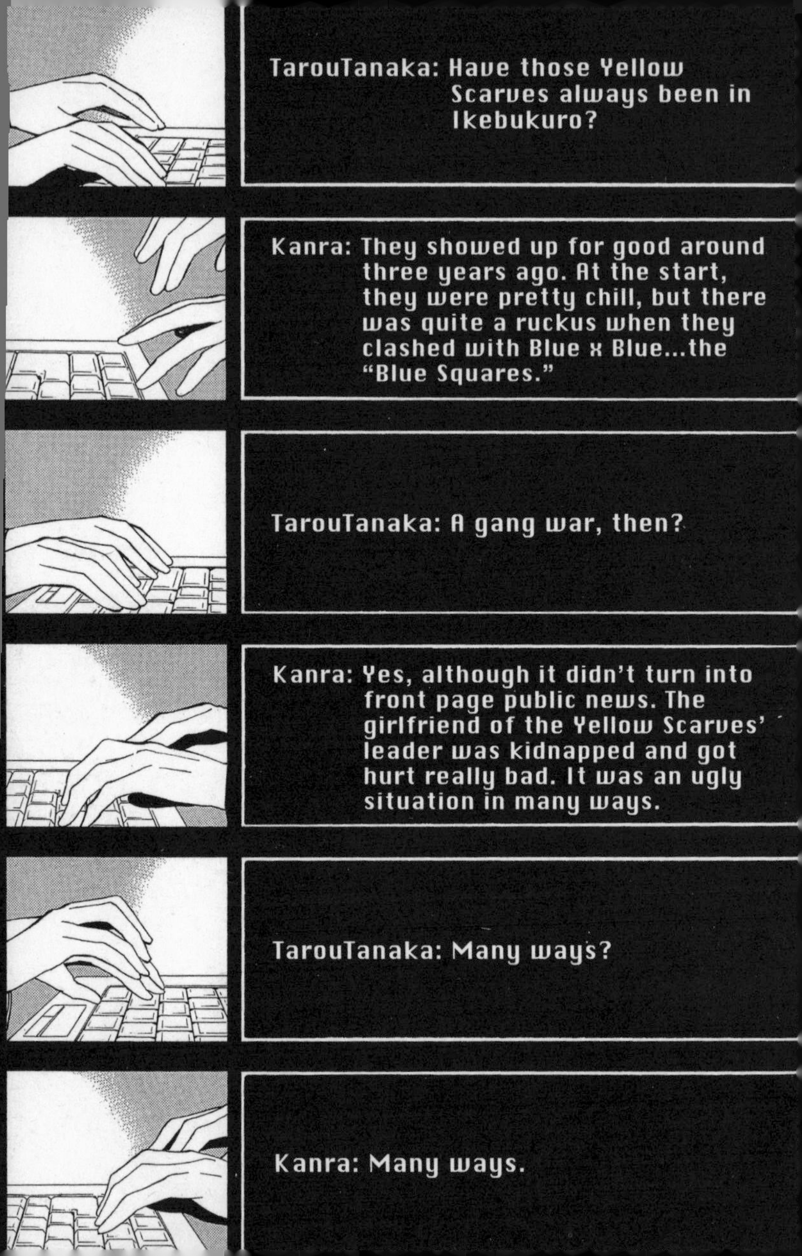
TarouTanaka: Have those Yellow Scarves always been in Ikebukuro?
Kanra: They showed up for good around three years ago. At the start, they were pretty chill, but there was quite a ruckus when they clashed with Blue x Blue...the "Blue Squares."
TarouTanaka: A gang war, then?
Kanra: Yes, although it didn't turn into front page public news. The girlfriend of the Yellow Scarves' leader was kidnapped and got hurt really bad. It was an ugly situation in many ways.
TarouTanaka: Many ways?
Kanra: Many ways.

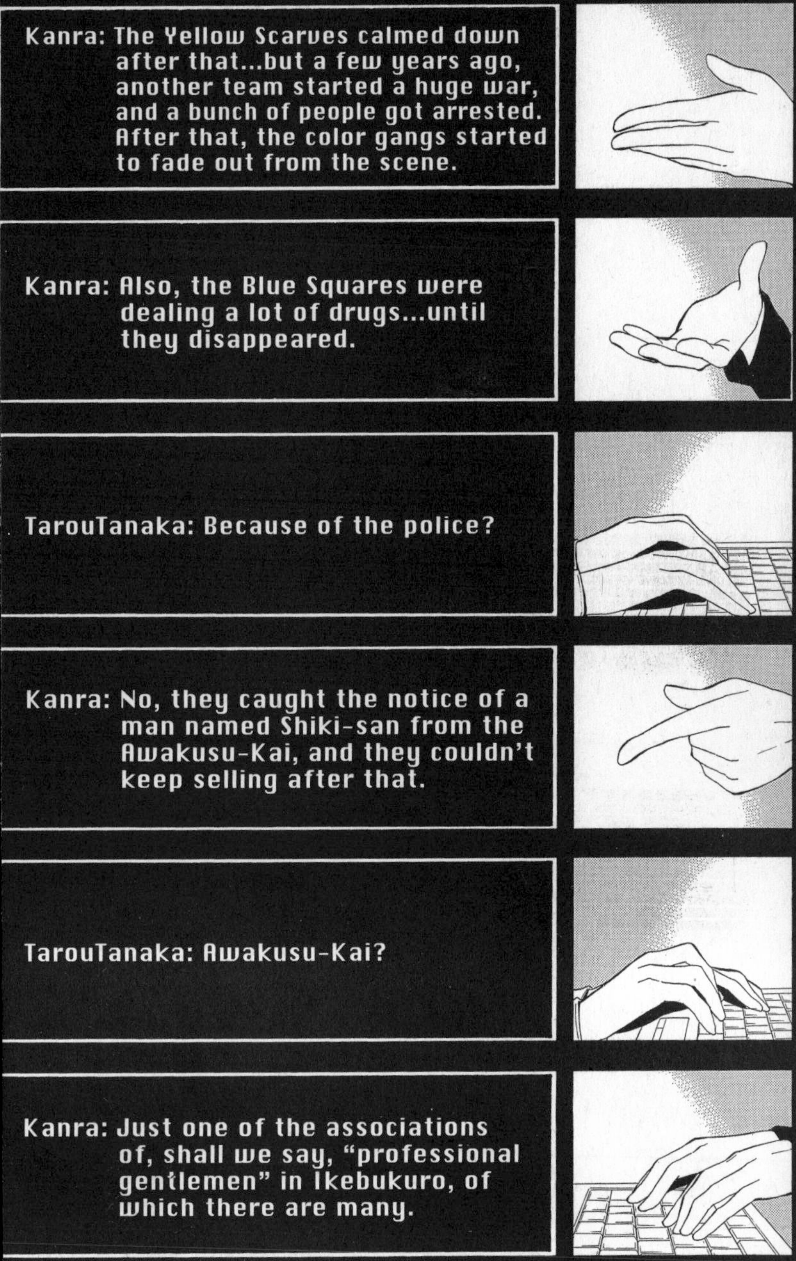
Kanra: The Yellow Scarves calmed down after that...but a few years ago, another team started a huge war, and a bunch of people got arrested. After that, the color gangs started to fade out from the scene.
Kanra: Also, the Blue Squares were dealing a lot of drugs...until they disappeared.
TarouTanaka: Because of the police?
Kanra: No, they caught the notice of a man named Shiki-san from the Awakusu-Kai, and they couldn't keep selling after that.
TarouTanaka: Awakusu-Kai?
Kanra: Just one of the associations of, shall we say, "professional gentlemen" in Ikebukuro, of which there are many.

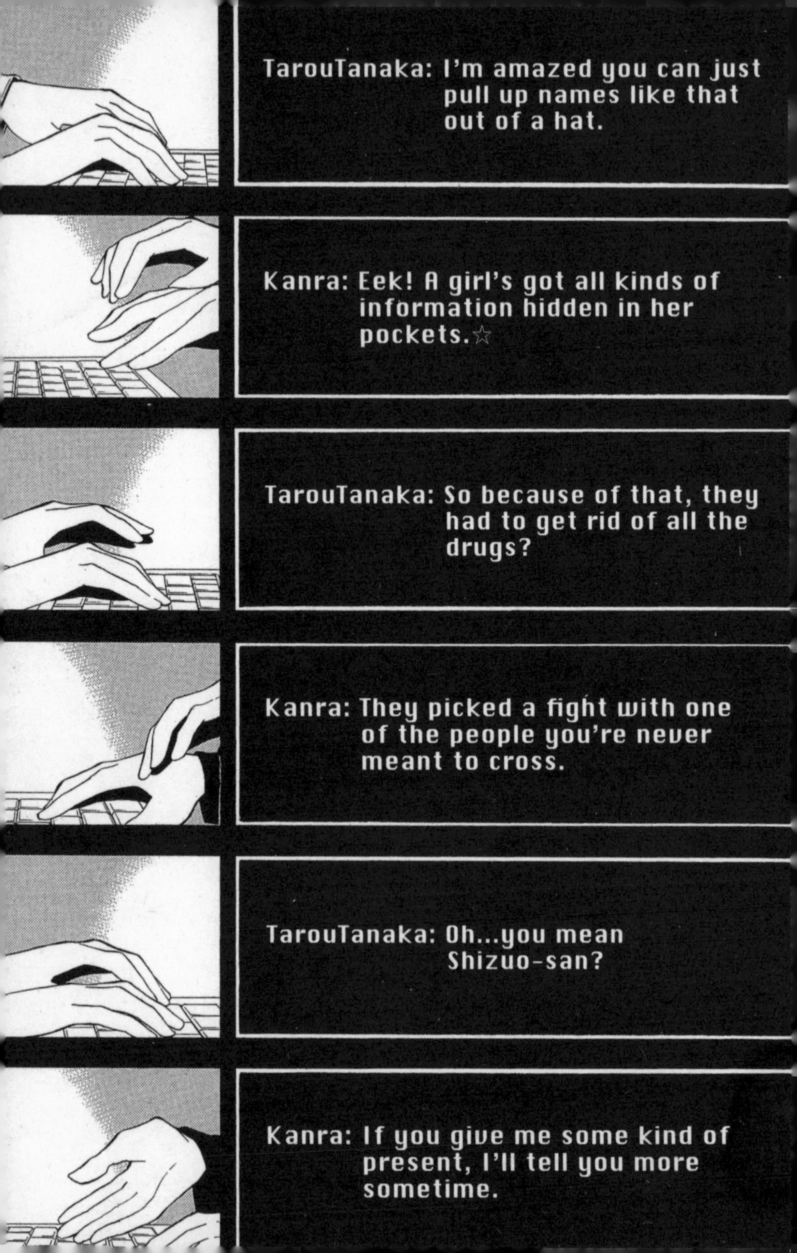

TarouTanaka: I'm amazed you can just pull up names like that out of a hat.
Kanra: Eek! A girl's got all kinds of information hidden in her pockets.☆
TarouTanaka: So because of that, they had to get rid of all the drugs?
Kanra: They picked a fight with one of the people you're never meant to cross.
TarouTanaka: Oh...you mean Shizuo-san?
Kanra: If you give me some kind of present, I'll tell you more sometime.

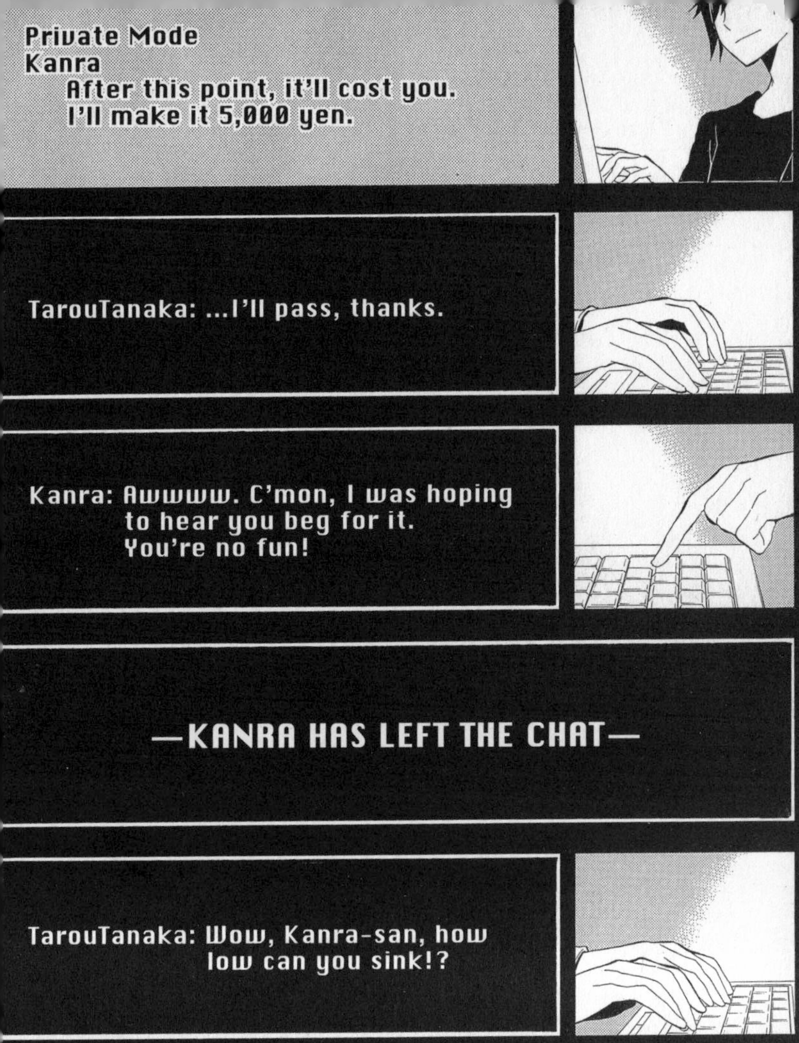
Private Mode
Kanra
After this point, it'll cost you.
I'll make it 5,000 yen.
TarouTanaka: ...I'll pass, thanks.
Kanra: Awwww. C'mon, I was hoping to hear you beg for it. You're no fun!
—KANRA HAS LEFT THE CHAT—
TarouTanaka: Wow, Kanra-san, how low can you sink!?

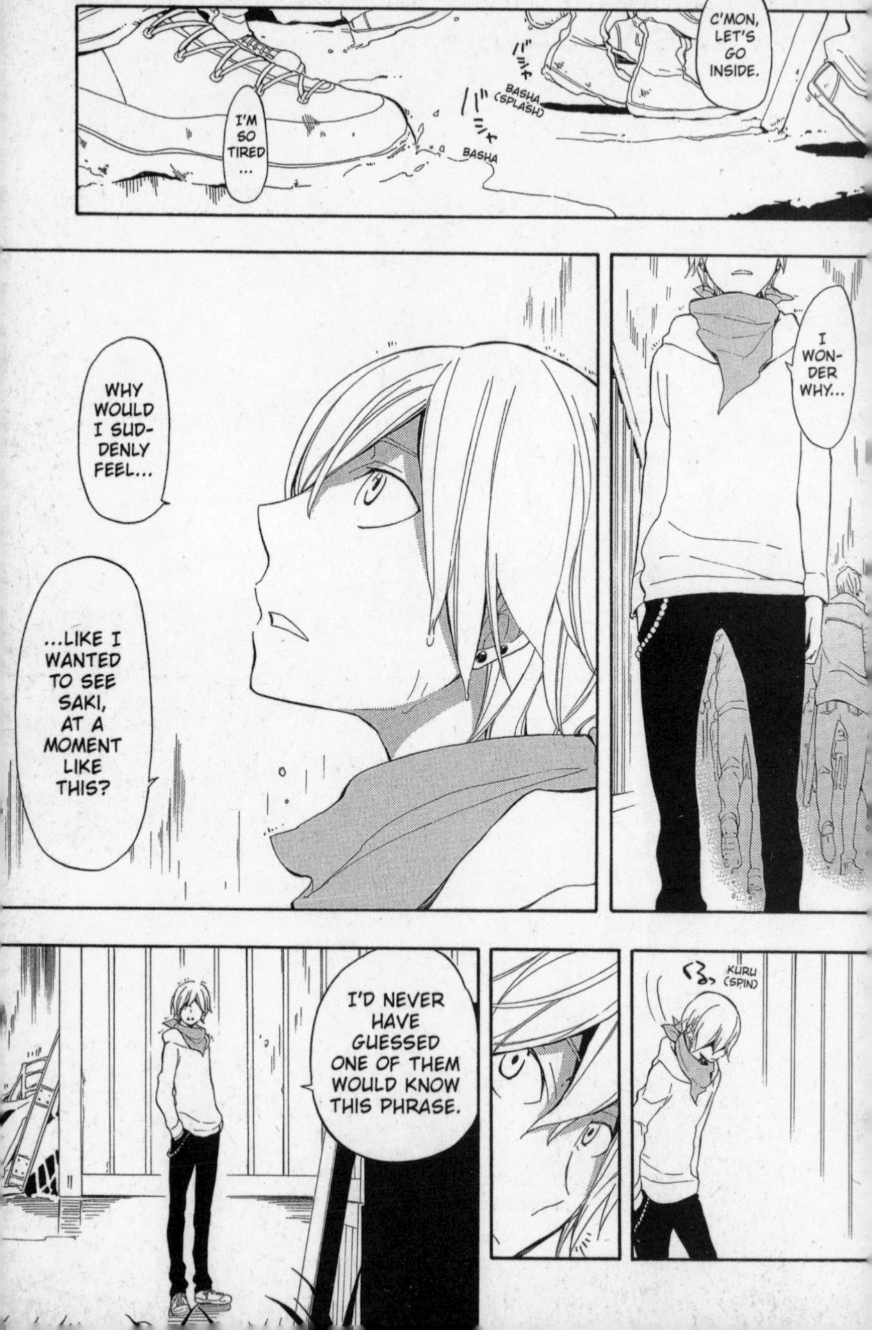
C'MON, LET'S GO INSIDE.
BASHA (SPLASH)
BASHA
I'M SO TIRED...
I WONDER WHY...
WHY WOULD I SUDDENLY FEEL...
...LIKE I WANTED TO SEE SAKI, AT A MOMENT LIKE THIS?
KURU (SPIN)
I'D NEVER HAVE GUESSED ONE OF THEM WOULD KNOW THIS PHRASE.

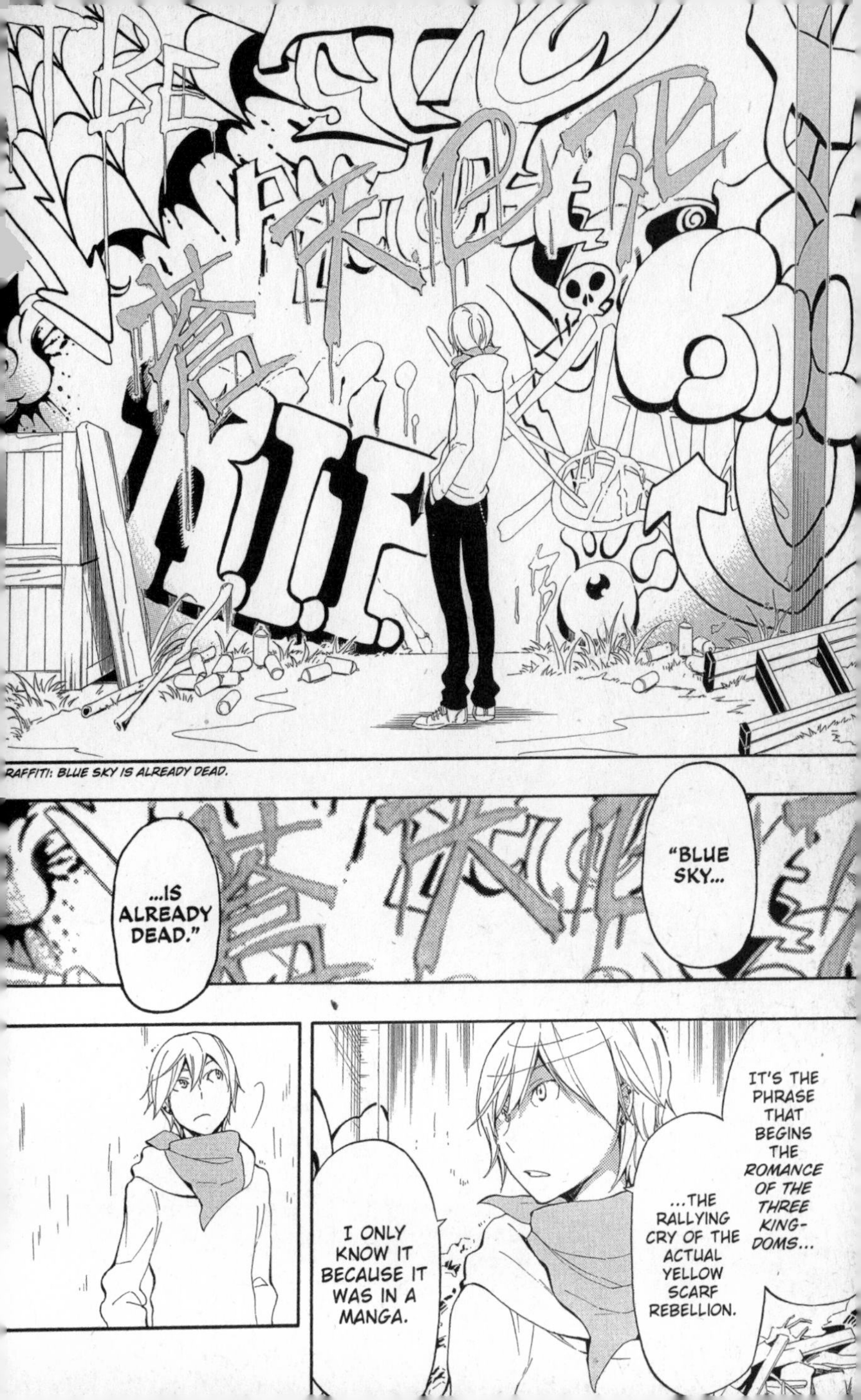
RAFFITI: BLUE SKY IS ALREADY DEAD.
"BLUE SKY...
...IS ALREADY DEAD."
IT'S THE PHRASE THAT BEGINS THE *ROMANCE OF THE THREE KINGDOMS*...
...THE RALLYING CRY OF THE ACTUAL YELLOW SCARF REBELLION.
I ONLY KNOW IT BECAUSE IT WAS IN A MANGA.

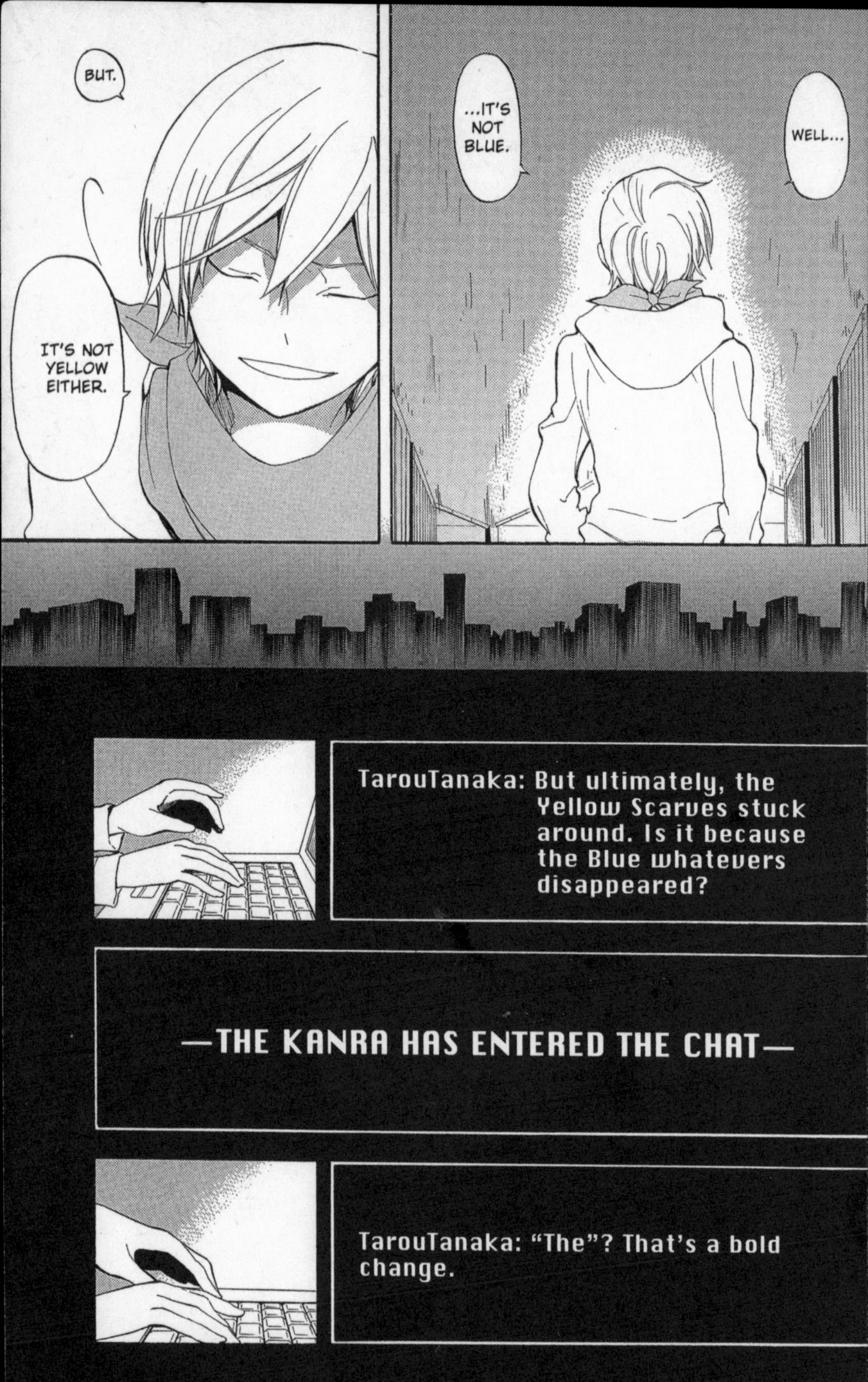
WELL...
...IT'S NOT BLUE.
BUT.
IT'S NOT YELLOW EITHER.
TarouTanaka: But ultimately, the Yellow Scarves stuck around. Is it because the Blue whatevers disappeared?
—THE KANRA HAS ENTERED THE CHAT—
TarouTanaka: "The"? That's a bold change.

The Kanra: Hee-hee, just a change of heart. Now, about the Yellow Scarves...

Private Mode
The Kanra
　The Blue Squares didn't die out. The Yellow Scarves' leader got tired of fighting and left the team...and they joined up with the remaining Yellow Scarves.

Private Mode
TarouTanaka
　Huh? They had a merger?

Private Mode
The Kanra
　Well, who's really going to keep track of which person is in which group, aside from the leaders and important members? If you take off your blue gear, then say you want in with the yellow side, who's going to care?

Private Mode
The Kanra
　Plus, when the Yellow Scarves were weakened after the loss of their leader, they might have welcomed the chance for some fresh blood.

Private Mode
TarouTanaka
　Then the former leader...?

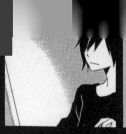

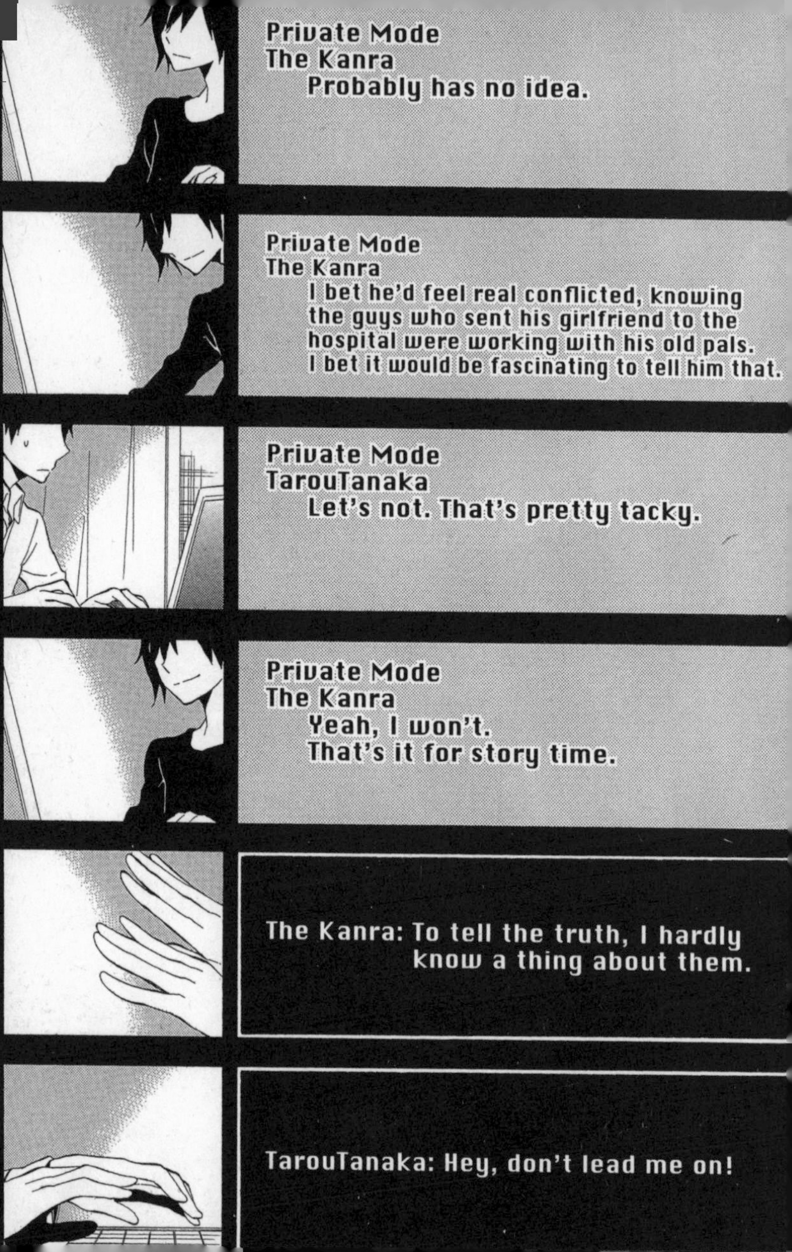
Private Mode
The Kanra
Probably has no idea.
Private Mode
The Kanra
I bet he'd feel real conflicted, knowing the guys who sent his girlfriend to the hospital were working with his old pals. I bet it would be fascinating to tell him that.
Private Mode
TarouTanaka
Let's not. That's pretty tacky.
Private Mode
The Kanra
Yeah, I won't.
That's it for story time.
The Kanra: To tell the truth, I hardly know a thing about them.
TarouTanaka: Hey, don't lead me on!

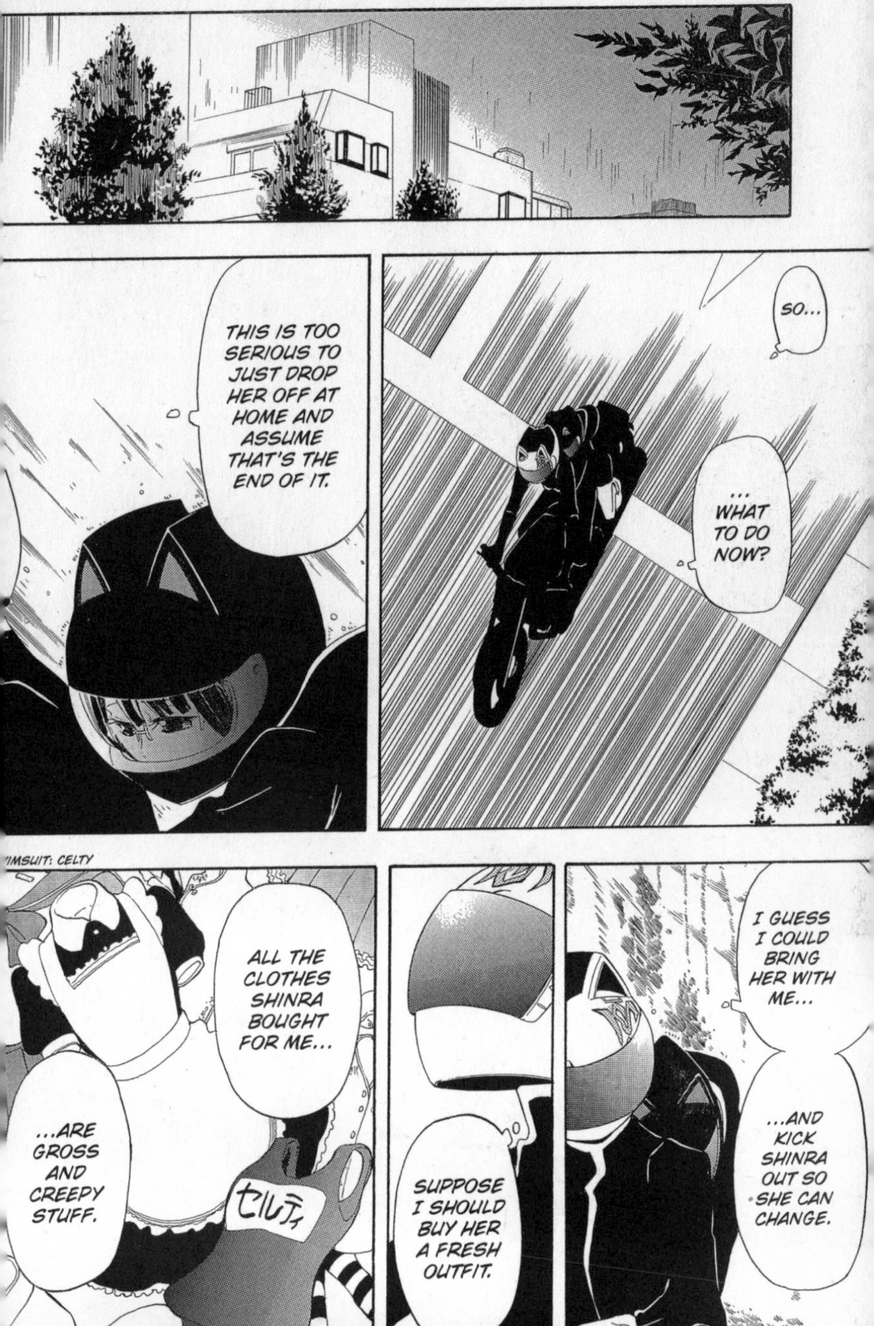
SO...
...WHAT TO DO NOW?
THIS IS TOO SERIOUS TO JUST DROP HER OFF AT HOME AND ASSUME THAT'S THE END OF IT.
I GUESS I COULD BRING HER WITH ME...
...AND KICK SHINRA OUT SO SHE CAN CHANGE.
SUPPOSE I SHOULD BUY HER A FRESH OUTFIT.
IMSUIT: CELTY
ALL THE CLOTHES SHINRA BOUGHT FOR ME...
...ARE GROSS AND CREEPY STUFF.
セルティ

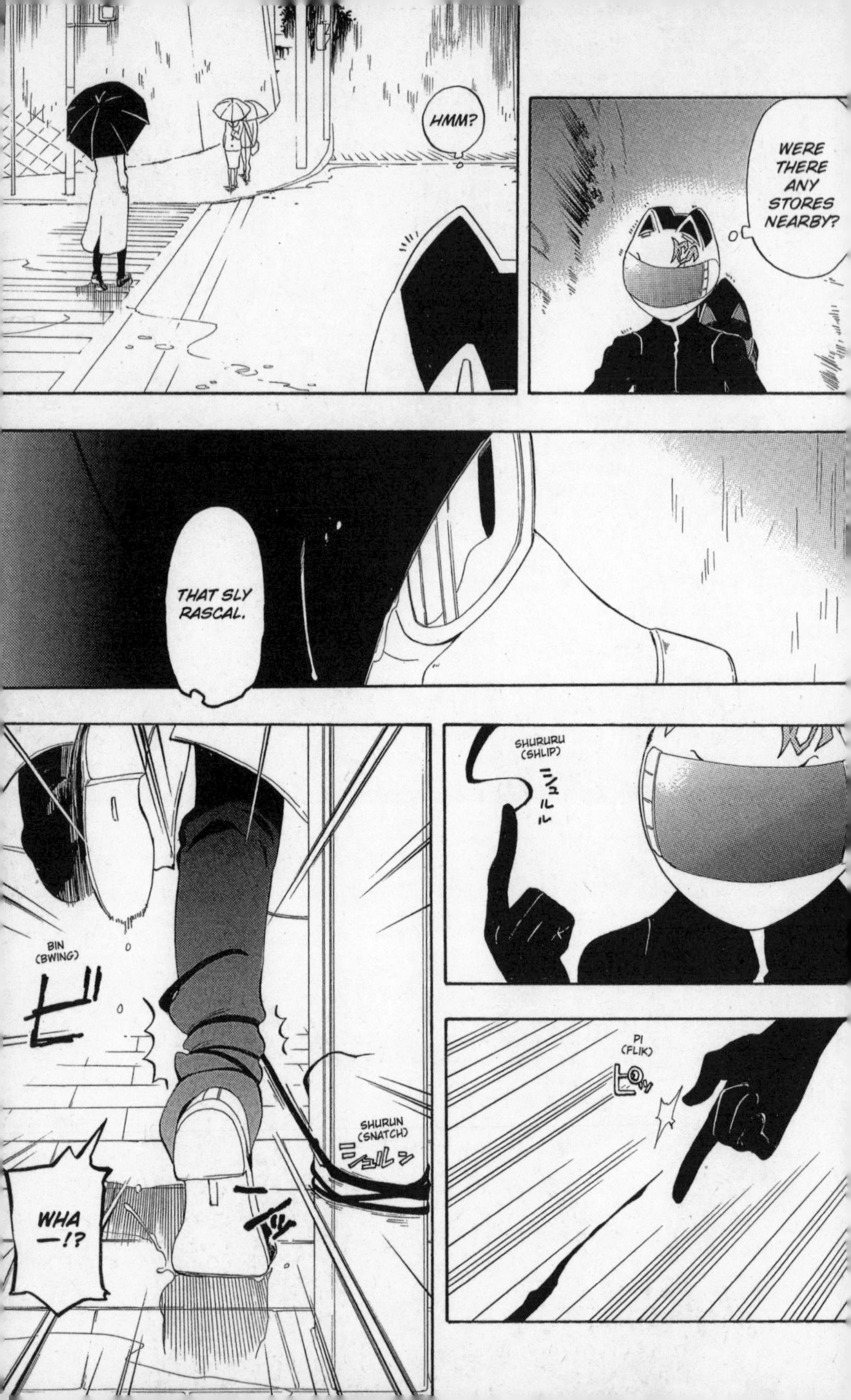
WERE THERE ANY STORES NEARBY?
HMM?
THAT SLY RASCAL.
SHURURU (SHLIP)
PI (FLIK)
BIN (BWING)
SHURUN (SNATCH)
WHA—!?

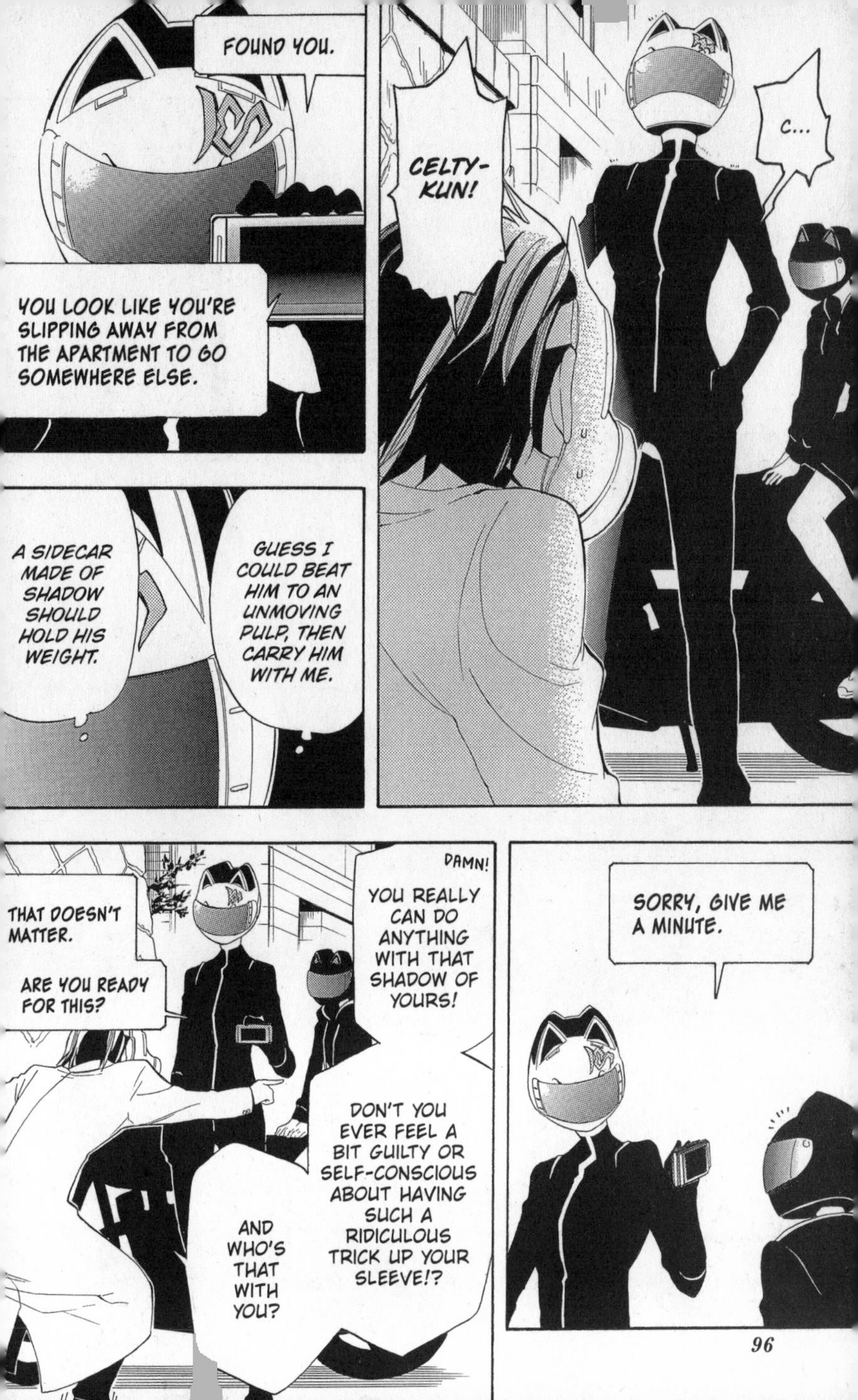
C...
CELTY-KUN!
FOUND YOU.
YOU LOOK LIKE YOU'RE SLIPPING AWAY FROM THE APARTMENT TO GO SOMEWHERE ELSE.
GUESS I COULD BEAT HIM TO AN UNMOVING PULP, THEN CARRY HIM WITH ME.
A SIDECAR MADE OF SHADOW SHOULD HOLD HIS WEIGHT.
SORRY, GIVE ME A MINUTE.
DAMN!
YOU REALLY CAN DO ANYTHING WITH THAT SHADOW OF YOURS!
THAT DOESN'T MATTER.
ARE YOU READY FOR THIS?
DON'T YOU EVER FEEL A BIT GUILTY OR SELF-CONSCIOUS ABOUT HAVING SUCH A RIDICULOUS TRICK UP YOUR SLEEVE!?
AND WHO'S THAT WITH YOU?

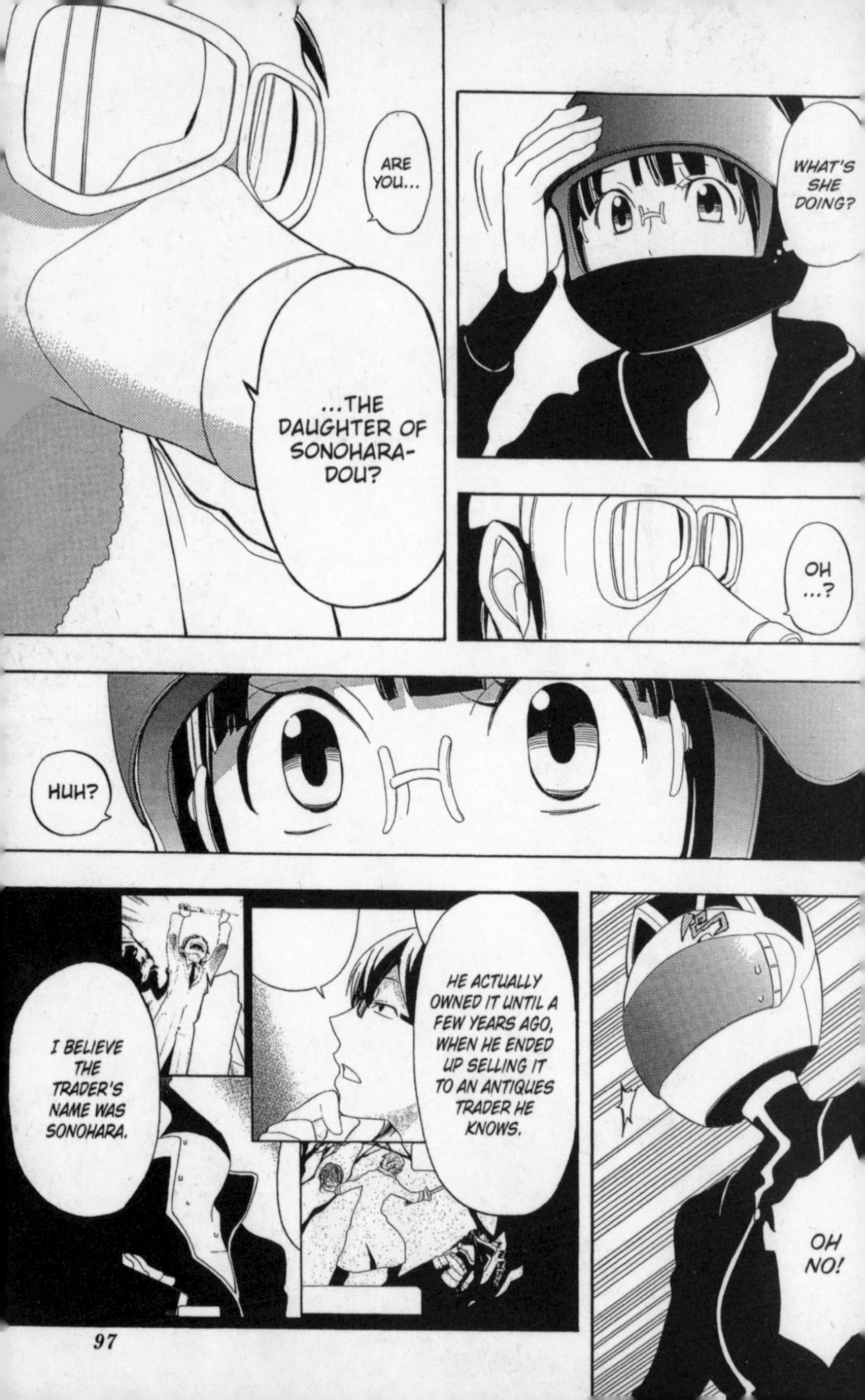
WHAT'S SHE DOING?
OH ...?
ARE YOU...
...THE DAUGHTER OF SONOHARA-DOU?
HUH?
OH NO!
HE ACTUALLY OWNED IT UNTIL A FEW YEARS AGO, WHEN HE ENDED UP SELLING IT TO AN ANTIQUES TRADER HE KNOWS.
I BELIEVE THE TRADER'S NAME WAS SONOHARA.

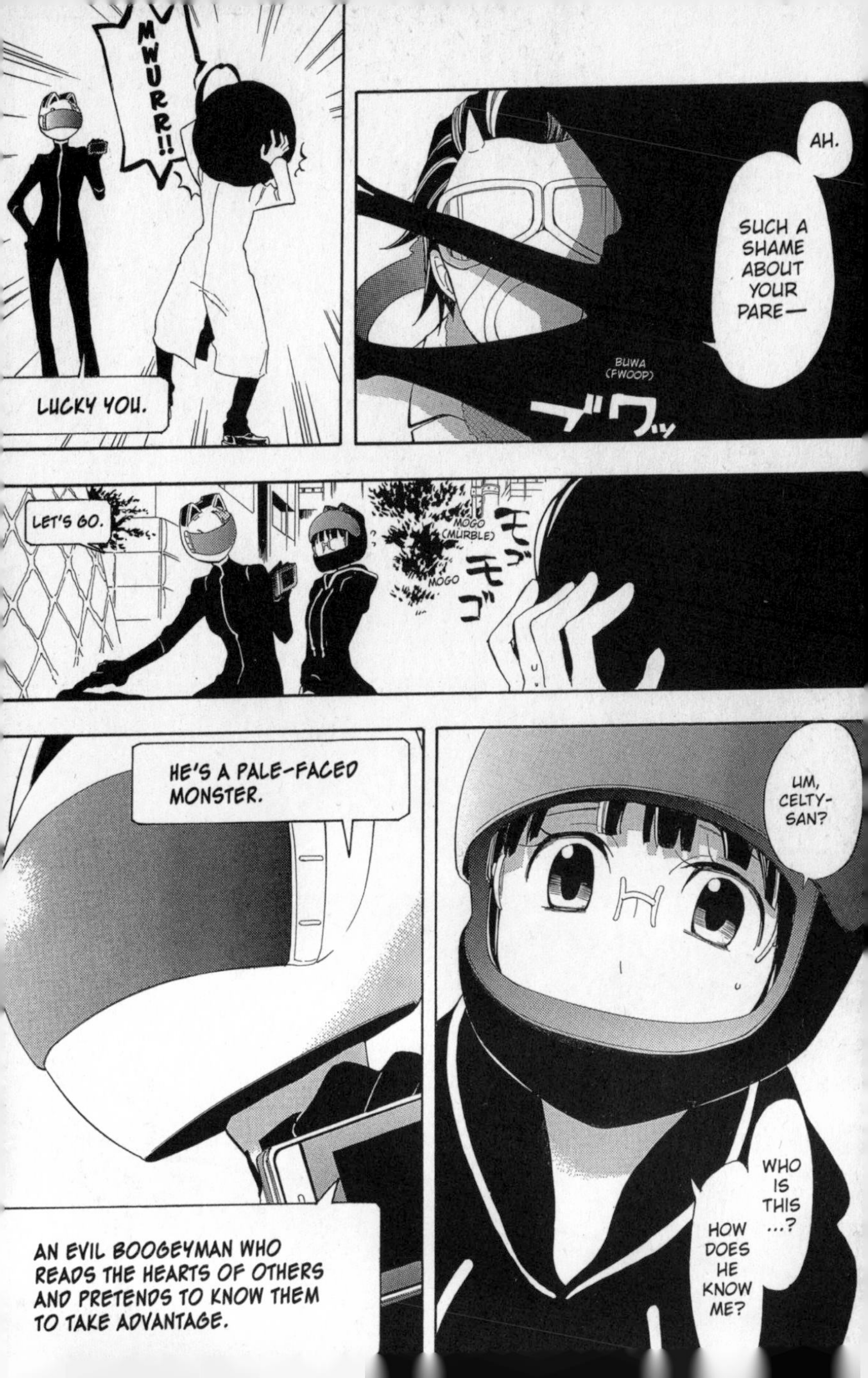
AH.
SUCH A SHAME ABOUT YOUR PARE—
BUWA (FWOOP)
ブワッ
MWURR!!
LUCKY YOU.
MOGO (MURBLE) MOGO
モゴモゴ
LET'S GO.
UM, CELTY-SAN?
WHO IS THIS ...?
HOW DOES HE KNOW ME?
HE'S A PALE-FACED MONSTER.
AN EVIL BOOGEYMAN WHO READS THE HEARTS OF OTHERS AND PRETENDS TO KNOW THEM TO TAKE ADVANTAGE.

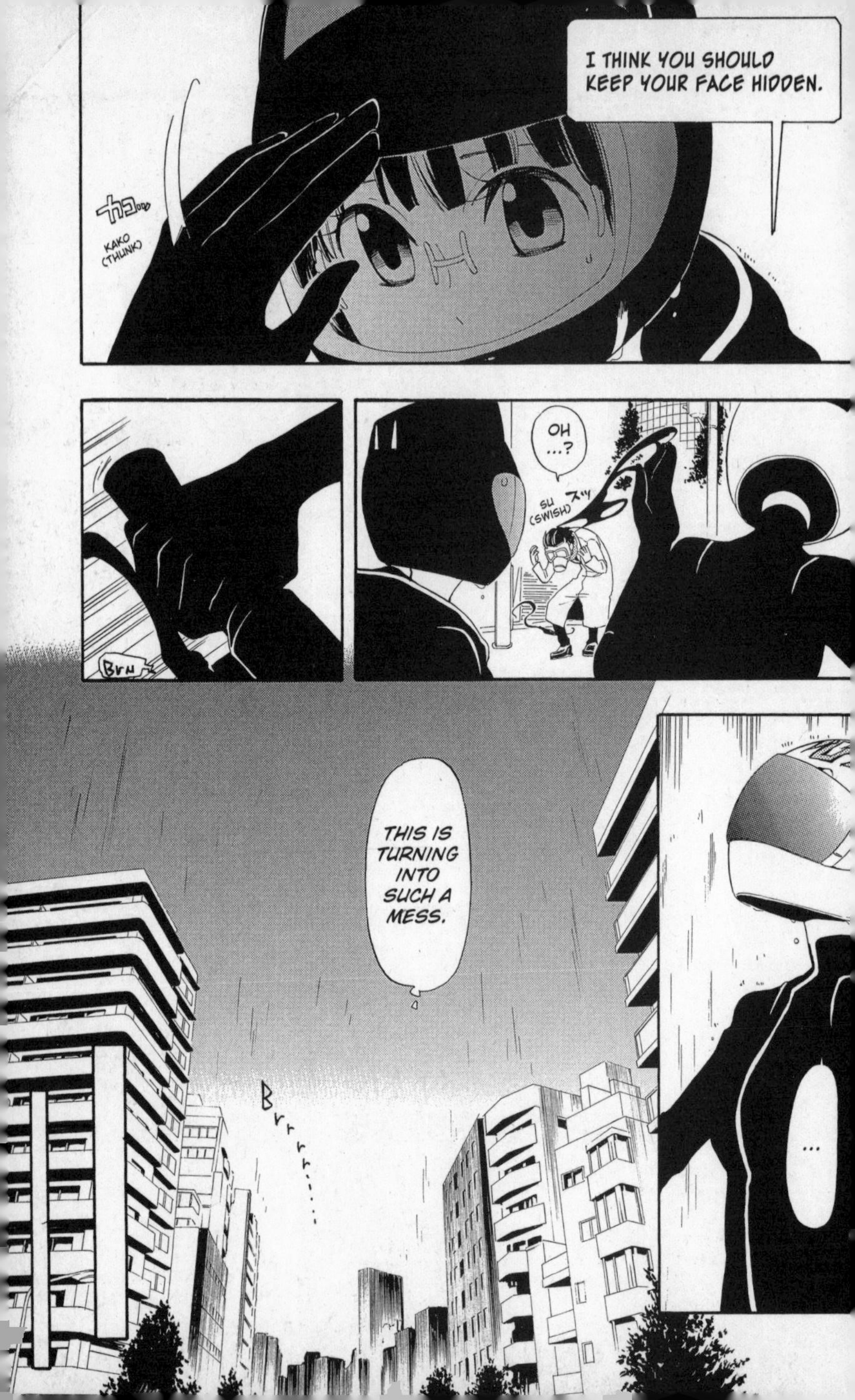
I THINK YOU SHOULD KEEP YOUR FACE HIDDEN.
カコッ
KAKO (THUNK)
OH ...?
ズッ
SU (SWISH)
Brn
...
THIS IS TURNING INTO SUCH A MESS.
Brrrr.....

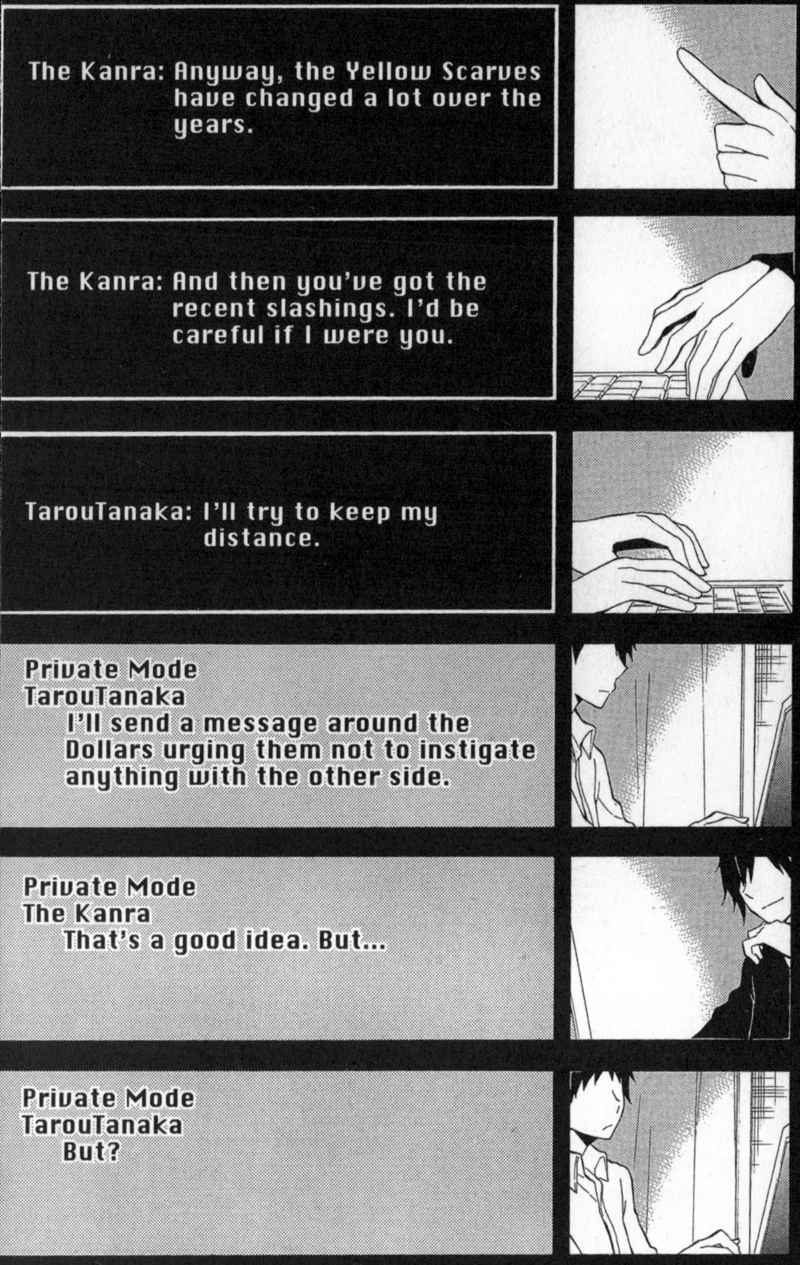
The Kanra: Anyway, the Yellow Scarves have changed a lot over the years.
The Kanra: And then you've got the recent slashings. I'd be careful if I were you.
TarouTanaka: I'll try to keep my distance.
Private Mode
TarouTanaka
I'll send a message around the Dollars urging them not to instigate anything with the other side.
Private Mode
The Kanra
That's a good idea. But...
Private Mode
TarouTanaka
But?

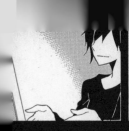

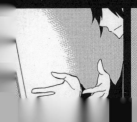

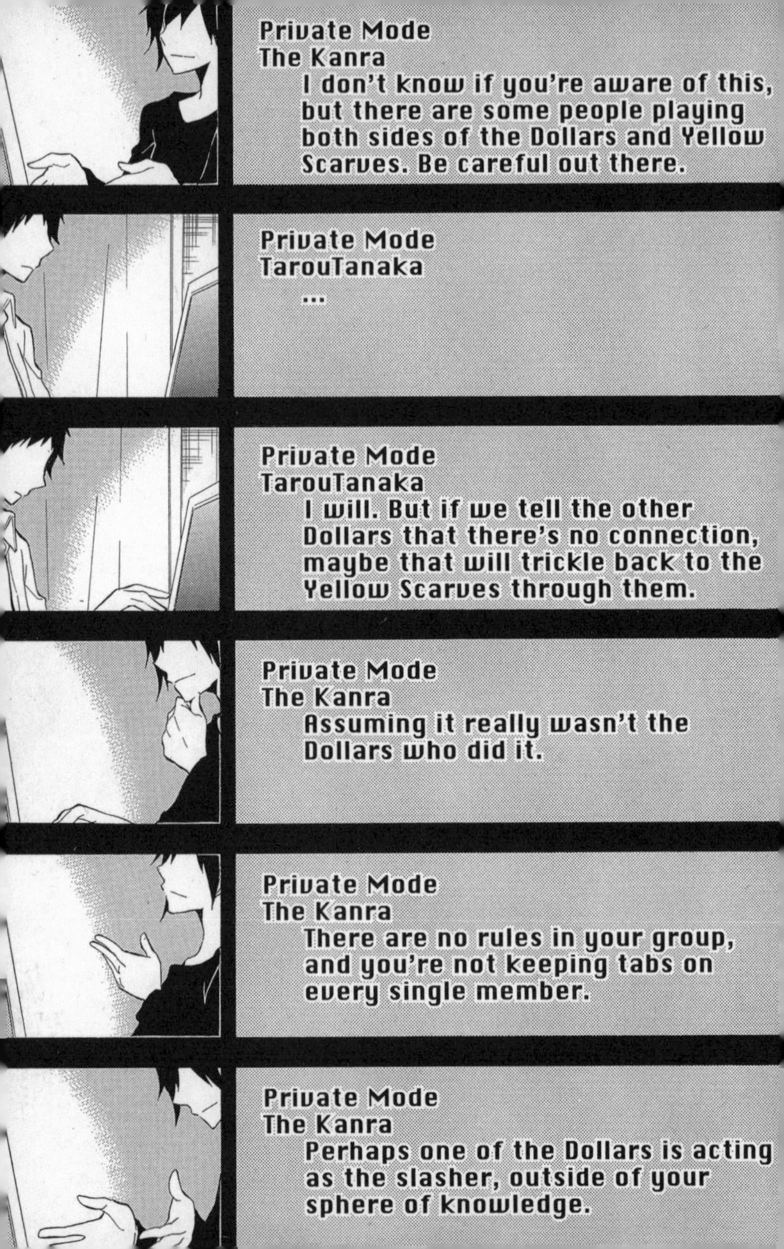
Private Mode
The Kanra
I don't know if you're aware of this, but there are some people playing both sides of the Dollars and Yellow Scarves. Be careful out there.
Private Mode
TarouTanaka
...
Private Mode
TarouTanaka
I will. But if we tell the other Dollars that there's no connection, maybe that will trickle back to the Yellow Scarves through them.
Private Mode
The Kanra
Assuming it really wasn't the Dollars who did it.
Private Mode
The Kanra
There are no rules in your group, and you're not keeping tabs on every single member.
Private Mode
The Kanra
Perhaps one of the Dollars is acting as the slasher, outside of your sphere of knowledge.

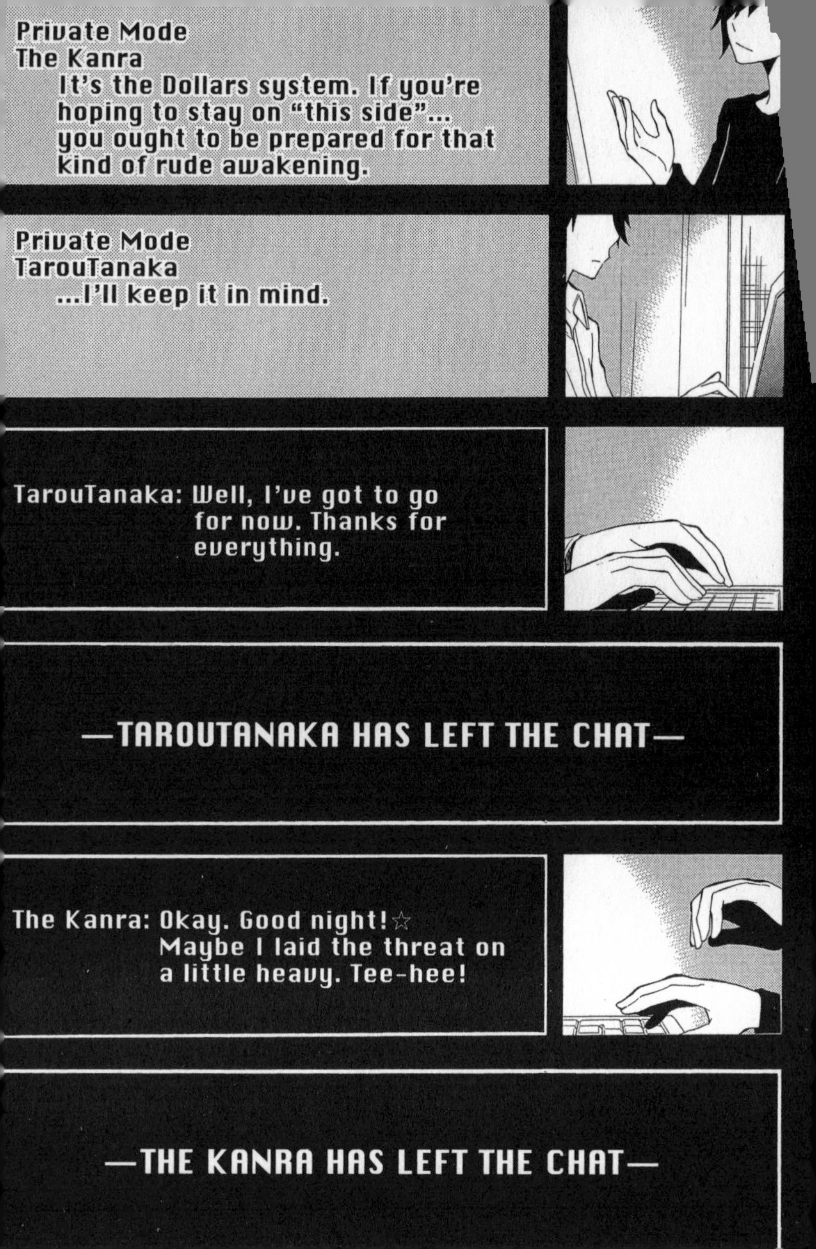
Private Mode
The Kanra
It's the Dollars system. If you're hoping to stay on "this side"... you ought to be prepared for that kind of rude awakening.
Private Mode
TarouTanaka
...I'll keep it in mind.
TarouTanaka: Well, I've got to go for now. Thanks for everything.
—TAROUTANAKA HAS LEFT THE CHAT—
The Kanra: Okay. Good night!☆ Maybe I laid the threat on a little heavy. Tee-hee!
—THE KANRA HAS LEFT THE CHAT—

DURARARA!!

ORRR!!

DRRR!!

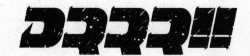

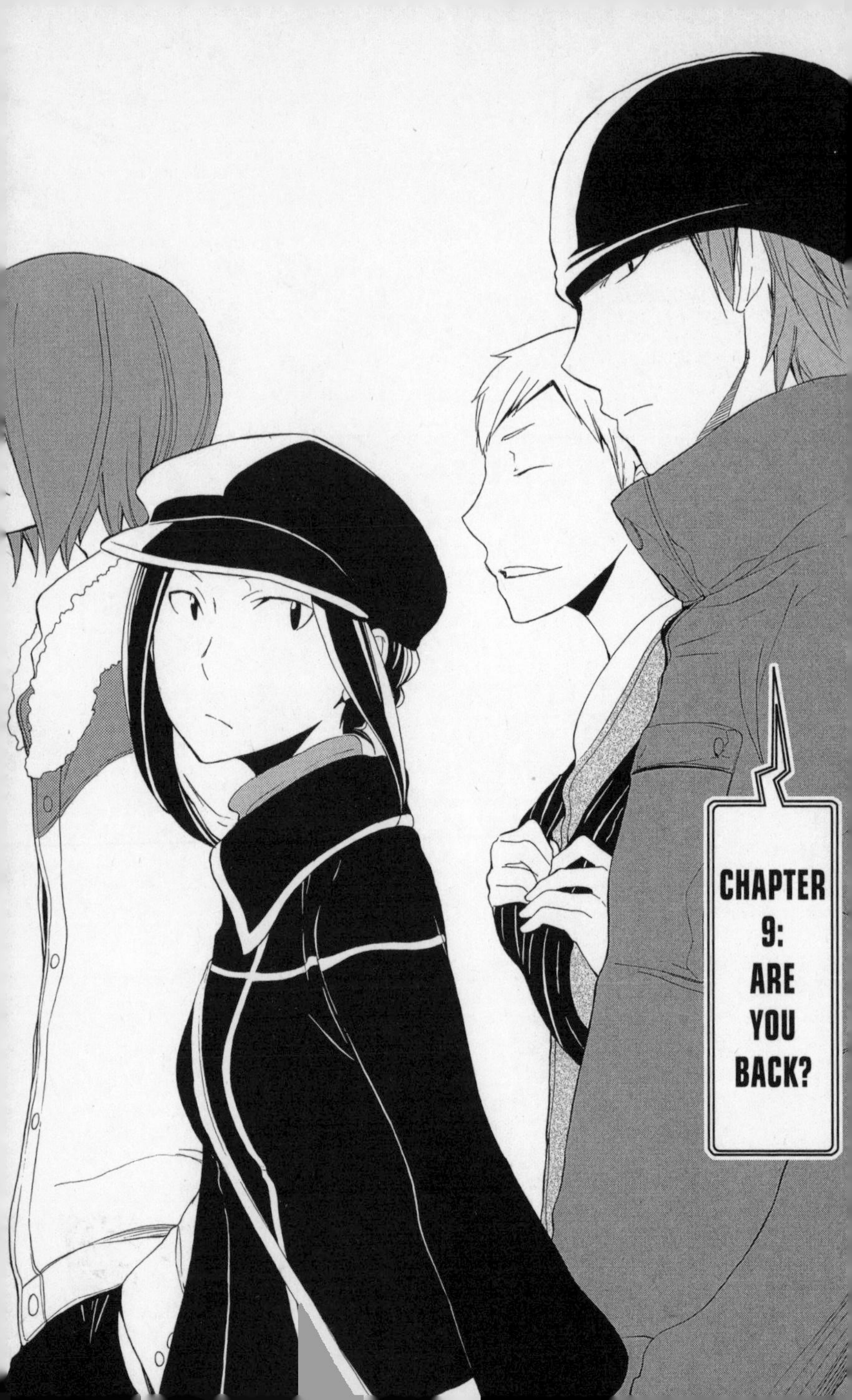
CHAPTER 9: ARE YOU BACK?

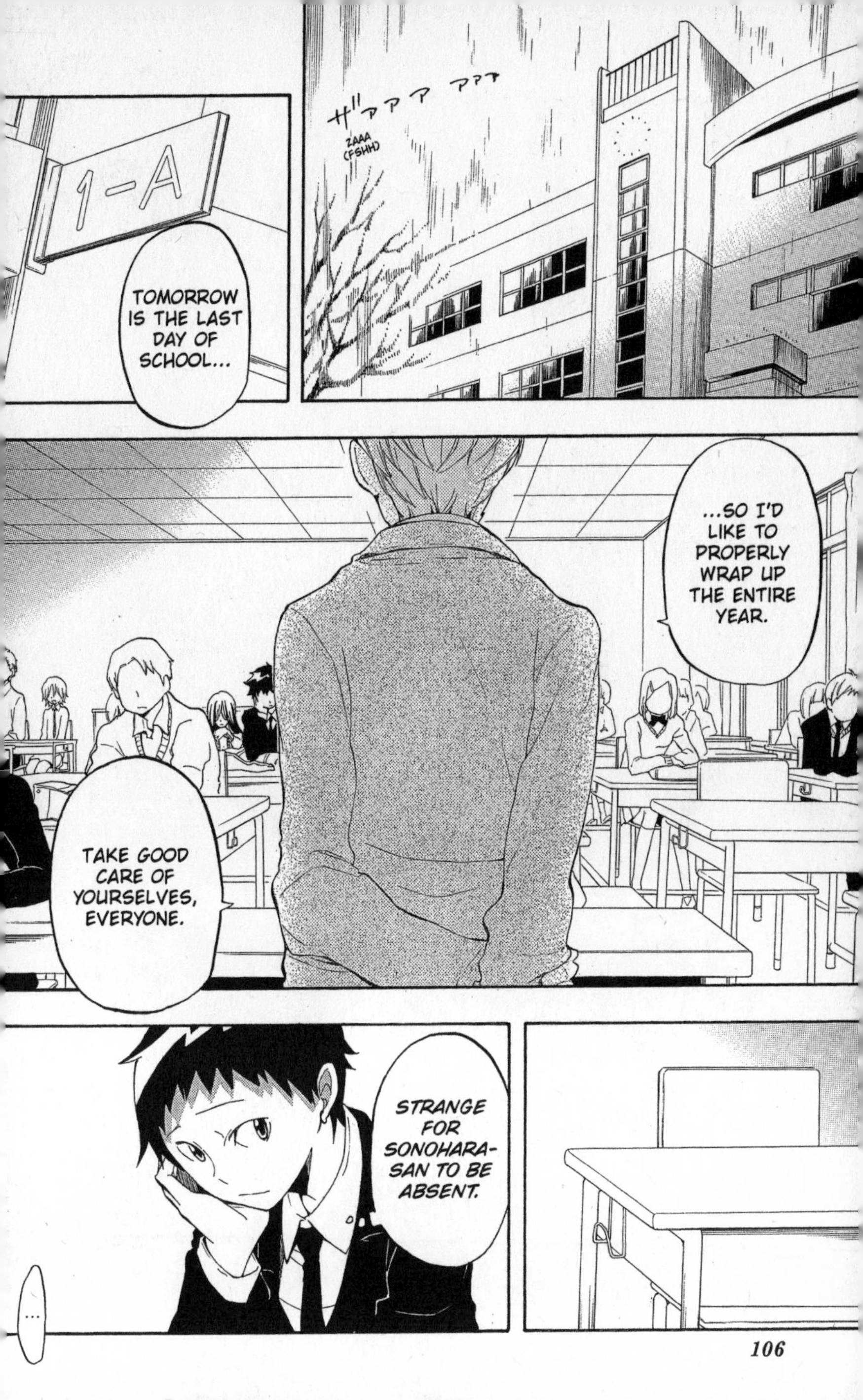
ザアアア アアア
ZAAA (FSHH)
1-A
TOMORROW IS THE LAST DAY OF SCHOOL...
...SO I'D LIKE TO PROPERLY WRAP UP THE ENTIRE YEAR.
TAKE GOOD CARE OF YOURSELVES, EVERYONE.
STRANGE FOR SONOHARA-SAN TO BE ABSENT.
...

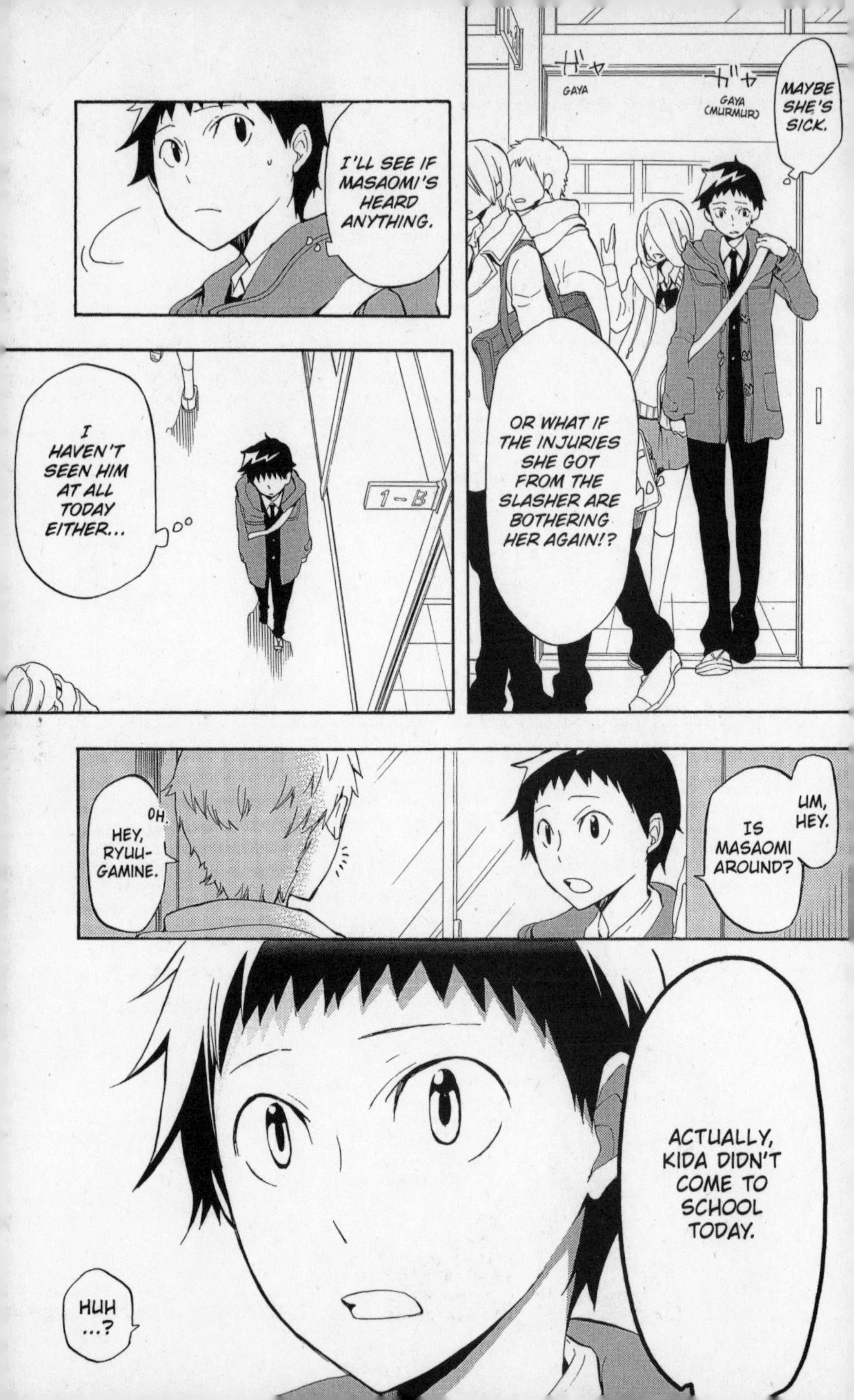
ガヤ
GAYA
ガヤ
GAYA (MURMUR)
MAYBE SHE'S SICK.
OR WHAT IF THE INJURIES SHE GOT FROM THE SLASHER ARE BOTHERING HER AGAIN!?
I'LL SEE IF MASAOMI'S HEARD ANYTHING.
1-B
I HAVEN'T SEEN HIM AT ALL TODAY EITHER...
UM, HEY. IS MASAOMI AROUND?
OH. HEY, RYUUGAMINE.
ACTUALLY, KIDA DIDN'T COME TO SCHOOL TODAY.
HUH ...?

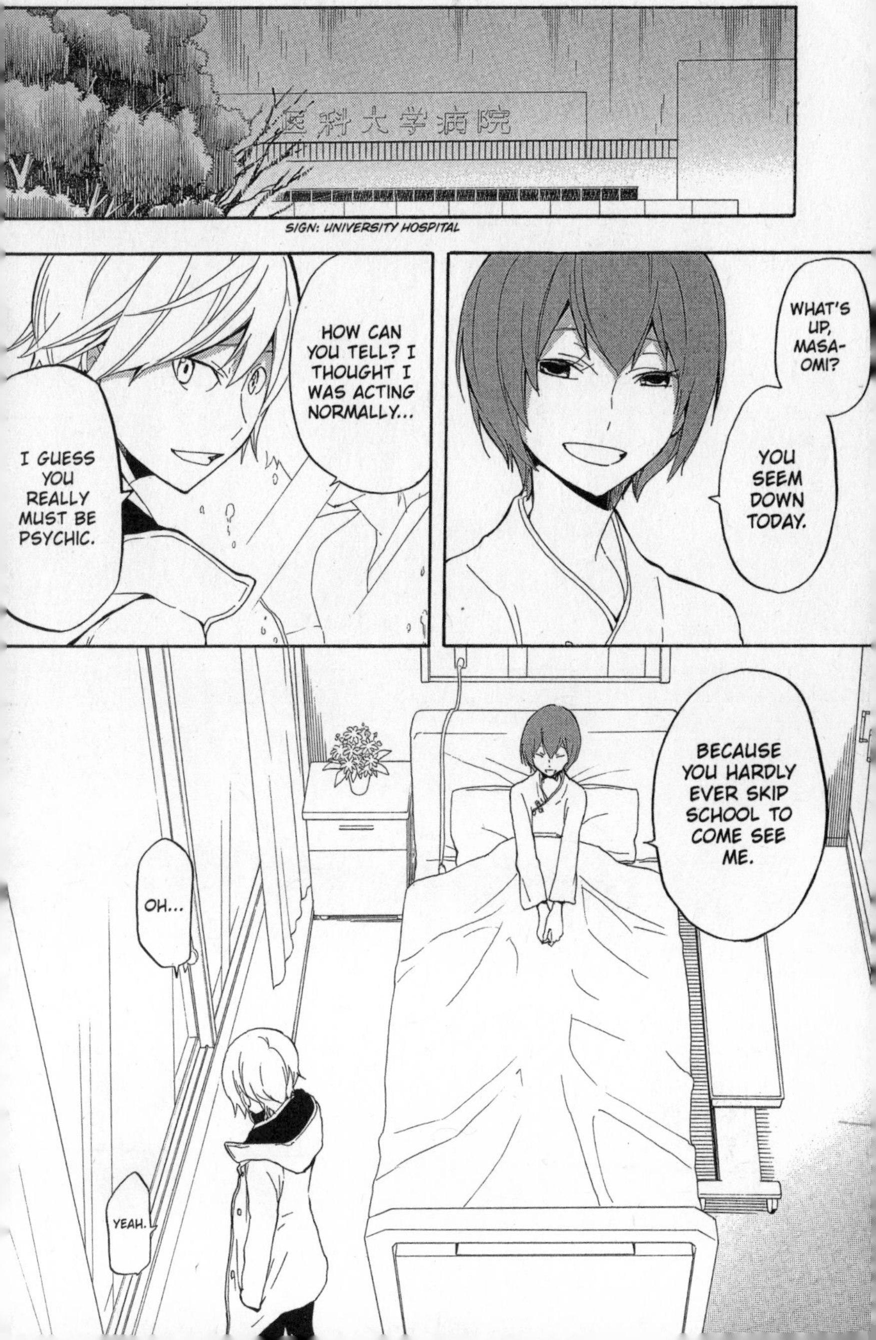
医科大学病院
SIGN: UNIVERSITY HOSPITAL
WHAT'S UP, MASA-OMI?
YOU SEEM DOWN TODAY.
HOW CAN YOU TELL? I THOUGHT I WAS ACTING NORMALLY...
I GUESS YOU REALLY MUST BE PSYCHIC.
BECAUSE YOU HARDLY EVER SKIP SCHOOL TO COME SEE ME.
OH...
YEAH.

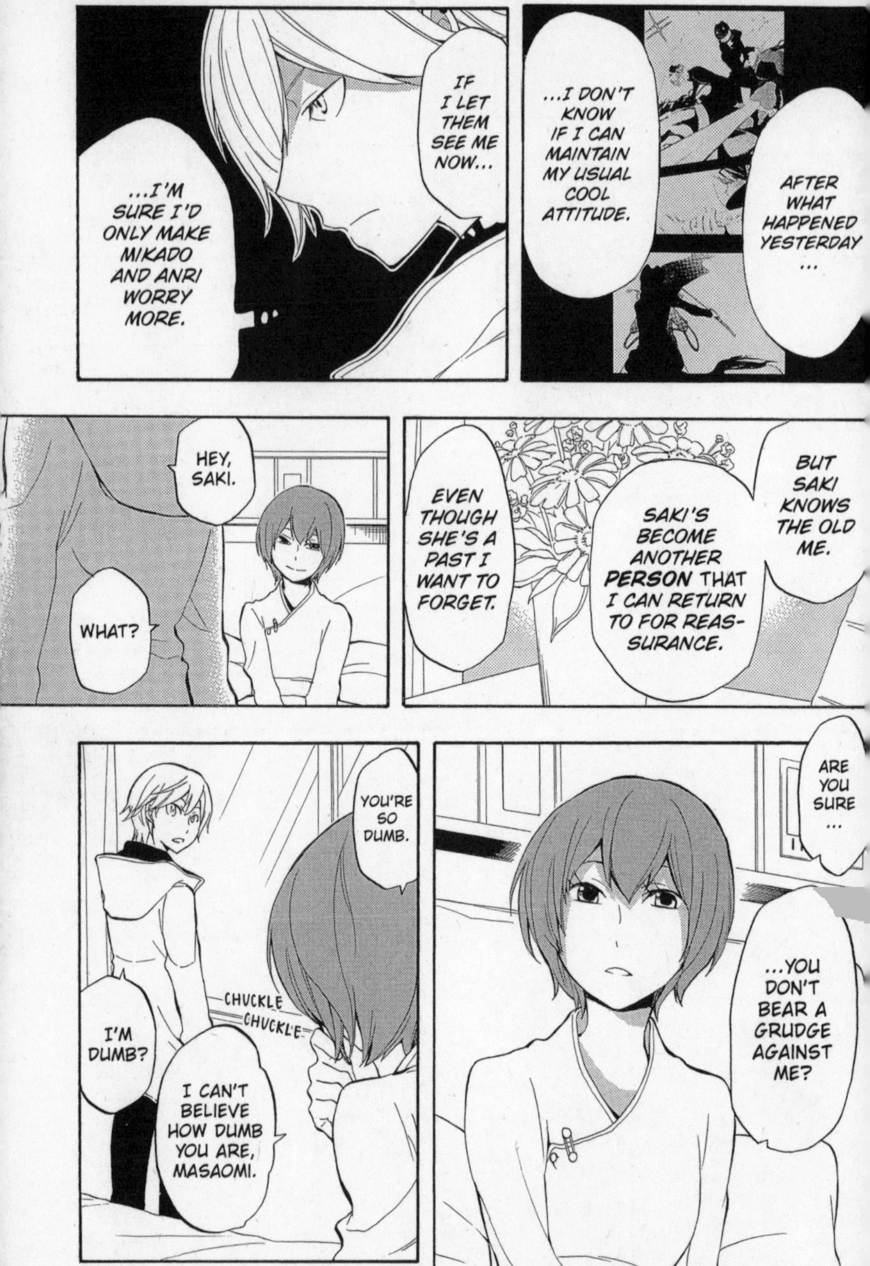
AFTER WHAT HAPPENED YESTERDAY...
...I DON'T KNOW IF I CAN MAINTAIN MY USUAL COOL ATTITUDE.
IF I LET THEM SEE ME NOW...
...I'M SURE I'D ONLY MAKE MIKADO AND ANRI WORRY MORE.
BUT SAKI KNOWS THE OLD ME.
SAKI'S BECOME ANOTHER **PERSON** THAT I CAN RETURN TO FOR REASSURANCE.
EVEN THOUGH SHE'S A PAST I WANT TO FORGET.
HEY, SAKI.
WHAT?
ARE YOU SURE...
...YOU DON'T BEAR A GRUDGE AGAINST ME?
YOU'RE SO DUMB.
CHUCKLE
CHUCKLE
I'M DUMB?
I CAN'T BELIEVE HOW DUMB YOU ARE, MASAOMI.

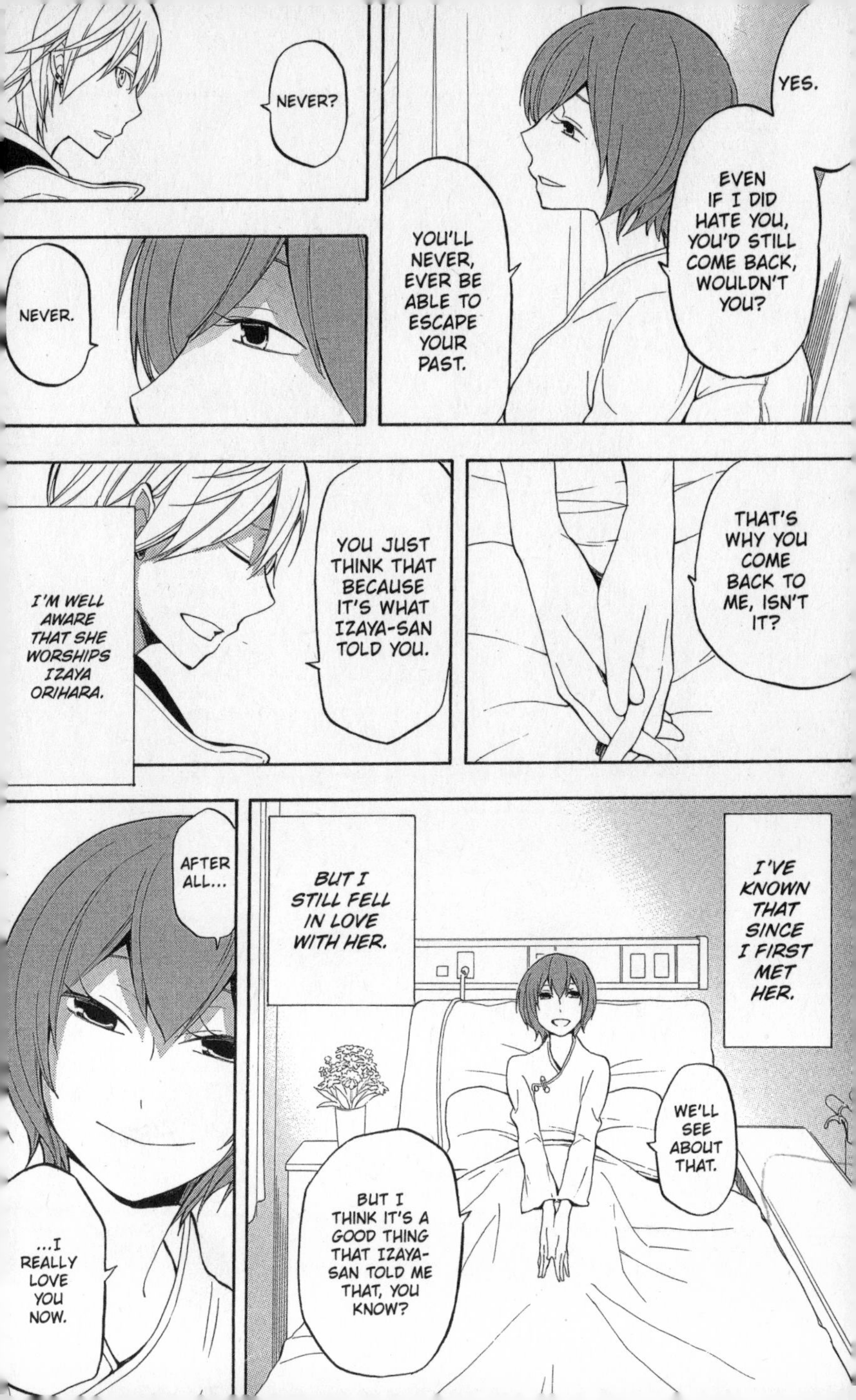
YES.
EVEN IF I DID HATE YOU, YOU'D STILL COME BACK, WOULDN'T YOU?
YOU'LL NEVER, EVER BE ABLE TO ESCAPE YOUR PAST.
NEVER?
NEVER.
THAT'S WHY YOU COME BACK TO ME, ISN'T IT?
YOU JUST THINK THAT BECAUSE IT'S WHAT IZAYA-SAN TOLD YOU.
I'M WELL AWARE THAT SHE WORSHIPS IZAYA ORIHARA.
I'VE KNOWN THAT SINCE I FIRST MET HER.
BUT I STILL FELL IN LOVE WITH HER.
WE'LL SEE ABOUT THAT.
BUT I THINK IT'S A GOOD THING THAT IZAYA-SAN TOLD ME THAT, YOU KNOW?
AFTER ALL...
...I REALLY LOVE YOU NOW.

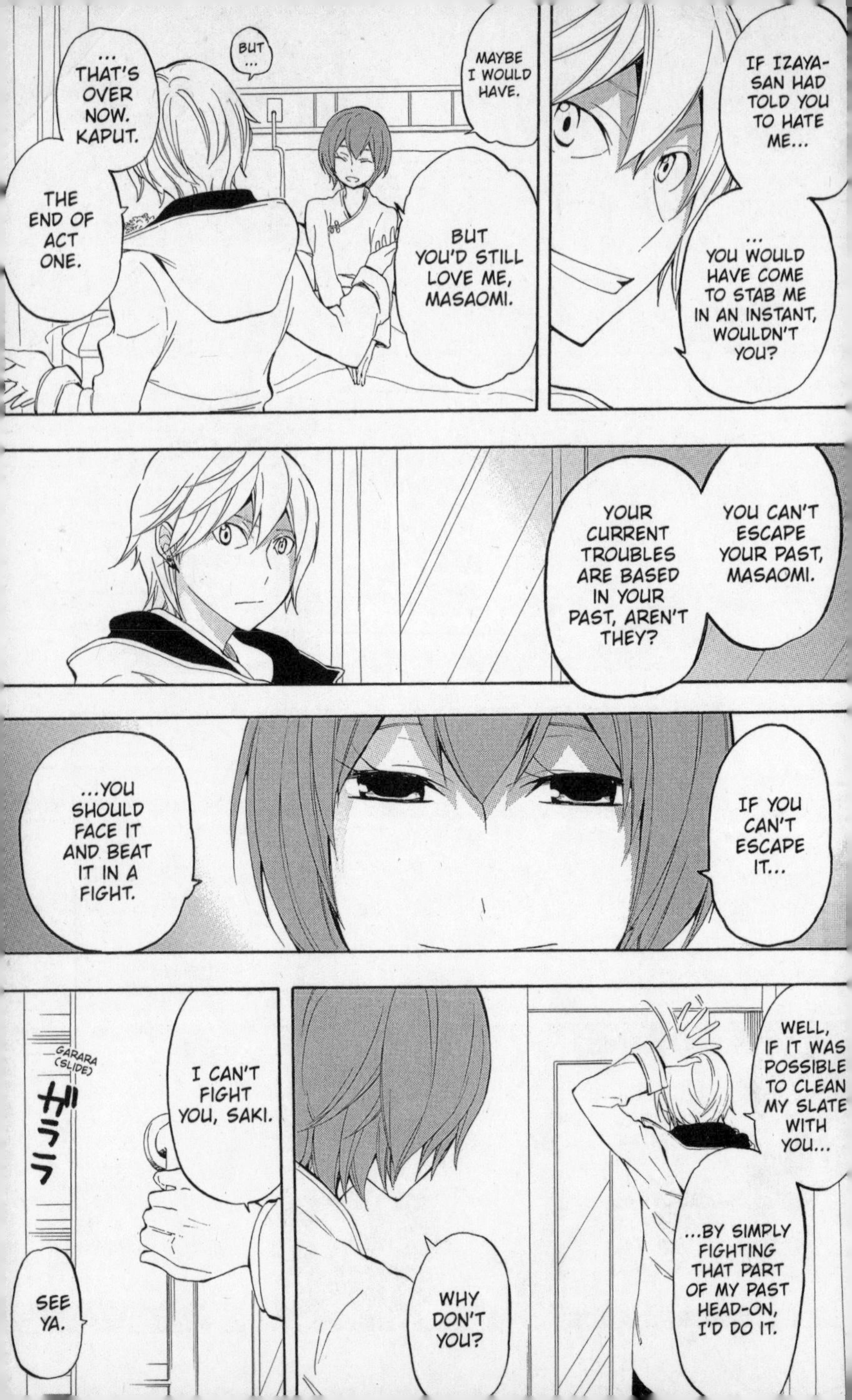
IF IZAYA-SAN HAD TOLD YOU TO HATE ME...
...YOU WOULD HAVE COME TO STAB ME IN AN INSTANT, WOULDN'T YOU?
MAYBE I WOULD HAVE.
BUT YOU'D STILL LOVE ME, MASAOMI.
BUT ...
... THAT'S OVER NOW. KAPUT.
THE END OF ACT ONE.
YOU CAN'T ESCAPE YOUR PAST, MASAOMI.
YOUR CURRENT TROUBLES ARE BASED IN YOUR PAST, AREN'T THEY?
IF YOU CAN'T ESCAPE IT...
...YOU SHOULD FACE IT AND BEAT IT IN A FIGHT.
WELL, IF IT WAS POSSIBLE TO CLEAN MY SLATE WITH YOU...
...BY SIMPLY FIGHTING THAT PART OF MY PAST HEAD-ON, I'D DO IT.
I CAN'T FIGHT YOU, SAKI.
WHY DON'T YOU?
GARARA (SLIDE)
ガララ
SEE YA.

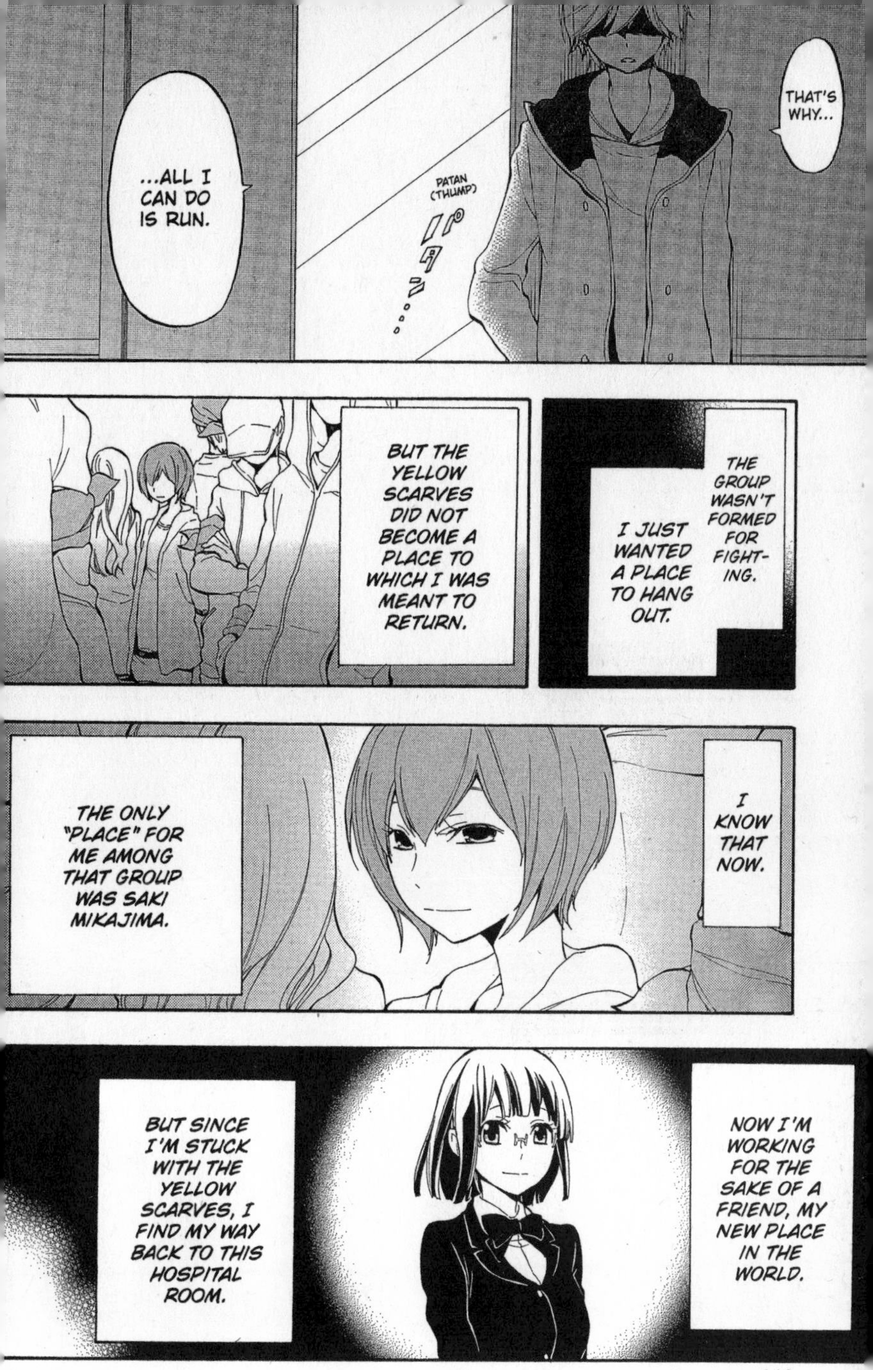
THAT'S WHY...
PATAN (THUMP)
...ALL I CAN DO IS RUN.
THE GROUP WASN'T FORMED FOR FIGHT-ING.
I JUST WANTED A PLACE TO HANG OUT.
BUT THE YELLOW SCARVES DID NOT BECOME A PLACE TO WHICH I WAS MEANT TO RETURN.
I KNOW THAT NOW.
THE ONLY "PLACE" FOR ME AMONG THAT GROUP WAS SAKI MIKAJIMA.
NOW I'M WORKING FOR THE SAKE OF A FRIEND, MY NEW PLACE IN THE WORLD.
BUT SINCE I'M STUCK WITH THE YELLOW SCARVES, I FIND MY WAY BACK TO THIS HOSPITAL ROOM.

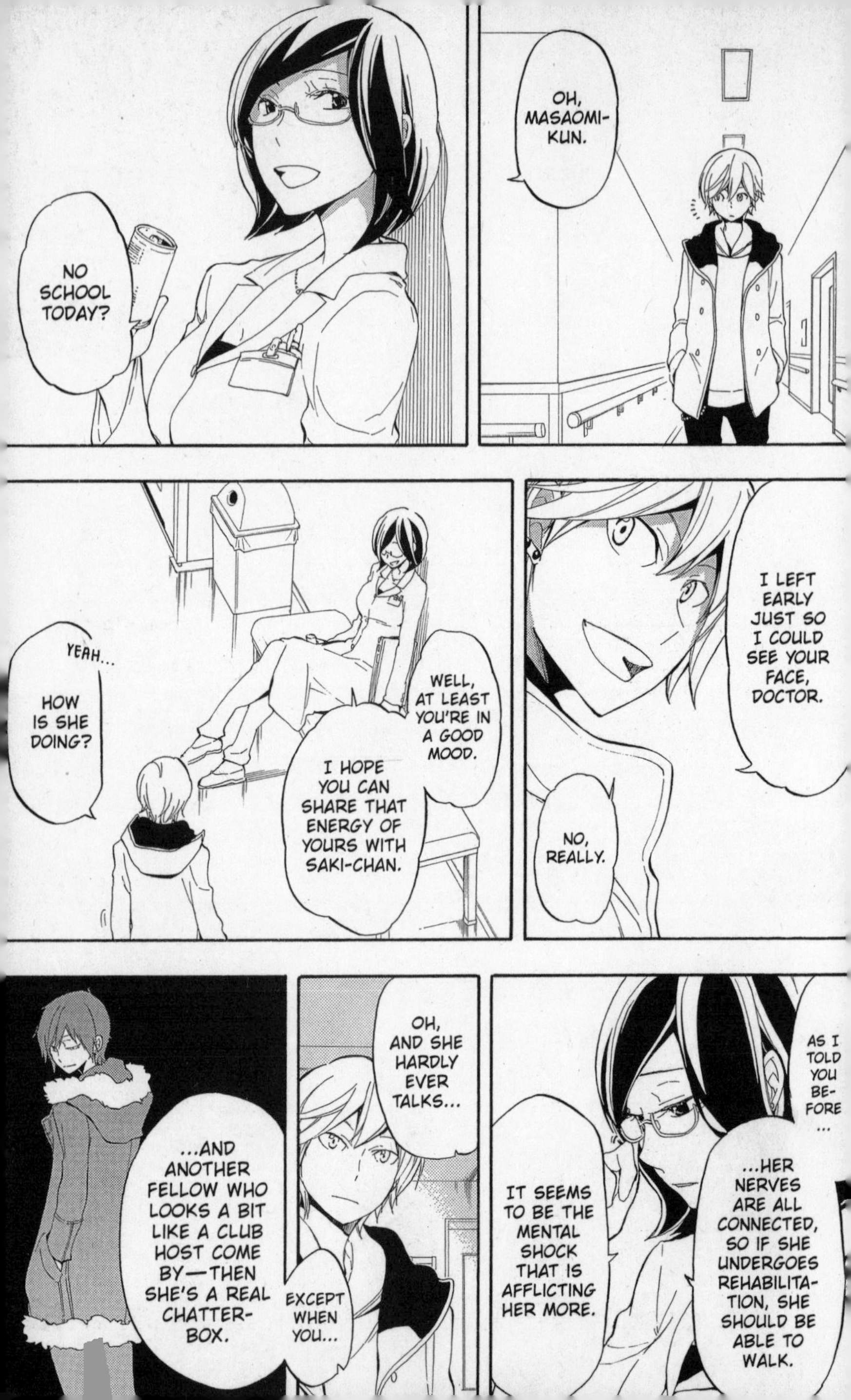
OH, MASAOMI-KUN.
NO SCHOOL TODAY?
I LEFT EARLY JUST SO I COULD SEE YOUR FACE, DOCTOR.
NO, REALLY.
WELL, AT LEAST YOU'RE IN A GOOD MOOD.
I HOPE YOU CAN SHARE THAT ENERGY OF YOURS WITH SAKI-CHAN.
YEAH...
HOW IS SHE DOING?
AS I TOLD YOU BEFORE...
...HER NERVES ARE ALL CONNECTED, SO IF SHE UNDERGOES REHABILITATION, SHE SHOULD BE ABLE TO WALK.
IT SEEMS TO BE THE MENTAL SHOCK THAT IS AFFLICTING HER MORE.
OH, AND SHE HARDLY EVER TALKS...
EXCEPT WHEN YOU...
...AND ANOTHER FELLOW WHO LOOKS A BIT LIKE A CLUB HOST COME BY—THEN SHE'S A REAL CHATTERBOX.

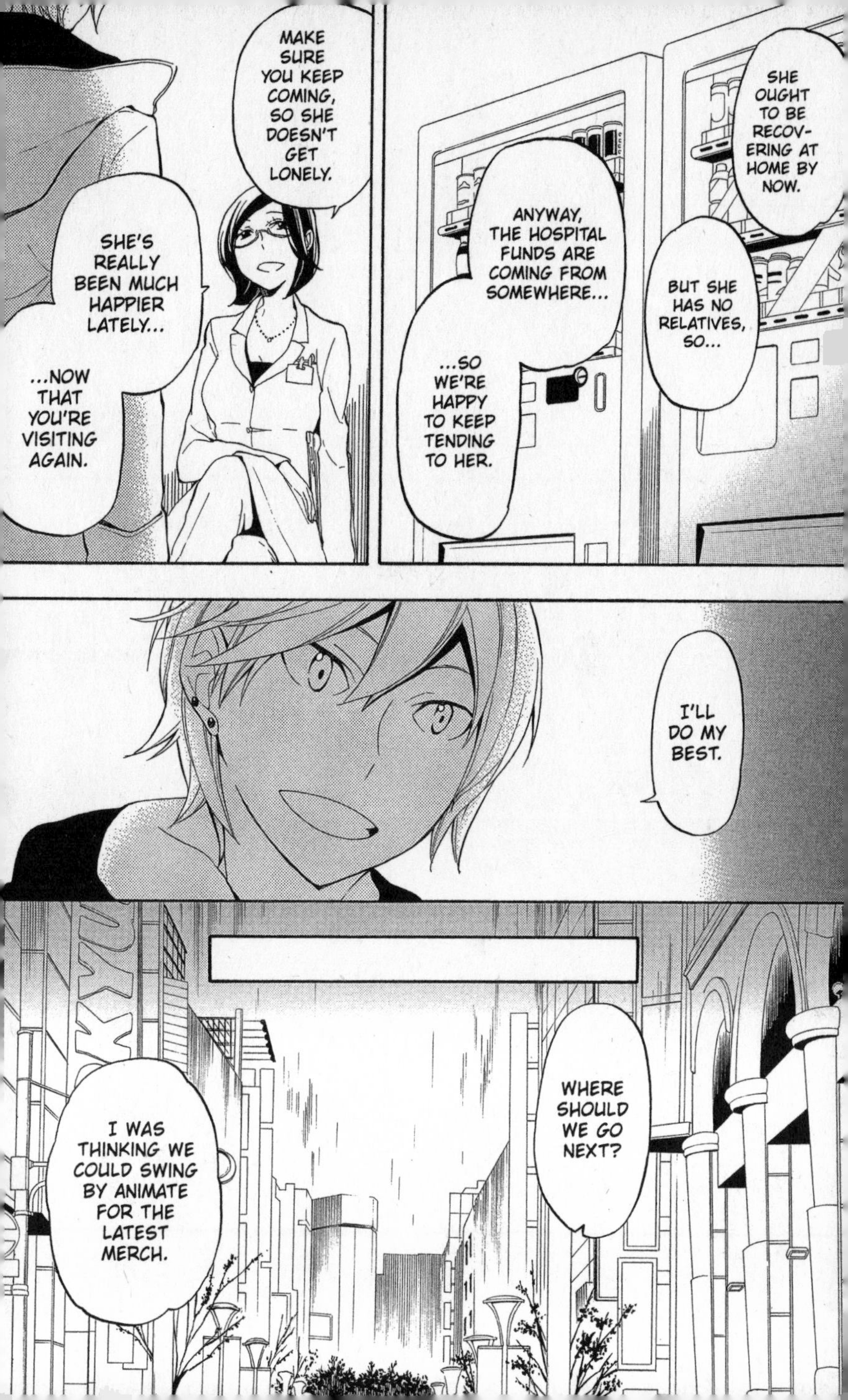
SHE OUGHT TO BE RECOV-ERING AT HOME BY NOW.
BUT SHE HAS NO RELATIVES, SO...
ANYWAY, THE HOSPITAL FUNDS ARE COMING FROM SOMEWHERE...
...SO WE'RE HAPPY TO KEEP TENDING TO HER.
MAKE SURE YOU KEEP COMING, SO SHE DOESN'T GET LONELY.
SHE'S REALLY BEEN MUCH HAPPIER LATELY...
...NOW THAT YOU'RE VISITING AGAIN.
I'LL DO MY BEST.
WHERE SHOULD WE GO NEXT?
I WAS THINKING WE COULD SWING BY ANIMATE FOR THE LATEST MERCH.

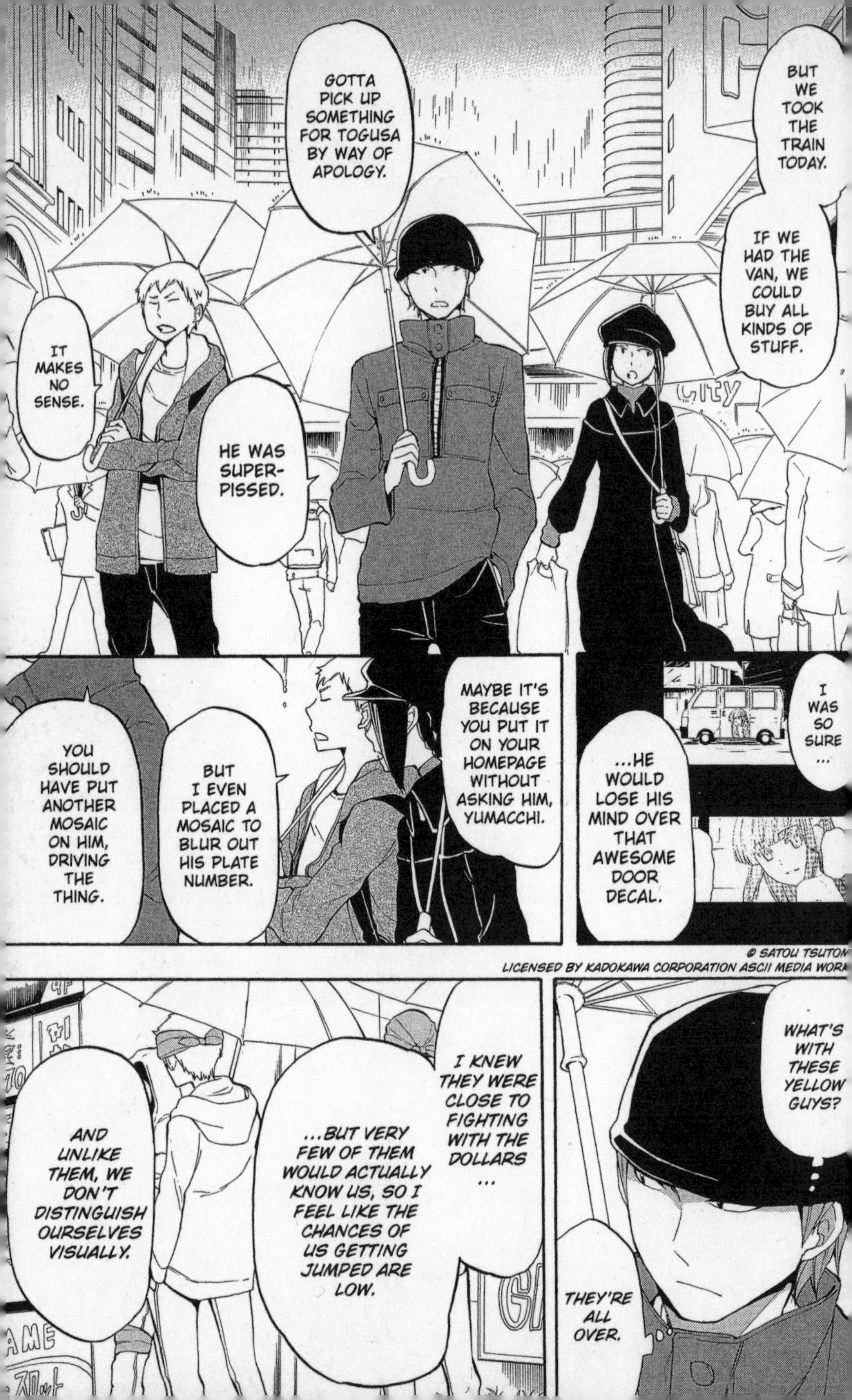
BUT WE TOOK THE TRAIN TODAY.
IF WE HAD THE VAN, WE COULD BUY ALL KINDS OF STUFF.
GOTTA PICK UP SOMETHING FOR TOGUSA BY WAY OF APOLOGY.
HE WAS SUPER-PISSED.
IT MAKES NO SENSE.
I WAS SO SURE...
...HE WOULD LOSE HIS MIND OVER THAT AWESOME DOOR DECAL.
MAYBE IT'S BECAUSE YOU PUT IT ON YOUR HOMEPAGE WITHOUT ASKING HIM, YUMACCHI.
BUT I EVEN PLACED A MOSAIC TO BLUR OUT HIS PLATE NUMBER.
YOU SHOULD HAVE PUT ANOTHER MOSAIC ON HIM, DRIVING THE THING.
WHAT'S WITH THESE YELLOW GUYS?
THEY'RE ALL OVER.
I KNEW THEY WERE CLOSE TO FIGHTING WITH THE DOLLARS...
...BUT VERY FEW OF THEM WOULD ACTUALLY KNOW US, SO I FEEL LIKE THE CHANCES OF US GETTING JUMPED ARE LOW.
AND UNLIKE THEM, WE DON'T DISTINGUISH OURSELVES VISUALLY.

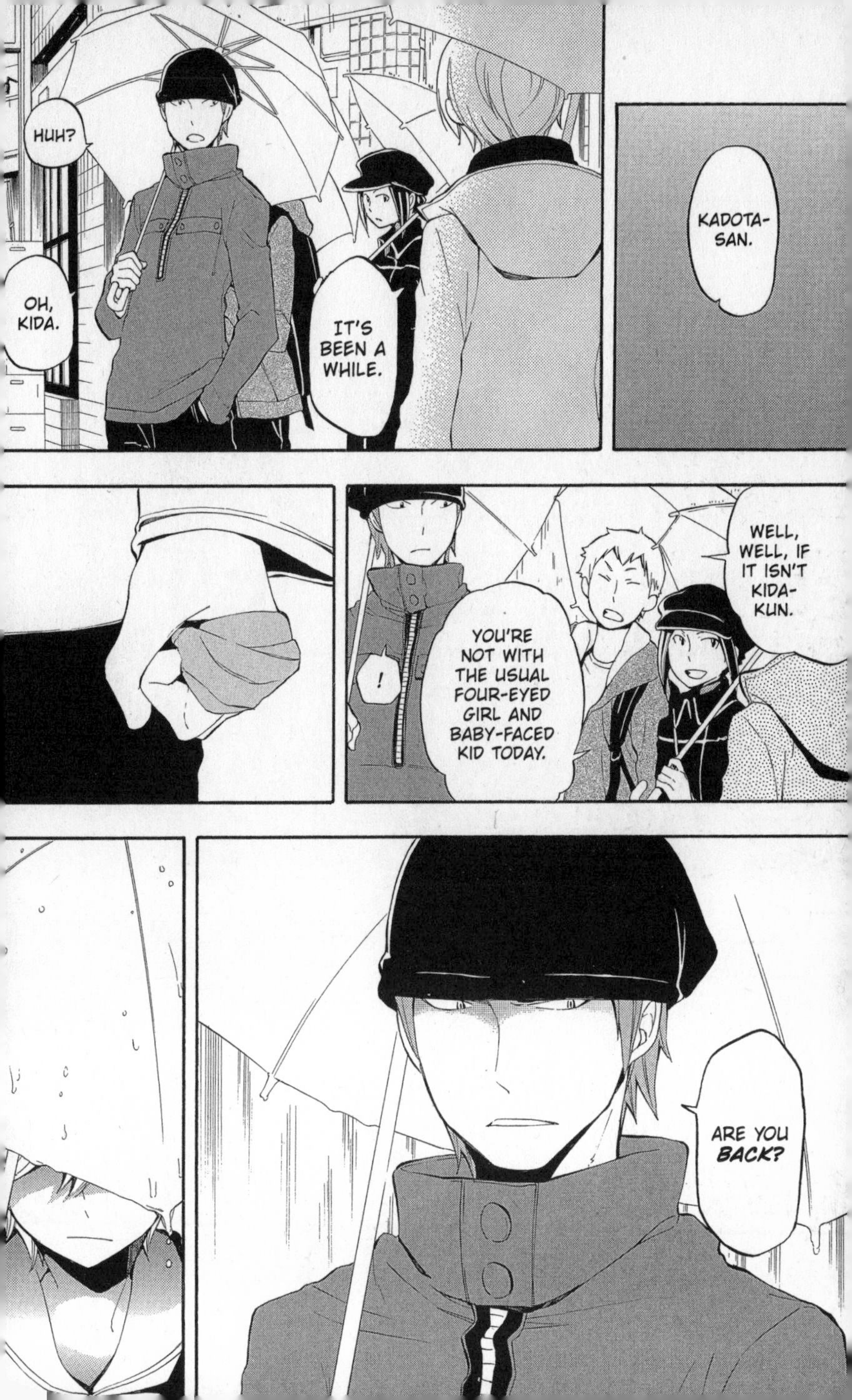
KADOTA-SAN.
HUH?
OH, KIDA.
IT'S BEEN A WHILE.
WELL, WELL, IF IT ISN'T KIDA-KUN.
YOU'RE NOT WITH THE USUAL FOUR-EYED GIRL AND BABY-FACED KID TODAY.
!
ARE YOU *BACK?*

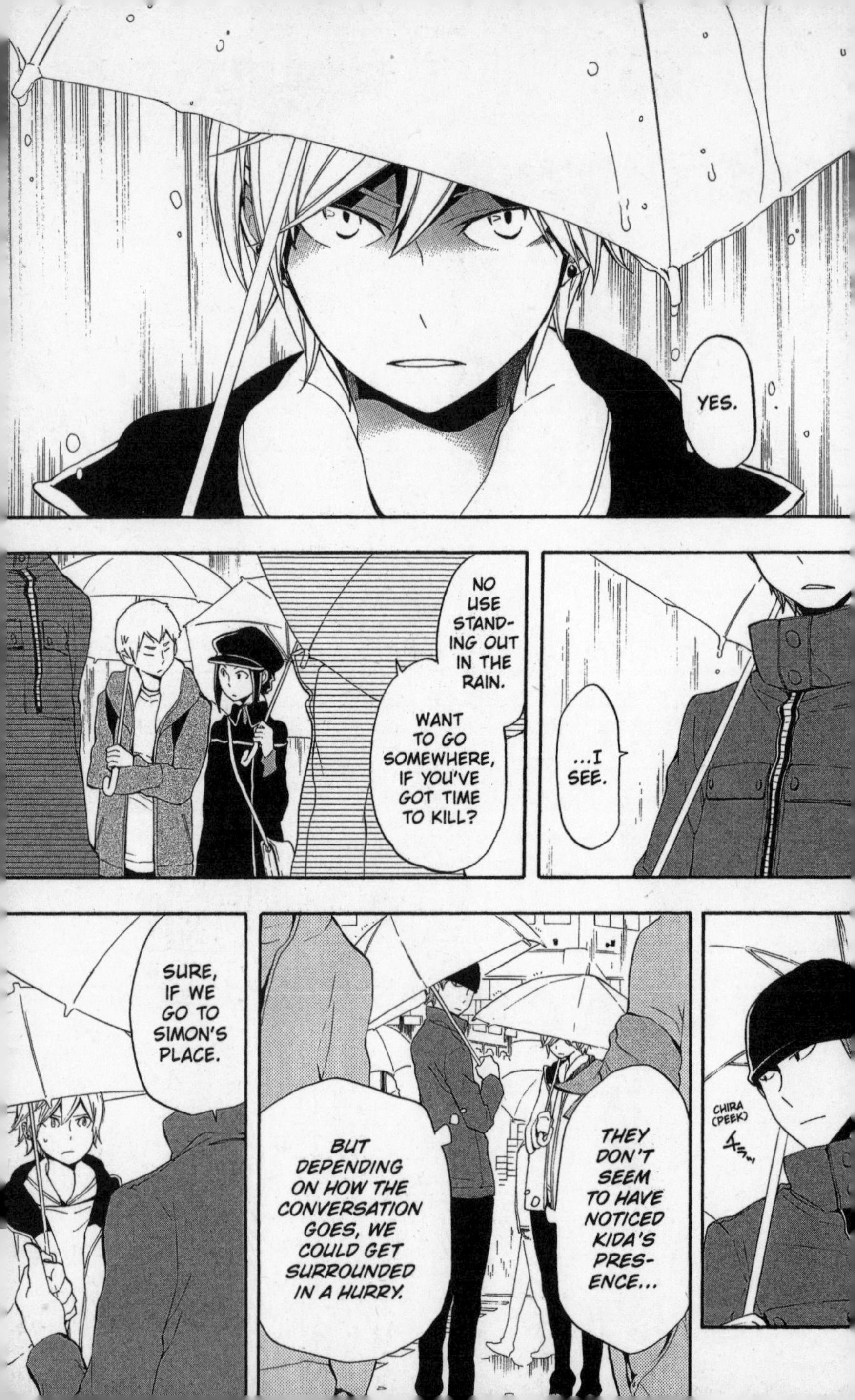
YES.
...I SEE.
NO USE STANDING-ING OUT IN THE RAIN.
WANT TO GO SOMEWHERE, IF YOU'VE GOT TIME TO KILL?
CHIRA (PEEK)
THEY DON'T SEEM TO HAVE NOTICED KIDA'S PRES-ENCE...
BUT DEPENDING ON HOW THE CONVERSATION GOES, WE COULD GET SURROUNDED IN A HURRY.
SURE, IF WE GO TO SIMON'S PLACE.

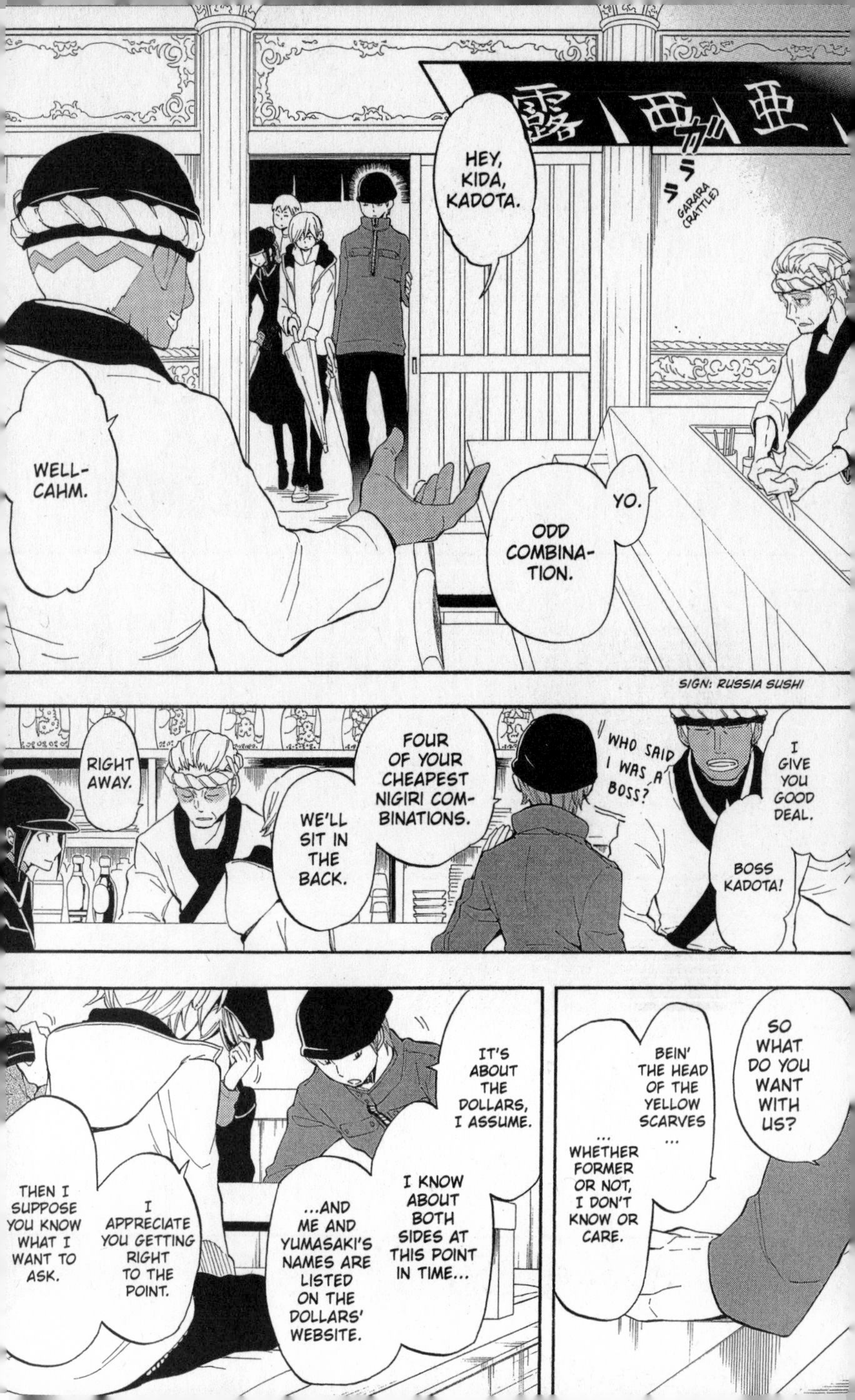
露西亜
GARARA (RATTLE)
HEY, KIDA, KADOTA.
YO.
ODD COMBINATION.
WELL-CAHM.
SIGN: RUSSIA SUSHI
I GIVE YOU GOOD DEAL.
BOSS KADOTA!
WHO SAID I WAS A BOSS?
FOUR OF YOUR CHEAPEST NIGIRI COMBINATIONS.
WE'LL SIT IN THE BACK.
RIGHT AWAY.
SO WHAT DO YOU WANT WITH US?
BEIN' THE HEAD OF THE YELLOW SCARVES...
...WHETHER FORMER OR NOT, I DON'T KNOW OR CARE.
IT'S ABOUT THE DOLLARS, I ASSUME.
I KNOW ABOUT BOTH SIDES AT THIS POINT IN TIME...
...AND ME AND YUMASAKI'S NAMES ARE LISTED ON THE DOLLARS' WEBSITE.
I APPRECIATE YOU GETTING RIGHT TO THE POINT.
THEN I SUPPOSE YOU KNOW WHAT I WANT TO ASK.

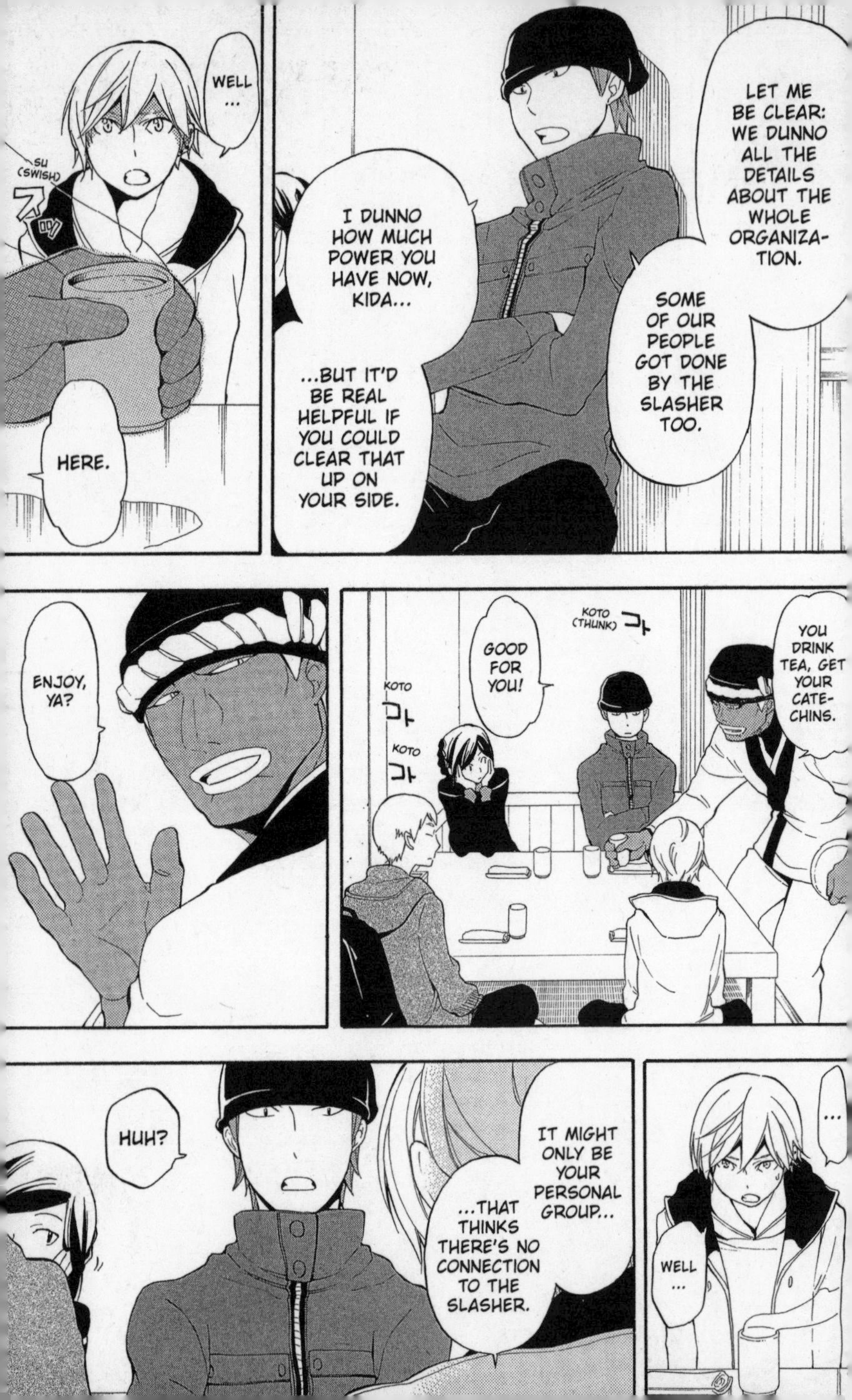
LET ME BE CLEAR: WE DUNNO ALL THE DETAILS ABOUT THE WHOLE ORGANIZATION.
SOME OF OUR PEOPLE GOT DONE BY THE SLASHER TOO.
I DUNNO HOW MUCH POWER YOU HAVE NOW, KIDA...
...BUT IT'D BE REAL HELPFUL IF YOU COULD CLEAR THAT UP ON YOUR SIDE.
WELL ...
SU (SWISH)
HERE.
YOU DRINK TEA, GET YOUR CATE-CHINS.
KOTO (THUNK)
GOOD FOR YOU!
KOTO
KOTO
ENJOY, YA?
...
WELL ...
IT MIGHT ONLY BE YOUR PERSONAL GROUP...
...THAT THINKS THERE'S NO CONNECTION TO THE SLASHER.
HUH?

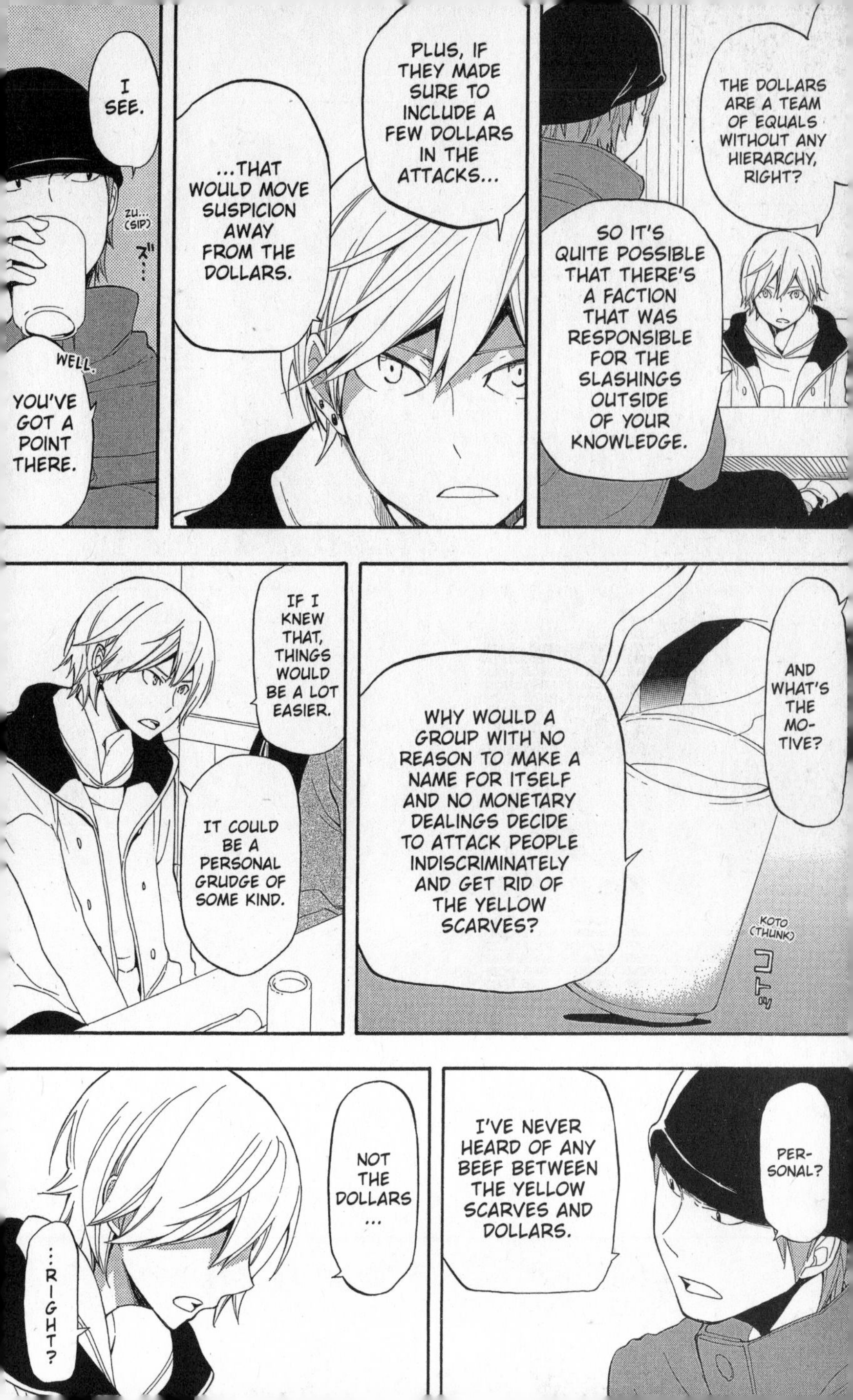
THE DOLLARS ARE A TEAM OF EQUALS WITHOUT ANY HIERARCHY, RIGHT?
SO IT'S QUITE POSSIBLE THAT THERE'S A FACTION THAT WAS RESPONSIBLE FOR THE SLASHINGS OUTSIDE OF YOUR KNOWLEDGE.
PLUS, IF THEY MADE SURE TO INCLUDE A FEW DOLLARS IN THE ATTACKS...
...THAT WOULD MOVE SUSPICION AWAY FROM THE DOLLARS.
I SEE.
ZU... (SIP)
WELL.
YOU'VE GOT A POINT THERE.
AND WHAT'S THE MO-TIVE?
WHY WOULD A GROUP WITH NO REASON TO MAKE A NAME FOR ITSELF AND NO MONETARY DEALINGS DECIDE TO ATTACK PEOPLE INDISCRIMINATELY AND GET RID OF THE YELLOW SCARVES?
KOTO (THUNK)
IF I KNEW THAT, THINGS WOULD BE A LOT EASIER.
IT COULD BE A PERSONAL GRUDGE OF SOME KIND.
PER-SONAL?
I'VE NEVER HEARD OF ANY BEEF BETWEEN THE YELLOW SCARVES AND DOLLARS.
NOT THE DOLLARS ...
...RIGHT?

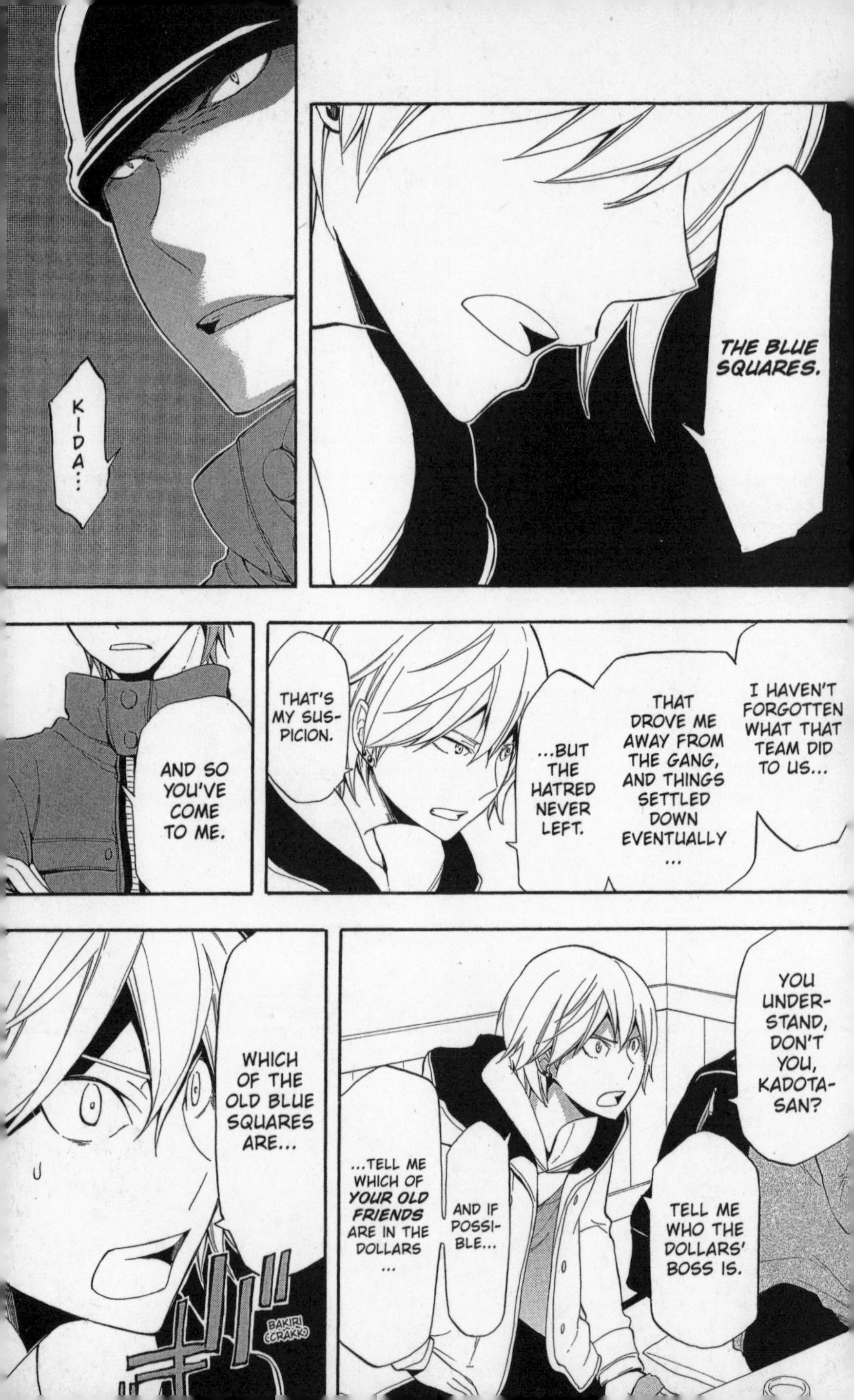
THE BLUE SQUARES.
KIDA...
I HAVEN'T FORGOTTEN WHAT THAT TEAM DID TO US...
THAT DROVE ME AWAY FROM THE GANG, AND THINGS SETTLED DOWN EVENTUALLY...
...BUT THE HATRED NEVER LEFT.
THAT'S MY SUSPICION.
AND SO YOU'VE COME TO ME.
YOU UNDERSTAND, DON'T YOU, KADOTA-SAN?
TELL ME WHO THE DOLLARS' BOSS IS.
AND IF POSSIBLE...
...TELL ME WHICH OF *YOUR OLD FRIENDS* ARE IN THE DOLLARS...
WHICH OF THE OLD BLUE SQUARES ARE...
BAKIRI (CRAKK)

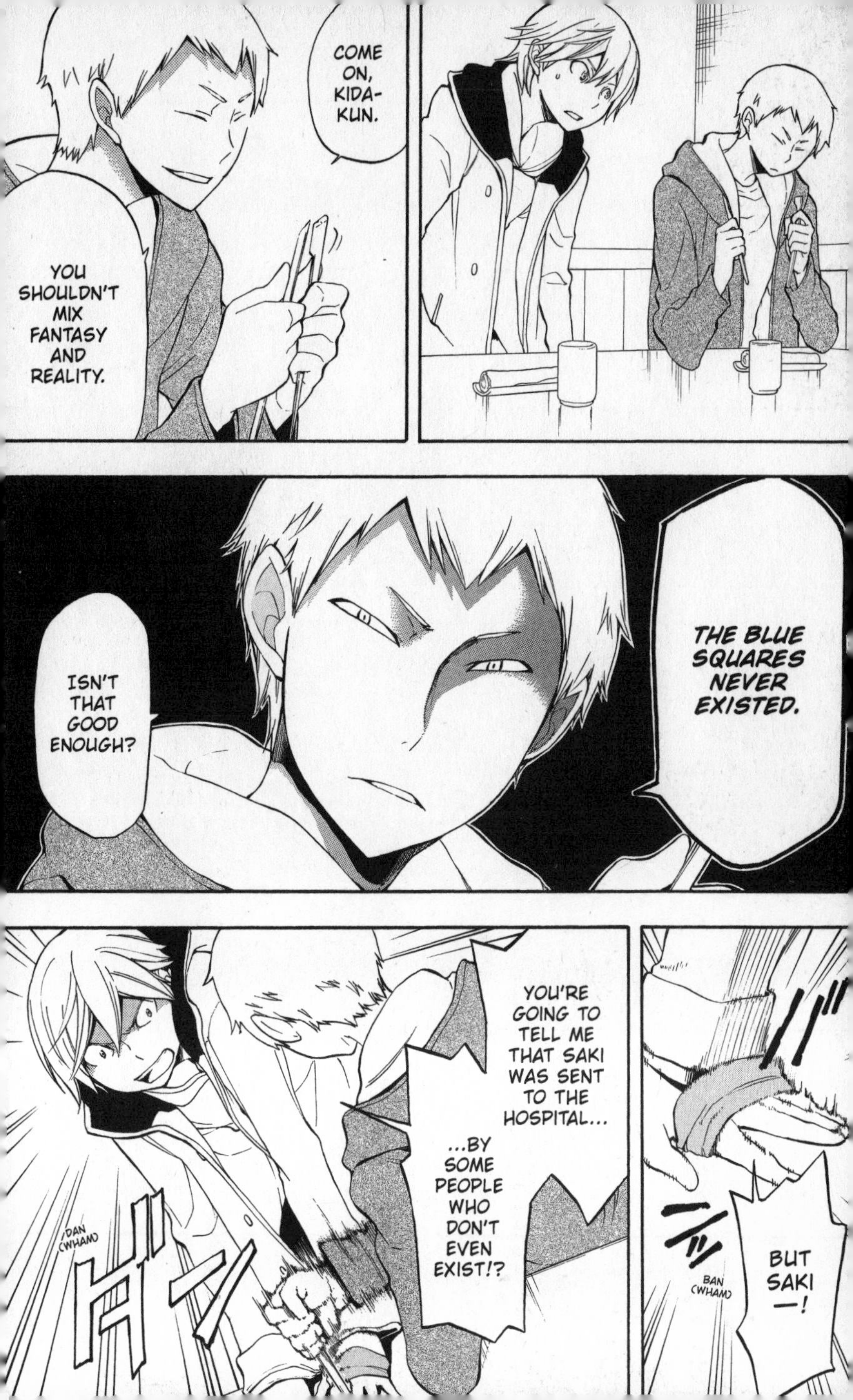
COME ON, KIDA-KUN.
YOU SHOULDN'T MIX FANTASY AND REALITY.
THE BLUE SQUARES NEVER EXISTED.
ISN'T THAT GOOD ENOUGH?
BUT SAKI—!
BAN (WHAM)
YOU'RE GOING TO TELL ME THAT SAKI WAS SENT TO THE HOSPITAL...
...BY SOME PEOPLE WHO DON'T EVEN EXIST!?
DAN (WHAM)

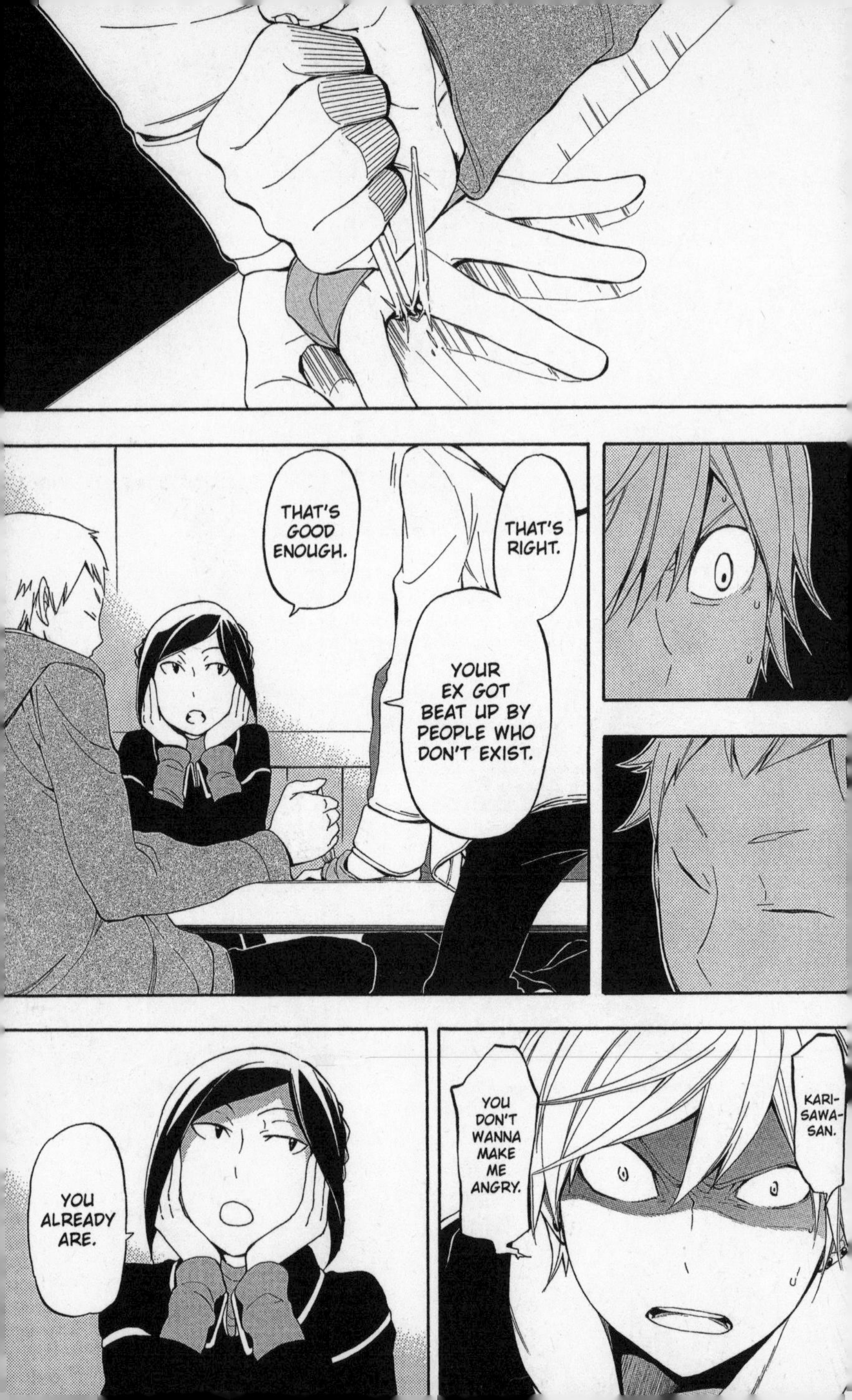
THAT'S GOOD ENOUGH.
THAT'S RIGHT.
YOUR EX GOT BEAT UP BY PEOPLE WHO DON'T EXIST.
KARI-SAWA-SAN.
YOU DON'T WANNA MAKE ME ANGRY.
YOU ALREADY ARE.

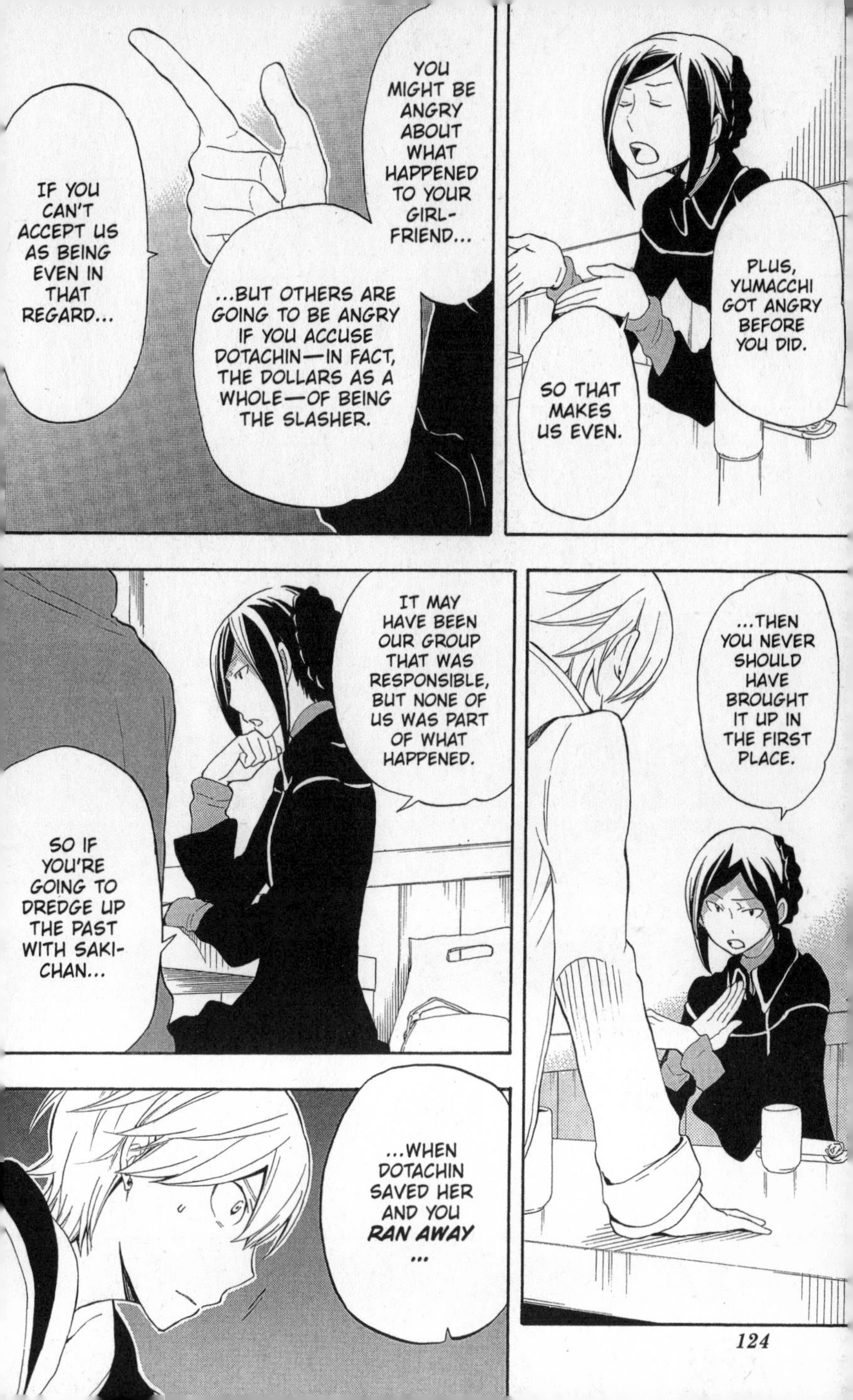
PLUS, YUMACCHI GOT ANGRY BEFORE YOU DID.
SO THAT MAKES US EVEN.
YOU MIGHT BE ANGRY ABOUT WHAT HAPPENED TO YOUR GIRL-FRIEND...
...BUT OTHERS ARE GOING TO BE ANGRY IF YOU ACCUSE DOTACHIN—IN FACT, THE DOLLARS AS A WHOLE—OF BEING THE SLASHER.
IF YOU CAN'T ACCEPT US AS BEING EVEN IN THAT REGARD...
...THEN YOU NEVER SHOULD HAVE BROUGHT IT UP IN THE FIRST PLACE.
IT MAY HAVE BEEN OUR GROUP THAT WAS RESPONSIBLE, BUT NONE OF US WAS PART OF WHAT HAPPENED.
SO IF YOU'RE GOING TO DREDGE UP THE PAST WITH SAKI-CHAN...
...WHEN DOTACHIN SAVED HER AND YOU ***RAN AWAY***...

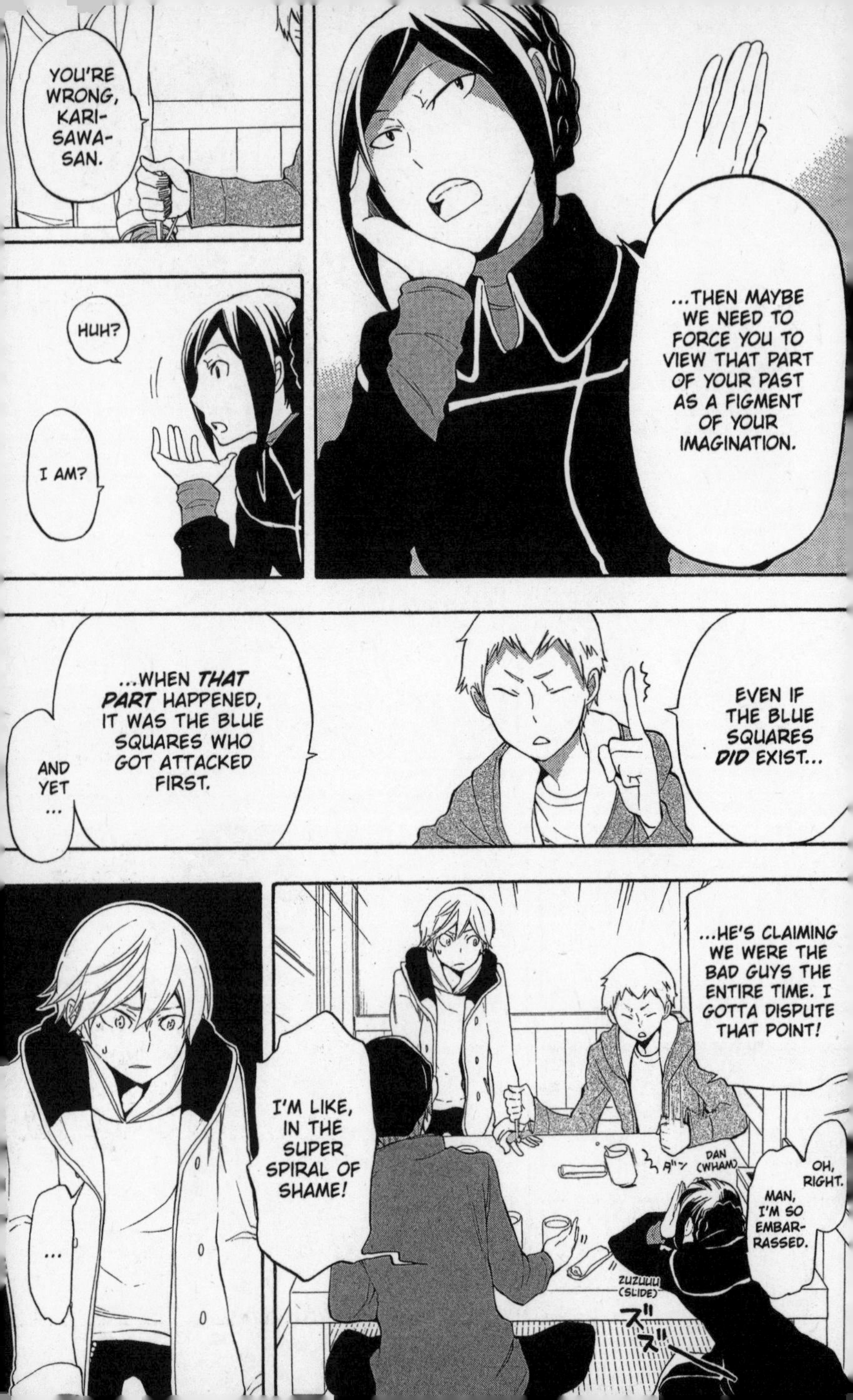
...THEN MAYBE WE NEED TO FORCE YOU TO VIEW THAT PART OF YOUR PAST AS A FIGMENT OF YOUR IMAGINATION.
YOU'RE WRONG, KARI-SAWA-SAN.
HUH?
I AM?
EVEN IF THE BLUE SQUARES *DID* EXIST...
...WHEN *THAT PART* HAPPENED, IT WAS THE BLUE SQUARES WHO GOT ATTACKED FIRST.
AND YET ...
...HE'S CLAIMING WE WERE THE BAD GUYS THE ENTIRE TIME. I GOTTA DISPUTE THAT POINT!
OH, RIGHT.
MAN, I'M SO EMBARRASSED.
DAN (WHAM)
I'M LIKE, IN THE SUPER SPIRAL OF SHAME!
ZUZUUU (SLIDE)
...

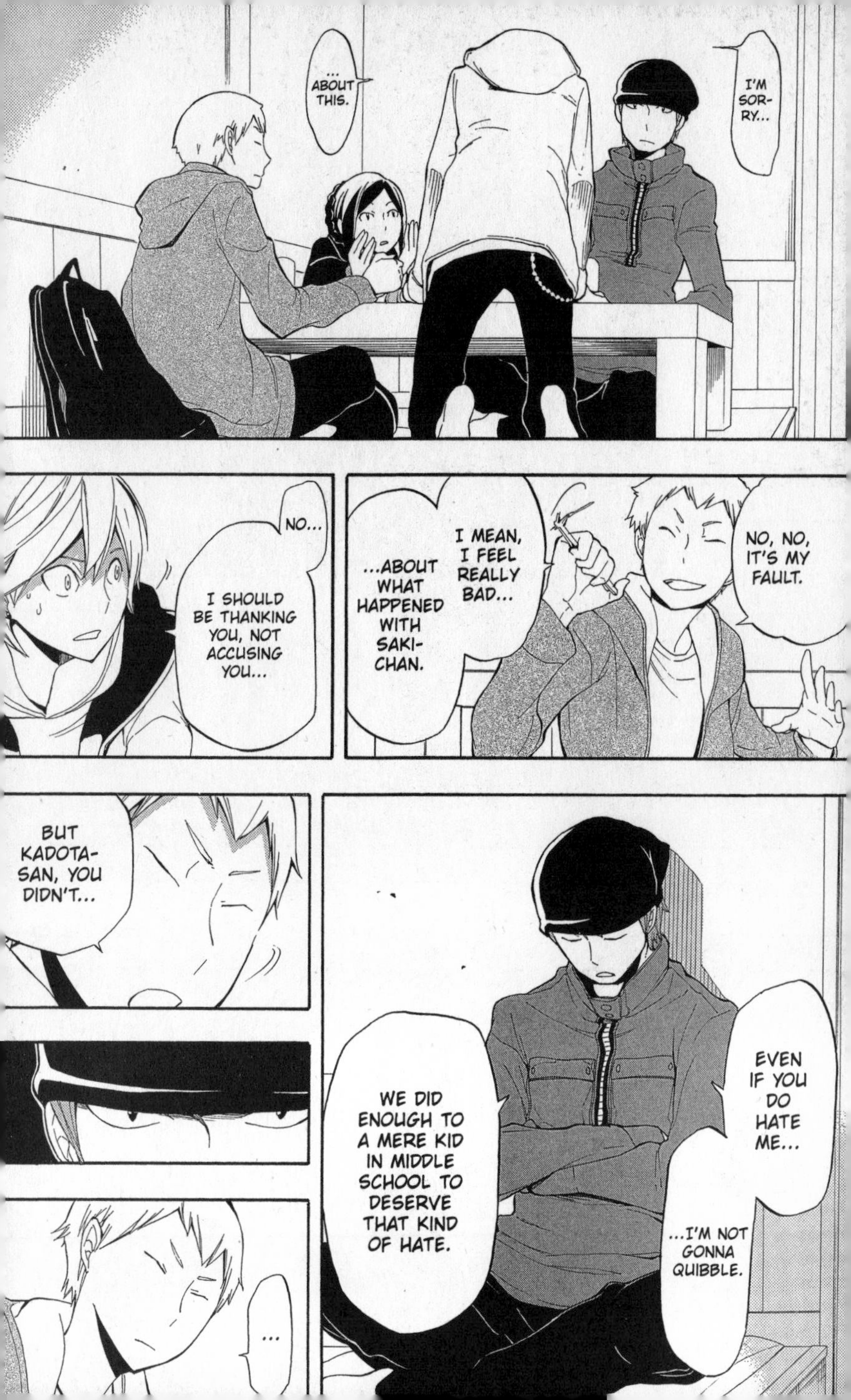
I'M SORRY...
...ABOUT THIS.
NO, NO, IT'S MY FAULT.
I MEAN, I FEEL REALLY BAD...
...ABOUT WHAT HAPPENED WITH SAKI-CHAN.
NO...
I SHOULD BE THANKING YOU, NOT ACCUSING YOU...
EVEN IF YOU DO HATE ME...
...I'M NOT GONNA QUIBBLE.
WE DID ENOUGH TO A MERE KID IN MIDDLE SCHOOL TO DESERVE THAT KIND OF HATE.
BUT KADOTA-SAN, YOU DIDN'T...
...

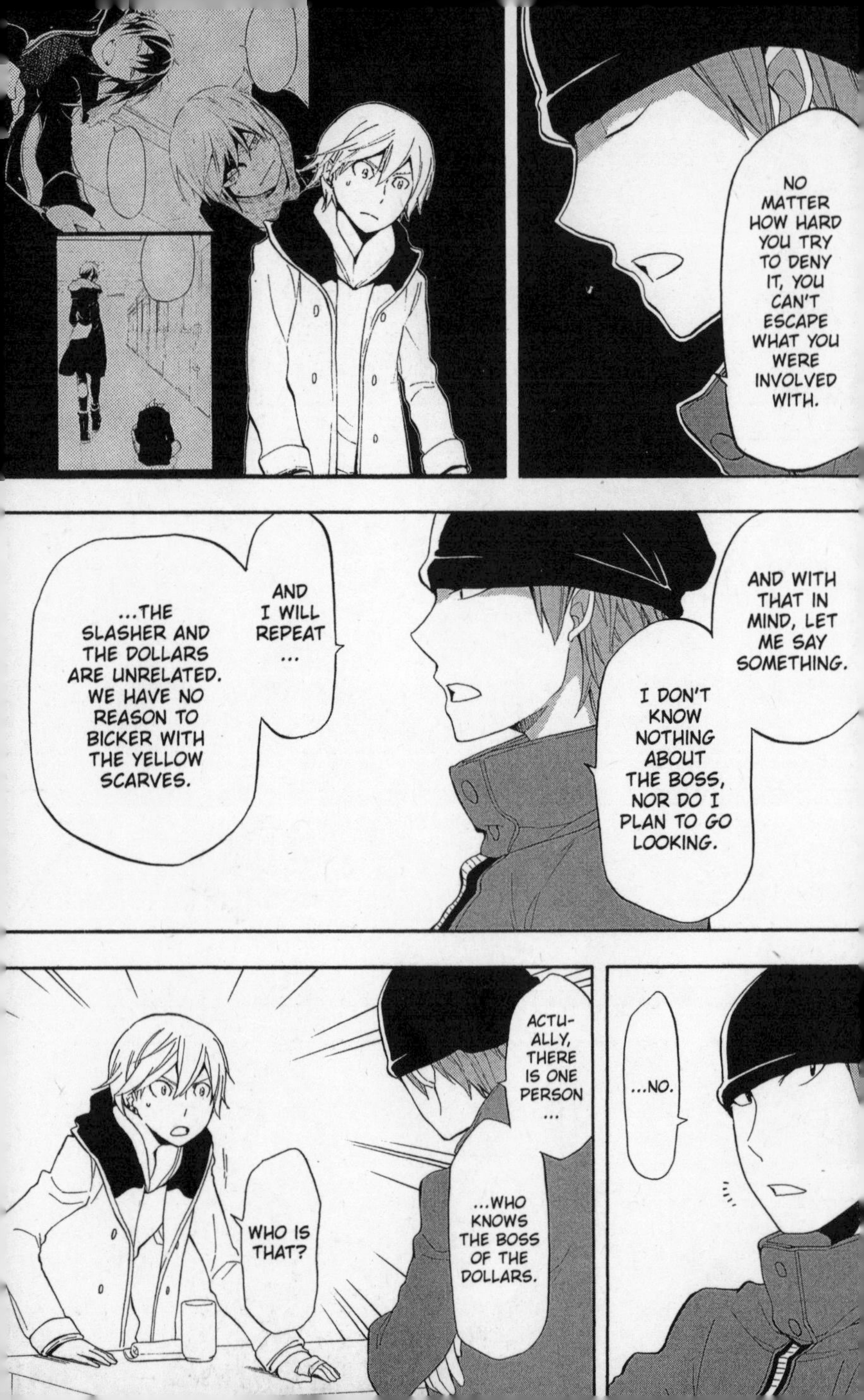
NO MATTER HOW HARD YOU TRY TO DENY IT, YOU CAN'T ESCAPE WHAT YOU WERE INVOLVED WITH.
AND WITH THAT IN MIND, LET ME SAY SOMETHING.
I DON'T KNOW NOTHING ABOUT THE BOSS, NOR DO I PLAN TO GO LOOKING.
AND I WILL REPEAT...
...THE SLASHER AND THE DOLLARS ARE UNRELATED. WE HAVE NO REASON TO BICKER WITH THE YELLOW SCARVES.
...NO.
ACTU-ALLY, THERE IS ONE PERSON...
...WHO KNOWS THE BOSS OF THE DOLLARS.
WHO IS THAT?

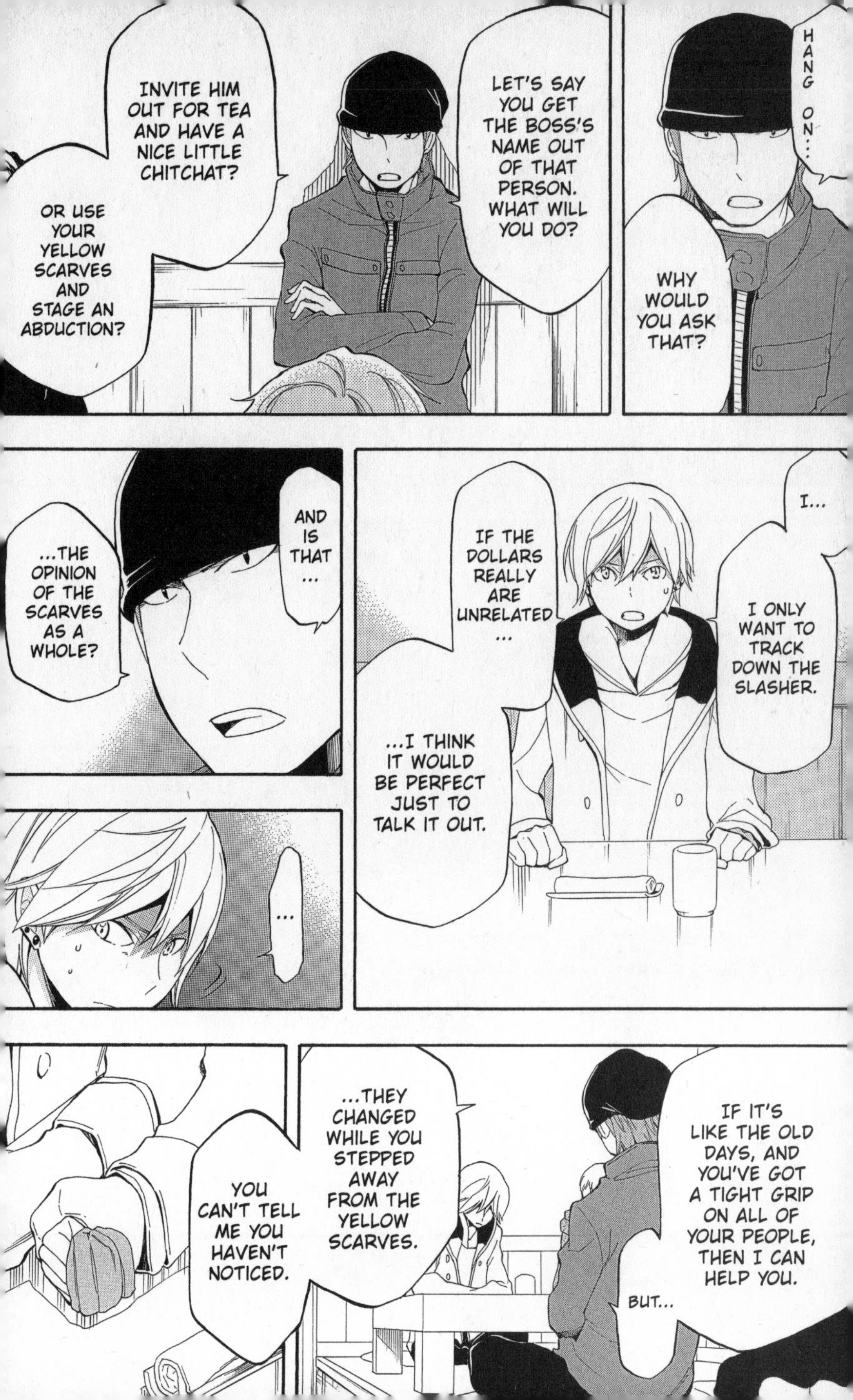
HANG ON...
WHY WOULD YOU ASK THAT?
LET'S SAY YOU GET THE BOSS'S NAME OUT OF THAT PERSON. WHAT WILL YOU DO?
INVITE HIM OUT FOR TEA AND HAVE A NICE LITTLE CHITCHAT?
OR USE YOUR YELLOW SCARVES AND STAGE AN ABDUCTION?
I...
I ONLY WANT TO TRACK DOWN THE SLASHER.
IF THE DOLLARS REALLY ARE UNRELATED...
...I THINK IT WOULD BE PERFECT JUST TO TALK IT OUT.
AND IS THAT...
...THE OPINION OF THE SCARVES AS A WHOLE?
...
IF IT'S LIKE THE OLD DAYS, AND YOU'VE GOT A TIGHT GRIP ON ALL OF YOUR PEOPLE, THEN I CAN HELP YOU.
BUT...
...THEY CHANGED WHILE YOU STEPPED AWAY FROM THE YELLOW SCARVES.
YOU CAN'T TELL ME YOU HAVEN'T NOTICED.

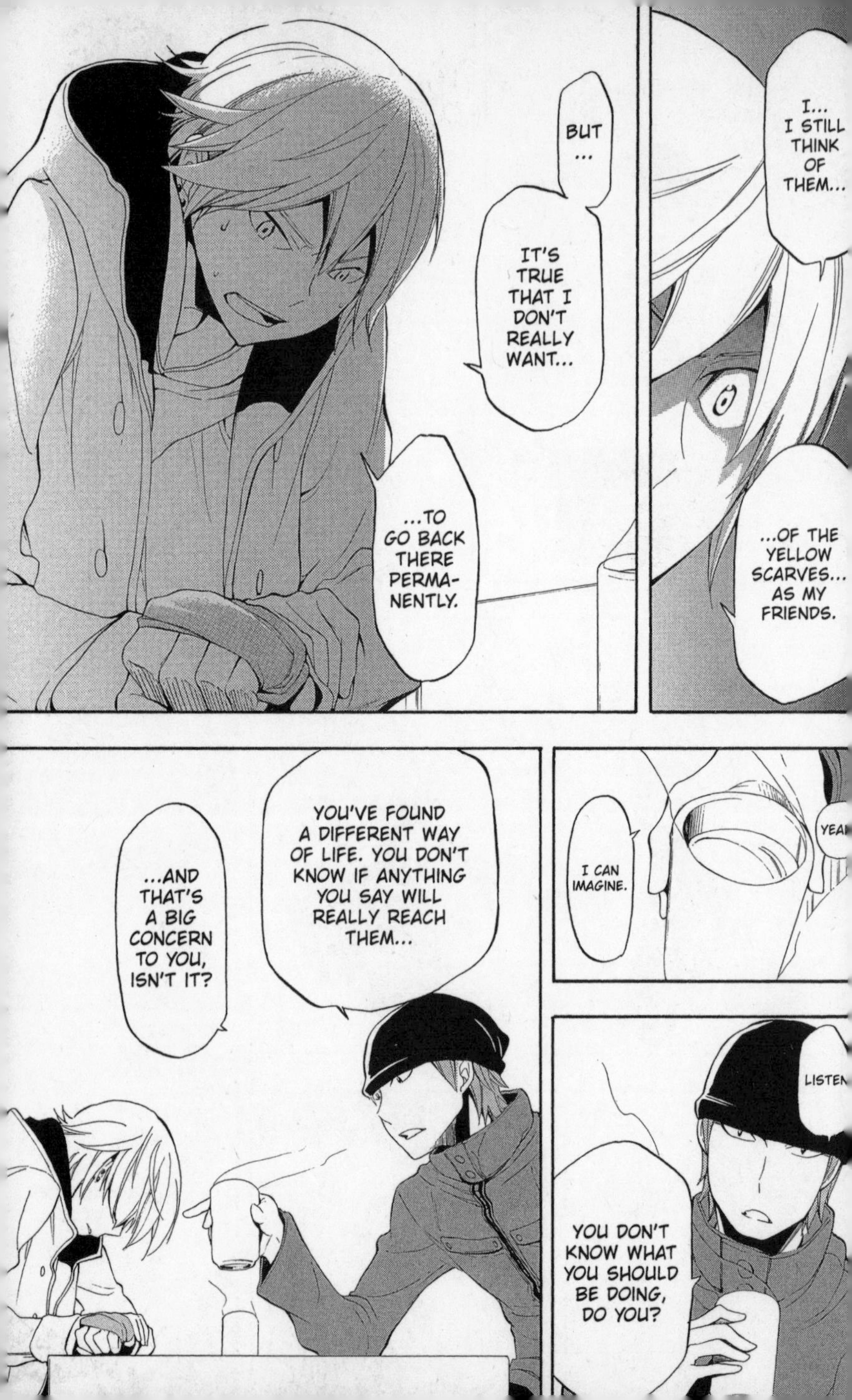
I... I STILL THINK OF THEM...
...OF THE YELLOW SCARVES... AS MY FRIENDS.
BUT ...
IT'S TRUE THAT I DON'T REALLY WANT...
...TO GO BACK THERE PERMANENTLY.
I CAN IMAGINE.
LISTEN
YOU DON'T KNOW WHAT YOU SHOULD BE DOING, DO YOU?
YOU'VE FOUND A DIFFERENT WAY OF LIFE. YOU DON'T KNOW IF ANYTHING YOU SAY WILL REALLY REACH THEM...
...AND THAT'S A BIG CONCERN TO YOU, ISN'T IT?

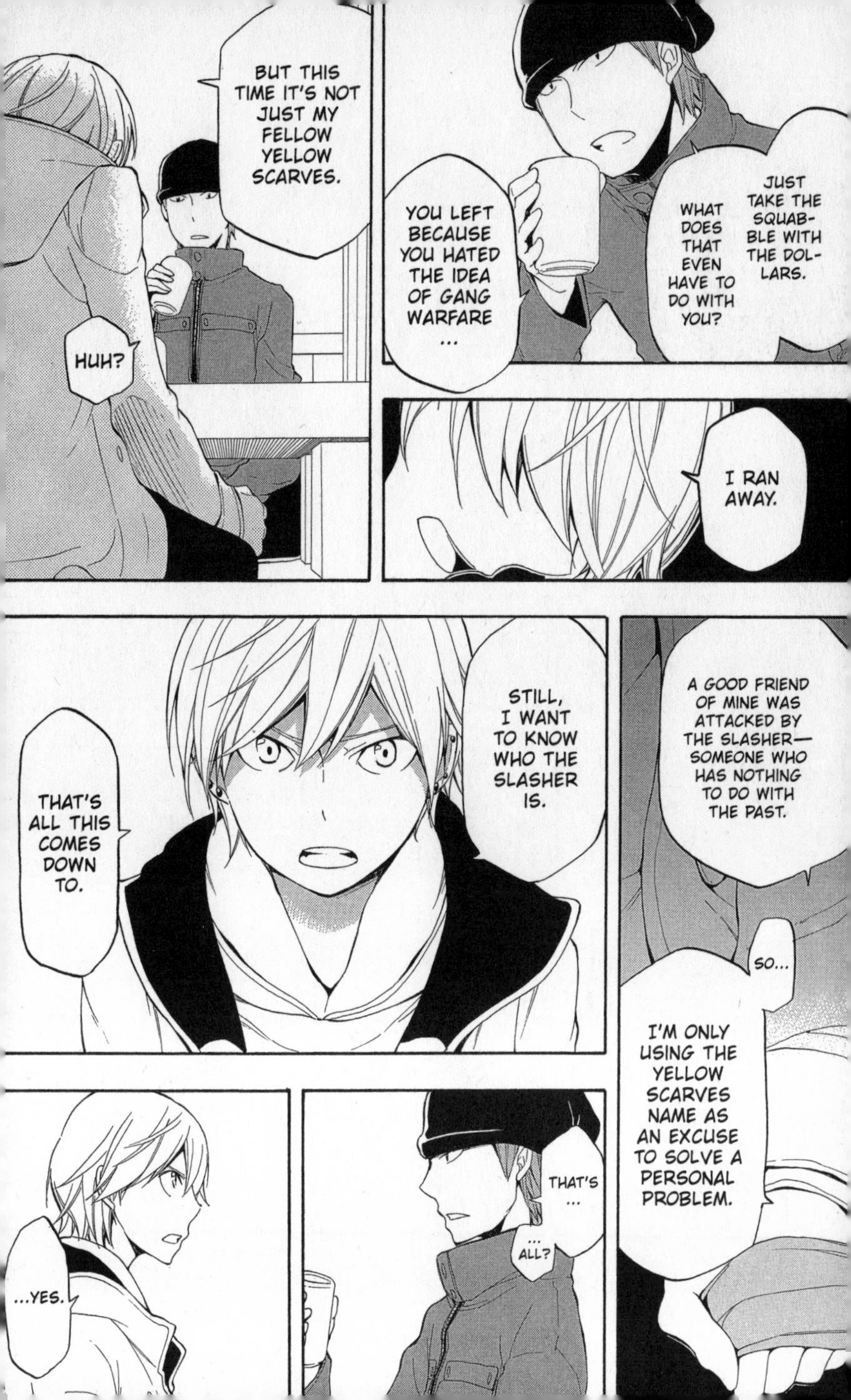
JUST TAKE THE SQUAB-BLE WITH THE DOL-LARS.
WHAT DOES THAT EVEN HAVE TO DO WITH YOU?
YOU LEFT BECAUSE YOU HATED THE IDEA OF GANG WARFARE ...
I RAN AWAY.
BUT THIS TIME IT'S NOT JUST MY FELLOW YELLOW SCARVES.
HUH?
A GOOD FRIEND OF MINE WAS ATTACKED BY THE SLASHER— SOMEONE WHO HAS NOTHING TO DO WITH THE PAST.
SO...
I'M ONLY USING THE YELLOW SCARVES NAME AS AN EXCUSE TO SOLVE A PERSONAL PROBLEM.
STILL, I WANT TO KNOW WHO THE SLASHER IS.
THAT'S ALL THIS COMES DOWN TO.
THAT'S ...
... ALL?
...YES.

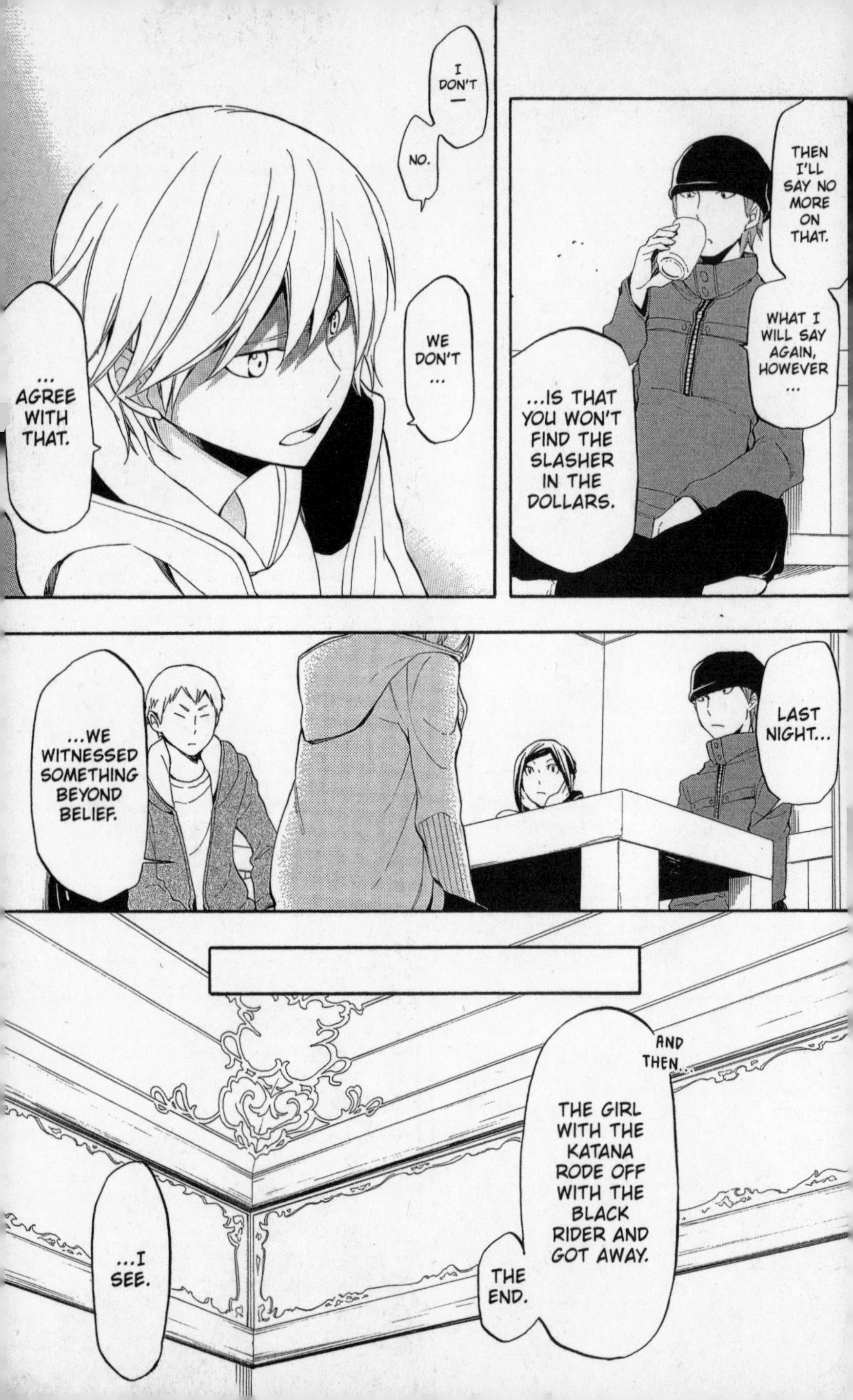
THEN I'LL SAY NO MORE ON THAT.
WHAT I WILL SAY AGAIN, HOWEVER...
...IS THAT YOU WON'T FIND THE SLASHER IN THE DOLLARS.
I DON'T —
NO.
WE DON'T...
...AGREE WITH THAT.
LAST NIGHT...
...WE WITNESSED SOMETHING BEYOND BELIEF.
AND THEN...
THE GIRL WITH THE KATANA RODE OFF WITH THE BLACK RIDER AND GOT AWAY.
THE END.
...I SEE.

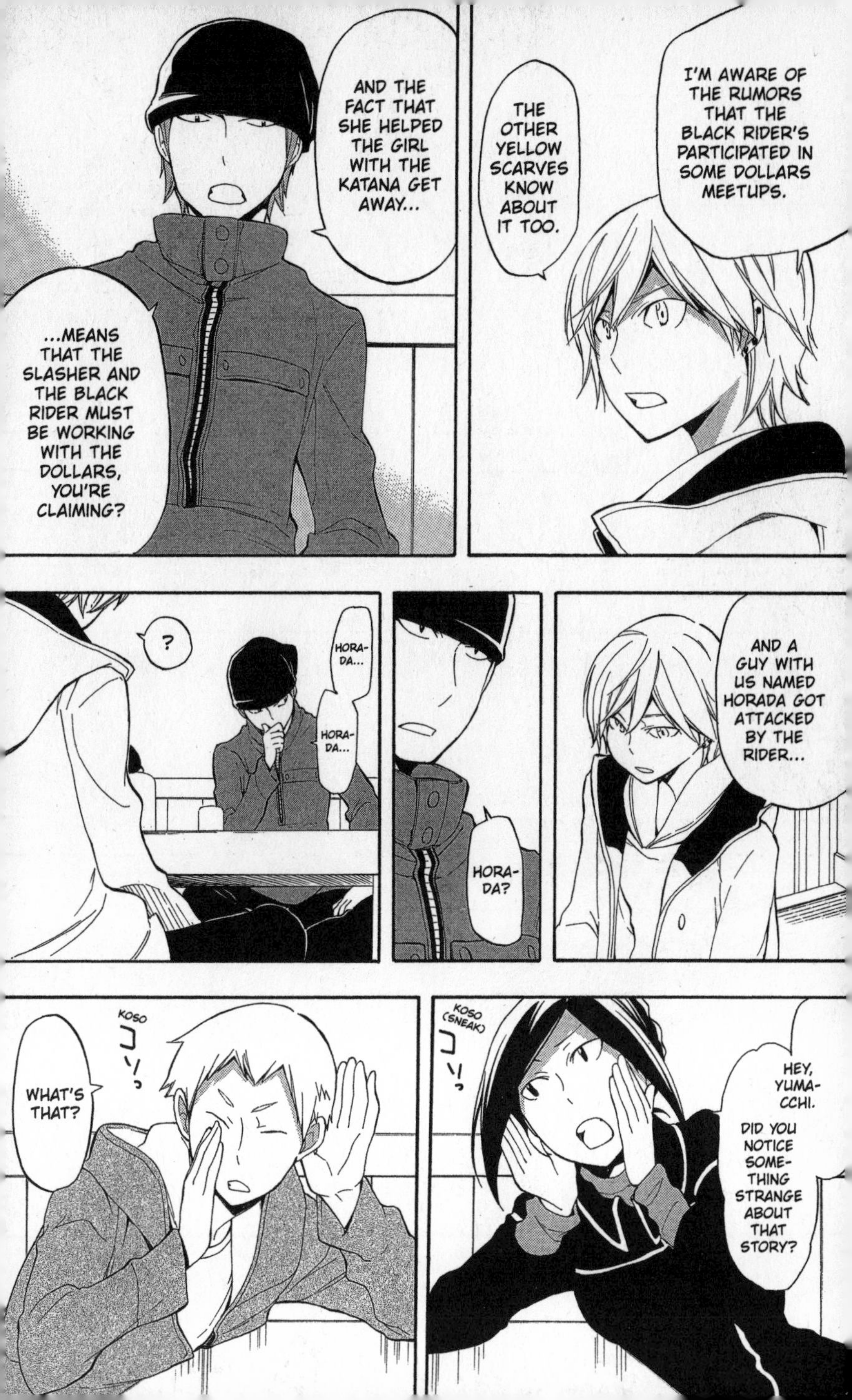
I'M AWARE OF THE RUMORS THAT THE BLACK RIDER'S PARTICIPATED IN SOME DOLLARS MEETUPS.
THE OTHER YELLOW SCARVES KNOW ABOUT IT TOO.
AND THE FACT THAT SHE HELPED THE GIRL WITH THE KATANA GET AWAY...
...MEANS THAT THE SLASHER AND THE BLACK RIDER MUST BE WORKING WITH THE DOLLARS, YOU'RE CLAIMING?
AND A GUY WITH US NAMED HORADA GOT ATTACKED BY THE RIDER...
HORA-DA?
HORA-DA...
HORA-DA...
?
KOSO (SNEAK)
コソッ
HEY, YUMACCHI.
DID YOU NOTICE SOME-THING STRANGE ABOUT THAT STORY?
KOSO
コソッ
WHAT'S THAT?

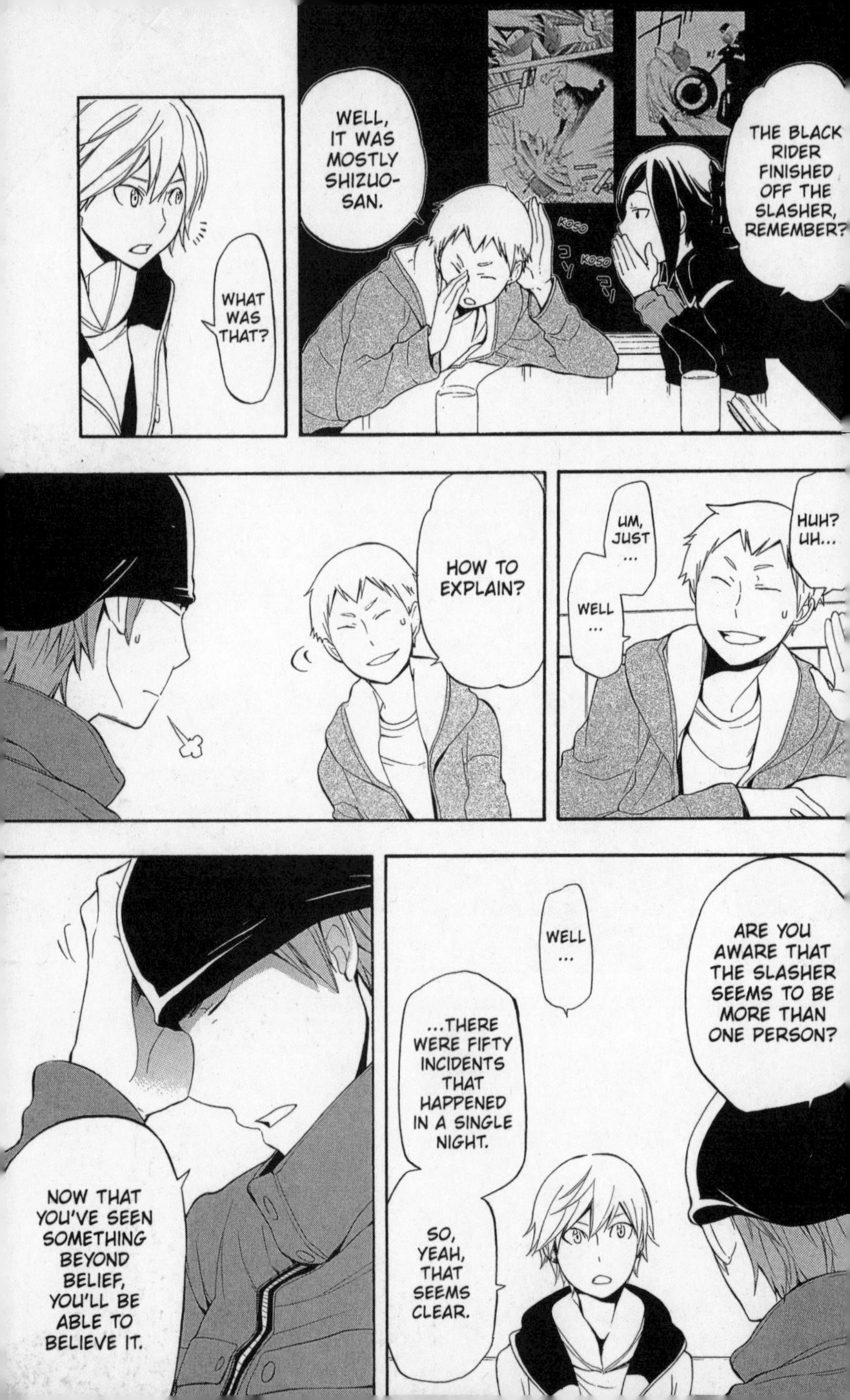
THE BLACK RIDER FINISHED OFF THE SLASHER, REMEMBER?
KOSO
KOSO
WELL, IT WAS MOSTLY SHIZUO-SAN.
WHAT WAS THAT?
HUH? UH...
UM, JUST...
WELL...
HOW TO EXPLAIN?
ARE YOU AWARE THAT THE SLASHER SEEMS TO BE MORE THAN ONE PERSON?
WELL...
...THERE WERE FIFTY INCIDENTS THAT HAPPENED IN A SINGLE NIGHT.
SO, YEAH, THAT SEEMS CLEAR.
NOW THAT YOU'VE SEEN SOMETHING BEYOND BELIEF, YOU'LL BE ABLE TO BELIEVE IT.

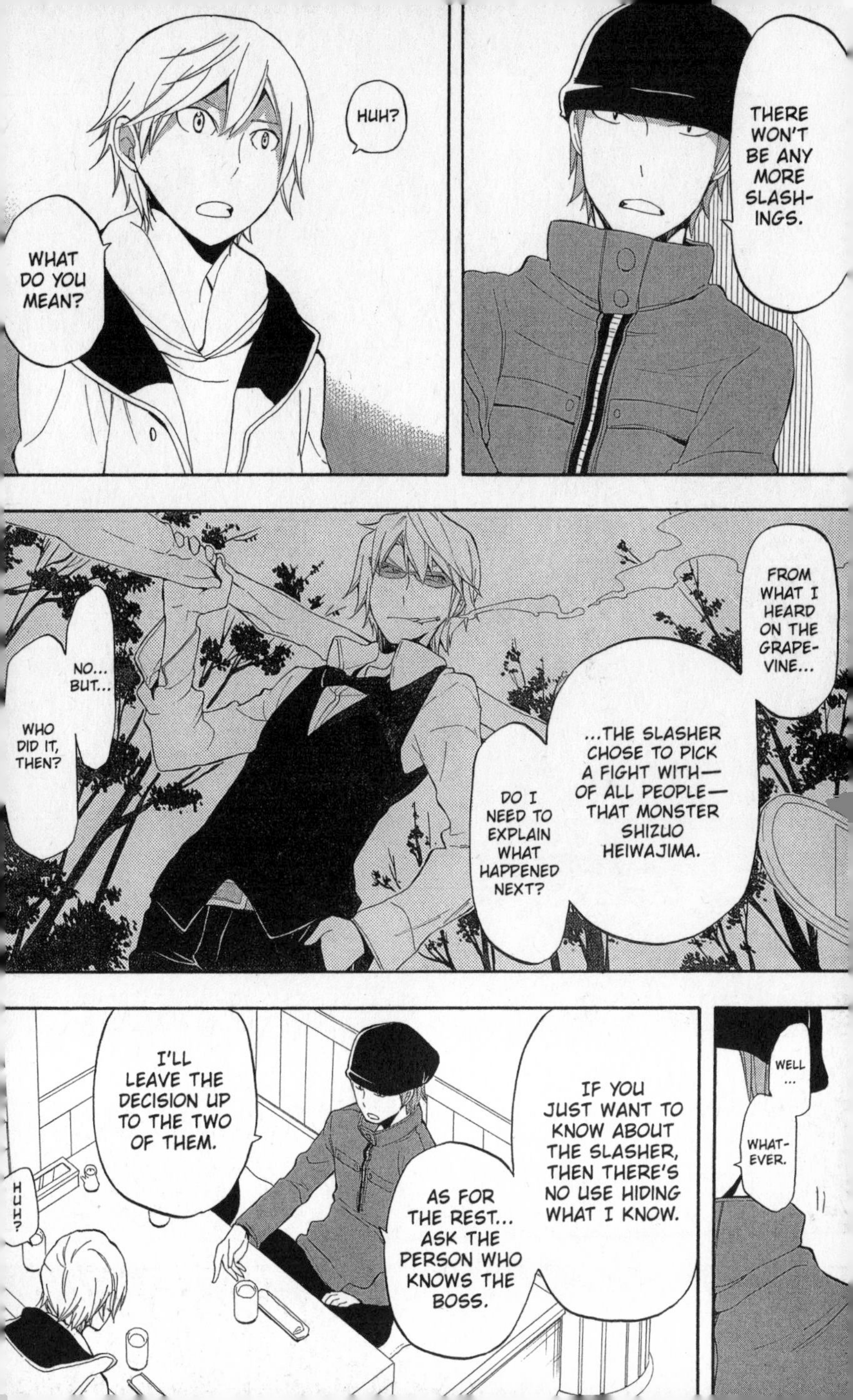
THERE WON'T BE ANY MORE SLASH-INGS.
HUH?
WHAT DO YOU MEAN?
FROM WHAT I HEARD ON THE GRAPE-VINE...
...THE SLASHER CHOSE TO PICK A FIGHT WITH—OF ALL PEOPLE—THAT MONSTER SHIZUO HEIWAJIMA.
DO I NEED TO EXPLAIN WHAT HAPPENED NEXT?
NO... BUT...
WHO DID IT, THEN?
WELL...
WHAT-EVER.
IF YOU JUST WANT TO KNOW ABOUT THE SLASHER, THEN THERE'S NO USE HIDING WHAT I KNOW.
AS FOR THE REST... ASK THE PERSON WHO KNOWS THE BOSS.
I'LL LEAVE THE DECISION UP TO THE TWO OF THEM.
HUH?

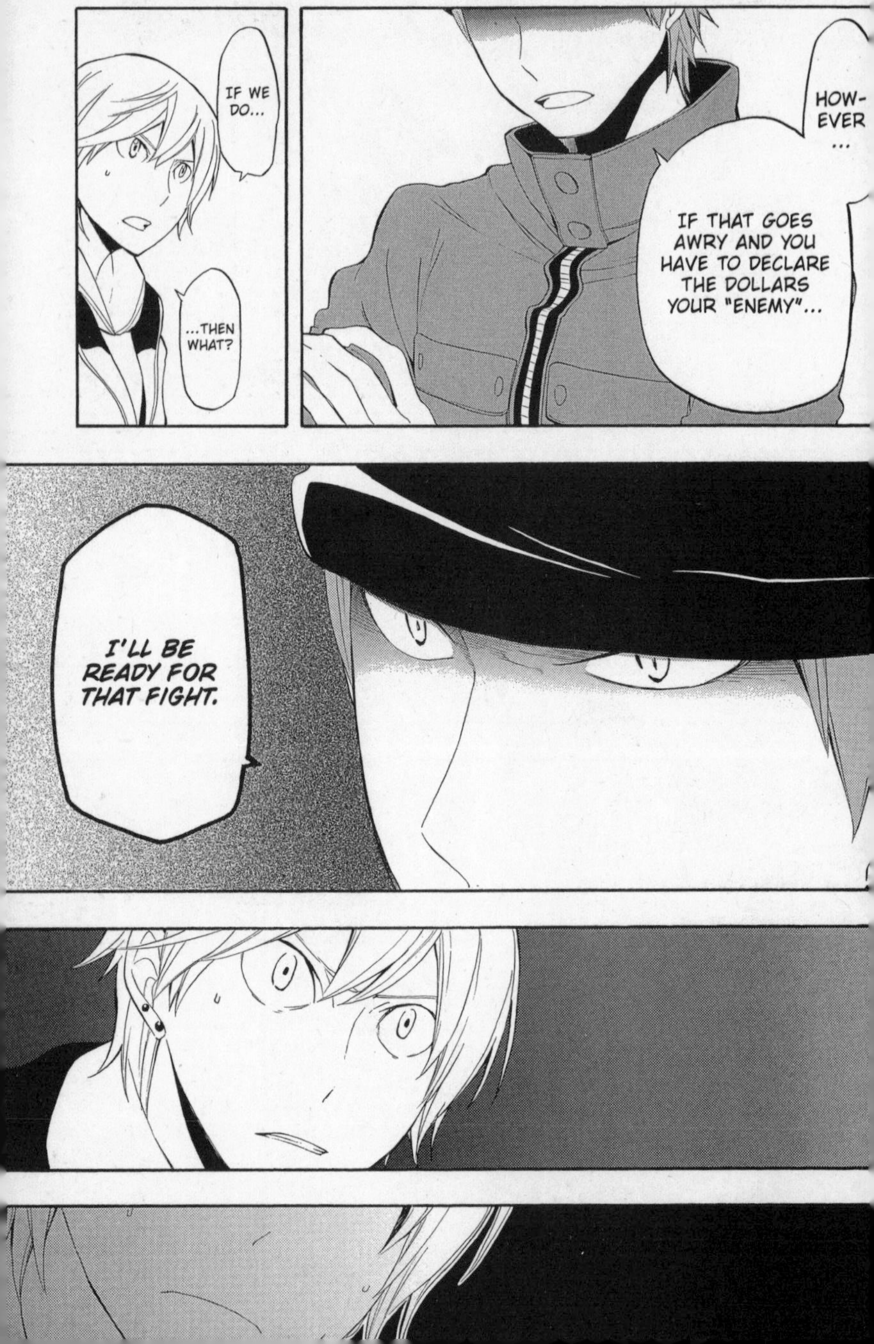
HOW-EVER...
IF THAT GOES AWRY AND YOU HAVE TO DECLARE THE DOLLARS YOUR "ENEMY"...
IF WE DO...
...THEN WHAT?
I'LL BE READY FOR THAT FIGHT.

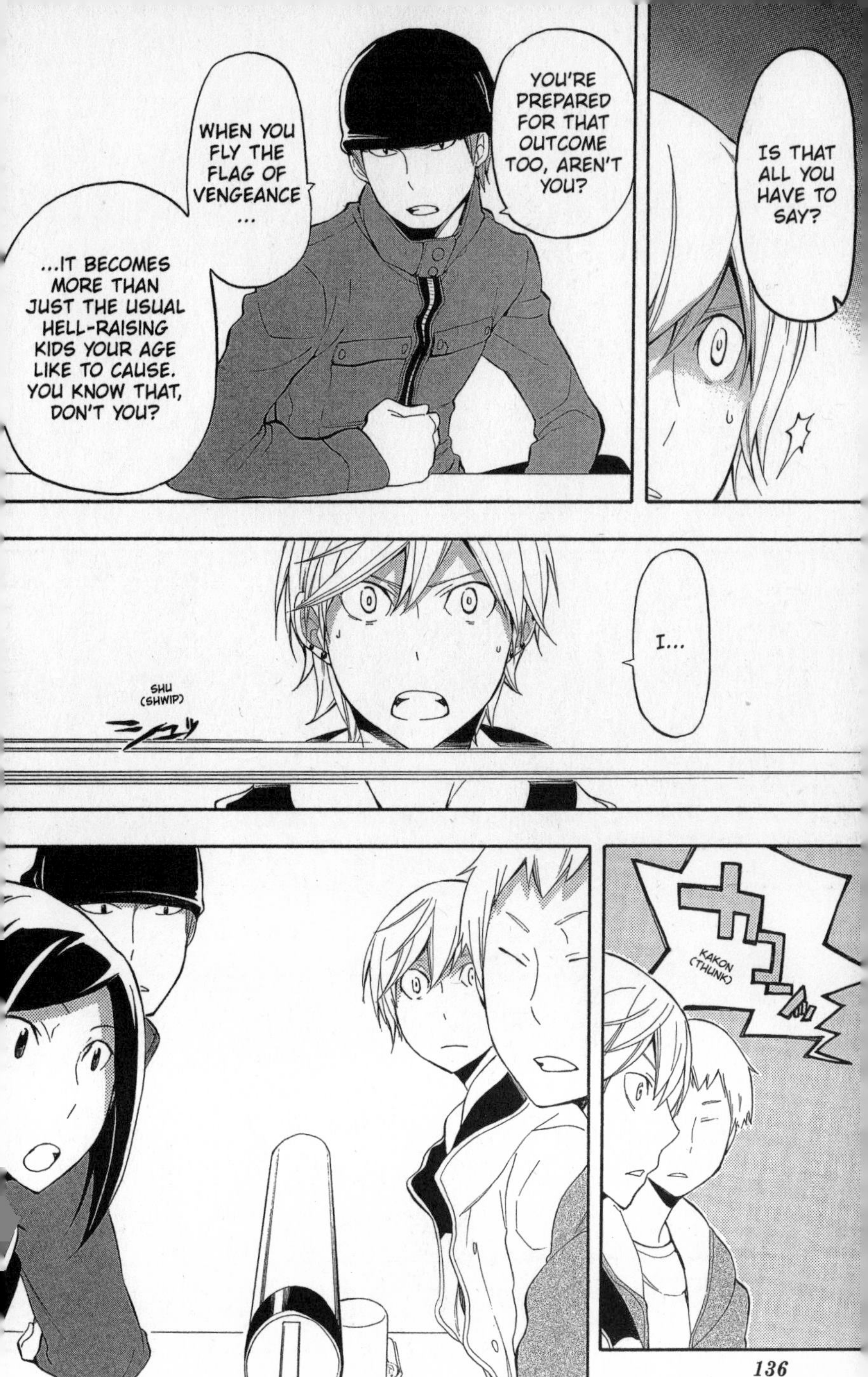
IS THAT ALL YOU HAVE TO SAY?
YOU'RE PREPARED FOR THAT OUTCOME TOO, AREN'T YOU?
WHEN YOU FLY THE FLAG OF VENGEANCE ...
...IT BECOMES MORE THAN JUST THE USUAL HELL-RAISING KIDS YOUR AGE LIKE TO CAUSE. YOU KNOW THAT, DON'T YOU?
I...
SHU (SHWIP)
KAKON (THUNK)

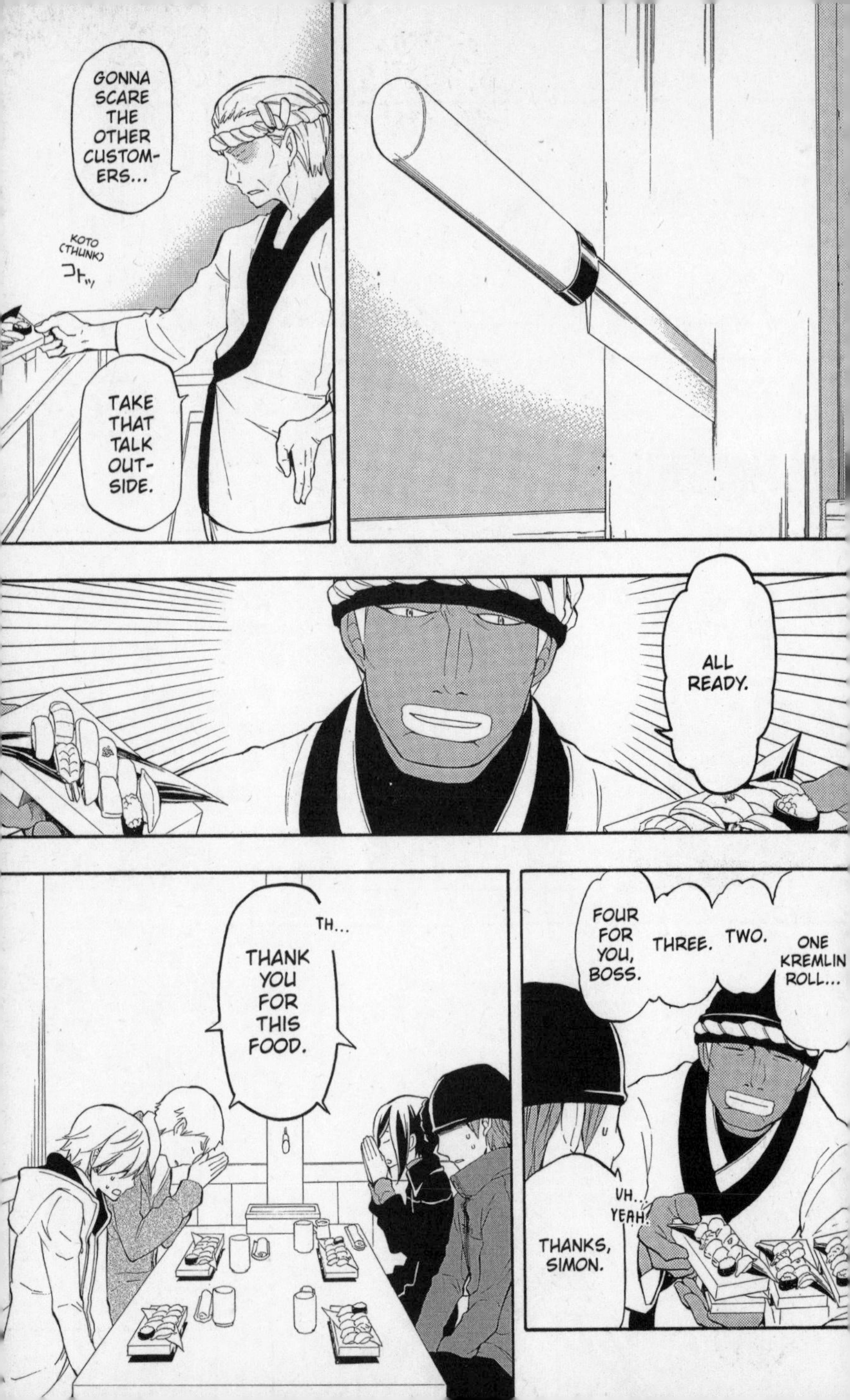
GONNA SCARE THE OTHER CUSTOMERS...
KOTO (THUNK)
コトッ
TAKE THAT TALK OUTSIDE.
ALL READY.
ONE KREMLIN ROLL...
TWO.
THREE.
FOUR FOR YOU, BOSS.
UH... YEAH.
THANKS, SIMON.
TH...
THANK YOU FOR THIS FOOD.

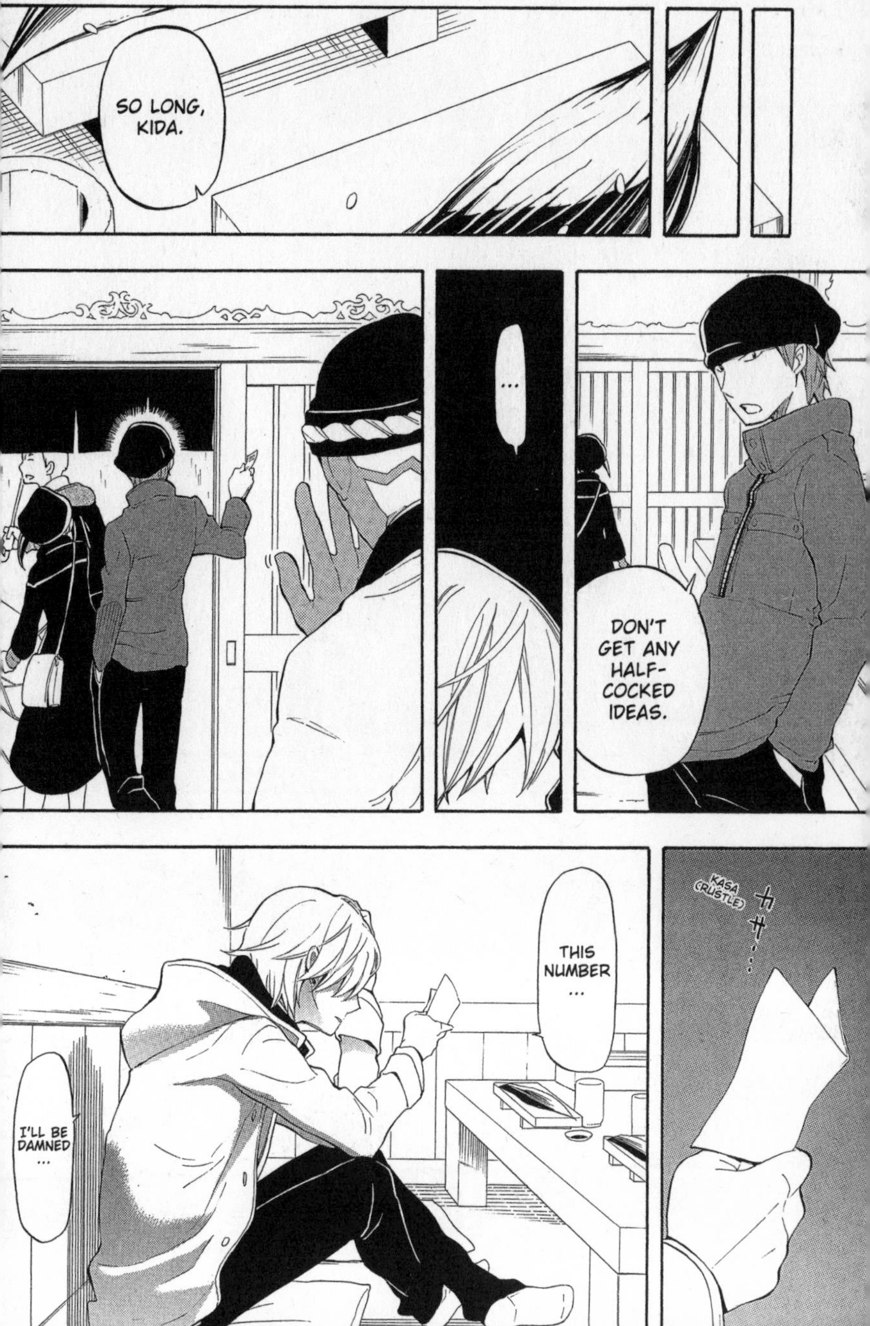
SO LONG, KIDA.
DON'T GET ANY HALF-COCKED IDEAS.
...
KASA (RUSTLE)
カサ…
THIS NUMBER ...
I'LL BE DAMNED ...

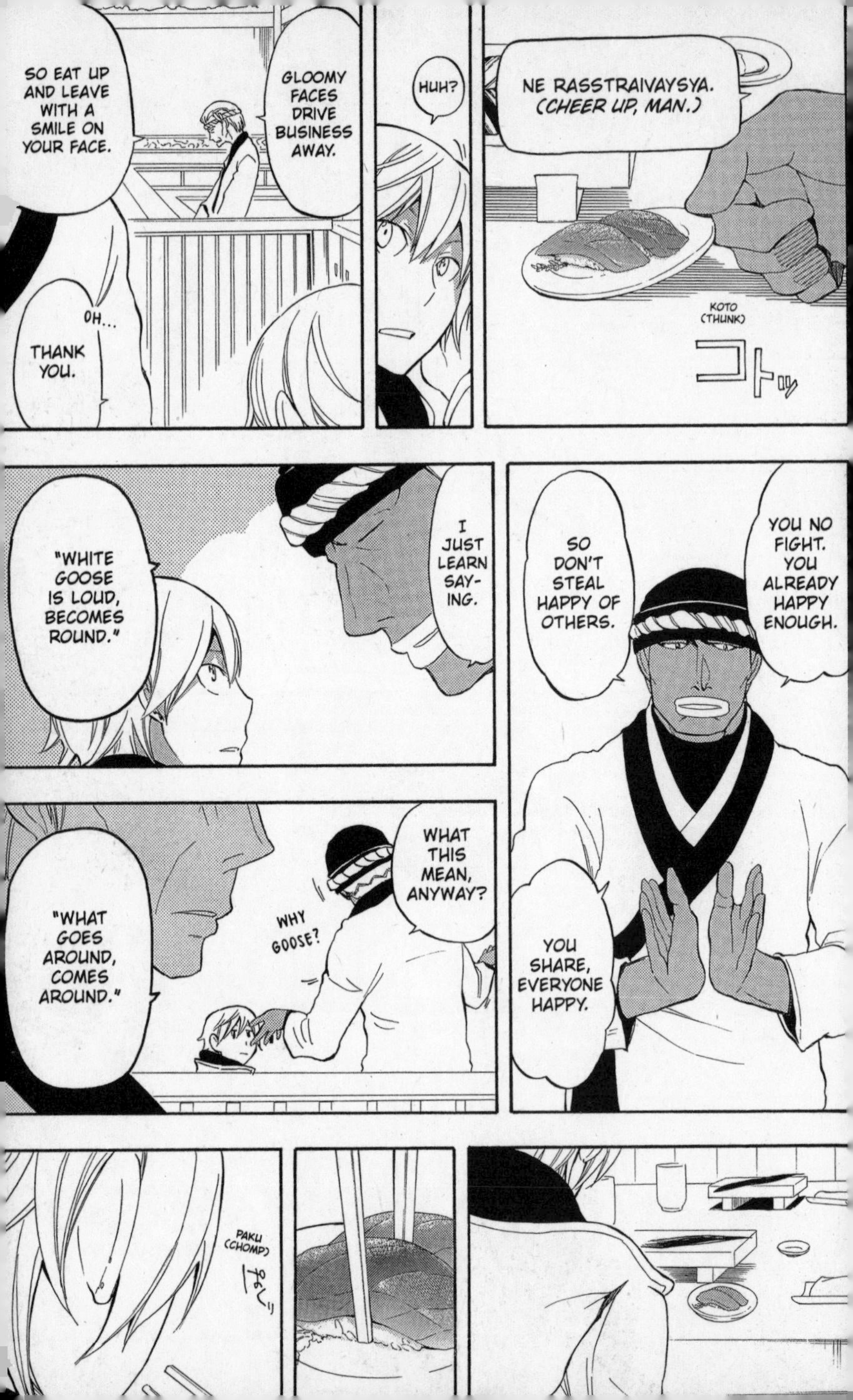
NE RASSTRAIVAYSYA. (CHEER UP, MAN.)
KOTO (THUNK)
コトッ
HUH?
GLOOMY FACES DRIVE BUSINESS AWAY.
SO EAT UP AND LEAVE WITH A SMILE ON YOUR FACE.
OH...
THANK YOU.
YOU NO FIGHT. YOU ALREADY HAPPY ENOUGH.
SO DON'T STEAL HAPPY OF OTHERS.
YOU SHARE, EVERYONE HAPPY.
I JUST LEARN SAYING.
"WHITE GOOSE IS LOUD, BECOMES ROUND."
WHAT THIS MEAN, ANYWAY?
WHY GOOSE?
"WHAT GOES AROUND, COMES AROUND."
PAKU (CHOMP)
ぱくり

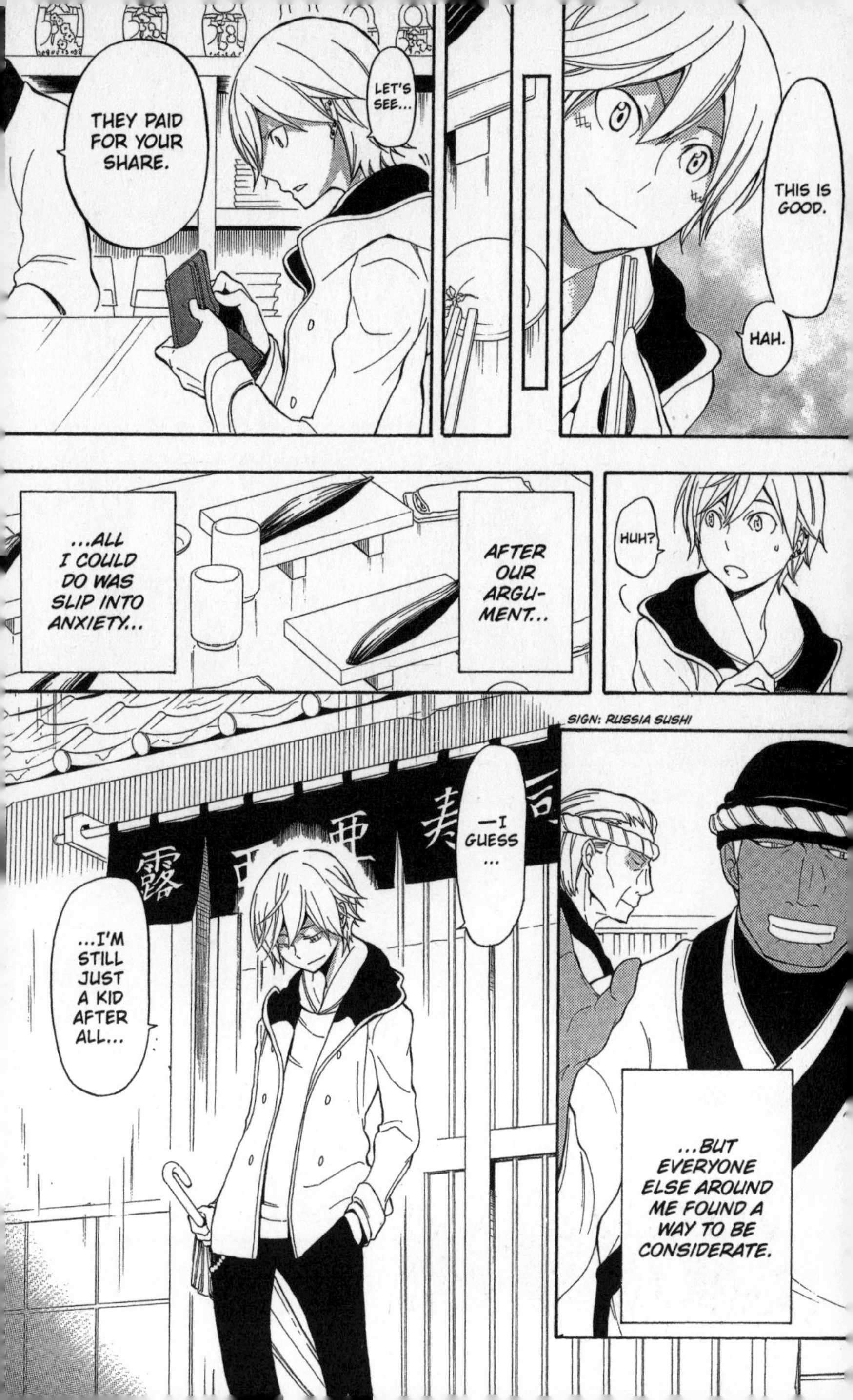
THIS IS GOOD.
HAH.
LET'S SEE...
THEY PAID FOR YOUR SHARE.
HUH?
AFTER OUR ARGUMENT...
...ALL I COULD DO WAS SLIP INTO ANXIETY...
...BUT EVERYONE ELSE AROUND ME FOUND A WAY TO BE CONSIDERATE.
SIGN: RUSSIA SUSHI
—I GUESS...
...I'M STILL JUST A KID AFTER ALL...

DURARARA!!

ORRR!!

DRRR!!

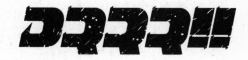

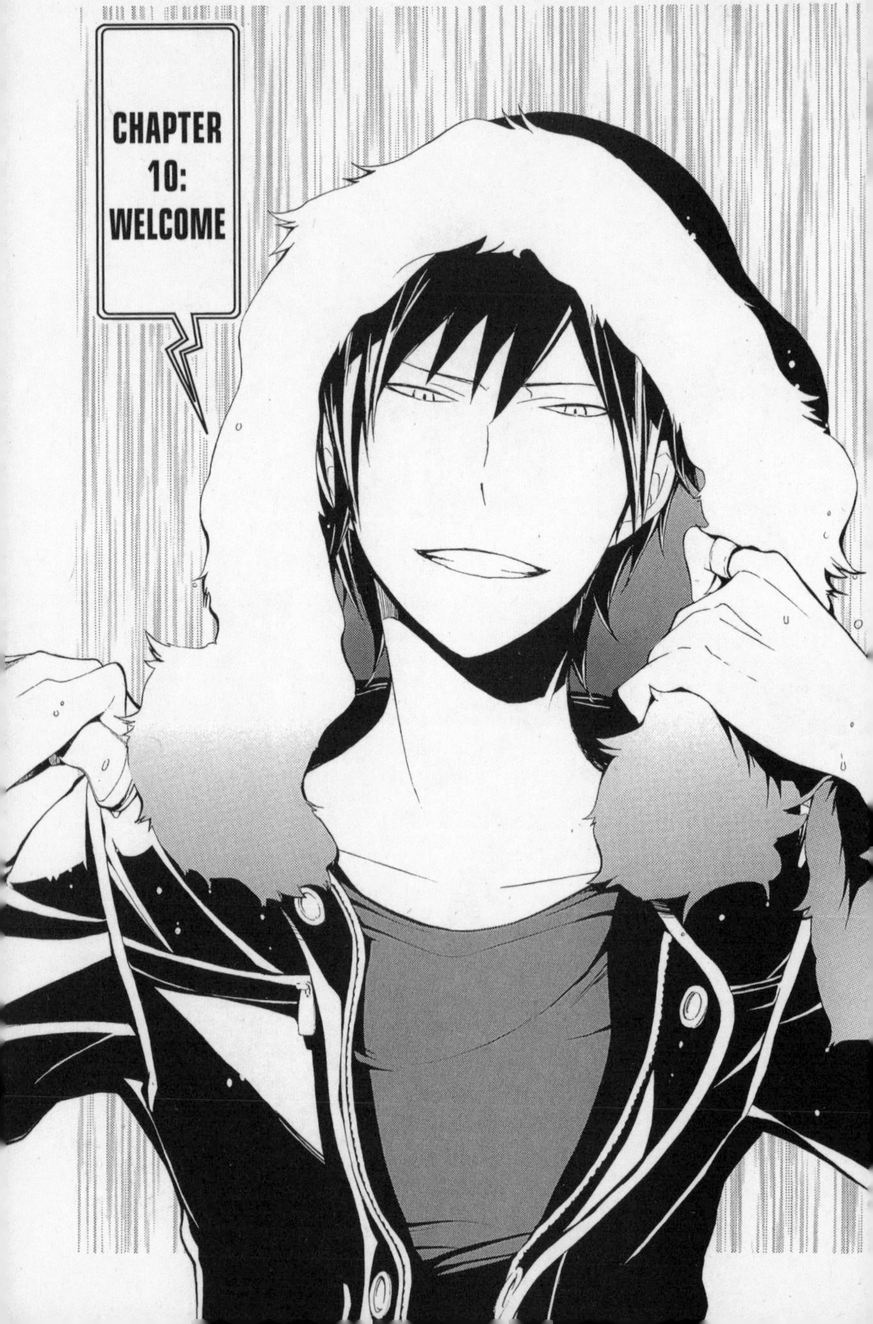
CHAPTER 10: WELCOME

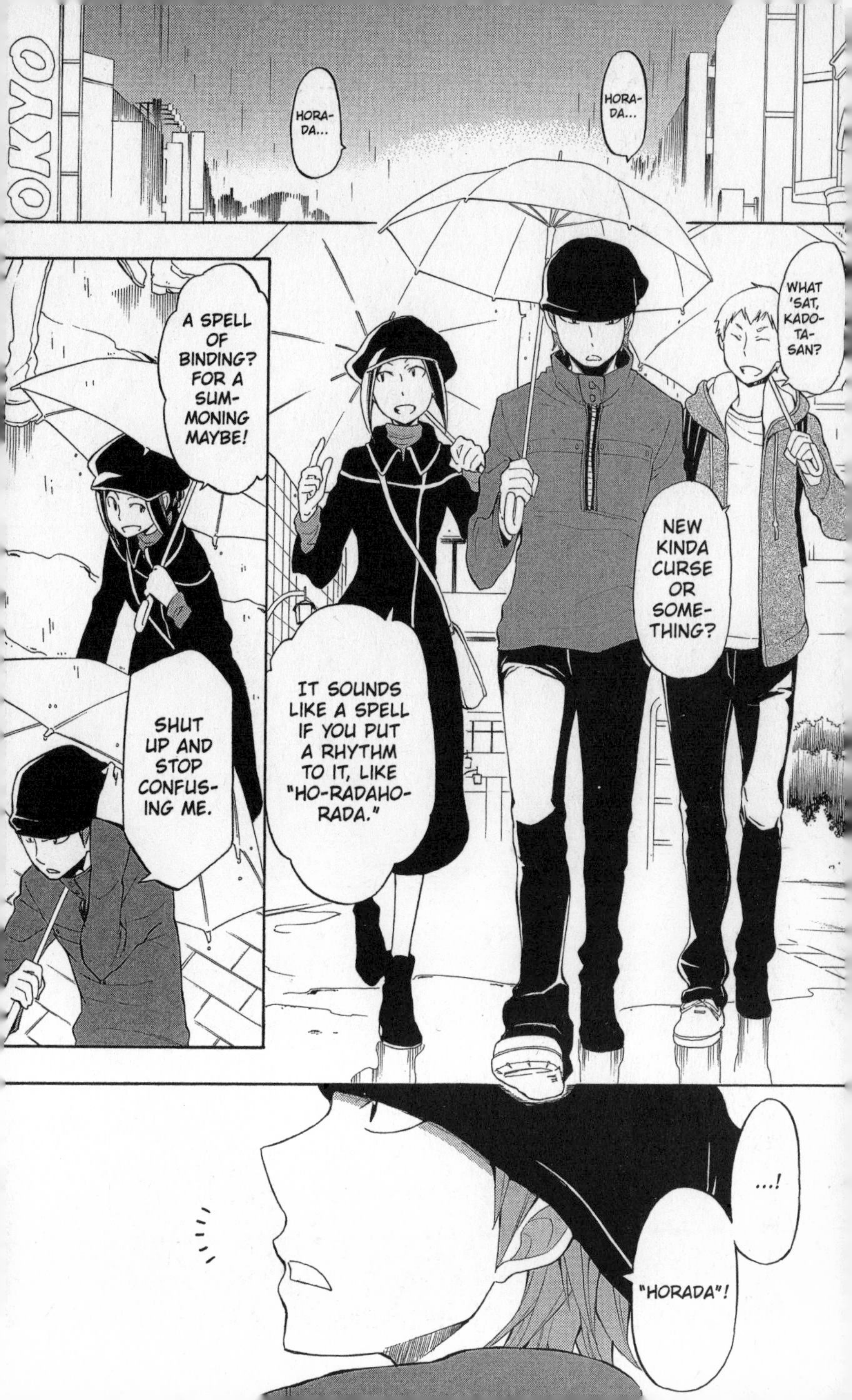
HORADA...
HORADA...
OKYO
WHAT 'SAT, KADOTA-SAN?
NEW KINDA CURSE OR SOMETHING?
IT SOUNDS LIKE A SPELL IF YOU PUT A RHYTHM TO IT, LIKE "HO-RADAHO-RADA."
A SPELL OF BINDING? FOR A SUMMONING MAYBE!
SHUT UP AND STOP CONFUSING ME.
...!
"HORADA"!

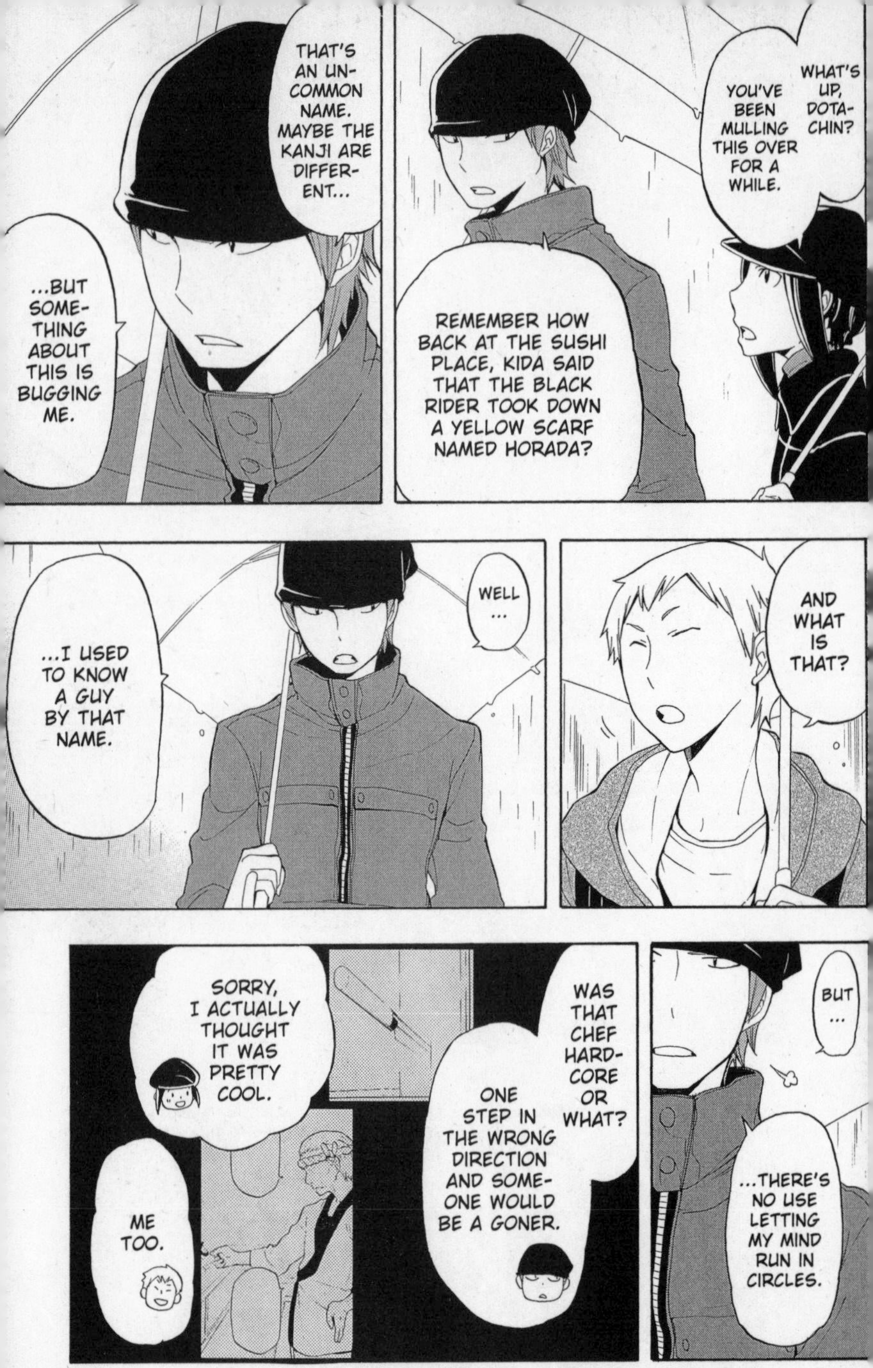
WHAT'S UP, DOTA-CHIN?
YOU'VE BEEN MULLING THIS OVER FOR A WHILE.
REMEMBER HOW BACK AT THE SUSHI PLACE, KIDA SAID THAT THE BLACK RIDER TOOK DOWN A YELLOW SCARF NAMED HORADA?
THAT'S AN UNCOMMON NAME. MAYBE THE KANJI ARE DIFFERENT...
...BUT SOMETHING ABOUT THIS IS BUGGING ME.
AND WHAT IS THAT?
WELL...
...I USED TO KNOW A GUY BY THAT NAME.
BUT...
...THERE'S NO USE LETTING MY MIND RUN IN CIRCLES.
WAS THAT CHEF HARDCORE OR WHAT?
ONE STEP IN THE WRONG DIRECTION AND SOMEONE WOULD BE A GONER.
SORRY, I ACTUALLY THOUGHT IT WAS PRETTY COOL.
ME TOO.

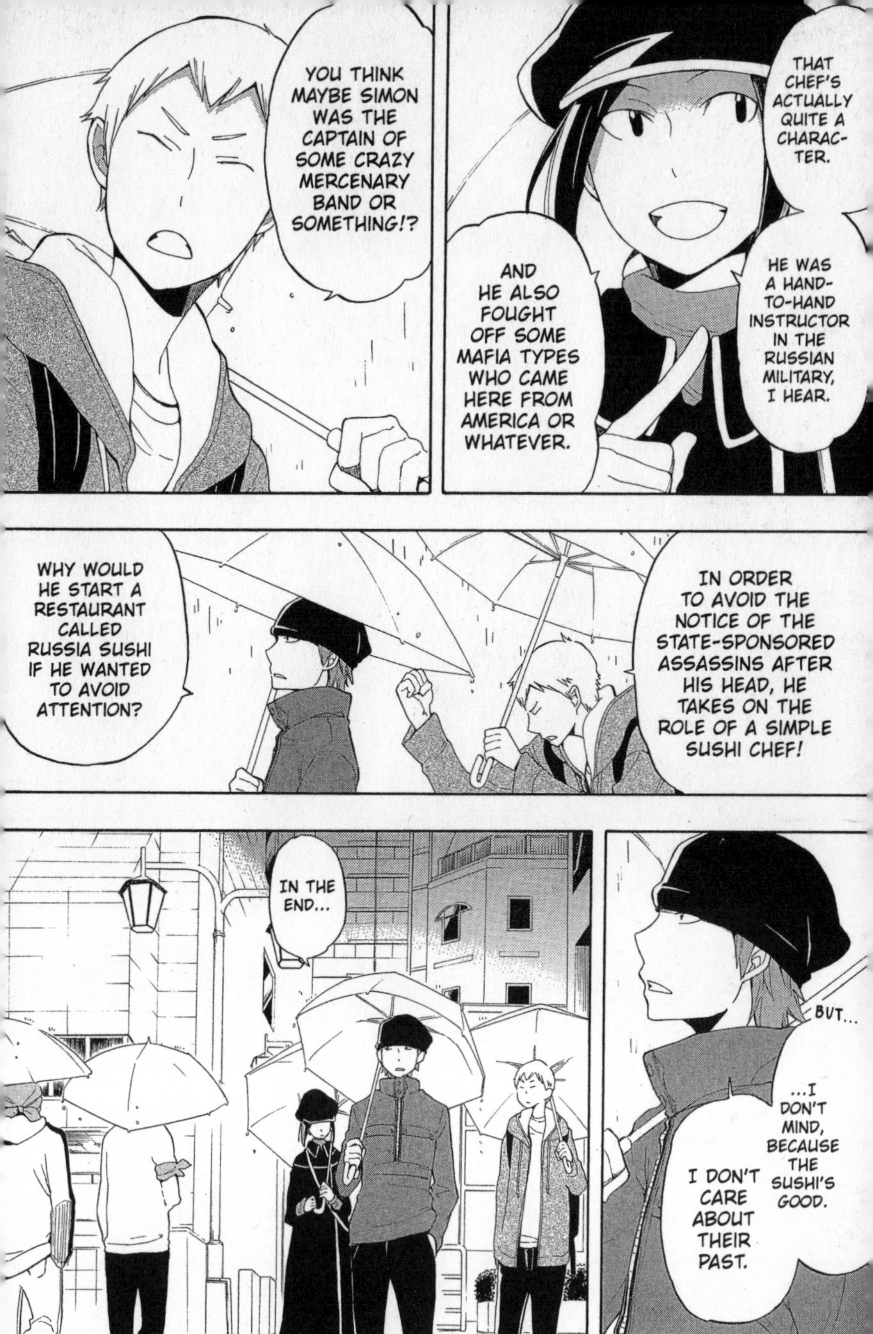
THAT CHEF'S ACTUALLY QUITE A CHARACTER.
HE WAS A HAND-TO-HAND INSTRUCTOR IN THE RUSSIAN MILITARY, I HEAR.
AND HE ALSO FOUGHT OFF SOME MAFIA TYPES WHO CAME HERE FROM AMERICA OR WHATEVER.
YOU THINK MAYBE SIMON WAS THE CAPTAIN OF SOME CRAZY MERCENARY BAND OR SOMETHING!?
IN ORDER TO AVOID THE NOTICE OF THE STATE-SPONSORED ASSASSINS AFTER HIS HEAD, HE TAKES ON THE ROLE OF A SIMPLE SUSHI CHEF!
WHY WOULD HE START A RESTAURANT CALLED RUSSIA SUSHI IF HE WANTED TO AVOID ATTENTION?
BUT...
...I DON'T MIND, BECAUSE THE SUSHI'S GOOD.
I DON'T CARE ABOUT THEIR PAST.
IN THE END...

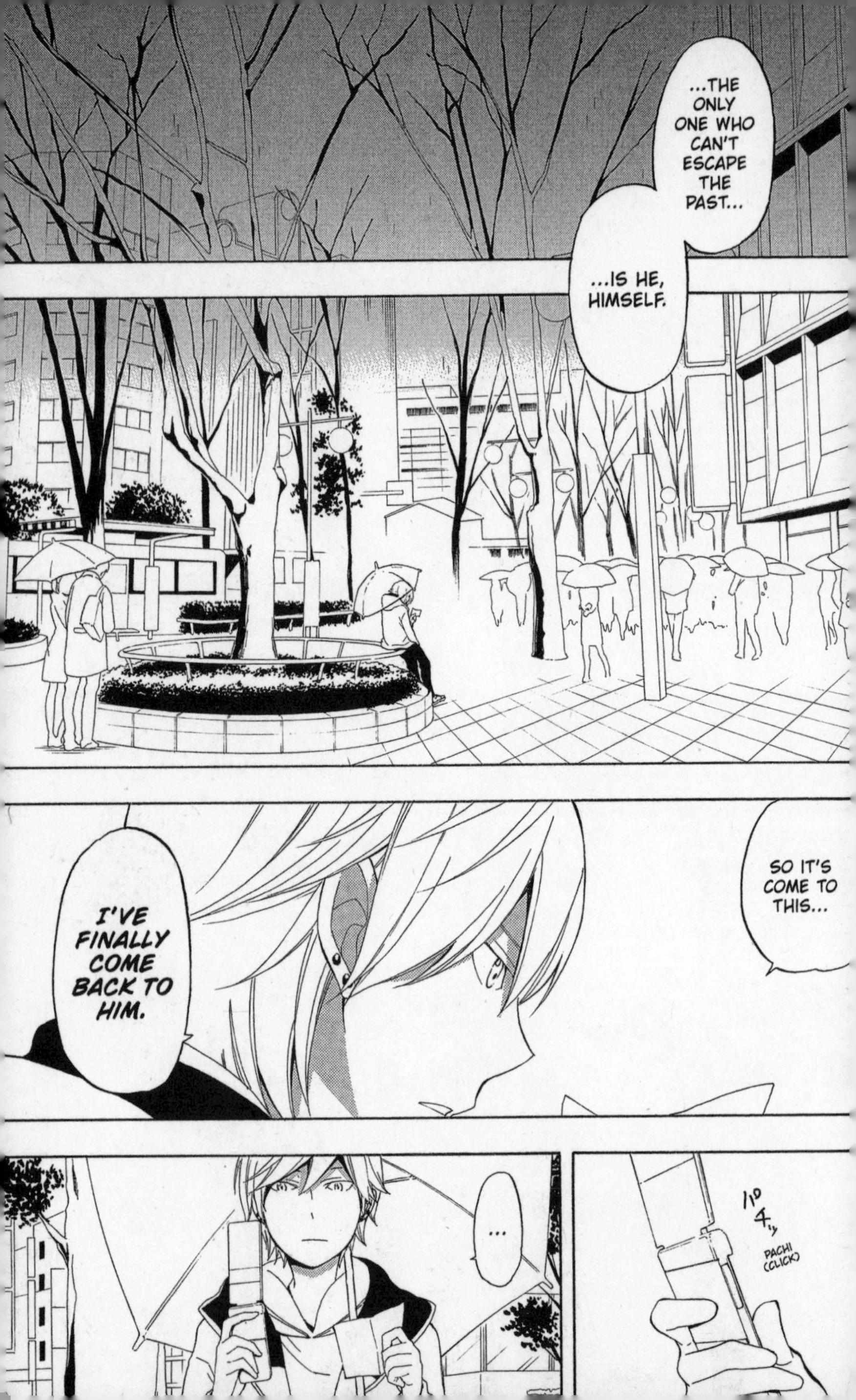
...THE ONLY ONE WHO CAN'T ESCAPE THE PAST...
...IS HE, HIMSELF.
SO IT'S COME TO THIS...
I'VE FINALLY COME BACK TO HIM.
PACHI (CLICK)
...

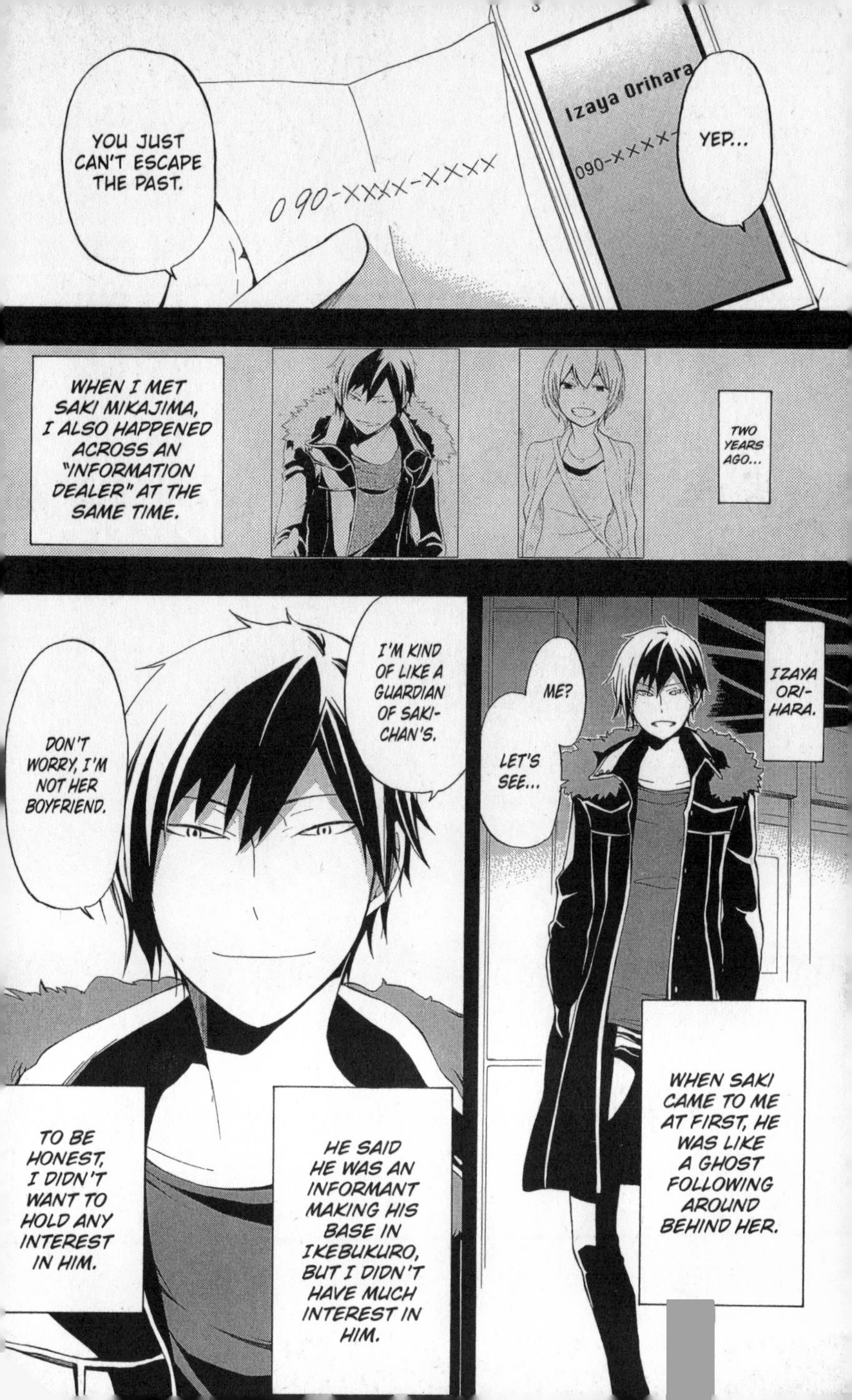
Izaya Orihara
YEP...
090-XXXX-
YOU JUST CAN'T ESCAPE THE PAST.
090-XXXX-XXXX
TWO YEARS AGO...
WHEN I MET SAKI MIKAJIMA, I ALSO HAPPENED ACROSS AN "INFORMATION DEALER" AT THE SAME TIME.
IZAYA ORIHARA.
ME?
LET'S SEE...
WHEN SAKI CAME TO ME AT FIRST, HE WAS LIKE A GHOST FOLLOWING AROUND BEHIND HER.
I'M KIND OF LIKE A GUARDIAN OF SAKI-CHAN'S.
DON'T WORRY, I'M NOT HER BOYFRIEND.
HE SAID HE WAS AN INFORMANT MAKING HIS BASE IN IKEBUKURO, BUT I DIDN'T HAVE MUCH INTEREST IN HIM.
TO BE HONEST, I DIDN'T WANT TO HOLD ANY INTEREST IN HIM.

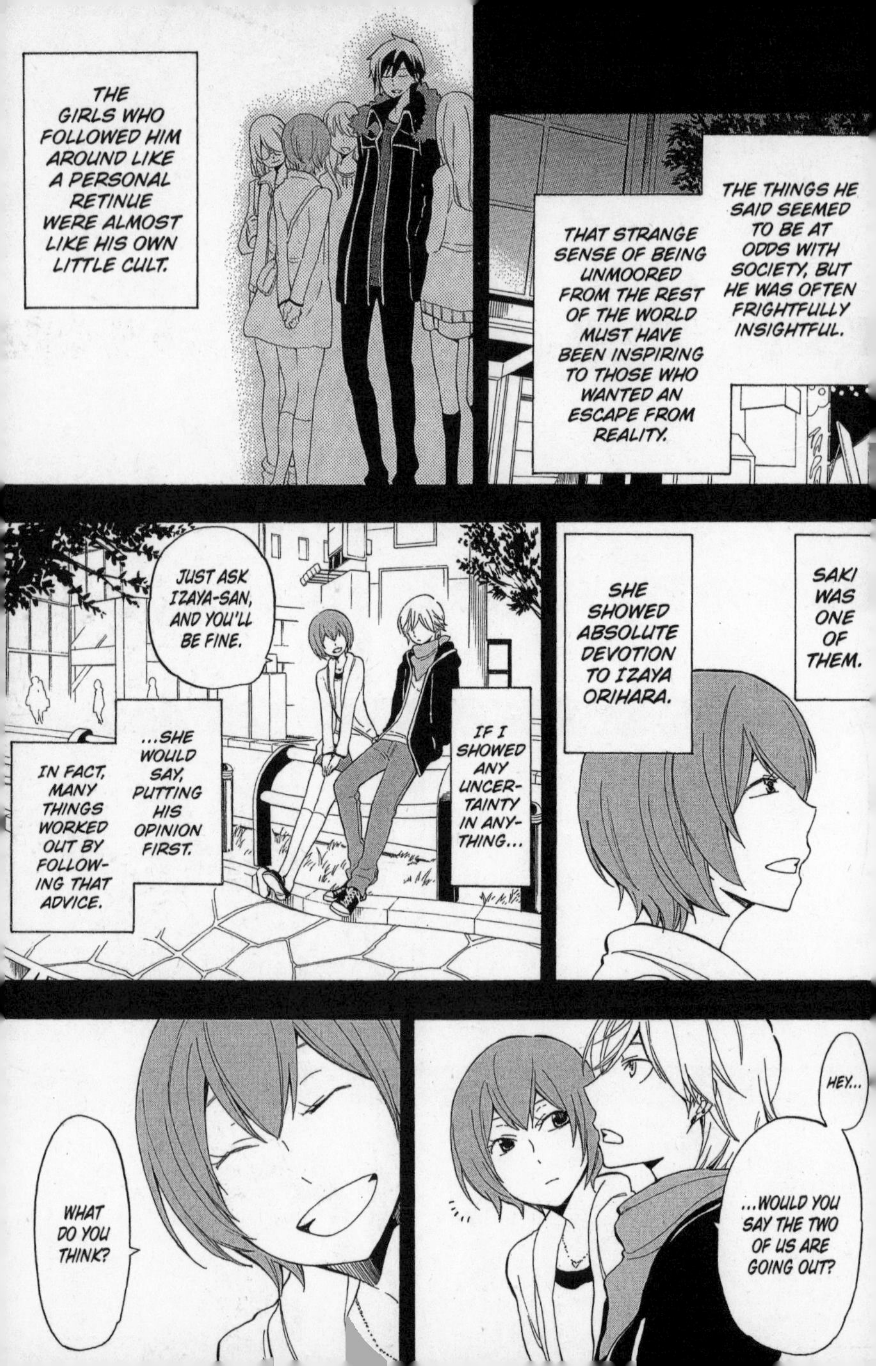

THE THINGS HE SAID SEEMED TO BE AT ODDS WITH SOCIETY, BUT HE WAS OFTEN FRIGHTFULLY INSIGHTFUL.
THAT STRANGE SENSE OF BEING UNMOORED FROM THE REST OF THE WORLD MUST HAVE BEEN INSPIRING TO THOSE WHO WANTED AN ESCAPE FROM REALITY.
THE GIRLS WHO FOLLOWED HIM AROUND LIKE A PERSONAL RETINUE WERE ALMOST LIKE HIS OWN LITTLE CULT.
SAKI WAS ONE OF THEM.
SHE SHOWED ABSOLUTE DEVOTION TO IZAYA ORIHARA.
IF I SHOWED ANY UNCER-TAINTY IN ANY-THING...
JUST ASK IZAYA-SAN, AND YOU'LL BE FINE.
...SHE WOULD SAY, PUTTING HIS OPINION FIRST.
IN FACT, MANY THINGS WORKED OUT BY FOLLOW-ING THAT ADVICE.
HEY...
...WOULD YOU SAY THE TWO OF US ARE GOING OUT?
WHAT DO YOU THINK?

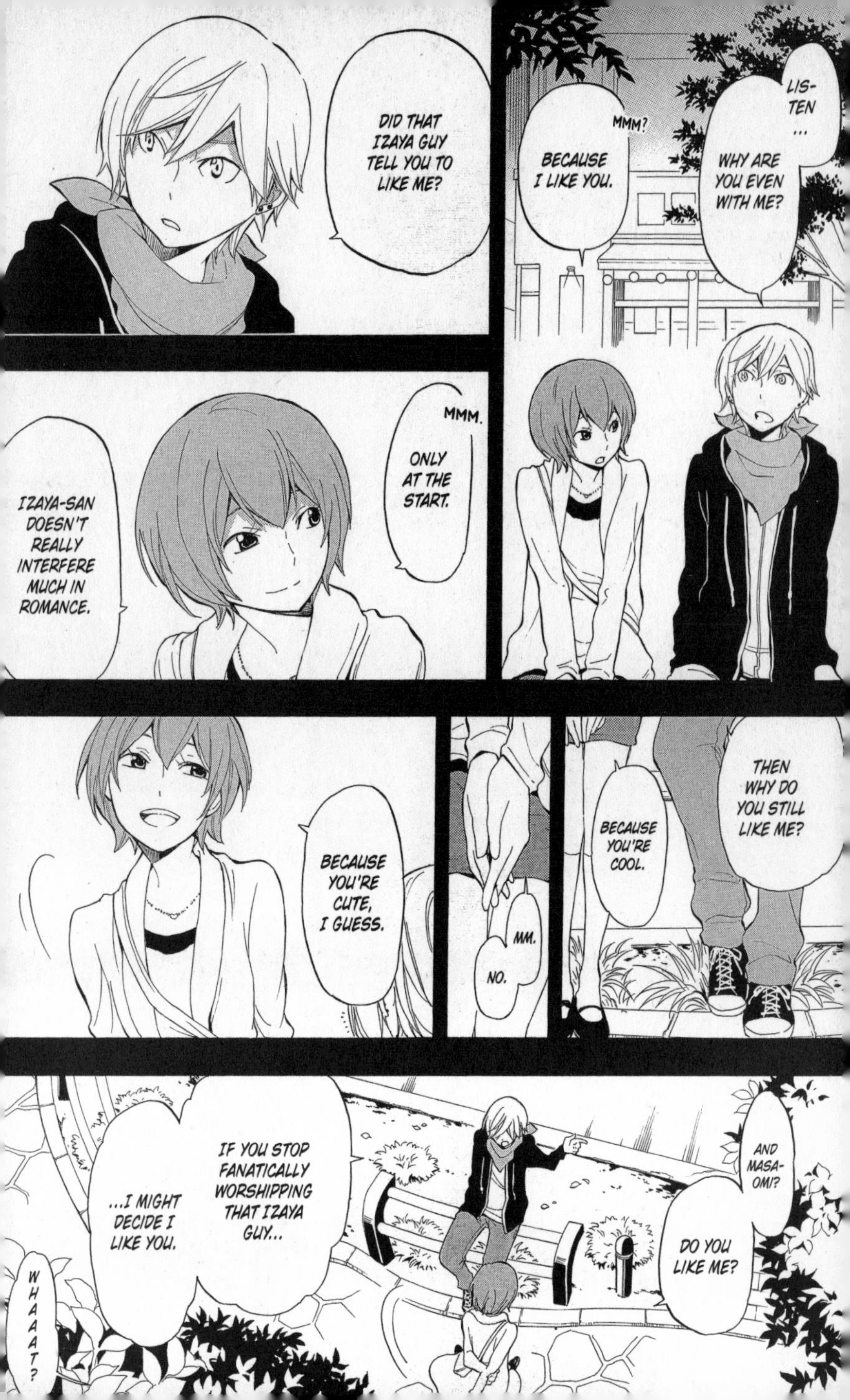

LIS-TEN...
WHY ARE YOU EVEN WITH ME?
MMM?
BECAUSE I LIKE YOU.
DID THAT IZAYA GUY TELL YOU TO LIKE ME?
MMM.
ONLY AT THE START.
IZAYA-SAN DOESN'T REALLY INTERFERE MUCH IN ROMANCE.
THEN WHY DO YOU STILL LIKE ME?
BECAUSE YOU'RE COOL.
MM.
NO.
BECAUSE YOU'RE CUTE, I GUESS.
AND MASA-OMI?
DO YOU LIKE ME?
IF YOU STOP FANATICALLY WORSHIPPING THAT IZAYA GUY...
...I MIGHT DECIDE I LIKE YOU.
WHAAAAT?

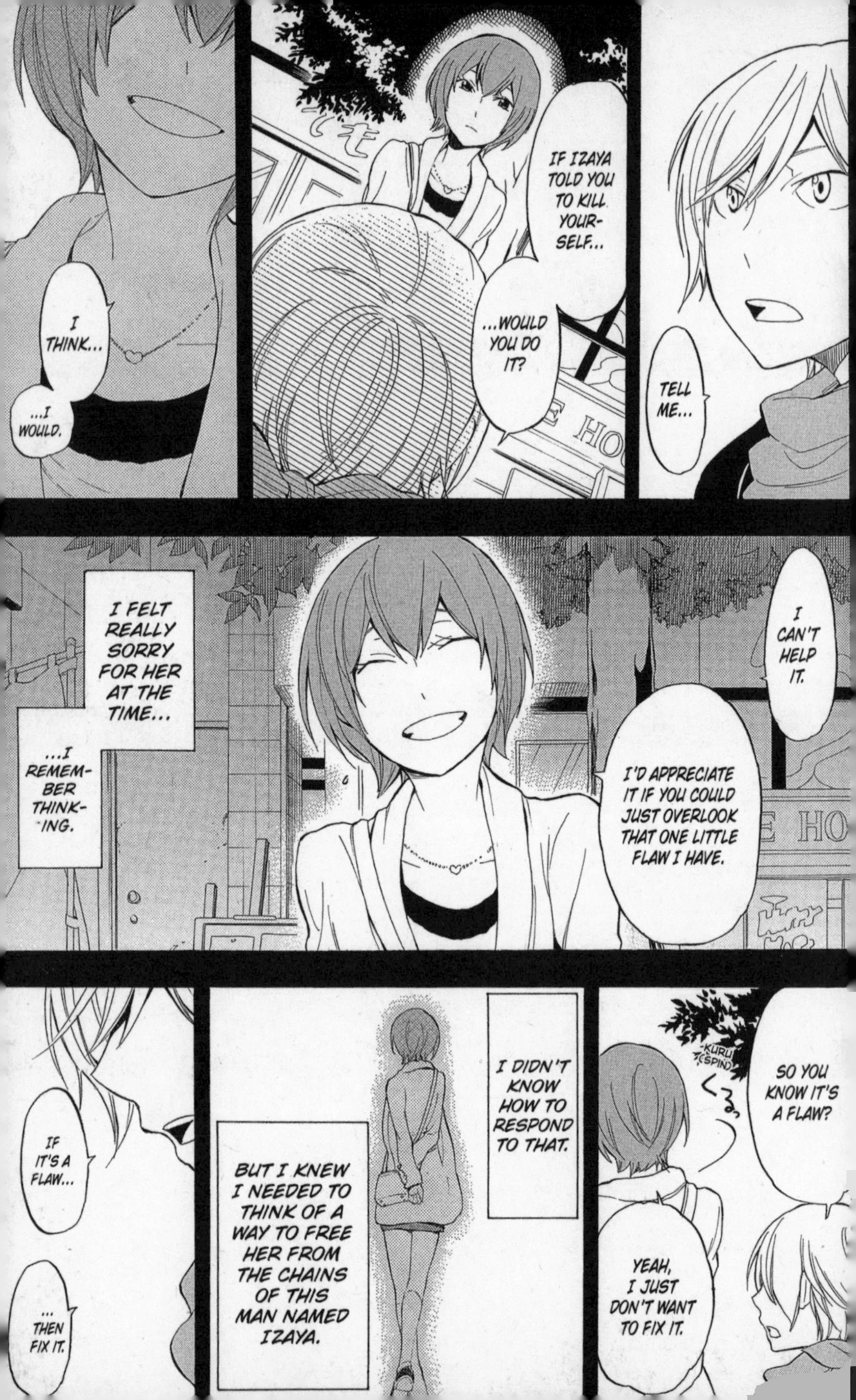
TELL ME...
IF IZAYA TOLD YOU TO KILL YOURSELF...
...WOULD YOU DO IT?
I THINK...
...I WOULD.
I CAN'T HELP IT.
I'D APPRECIATE IT IF YOU COULD JUST OVERLOOK THAT ONE LITTLE FLAW I HAVE.
I FELT REALLY SORRY FOR HER AT THE TIME...
...I REMEMBER THINKING.
SO YOU KNOW IT'S A FLAW?
-KURU (SPIN)
YEAH, I JUST DON'T WANT TO FIX IT.
I DIDN'T KNOW HOW TO RESPOND TO THAT.
BUT I KNEW I NEEDED TO THINK OF A WAY TO FREE HER FROM THE CHAINS OF THIS MAN NAMED IZAYA.
IF IT'S A FLAW...
...THEN FIX IT.

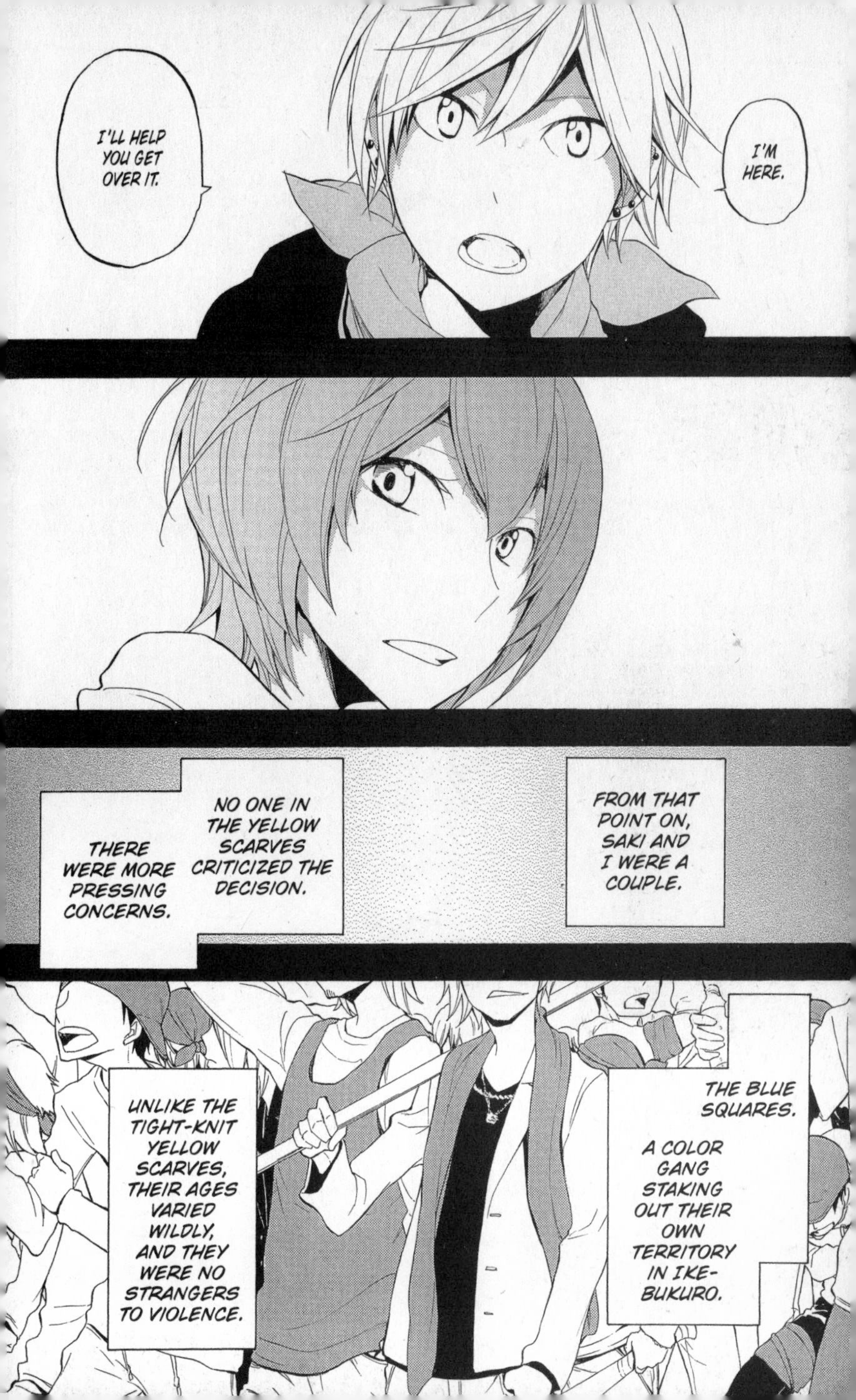
I'M HERE.
I'LL HELP YOU GET OVER IT.
FROM THAT POINT ON, SAKI AND I WERE A COUPLE.
NO ONE IN THE YELLOW SCARVES CRITICIZED THE DECISION.
THERE WERE MORE PRESSING CONCERNS.
THE BLUE SQUARES.
A COLOR GANG STAKING OUT THEIR OWN TERRITORY IN IKE-BUKURO.
UNLIKE THE TIGHT-KNIT YELLOW SCARVES, THEIR AGES VARIED WILDLY, AND THEY WERE NO STRANGERS TO VIOLENCE.

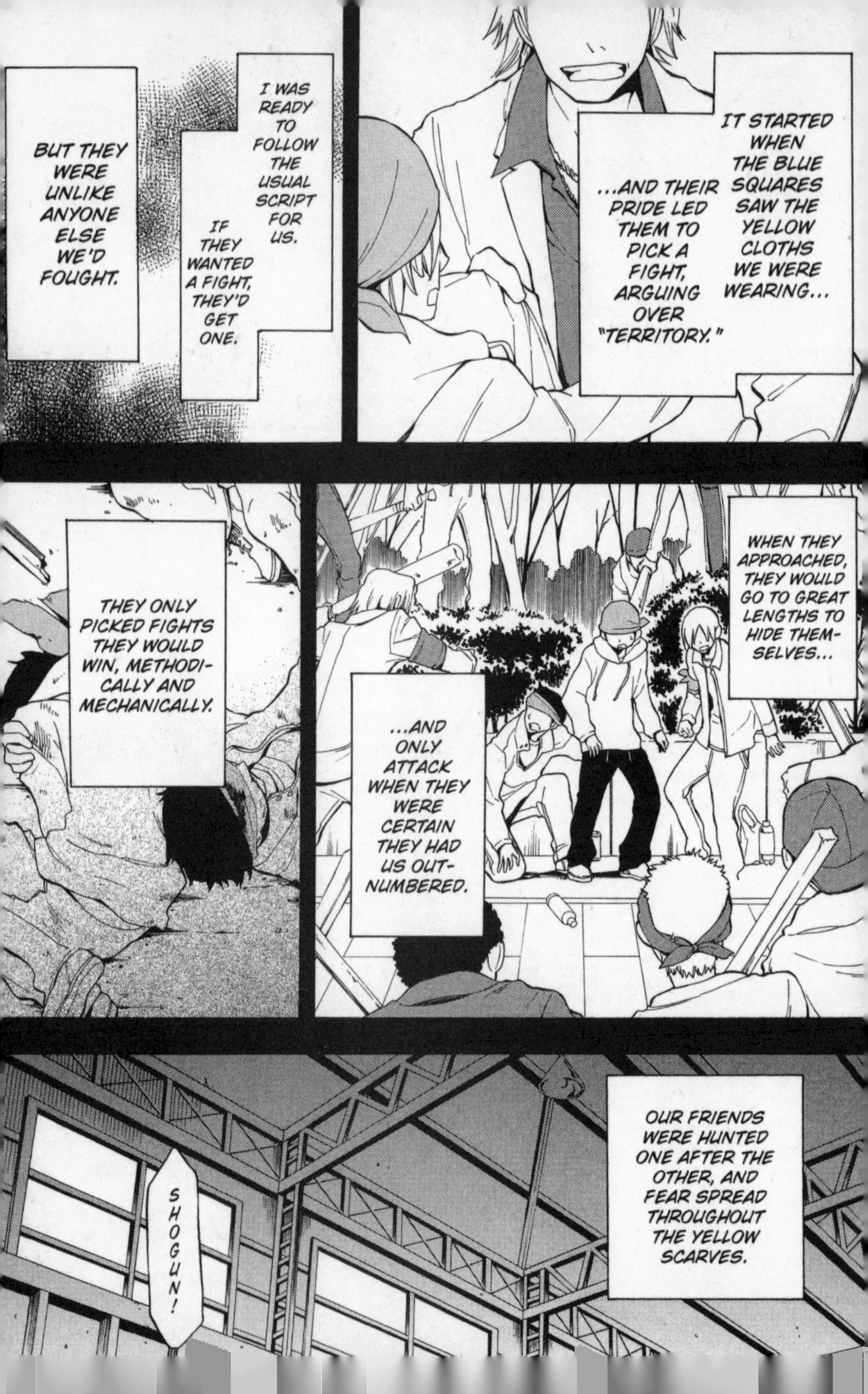
IT STARTED WHEN THE BLUE SQUARES SAW THE YELLOW CLOTHS WE WERE WEARING...
...AND THEIR PRIDE LED THEM TO PICK A FIGHT, ARGUING OVER "TERRITORY."
I WAS READY TO FOLLOW THE USUAL SCRIPT FOR US.
IF THEY WANTED A FIGHT, THEY'D GET ONE.
BUT THEY WERE UNLIKE ANYONE ELSE WE'D FOUGHT.
WHEN THEY APPROACHED, THEY WOULD GO TO GREAT LENGTHS TO HIDE THEM-SELVES...
...AND ONLY ATTACK WHEN THEY WERE CERTAIN THEY HAD US OUT-NUMBERED.
THEY ONLY PICKED FIGHTS THEY WOULD WIN, METHODI-CALLY AND MECHANICALLY.
OUR FRIENDS WERE HUNTED ONE AFTER THE OTHER, AND FEAR SPREAD THROUGHOUT THE YELLOW SCARVES.
SHOGUN!

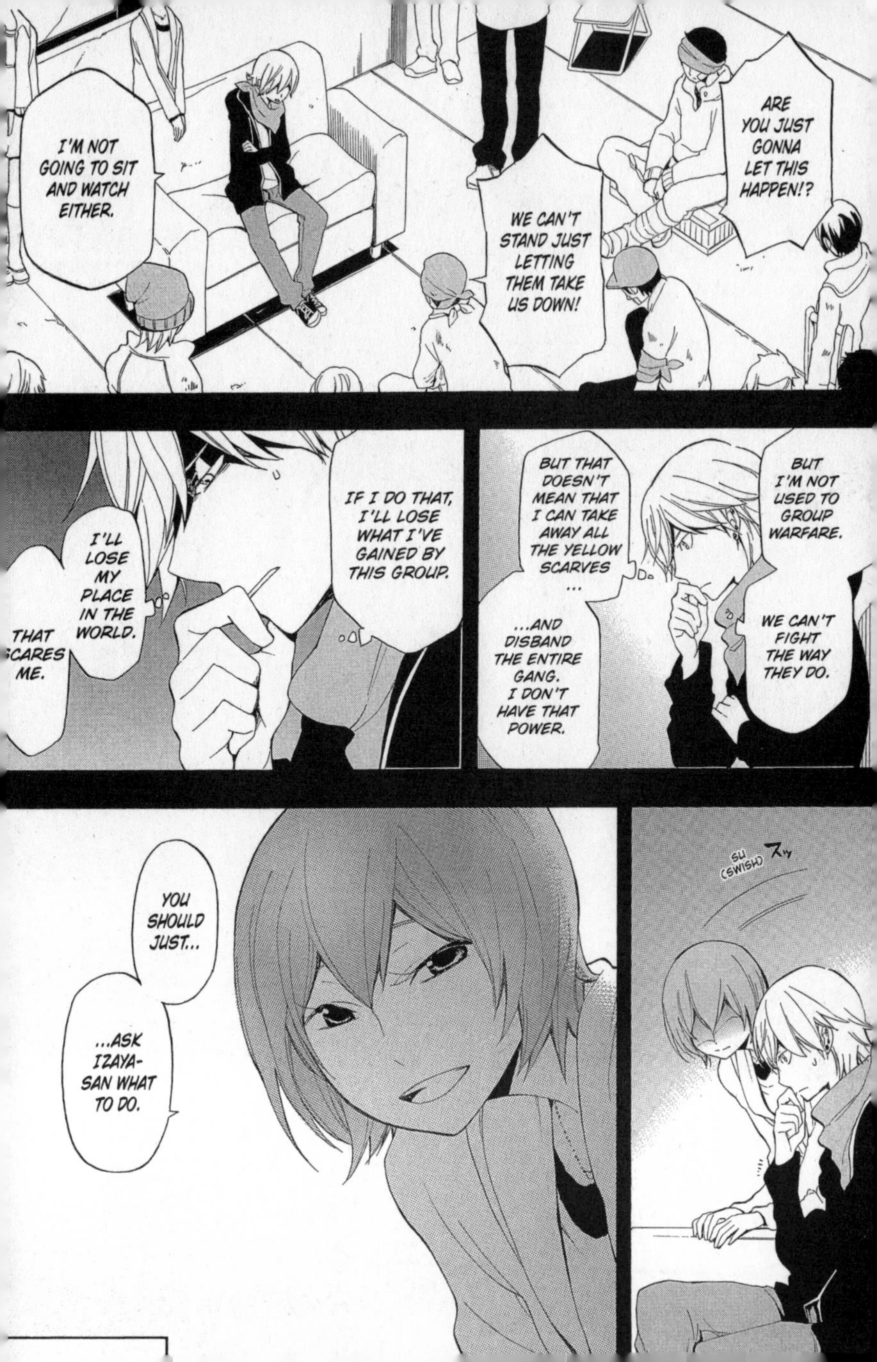
ARE YOU JUST GONNA LET THIS HAPPEN!?
WE CAN'T STAND JUST LETTING THEM TAKE US DOWN!
I'M NOT GOING TO SIT AND WATCH EITHER.
BUT I'M NOT USED TO GROUP WARFARE.
WE CAN'T FIGHT THE WAY THEY DO.
BUT THAT DOESN'T MEAN THAT I CAN TAKE AWAY ALL THE YELLOW SCARVES...
...AND DISBAND THE ENTIRE GANG. I DON'T HAVE THAT POWER.
IF I DO THAT, I'LL LOSE WHAT I'VE GAINED BY THIS GROUP.
I'LL LOSE MY PLACE IN THE WORLD.
THAT SCARES ME.
SU (SWISH) スッ
YOU SHOULD JUST...
...ASK IZAYA-SAN WHAT TO DO.

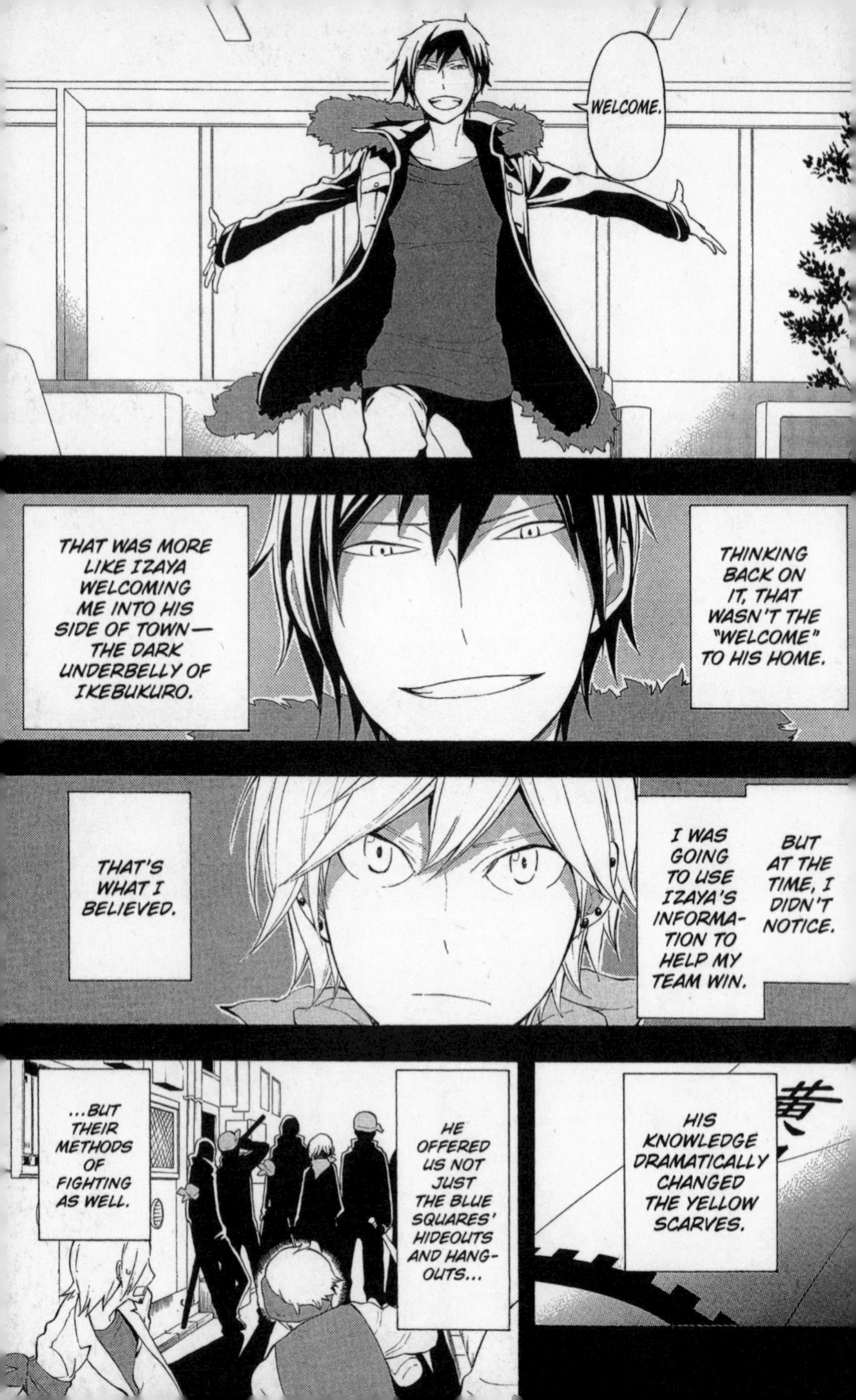
WELCOME.
THINKING BACK ON IT, THAT WASN'T THE "WELCOME" TO HIS HOME.
THAT WAS MORE LIKE IZAYA WELCOMING ME INTO HIS SIDE OF TOWN—THE DARK UNDERBELLY OF IKEBUKURO.
BUT AT THE TIME, I DIDN'T NOTICE.
I WAS GOING TO USE IZAYA'S INFORMATION TO HELP MY TEAM WIN.
THAT'S WHAT I BELIEVED.
HIS KNOWLEDGE DRAMATICALLY CHANGED THE YELLOW SCARVES.
HE OFFERED US NOT JUST THE BLUE SQUARES' HIDEOUTS AND HANG-OUTS...
...BUT THEIR METHODS OF FIGHTING AS WELL.

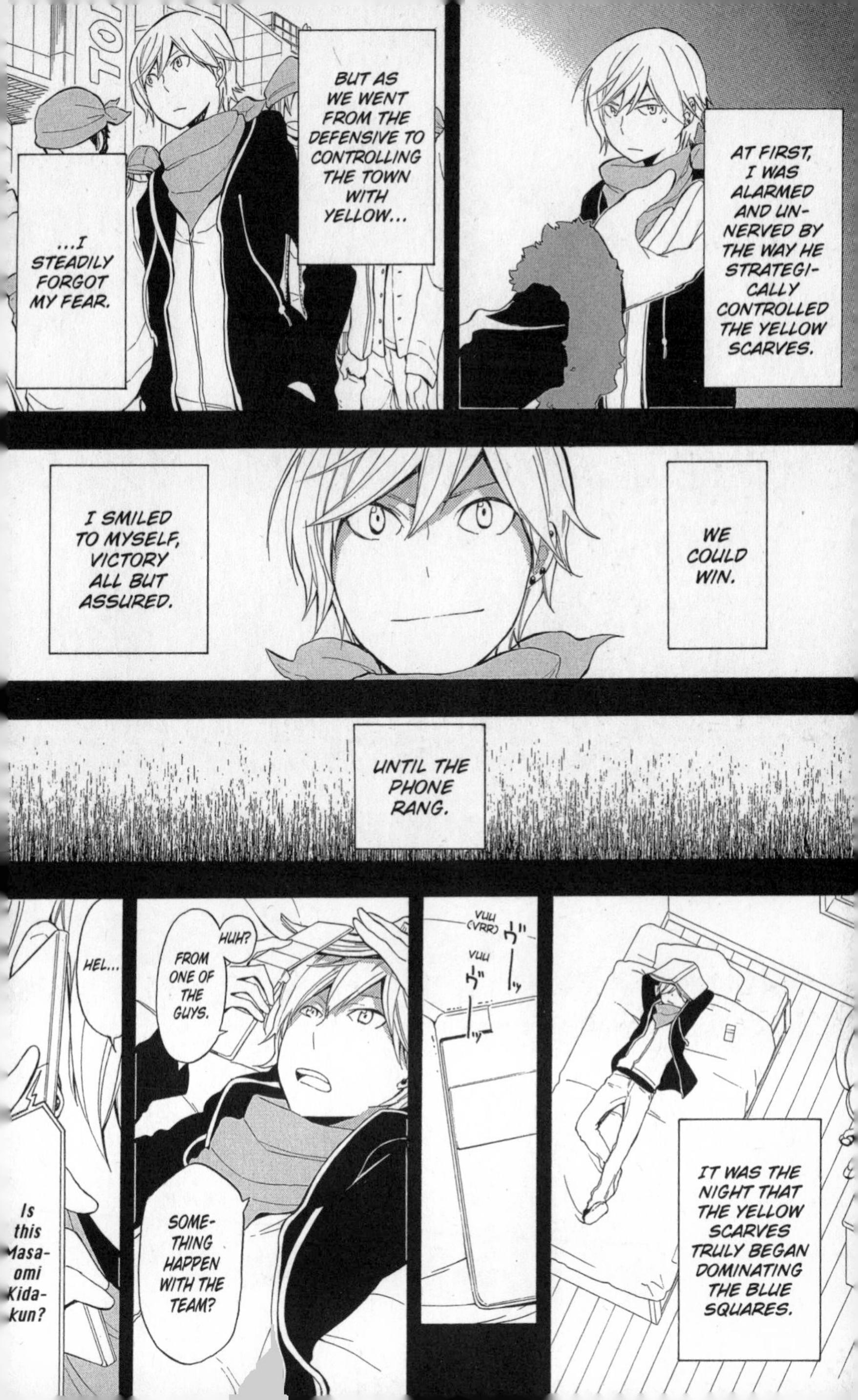
AT FIRST, I WAS ALARMED AND UNNERVED BY THE WAY HE STRATEGICALLY CONTROLLED THE YELLOW SCARVES.
BUT AS WE WENT FROM THE DEFENSIVE TO CONTROLLING THE TOWN WITH YELLOW...
...I STEADILY FORGOT MY FEAR.
WE COULD WIN.
I SMILED TO MYSELF, VICTORY ALL BUT ASSURED.
UNTIL THE PHONE RANG.
IT WAS THE NIGHT THAT THE YELLOW SCARVES TRULY BEGAN DOMINATING THE BLUE SQUARES.
VUU (VRR) ヴーッ
VUU ヴーッ
HUH?
FROM ONE OF THE GUYS.
SOMETHING HAPPEN WITH THE TEAM?
HEL...
Is this Masaomi Kida-kun?

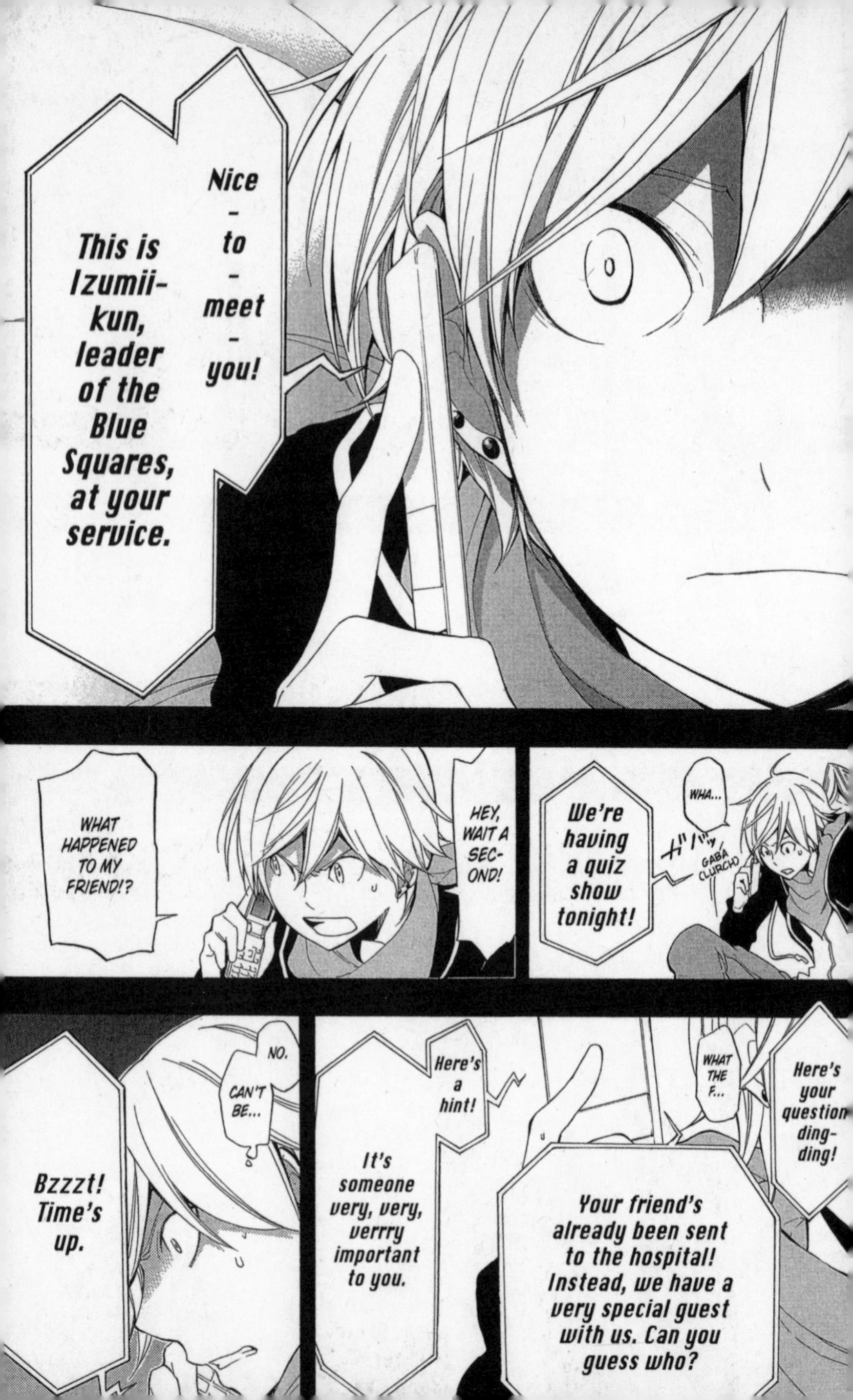

Nice - to - meet - you!
This is Izumii-kun, leader of the Blue Squares, at your service.
WHA...
We're having a quiz show tonight!
GABA (LURCH)
HEY, WAIT A SEC-OND!
WHAT HAPPENED TO MY FRIEND!?
Here's your question ding-ding!
WHAT THE F...
Your friend's already been sent to the hospital! Instead, we have a very special guest with us. Can you guess who?
Here's a hint!
It's someone very, very, verrry important to you.
NO.
CAN'T BE...
Bzzzt! Time's up.

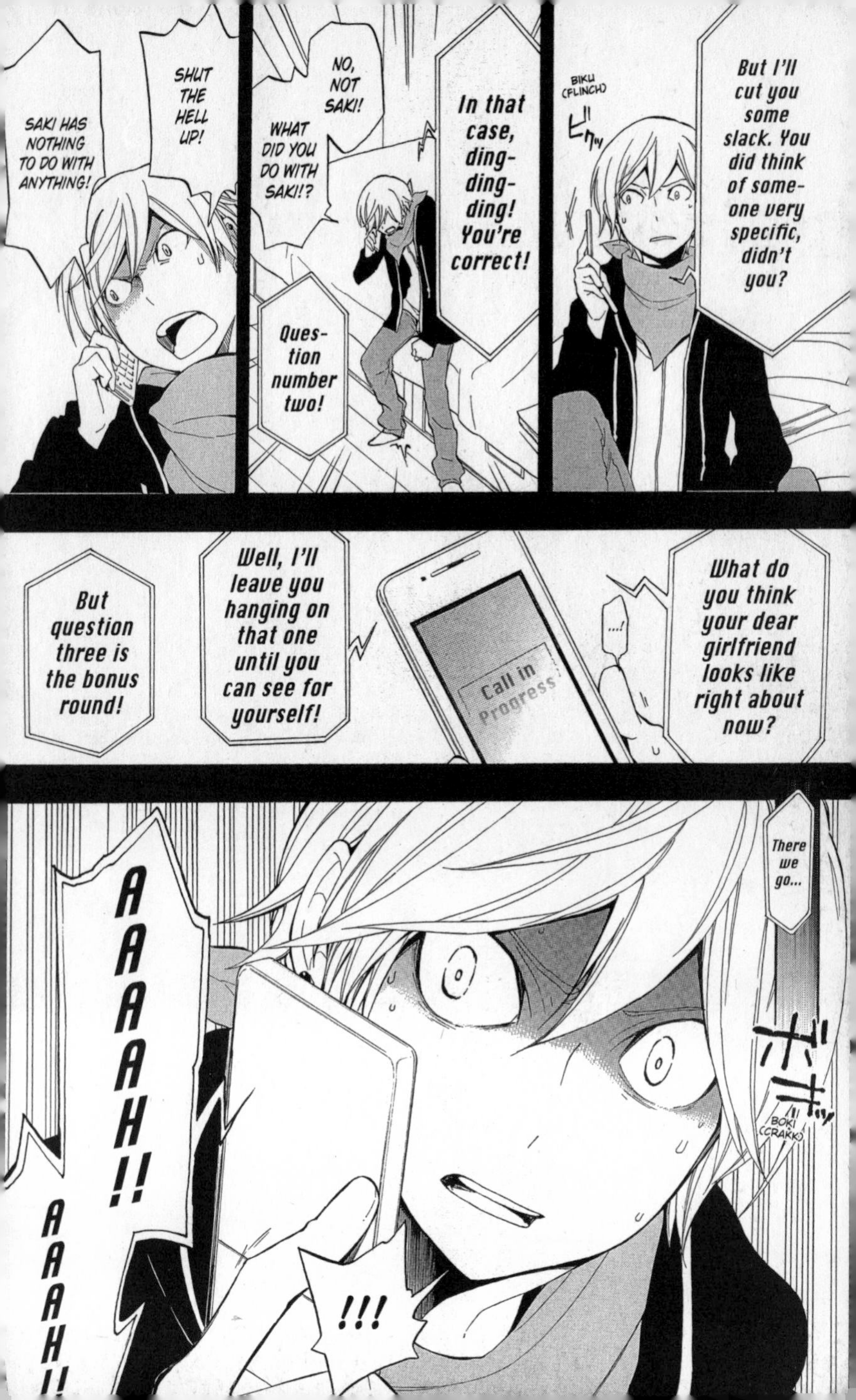
BIKU (FLINCH)
ビクッ
But I'll cut you some slack. You did think of some-one very specific, didn't you?
In that case, ding-ding-ding! You're correct!
NO, NOT SAKI!
WHAT DID YOU DO WITH SAKI!?
Question number two!
SHUT THE HELL UP!
SAKI HAS NOTHING TO DO WITH ANYTHING!
What do you think your dear girlfriend looks like right about now?
...!
Call in Progress
Well, I'll leave you hanging on that one until you can see for yourself!
But question three is the bonus round!
There we go...
ボキッ
BOKI (CRAKK)
AAAAAH!!
AAAAH!!
!!!

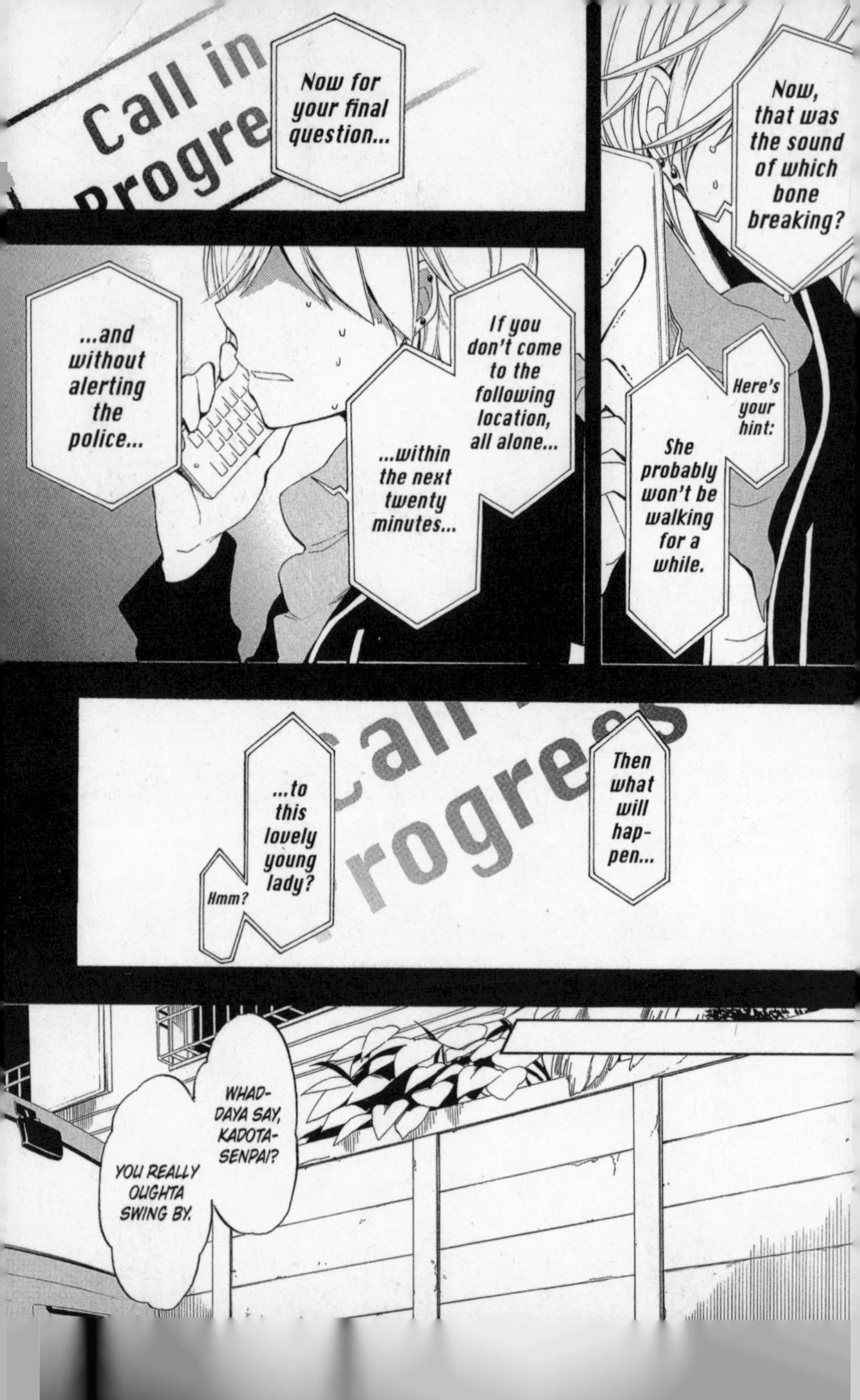

Now, that was the sound of which bone breaking?
Here's your hint:
She probably won't be walking for a while.
Call in Progre
Now for your final question...
If you don't come to the following location, all alone...
...within the next twenty minutes...
...and without alerting the police...
Then what will hap-pen...
...to this lovely young lady?
Hmm?
WHAD-DAYA SAY, KADOTA-SENPAI?
YOU REALLY OUGHTA SWING BY.

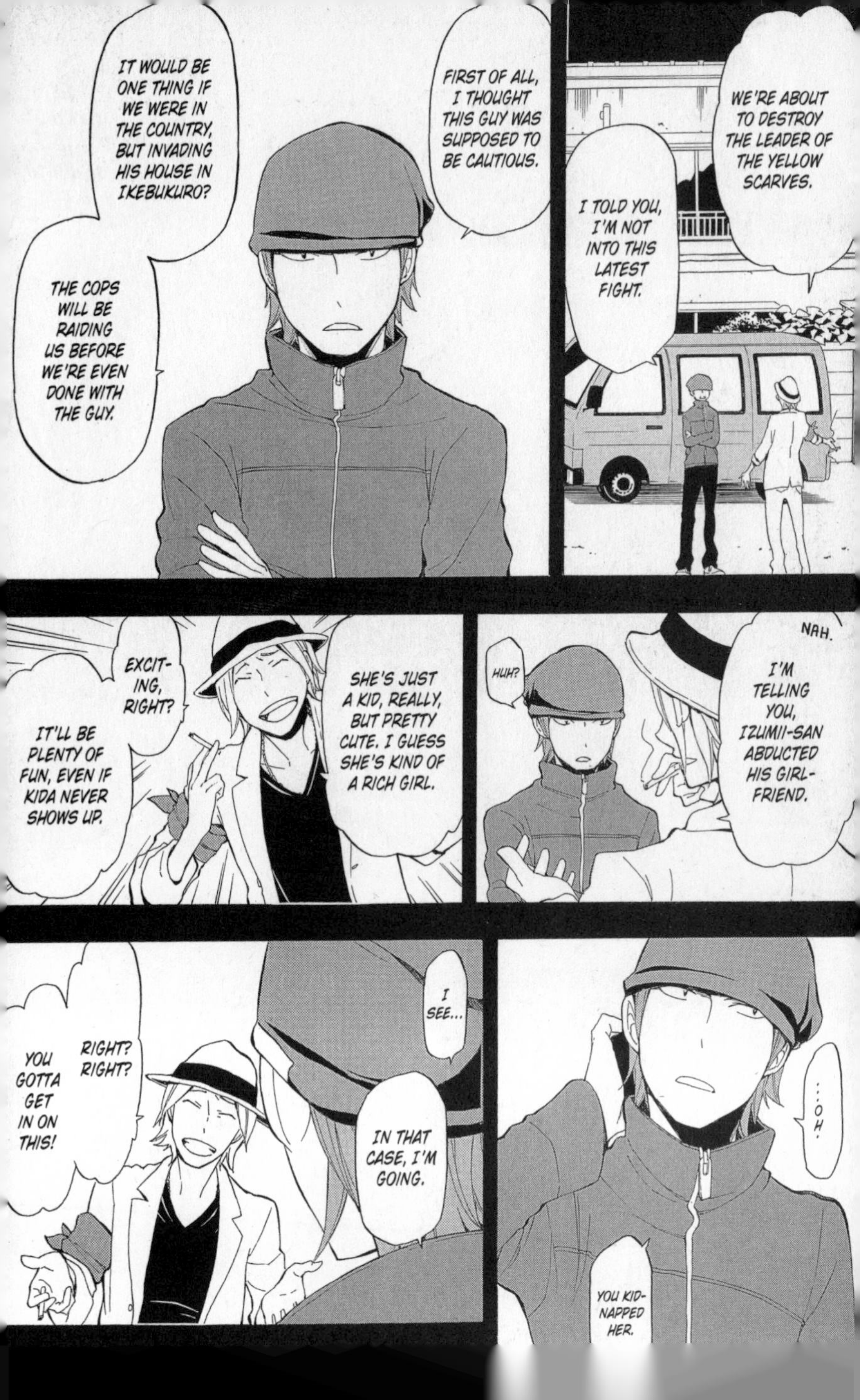
WE'RE ABOUT TO DESTROY THE LEADER OF THE YELLOW SCARVES.
I TOLD YOU, I'M NOT INTO THIS LATEST FIGHT.
FIRST OF ALL, I THOUGHT THIS GUY WAS SUPPOSED TO BE CAUTIOUS.
IT WOULD BE ONE THING IF WE WERE IN THE COUNTRY, BUT INVADING HIS HOUSE IN IKEBUKURO?
THE COPS WILL BE RAIDING US BEFORE WE'RE EVEN DONE WITH THE GUY.
NAH.
I'M TELLING YOU, IZUMII-SAN ABDUCTED HIS GIRL-FRIEND.
HUH?
SHE'S JUST A KID, REALLY, BUT PRETTY CUTE. I GUESS SHE'S KIND OF A RICH GIRL.
EXCIT-ING, RIGHT?
IT'LL BE PLENTY OF FUN, EVEN IF KIDA NEVER SHOWS UP.
...OH.
YOU KID-NAPPED HER.
I SEE...
IN THAT CASE, I'M GOING.
RIGHT? RIGHT?
YOU GOTTA GET IN ON THIS!

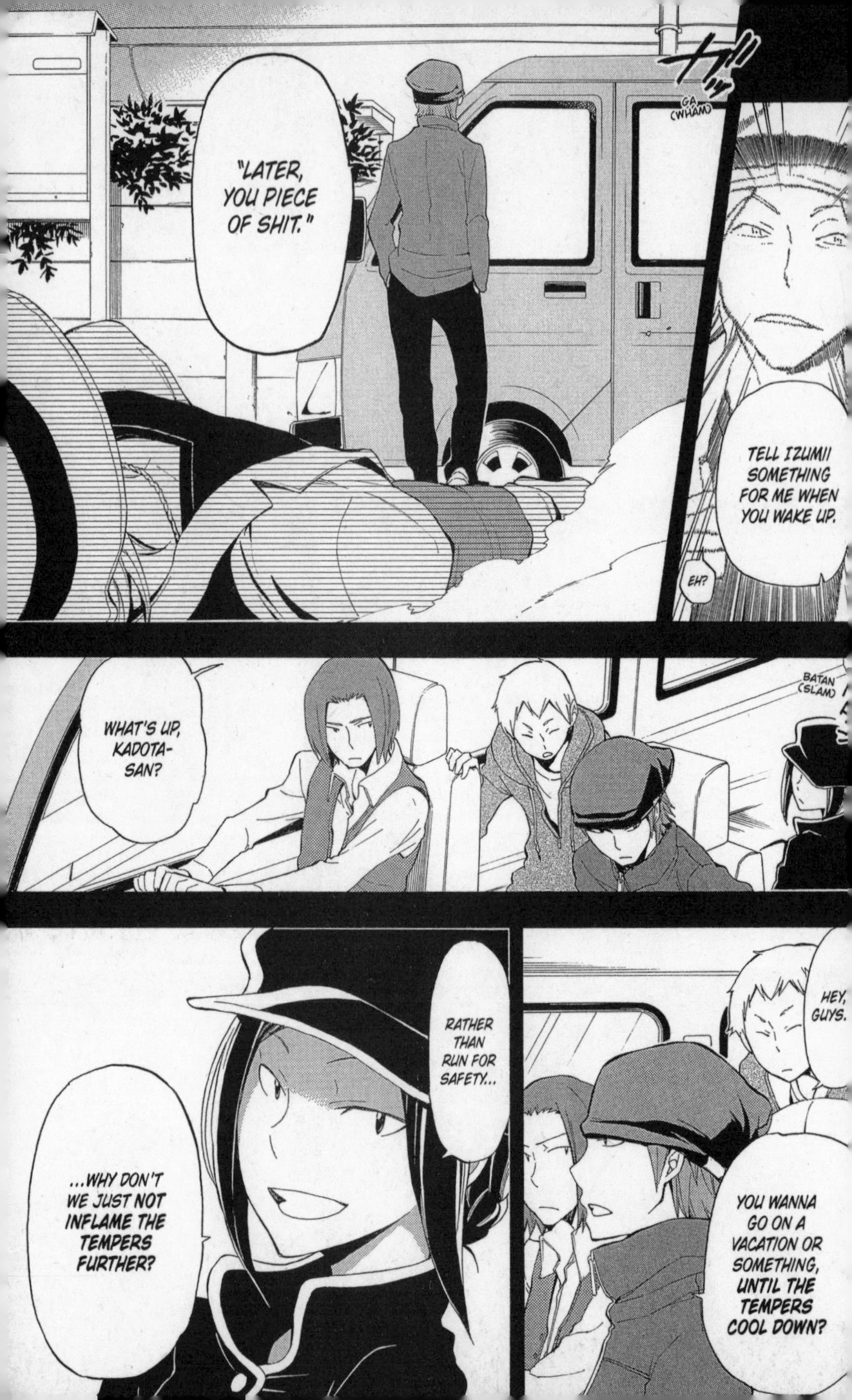
GA (WHAM)
TELL IZUMII SOMETHING FOR ME WHEN YOU WAKE UP.
EH?
"LATER, YOU PIECE OF SHIT."
BATAN (SLAM)
WHAT'S UP, KADOTA-SAN?
HEY, GUYS.
YOU WANNA GO ON A VACATION OR SOMETHING, UNTIL THE TEMPERS COOL DOWN?
RATHER THAN RUN FOR SAFETY...
...WHY DON'T WE JUST NOT INFLAME THE TEMPERS FURTHER?

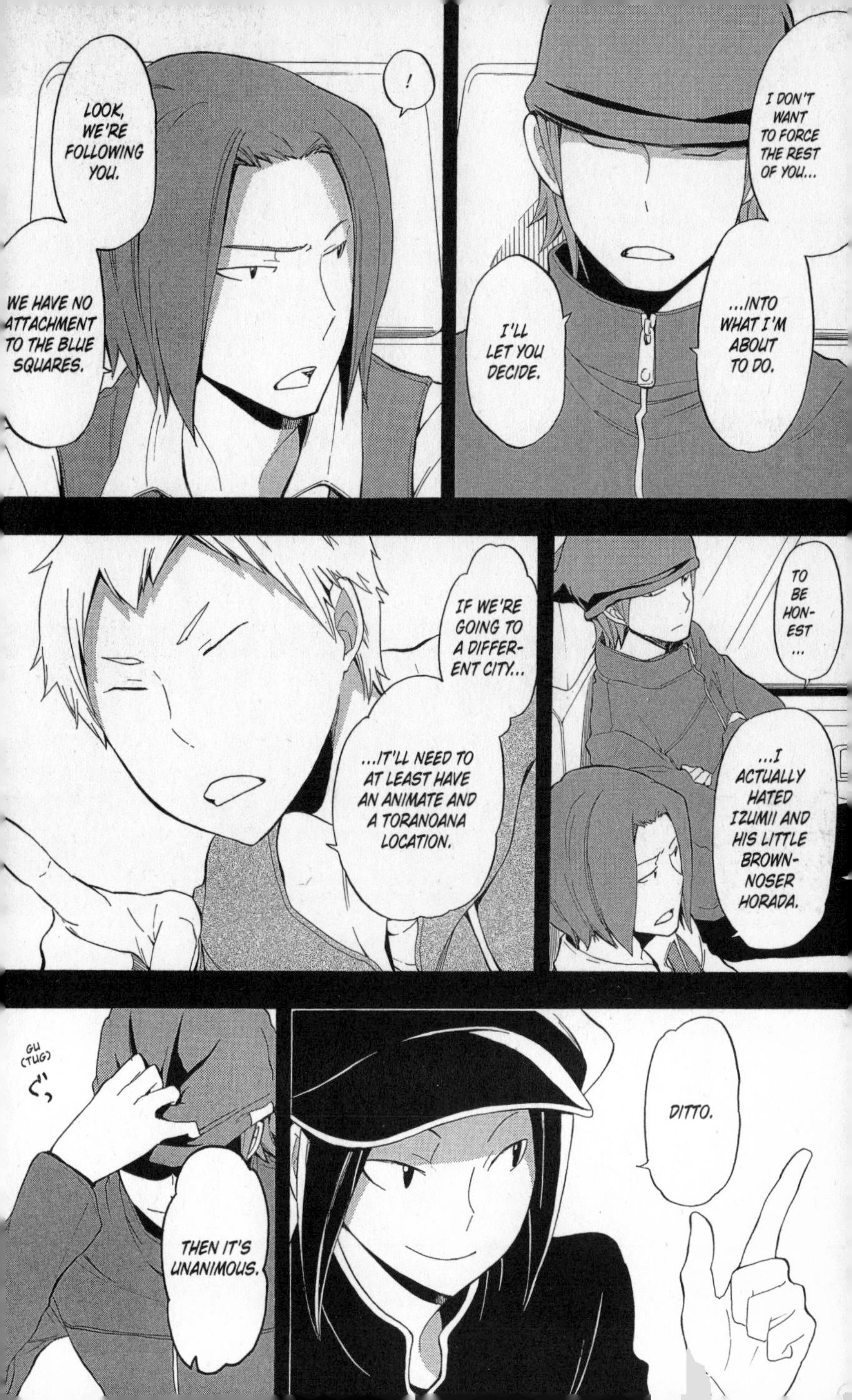
I DON'T WANT TO FORCE THE REST OF YOU...
...INTO WHAT I'M ABOUT TO DO.
I'LL LET YOU DECIDE.
!
LOOK, WE'RE FOLLOWING YOU.
WE HAVE NO ATTACHMENT TO THE BLUE SQUARES.
TO BE HON-EST...
...I ACTUALLY HATED IZUMII AND HIS LITTLE BROWN-NOSER HORADA.
IF WE'RE GOING TO A DIFFER-ENT CITY...
...IT'LL NEED TO AT LEAST HAVE AN ANIMATE AND A TORANOANA LOCATION.
DITTO.
GU (TUG)
THEN IT'S UNANIMOUS.

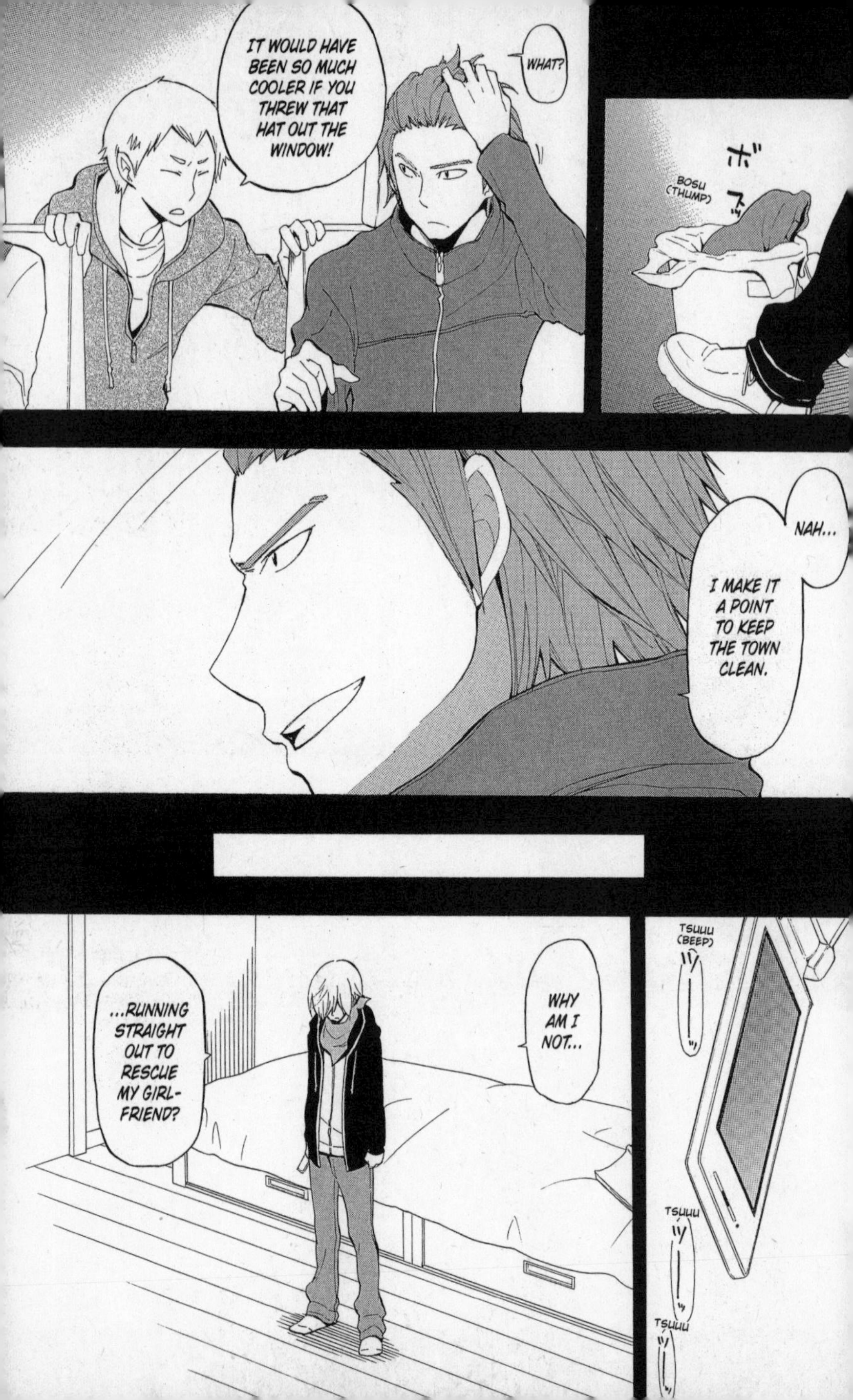
BOSU (THUMP)
WHAT?
IT WOULD HAVE BEEN SO MUCH COOLER IF YOU THREW THAT HAT OUT THE WINDOW!
NAH...
I MAKE IT A POINT TO KEEP THE TOWN CLEAN.
TSUUU (BEEP)
TSUUU
TSUUU
WHY AM I NOT...
...RUNNING STRAIGHT OUT TO RESCUE MY GIRL-FRIEND?

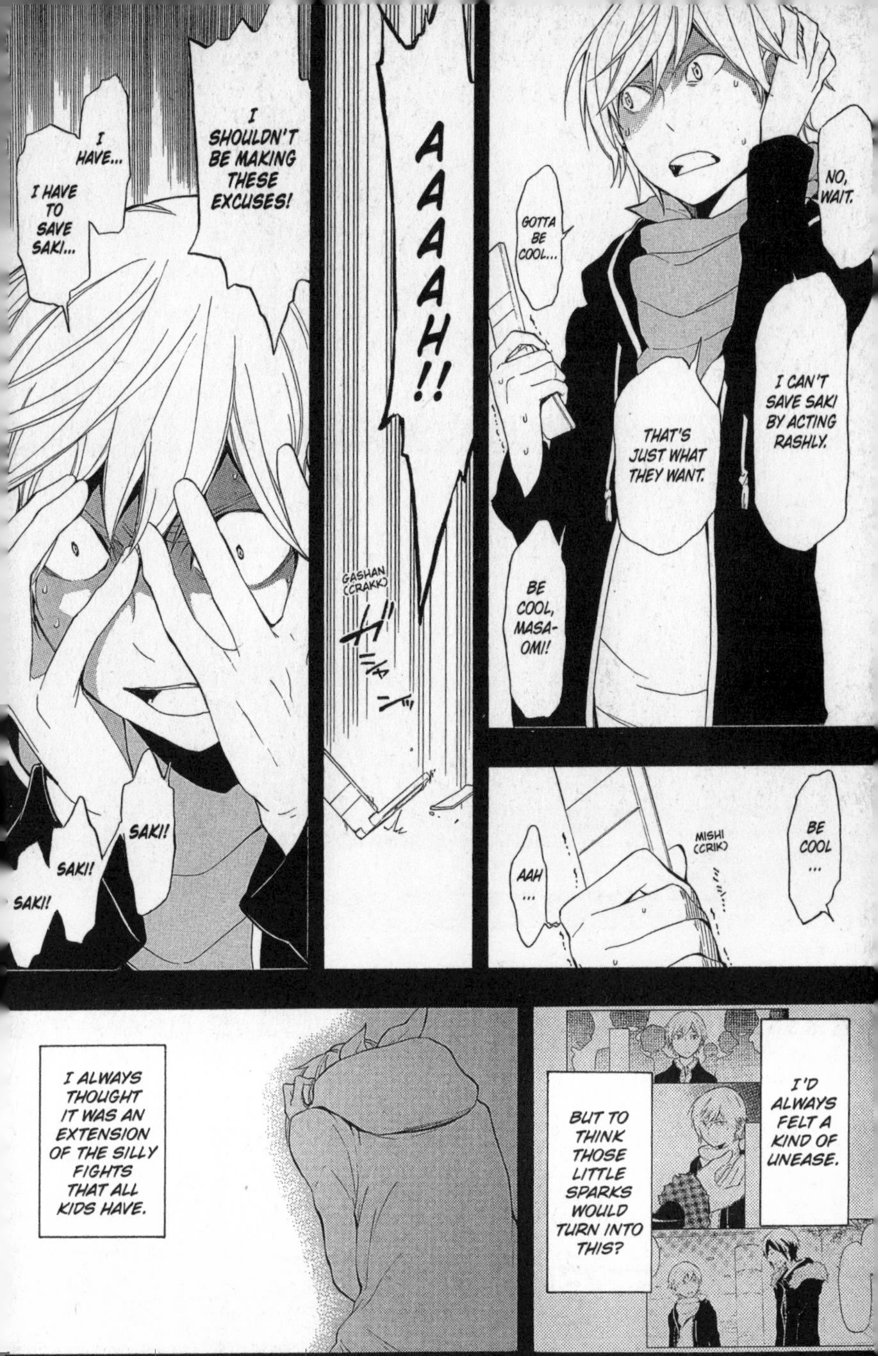
NO, WAIT.
GOTTA BE COOL...
I CAN'T SAVE SAKI BY ACTING RASHLY.
THAT'S JUST WHAT THEY WANT.
BE COOL, MASA-OMI!
BE COOL ...
MISHI (CRIK)
AAH ...
AAAAH!!
GASHAN (CRAKK)
I SHOULDN'T BE MAKING THESE EXCUSES!
I HAVE...
I HAVE TO SAVE SAKI...
SAKI!
SAKI!
SAKI!
I'D ALWAYS FELT A KIND OF UNEASE.
BUT TO THINK THOSE LITTLE SPARKS WOULD TURN INTO THIS?
I ALWAYS THOUGHT IT WAS AN EXTENSION OF THE SILLY FIGHTS THAT ALL KIDS HAVE.

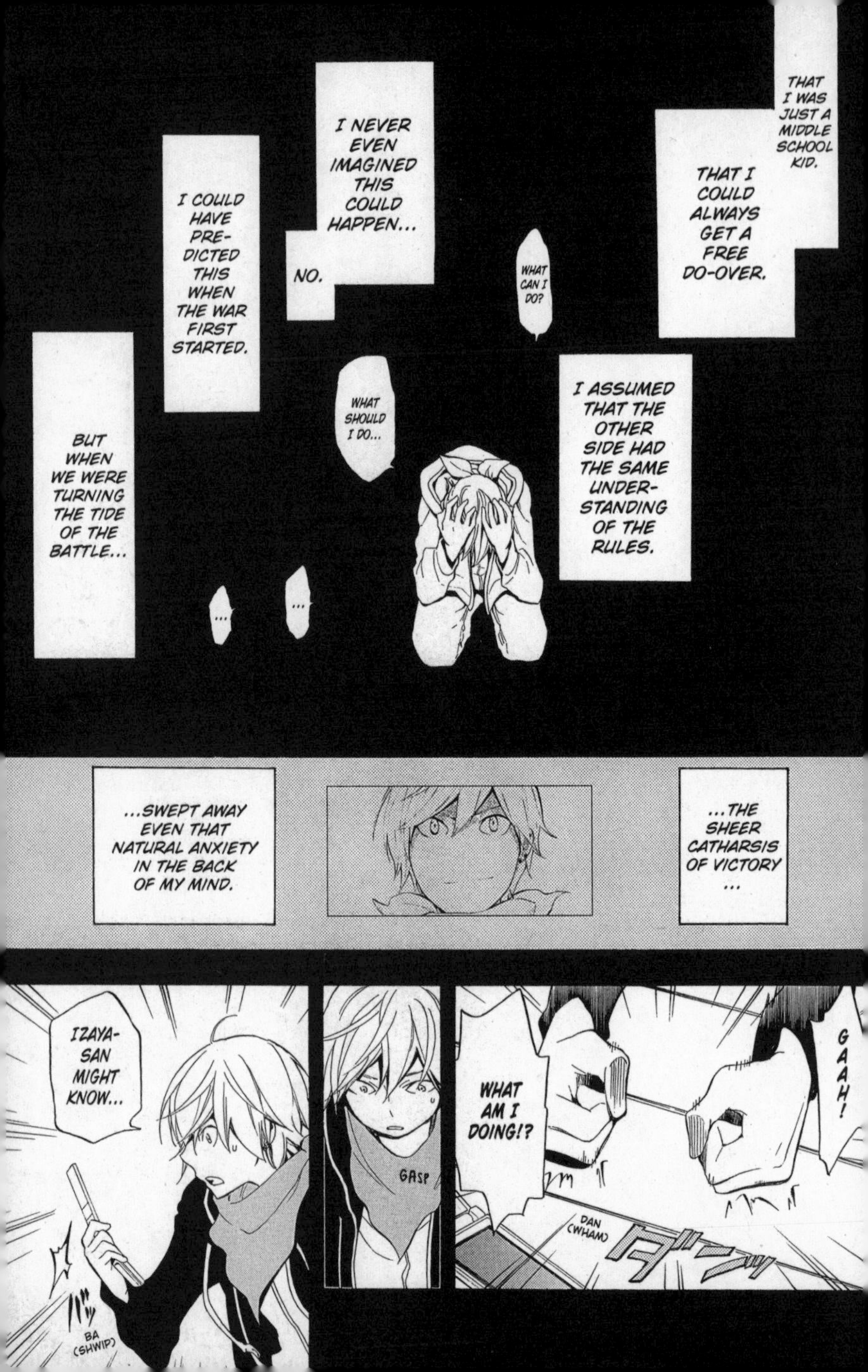
THAT I WAS JUST A MIDDLE SCHOOL KID.
THAT I COULD ALWAYS GET A FREE DO-OVER.
I NEVER EVEN IMAGINED THIS COULD HAPPEN...
WHAT CAN I DO?
NO.
I COULD HAVE PRE-DICTED THIS WHEN THE WAR FIRST STARTED.
I ASSUMED THAT THE OTHER SIDE HAD THE SAME UNDER-STANDING OF THE RULES.
WHAT SHOULD I DO...
BUT WHEN WE WERE TURNING THE TIDE OF THE BATTLE...
...
...
...THE SHEER CATHARSIS OF VICTORY ...
...SWEPT AWAY EVEN THAT NATURAL ANXIETY IN THE BACK OF MY MIND.
GAAH!
WHAT AM I DOING!?
DAN (WHAM)
GASP
IZAYA-SAN MIGHT KNOW...
BA (SHWIP)

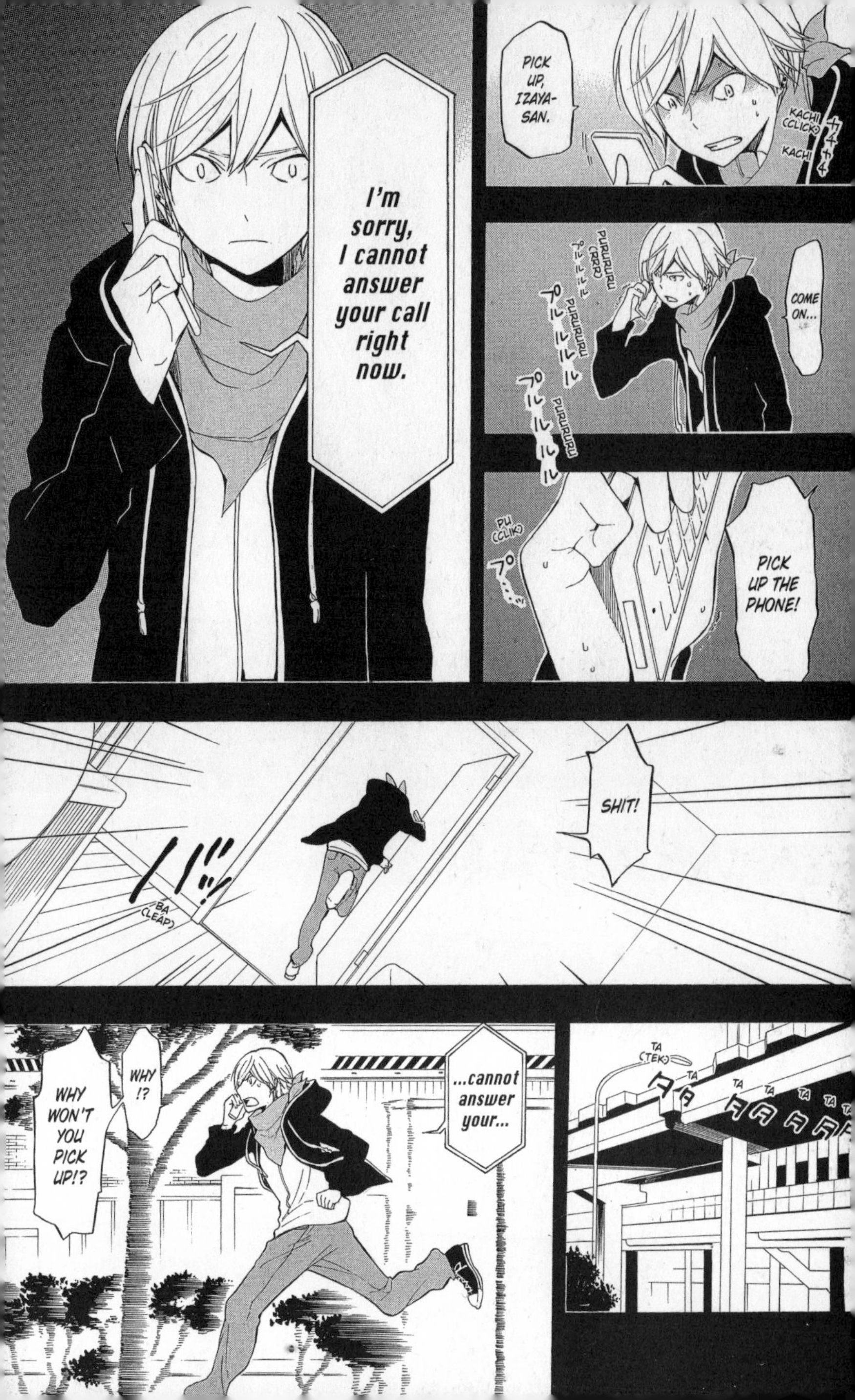
PICK UP, IZAYA-SAN.
KACHI (CLICK) KACHI
COME ON...
PURURURU (RRR) PURURURU PURURURU
PICK UP THE PHONE!
PU (CLIK)
I'm sorry, I cannot answer your call right now.
SHIT!
BA (LEAP)
TA (TEK) TA TA TA TA TA TA
...cannot answer your...
WHY!?
WHY WON'T YOU PICK UP!?

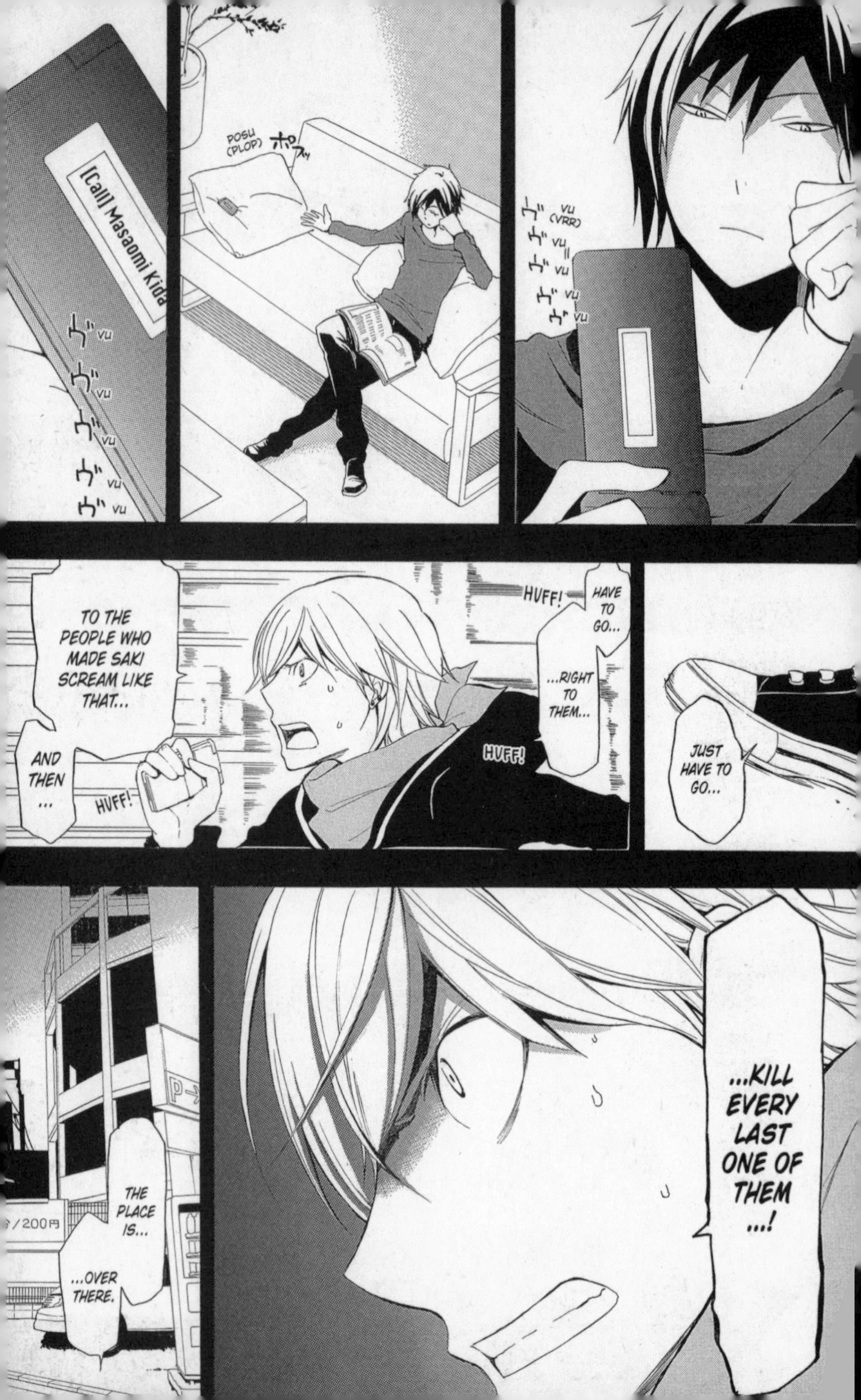

VU (VRR)
VU
VU
VU
VU
POSU (PLOP)
[Call] Masaomi Kida
VU
VU
VU
VU
VU
JUST HAVE TO GO...
HUFF!
HAVE TO GO...
...RIGHT TO THEM...
HUFF!
TO THE PEOPLE WHO MADE SAKI SCREAM LIKE THAT...
AND THEN...
HUFF!
...KILL EVERY LAST ONE OF THEM...!
THE PLACE IS...
...OVER THERE.

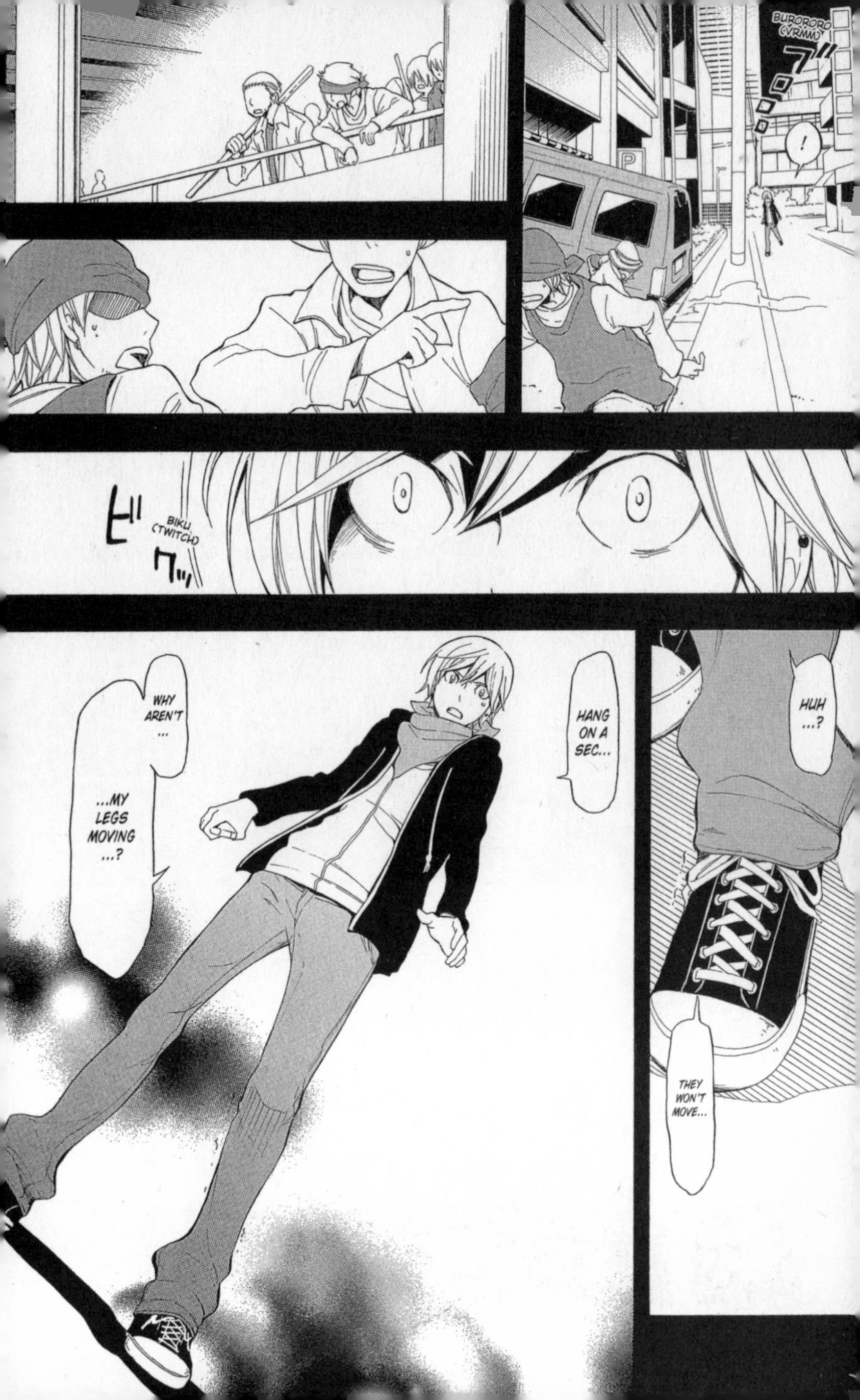
BURORORO (VRMM)
!
BIKU (TWITCH)
HUH ...?
THEY WON'T MOVE...
HANG ON A SEC...
WHY AREN'T ...
...MY LEGS MOVING ...?

DURARARA!!

DRRR!!

DRRR!!

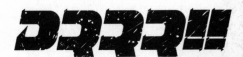

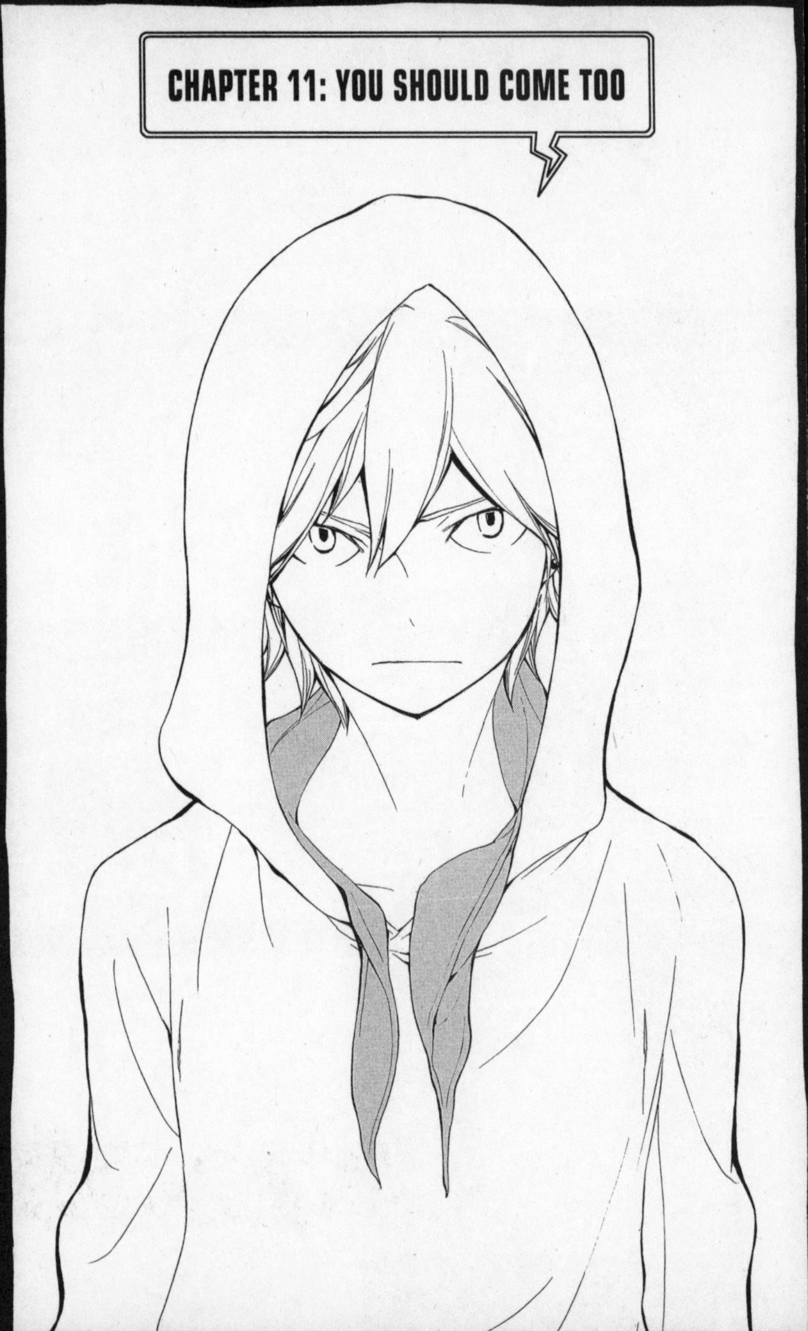
CHAPTER 11: YOU SHOULD COME TOO

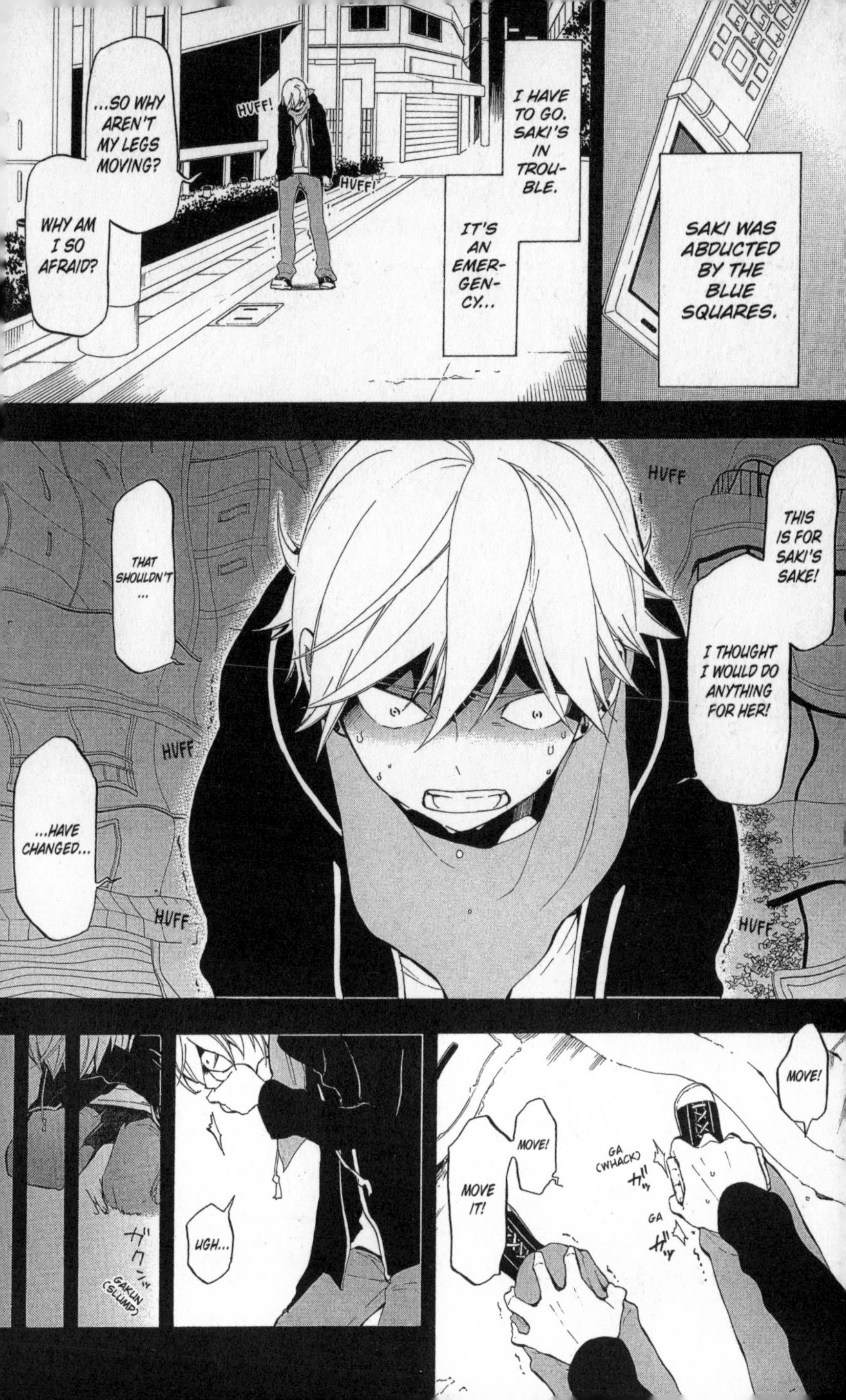
SAKI WAS ABDUCTED BY THE BLUE SQUARES.
I HAVE TO GO. SAKI'S IN TROUBLE.
IT'S AN EMERGENCY...
HUFF!
HUFF!
...SO WHY AREN'T MY LEGS MOVING?
WHY AM I SO AFRAID?
THIS IS FOR SAKI'S SAKE!
I THOUGHT I WOULD DO ANYTHING FOR HER!
HUFF
THAT SHOULDN'T ...
HUFF
...HAVE CHANGED...
HUFF
HUFF
MOVE!
MOVE!
MOVE IT!
GA (WHACK)
GA
UGH...
GAKUN (SLUMP)

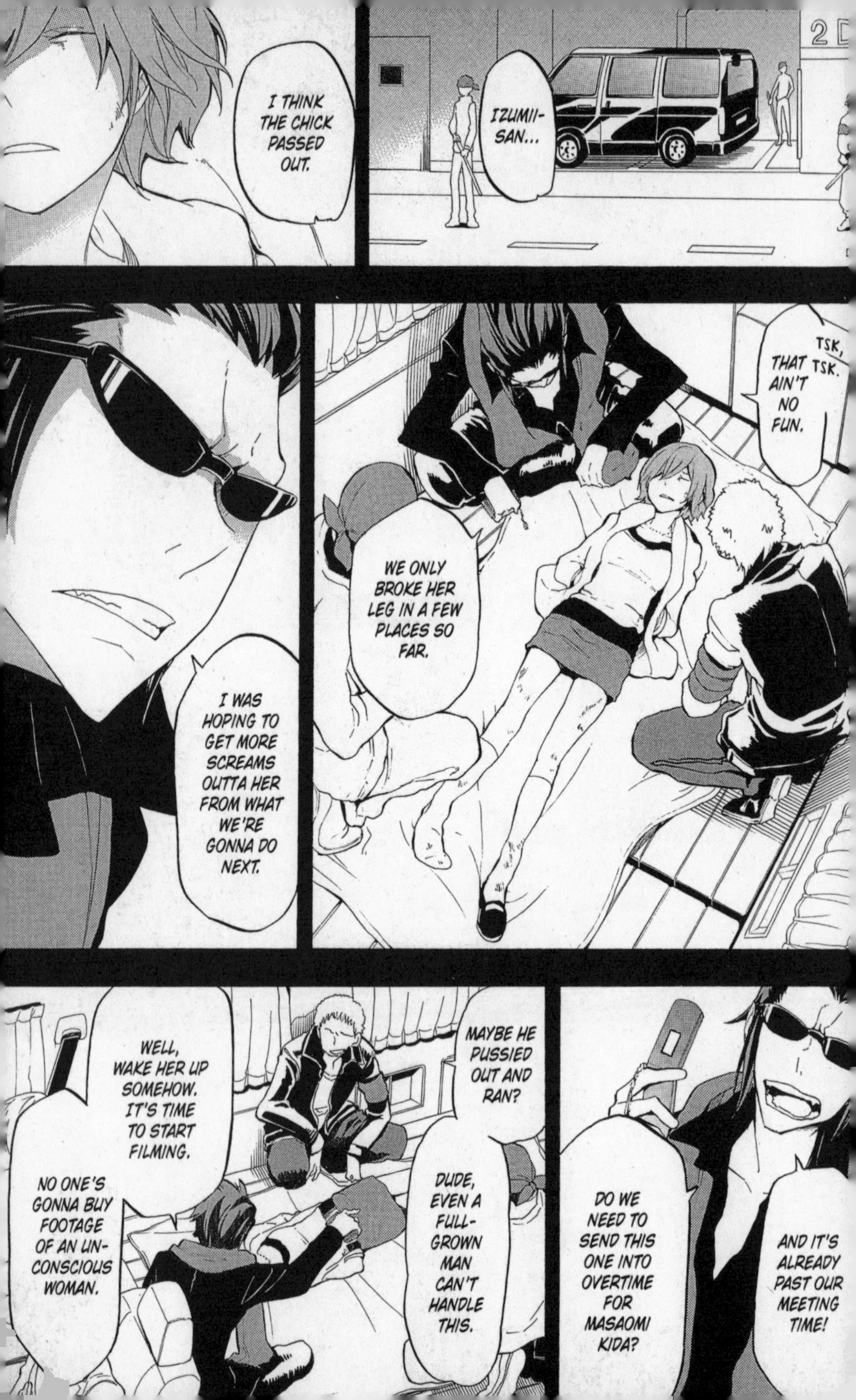
IZUMII-SAN...
I THINK THE CHICK PASSED OUT.
TSK, TSK.
THAT AIN'T NO FUN.
WE ONLY BROKE HER LEG IN A FEW PLACES SO FAR.
I WAS HOPING TO GET MORE SCREAMS OUTTA HER FROM WHAT WE'RE GONNA DO NEXT.
AND IT'S ALREADY PAST OUR MEETING TIME!
DO WE NEED TO SEND THIS ONE INTO OVERTIME FOR MASAOMI KIDA?
MAYBE HE PUSSIED OUT AND RAN?
WELL, WAKE HER UP SOMEHOW. IT'S TIME TO START FILMING.
DUDE, EVEN A FULL-GROWN MAN CAN'T HANDLE THIS.
NO ONE'S GONNA BUY FOOTAGE OF AN UN-CONSCIOUS WOMAN.

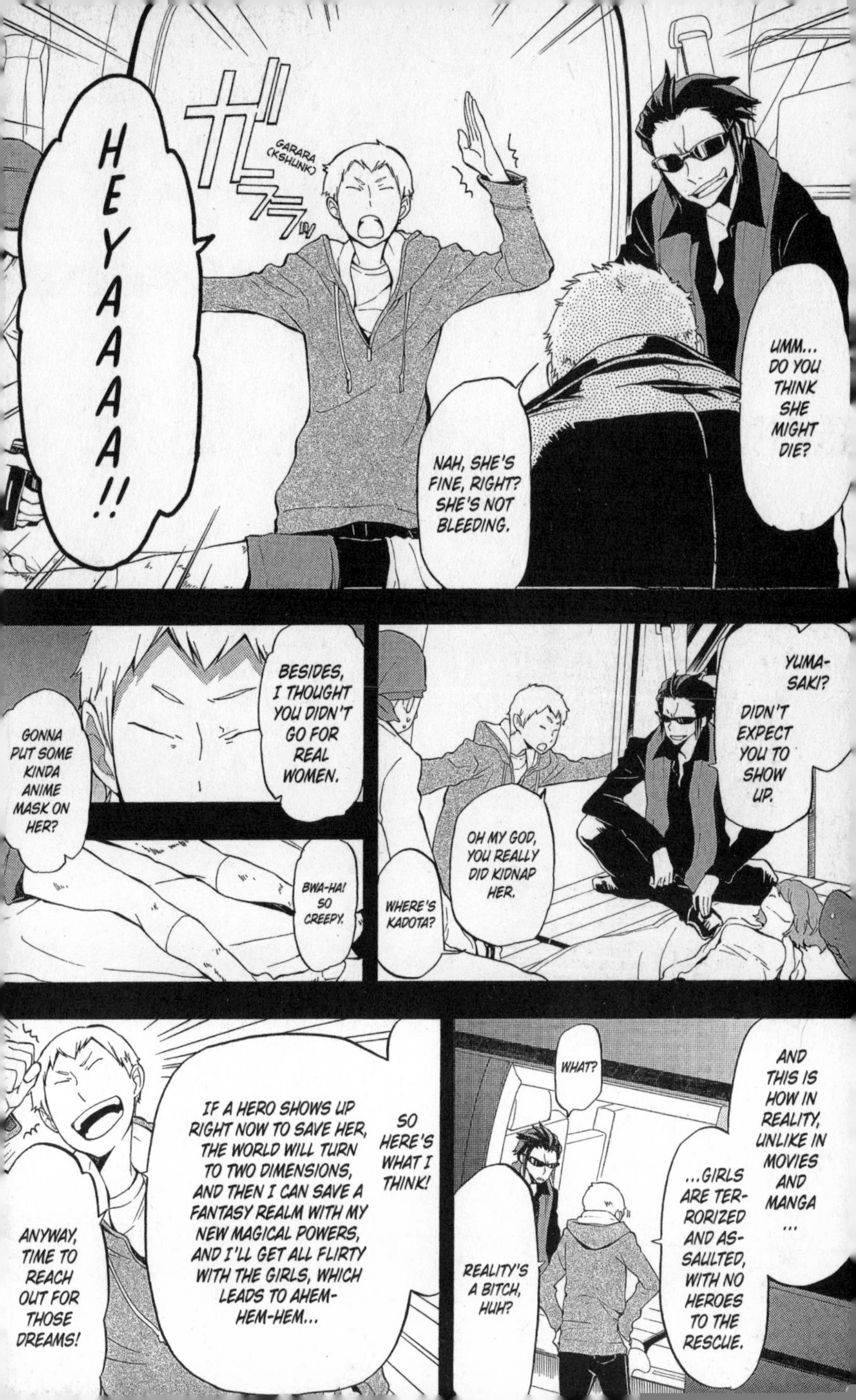
UMM... DO YOU THINK SHE MIGHT DIE?
NAH, SHE'S FINE, RIGHT? SHE'S NOT BLEEDING.
GARARA (KSHUNK)
HEYAAAAA!!
YUMASAKI? DIDN'T EXPECT YOU TO SHOW UP.
OH MY GOD, YOU REALLY DID KIDNAP HER.
WHERE'S KADOTA?
BESIDES, I THOUGHT YOU DIDN'T GO FOR REAL WOMEN.
GONNA PUT SOME KINDA ANIME MASK ON HER?
BWA-HA! SO CREEPY.
AND THIS IS HOW IN REALITY, UNLIKE IN MOVIES AND MANGA...
...GIRLS ARE TERRORIZED AND ASSAULTED, WITH NO HEROES TO THE RESCUE.
WHAT?
REALITY'S A BITCH, HUH?
SO HERE'S WHAT I THINK!
IF A HERO SHOWS UP RIGHT NOW TO SAVE HER, THE WORLD WILL TURN TO TWO DIMENSIONS, AND THEN I CAN SAVE A FANTASY REALM WITH MY NEW MAGICAL POWERS, AND I'LL GET ALL FLIRTY WITH THE GIRLS, WHICH LEADS TO AHEM-HEM-HEM...
ANYWAY, TIME TO REACH OUT FOR THOSE DREAMS!

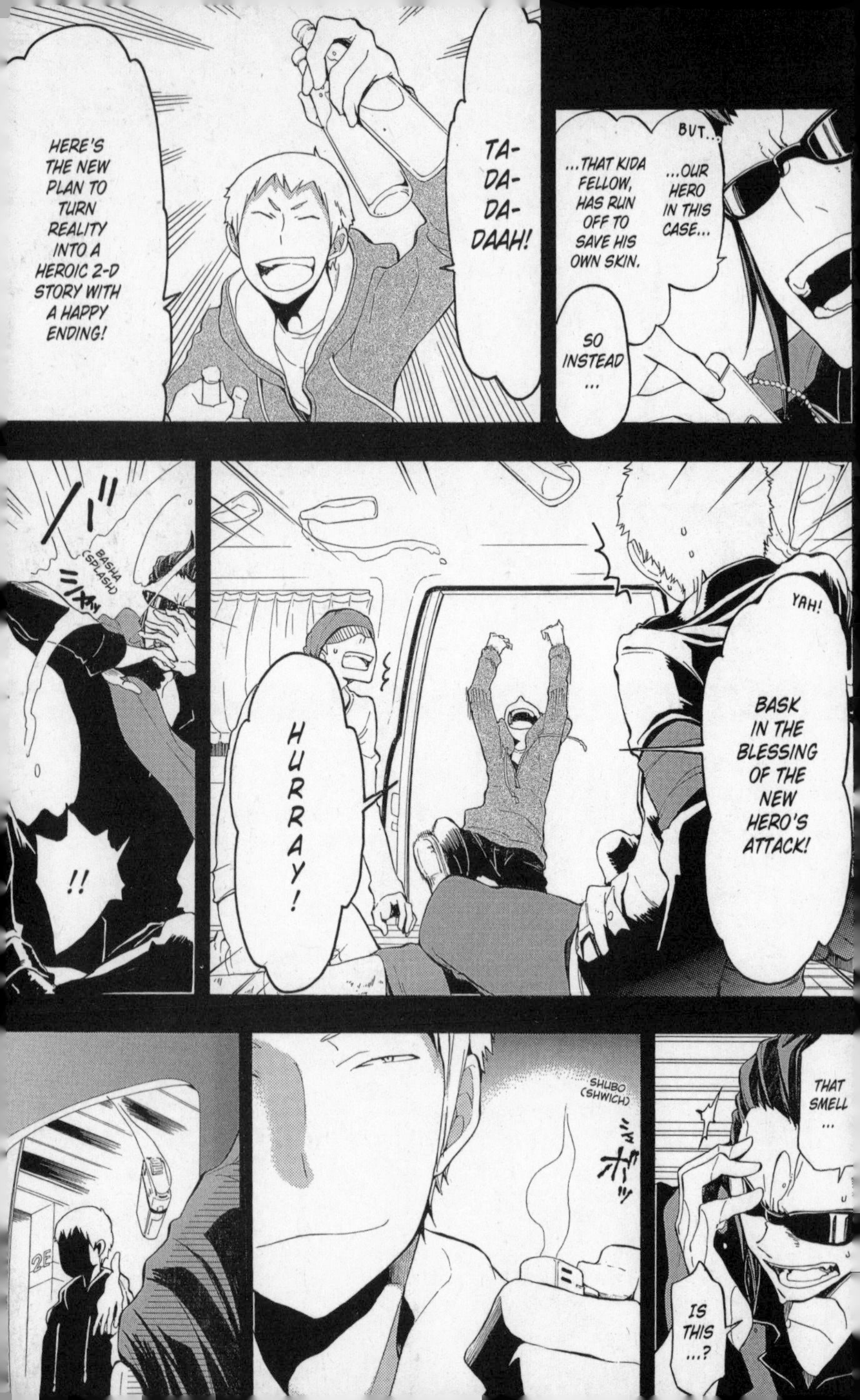
BUT...
...OUR HERO IN THIS CASE...
...THAT KIDA FELLOW, HAS RUN OFF TO SAVE HIS OWN SKIN.
SO INSTEAD ...
TA-DA-DA-DAAH!
HERE'S THE NEW PLAN TO TURN REALITY INTO A HEROIC 2-D STORY WITH A HAPPY ENDING!
YAH!
BASK IN THE BLESSING OF THE NEW HERO'S ATTACK!
HURRAY!
BASHA (SPLASH)
!!
THAT SMELL ...
IS THIS ...?
SHUBO (SHWICH)
2E

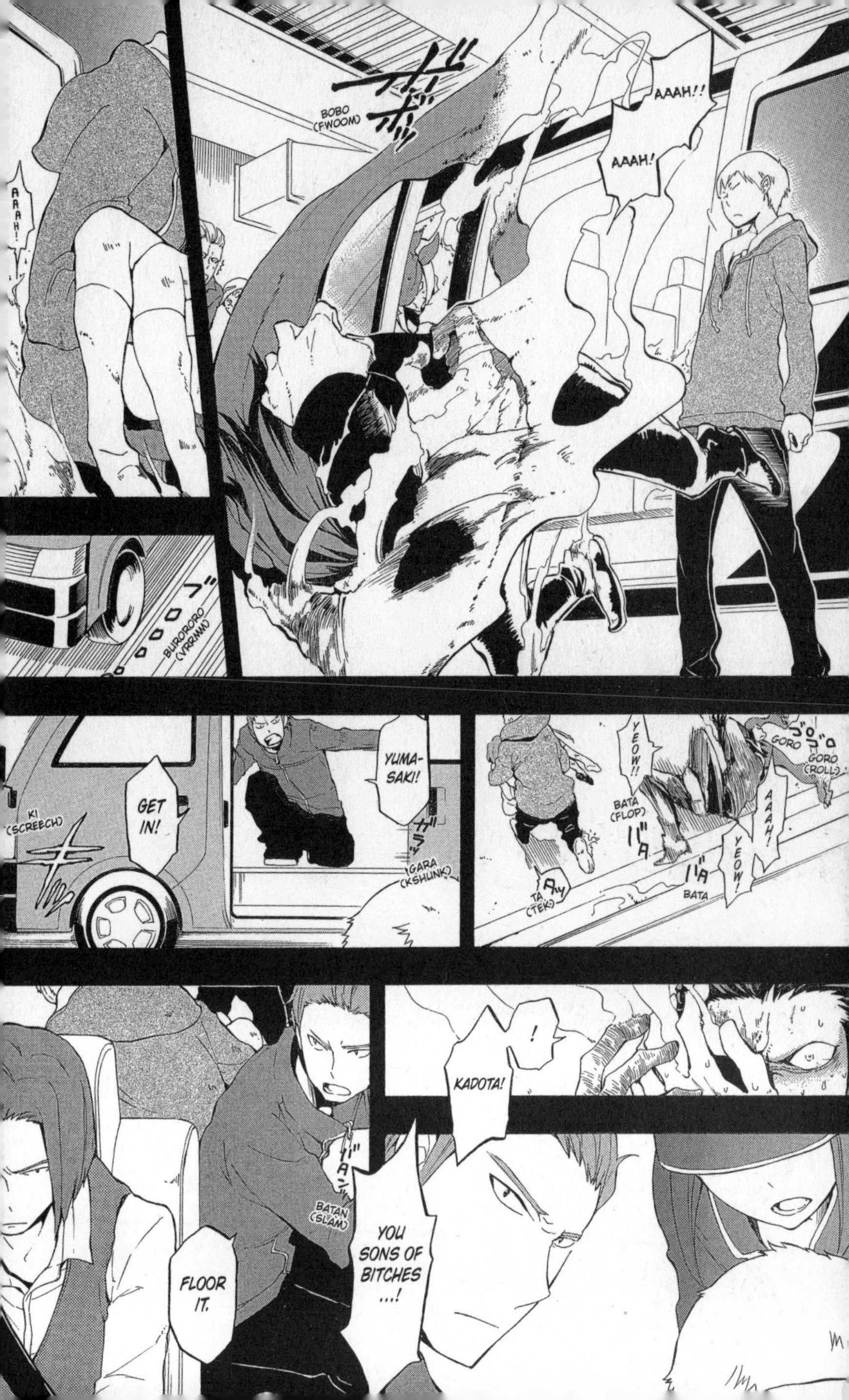
AAAH!!
AAAH!
BOBO (FWOOM)
AAAH!
BURORORO (VRRMM)
GORO GORO (ROLL)
YEOW!!
AAAH!
BATA (FLOP)
YEOW!
BATA
TA (TEK)
YUMA-SAKI!
GARA (KSHUNK)
GET IN!
KI (SCREECH)
!
KADOTA!
YOU SONS OF BITCHES ...!
BATAN (SLAM)
FLOOR IT.

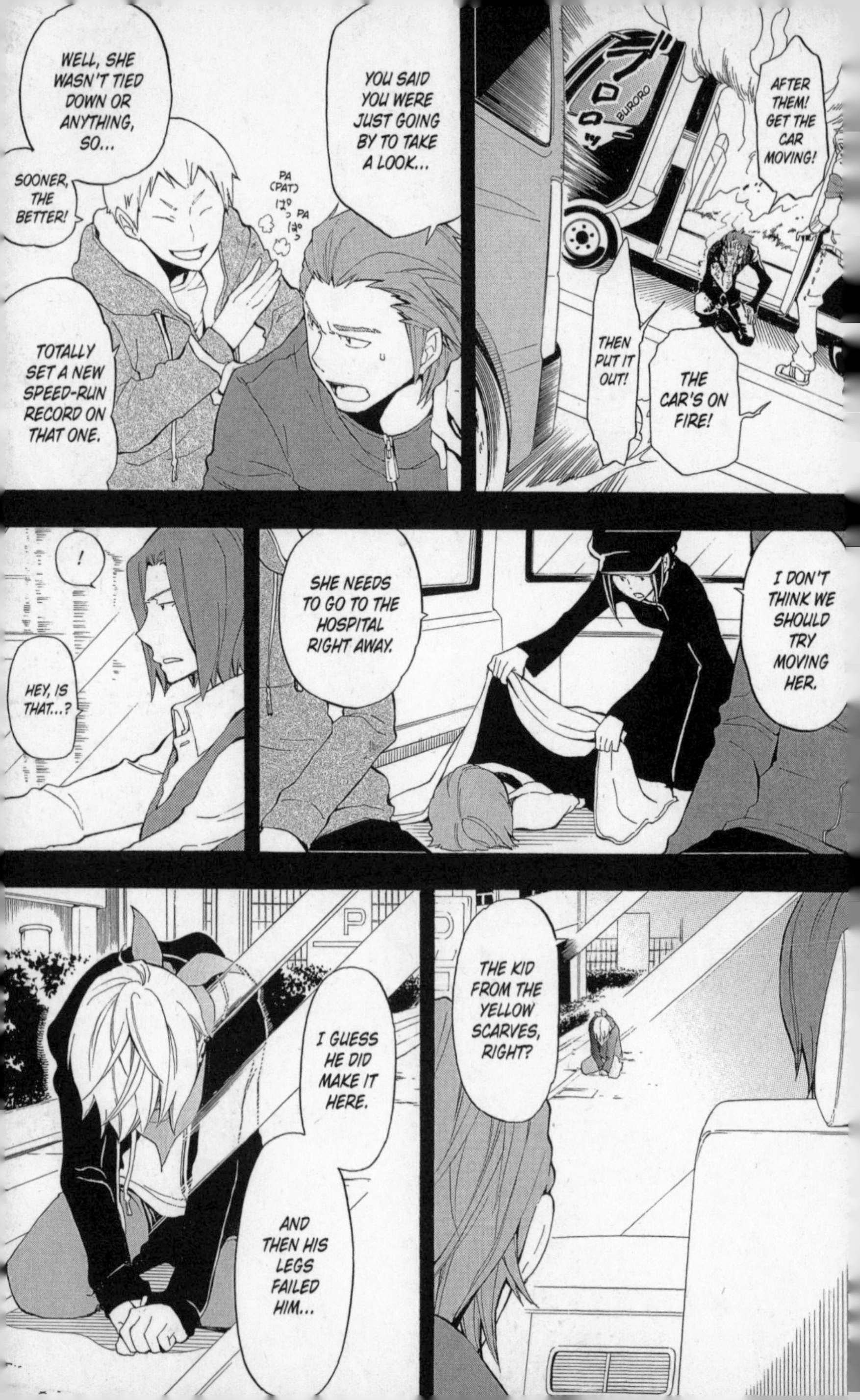
AFTER THEM! GET THE CAR MOVING!
BURORO
THE CAR'S ON FIRE!
THEN PUT IT OUT!
YOU SAID YOU WERE JUST GOING BY TO TAKE A LOOK...
PA (PAT) PA
WELL, SHE WASN'T TIED DOWN OR ANYTHING, SO...
SOONER, THE BETTER!
TOTALLY SET A NEW SPEED-RUN RECORD ON THAT ONE.
I DON'T THINK WE SHOULD TRY MOVING HER.
SHE NEEDS TO GO TO THE HOSPITAL RIGHT AWAY.
!
HEY, IS THAT...?
THE KID FROM THE YELLOW SCARVES, RIGHT?
I GUESS HE DID MAKE IT HERE.
AND THEN HIS LEGS FAILED HIM...

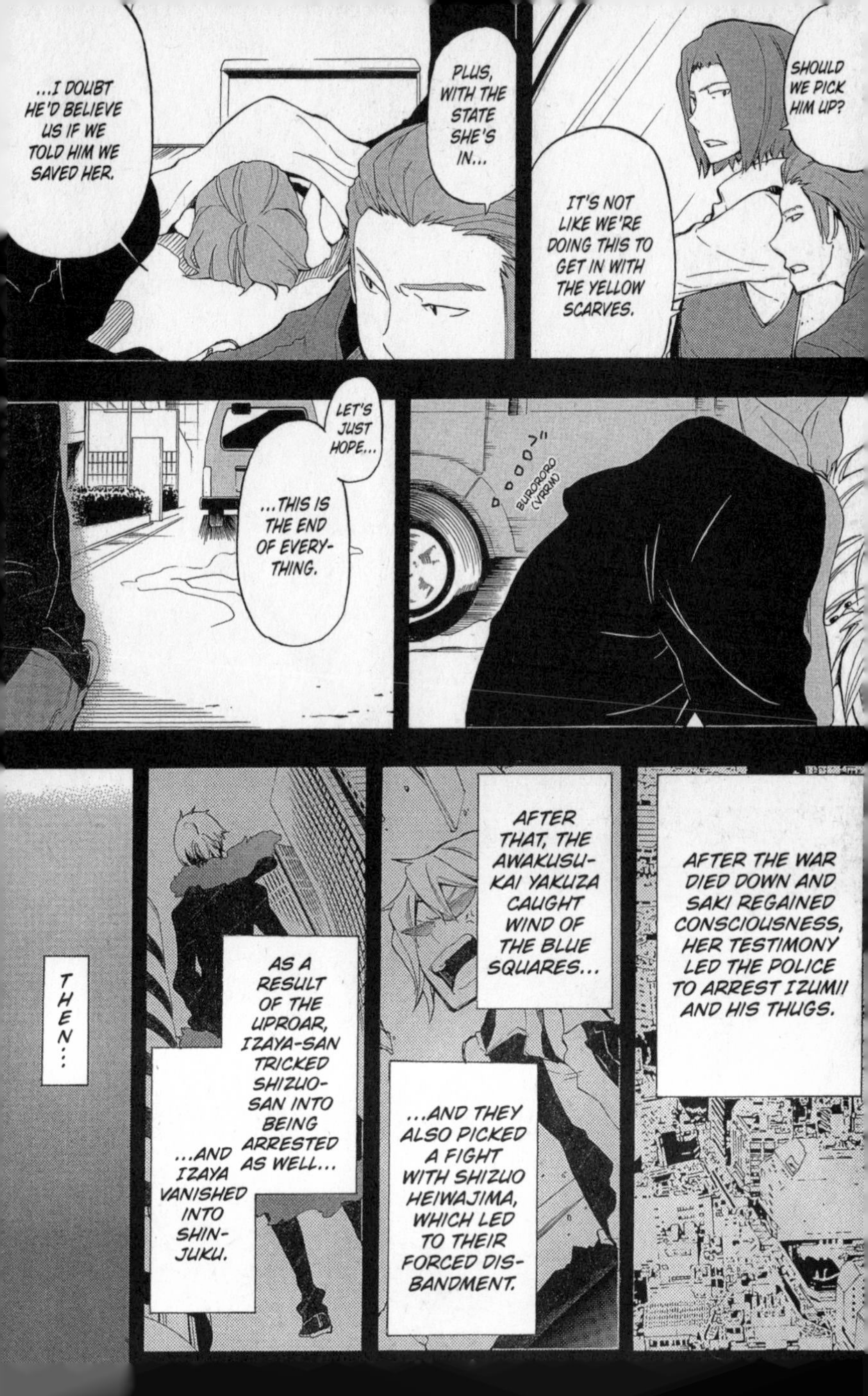
SHOULD WE PICK HIM UP?
IT'S NOT LIKE WE'RE DOING THIS TO GET IN WITH THE YELLOW SCARVES.
PLUS, WITH THE STATE SHE'S IN...
...I DOUBT HE'D BELIEVE US IF WE TOLD HIM WE SAVED HER.
BURORORO (VRRM)
LET'S JUST HOPE...
...THIS IS THE END OF EVERY-THING.
AFTER THE WAR DIED DOWN AND SAKI REGAINED CONSCIOUSNESS, HER TESTIMONY LED THE POLICE TO ARREST IZUMII AND HIS THUGS.
AFTER THAT, THE AWAKUSU-KAI YAKUZA CAUGHT WIND OF THE BLUE SQUARES...
...AND THEY ALSO PICKED A FIGHT WITH SHIZUO HEIWAJIMA, WHICH LED TO THEIR FORCED DIS-BANDMENT.
AS A RESULT OF THE UPROAR, IZAYA-SAN TRICKED SHIZUO-SAN INTO BEING ARRESTED AS WELL...
...AND IZAYA VANISHED INTO SHIN-JUKU.
THEN...

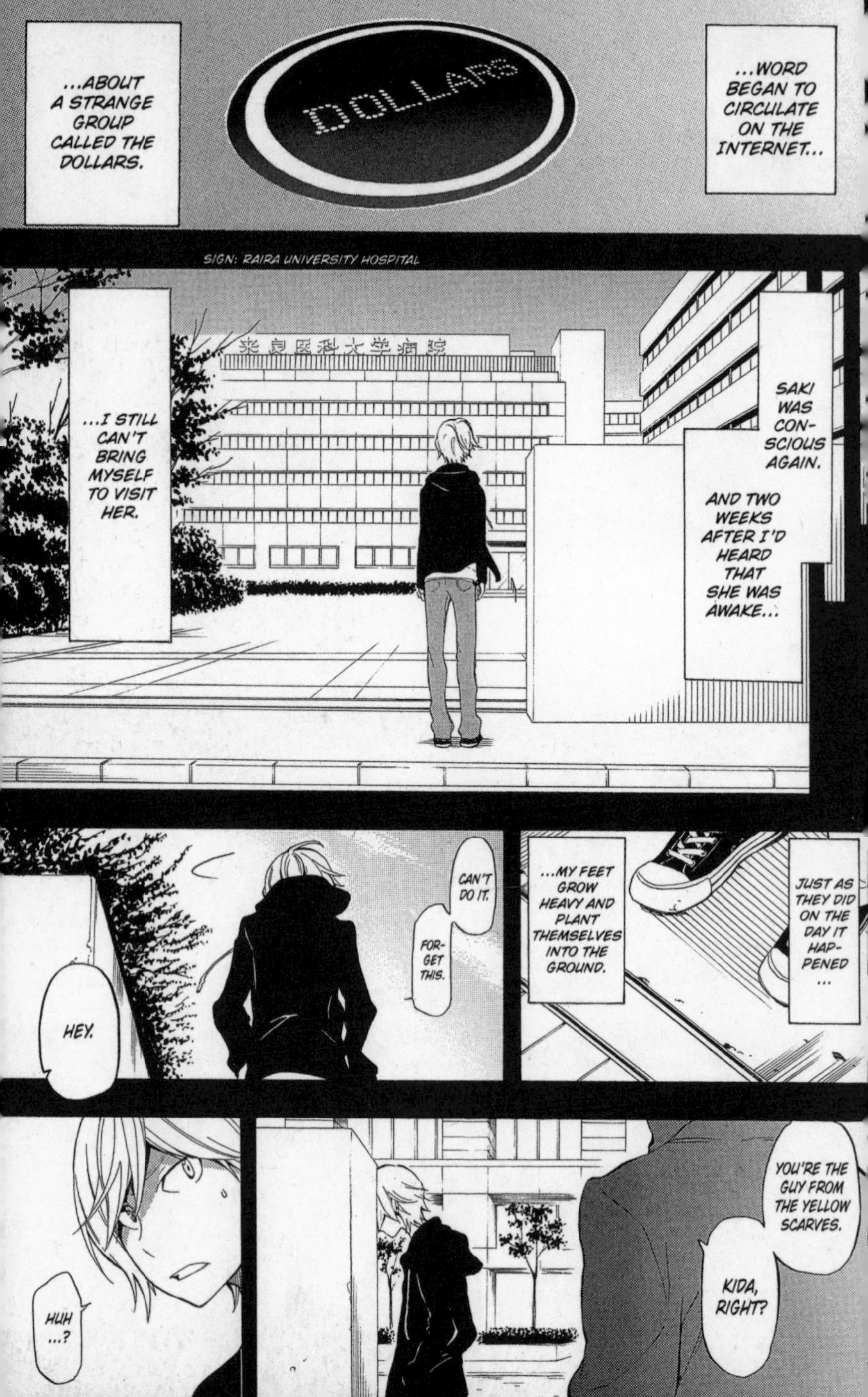
...WORD BEGAN TO CIRCULATE ON THE INTERNET...
DOLLARS
...ABOUT A STRANGE GROUP CALLED THE DOLLARS.
SIGN: RAIRA UNIVERSITY HOSPITAL
SAKI WAS CON-SCIOUS AGAIN.
AND TWO WEEKS AFTER I'D HEARD THAT SHE WAS AWAKE...
...I STILL CAN'T BRING MYSELF TO VISIT HER.
JUST AS THEY DID ON THE DAY IT HAP-PENED...
...MY FEET GROW HEAVY AND PLANT THEMSELVES INTO THE GROUND.
CAN'T DO IT.
FOR-GET THIS.
HEY.
YOU'RE THE GUY FROM THE YELLOW SCARVES.
KIDA, RIGHT?
HUH ...?

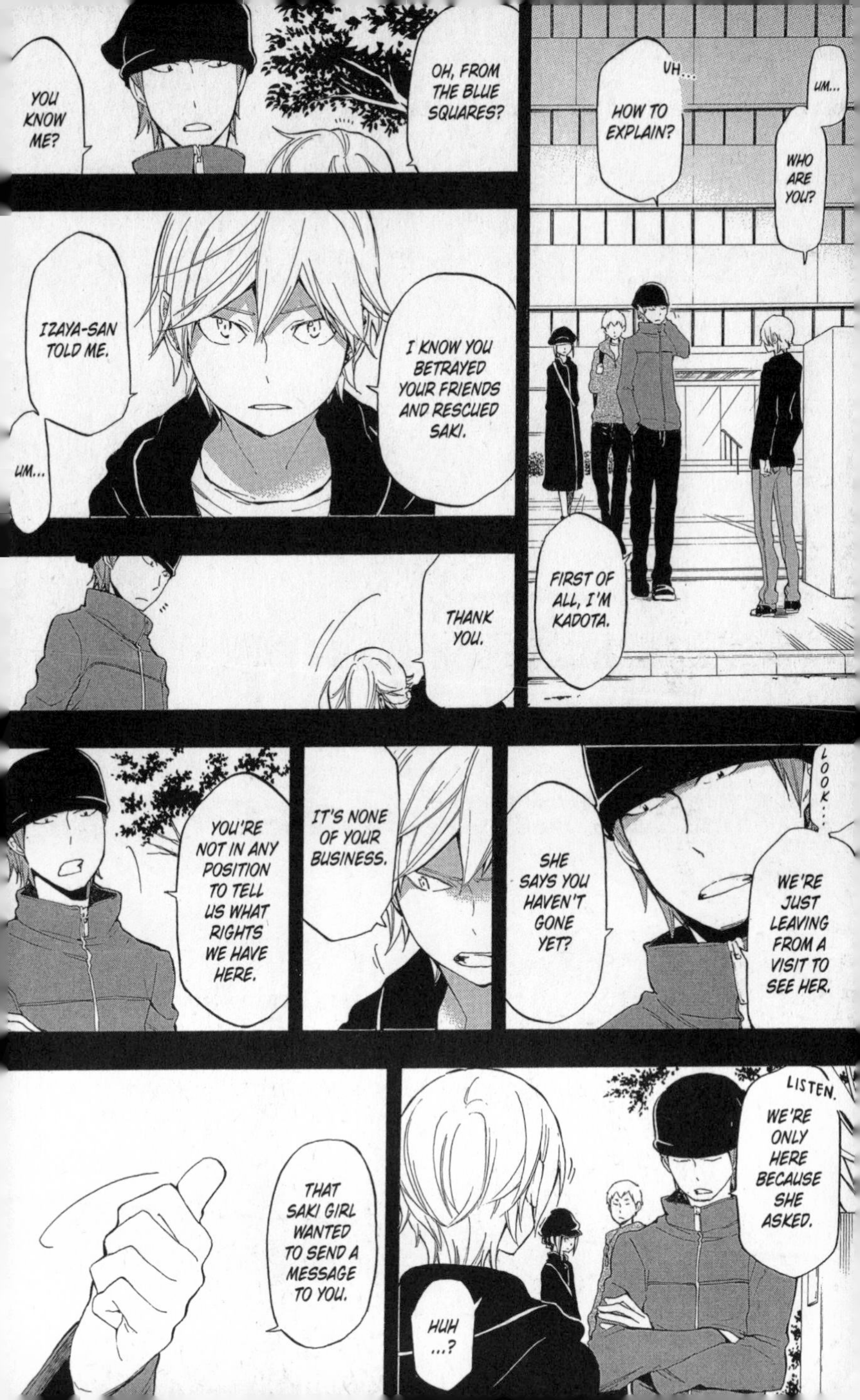
UM...
WHO ARE YOU?
UH...
HOW TO EXPLAIN?
FIRST OF ALL, I'M KADOTA.
OH, FROM THE BLUE SQUARES?
YOU KNOW ME?
I KNOW YOU BETRAYED YOUR FRIENDS AND RESCUED SAKI.
IZAYA-SAN TOLD ME.
UM...
THANK YOU.
LOOK...
WE'RE JUST LEAVING FROM A VISIT TO SEE HER.
SHE SAYS YOU HAVEN'T GONE YET?
IT'S NONE OF YOUR BUSINESS.
YOU'RE NOT IN ANY POSITION TO TELL US WHAT RIGHTS WE HAVE HERE.
LISTEN.
WE'RE ONLY HERE BECAUSE SHE ASKED.
HUH ...?
THAT SAKI GIRL WANTED TO SEND A MESSAGE TO YOU.

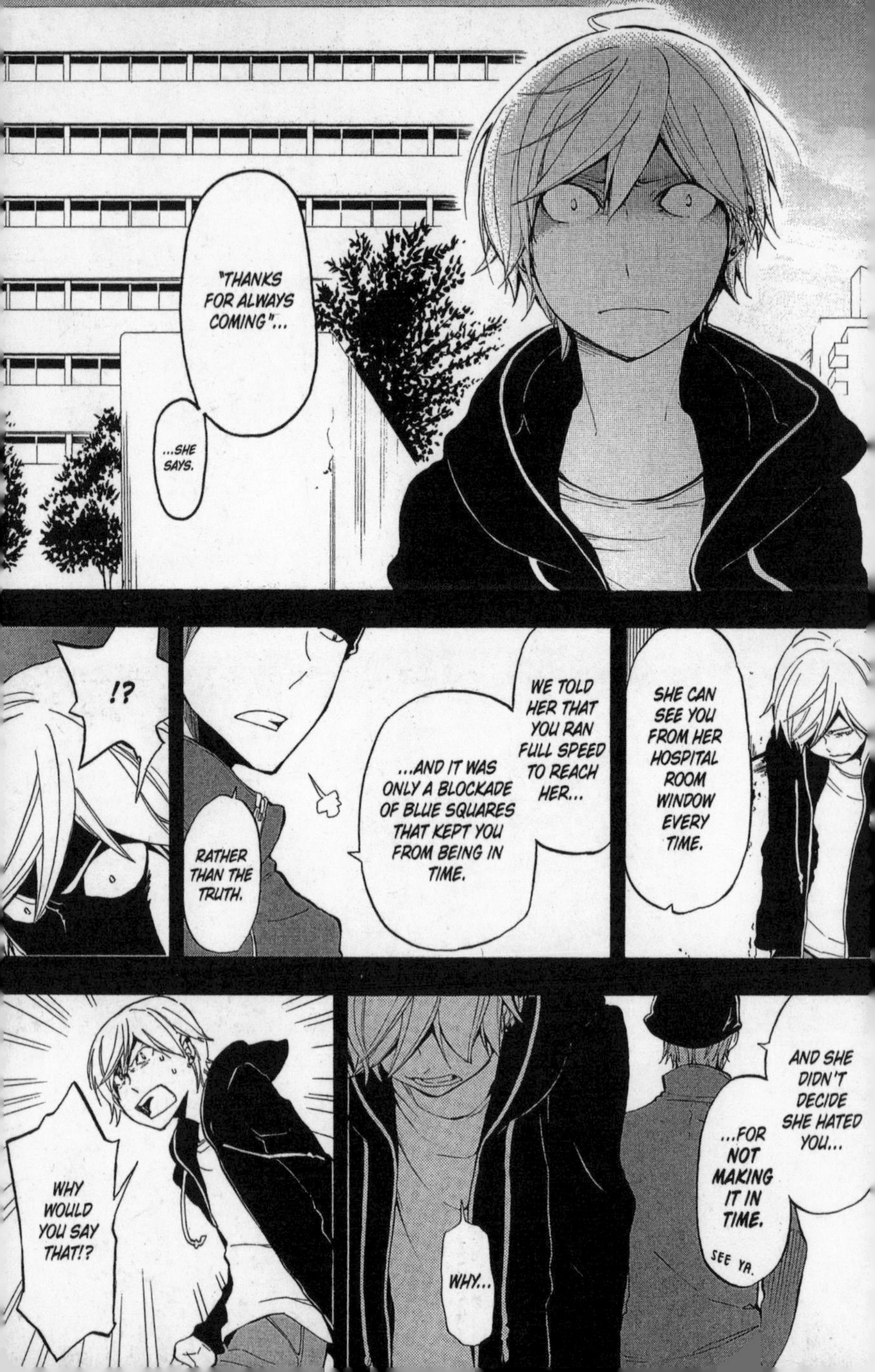
"THANKS FOR ALWAYS COMING"...
...SHE SAYS.
SHE CAN SEE YOU FROM HER HOSPITAL ROOM WINDOW EVERY TIME.
WE TOLD HER THAT YOU RAN FULL SPEED TO REACH HER...
...AND IT WAS ONLY A BLOCKADE OF BLUE SQUARES THAT KEPT YOU FROM BEING IN TIME.
RATHER THAN THE TRUTH.
!?
AND SHE DIDN'T DECIDE SHE HATED YOU...
...FOR NOT MAKING IT IN TIME.
SEE YA.
WHY...
WHY WOULD YOU SAY THAT!?

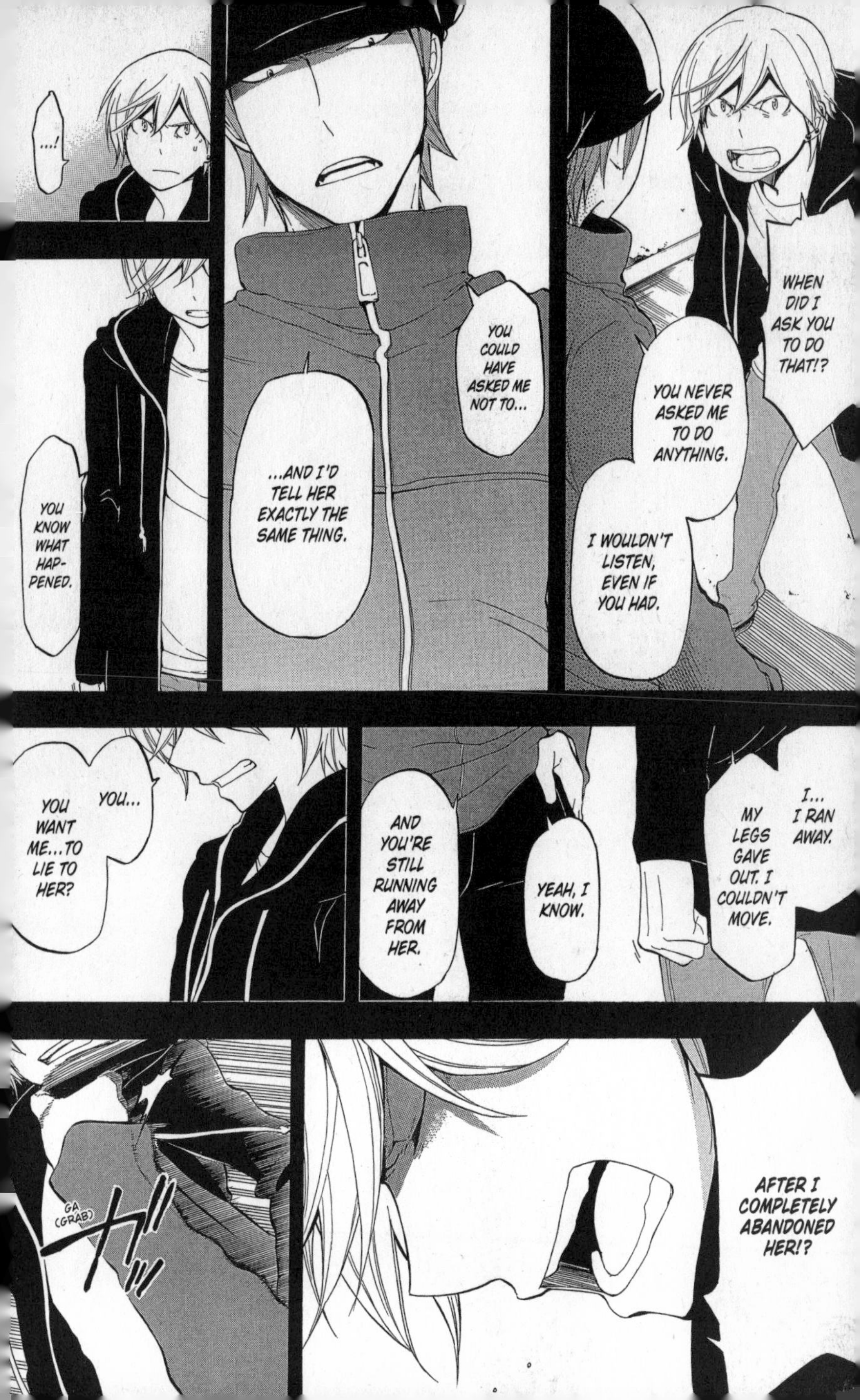
WHEN DID I ASK YOU TO DO THAT!?
YOU NEVER ASKED ME TO DO ANYTHING.
I WOULDN'T LISTEN, EVEN IF YOU HAD.
YOU COULD HAVE ASKED ME NOT TO...
...AND I'D TELL HER EXACTLY THE SAME THING.
...!
YOU KNOW WHAT HAP-PENED.
I... I RAN AWAY.
MY LEGS GAVE OUT. I COULDN'T MOVE.
YEAH, I KNOW.
AND YOU'RE STILL RUNNING AWAY FROM HER.
YOU...
YOU WANT ME...TO LIE TO HER?
AFTER I COMPLETELY ABANDONED HER!?
GA (GRAB)

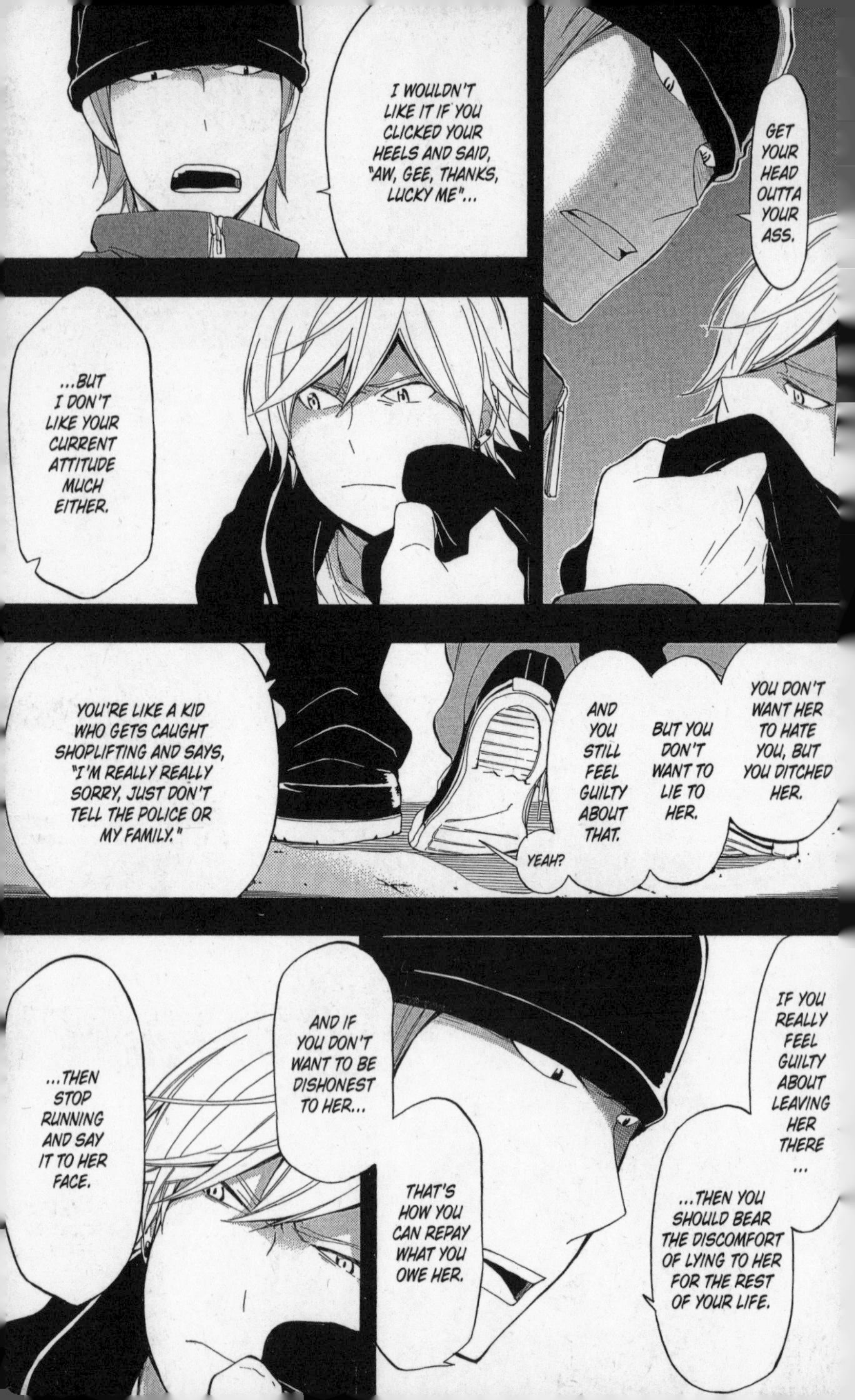
GET YOUR HEAD OUTTA YOUR ASS.
I WOULDN'T LIKE IT IF YOU CLICKED YOUR HEELS AND SAID, "AW, GEE, THANKS, LUCKY ME"...
...BUT I DON'T LIKE YOUR CURRENT ATTITUDE MUCH EITHER.
YOU DON'T WANT HER TO HATE YOU, BUT YOU DITCHED HER.
BUT YOU DON'T WANT TO LIE TO HER.
AND YOU STILL FEEL GUILTY ABOUT THAT.
YEAH?
YOU'RE LIKE A KID WHO GETS CAUGHT SHOPLIFTING AND SAYS, "I'M REALLY REALLY SORRY, JUST DON'T TELL THE POLICE OR MY FAMILY."
IF YOU REALLY FEEL GUILTY ABOUT LEAVING HER THERE...
...THEN YOU SHOULD BEAR THE DISCOMFORT OF LYING TO HER FOR THE REST OF YOUR LIFE.
AND IF YOU DON'T WANT TO BE DISHONEST TO HER...
...THEN STOP RUNNING AND SAY IT TO HER FACE.
THAT'S HOW YOU CAN REPAY WHAT YOU OWE HER.

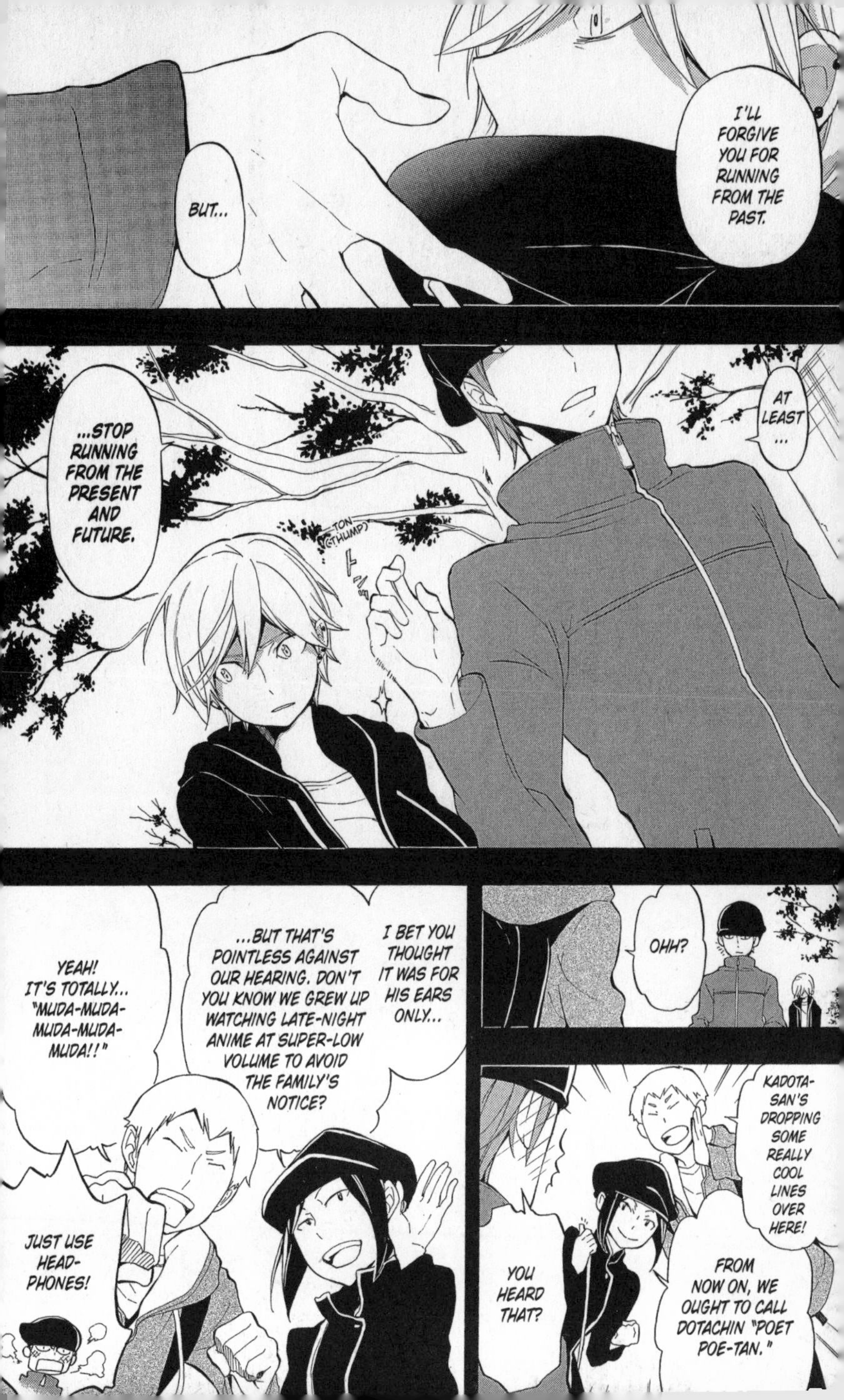

I'LL FORGIVE YOU FOR RUNNING FROM THE PAST.
BUT...
AT LEAST...
...STOP RUNNING FROM THE PRESENT AND FUTURE.
TON (THUMP)
OHH?
KADOTA-SAN'S DROPPING SOME REALLY COOL LINES OVER HERE!
FROM NOW ON, WE OUGHT TO CALL DOTACHIN "POET POE-TAN."
YOU HEARD THAT?
I BET YOU THOUGHT IT WAS FOR HIS EARS ONLY...
...BUT THAT'S POINTLESS AGAINST OUR HEARING. DON'T YOU KNOW WE GREW UP WATCHING LATE-NIGHT ANIME AT SUPER-LOW VOLUME TO AVOID THE FAMILY'S NOTICE?
YEAH! IT'S TOTALLY... "MUDA-MUDA-MUDA-MUDA-MUDA!!"
JUST USE HEAD-PHONES!

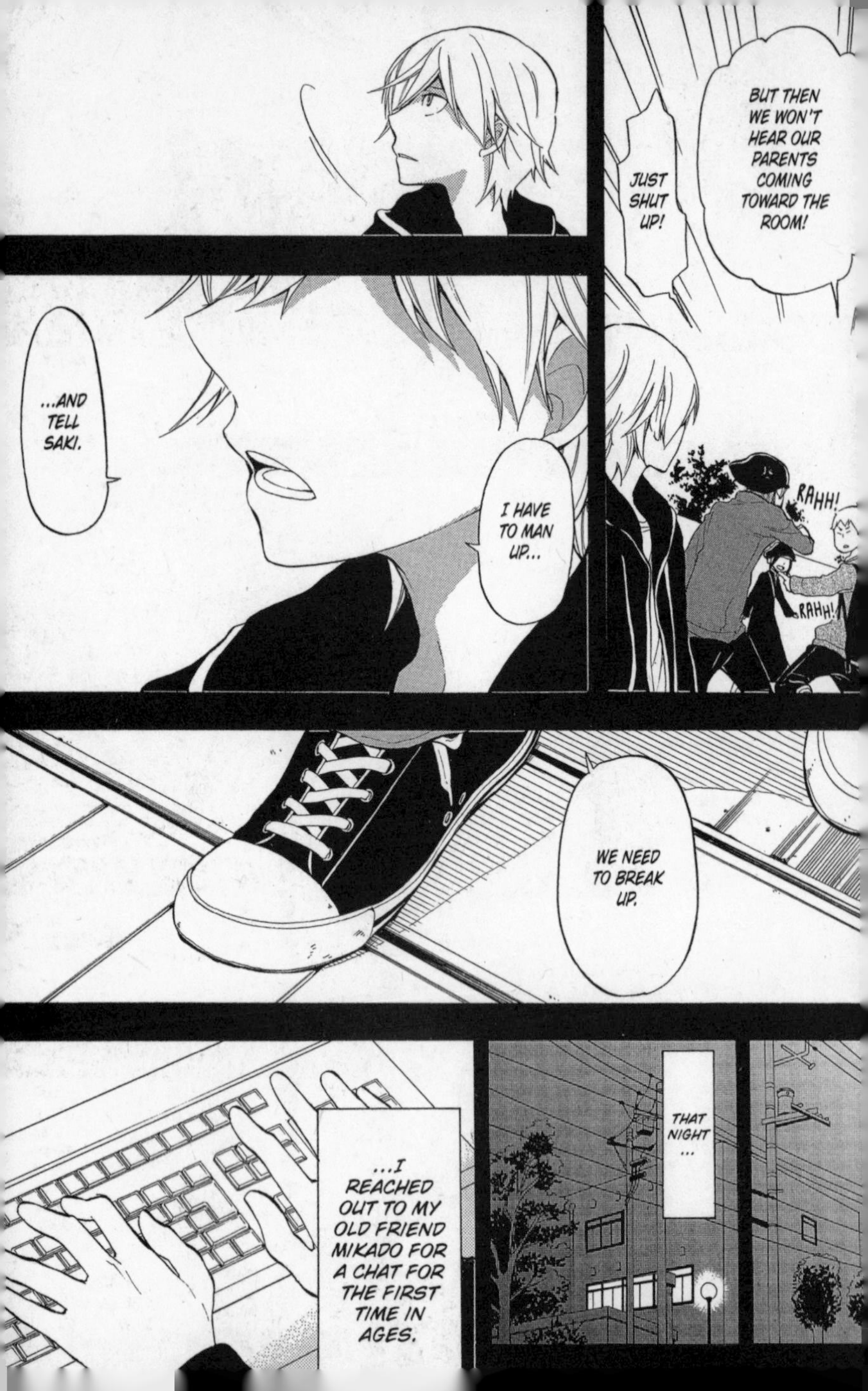
BUT THEN WE WON'T HEAR OUR PARENTS COMING TOWARD THE ROOM!
JUST SHUT UP!
RAHH!
RAHH!
I HAVE TO MAN UP...
...AND TELL SAKI.
WE NEED TO BREAK UP.
THAT NIGHT...
...I REACHED OUT TO MY OLD FRIEND MIKADO FOR A CHAT FOR THE FIRST TIME IN AGES.

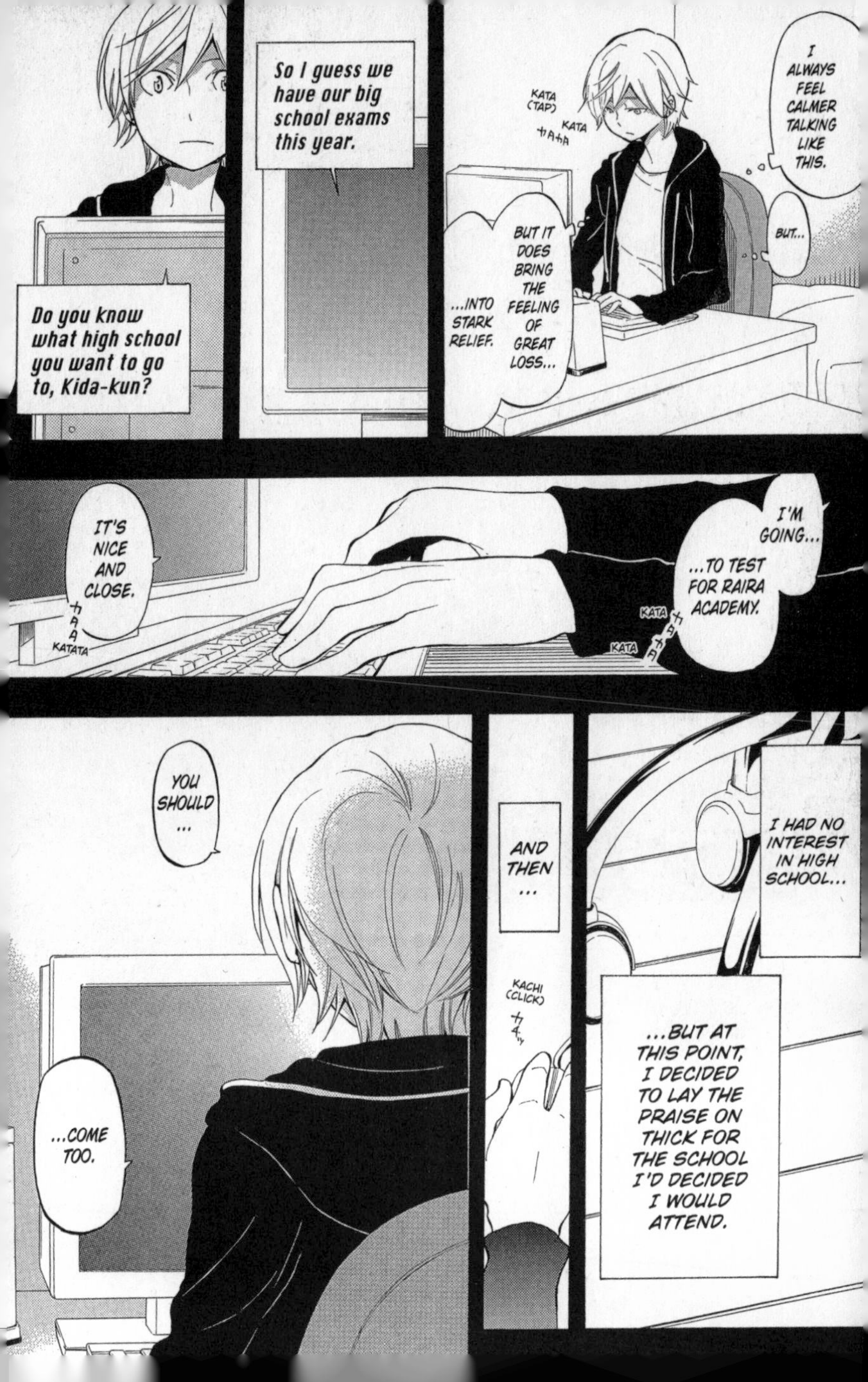
I ALWAYS FEEL CALMER TALKING LIKE THIS.
KATA (TAP)
KATA
BUT...
BUT IT DOES BRING THE FEELING OF GREAT LOSS...
...INTO STARK RELIEF.
So I guess we have our big school exams this year.
Do you know what high school you want to go to, Kida-kun?
I'M GOING...
...TO TEST FOR RAIRA ACADEMY.
KATA
KATA
IT'S NICE AND CLOSE.
KATATA
I HAD NO INTEREST IN HIGH SCHOOL...
...BUT AT THIS POINT, I DECIDED TO LAY THE PRAISE ON THICK FOR THE SCHOOL I'D DECIDED I WOULD ATTEND.
KACHI (CLICK)
AND THEN...
YOU SHOULD...
...COME TOO.

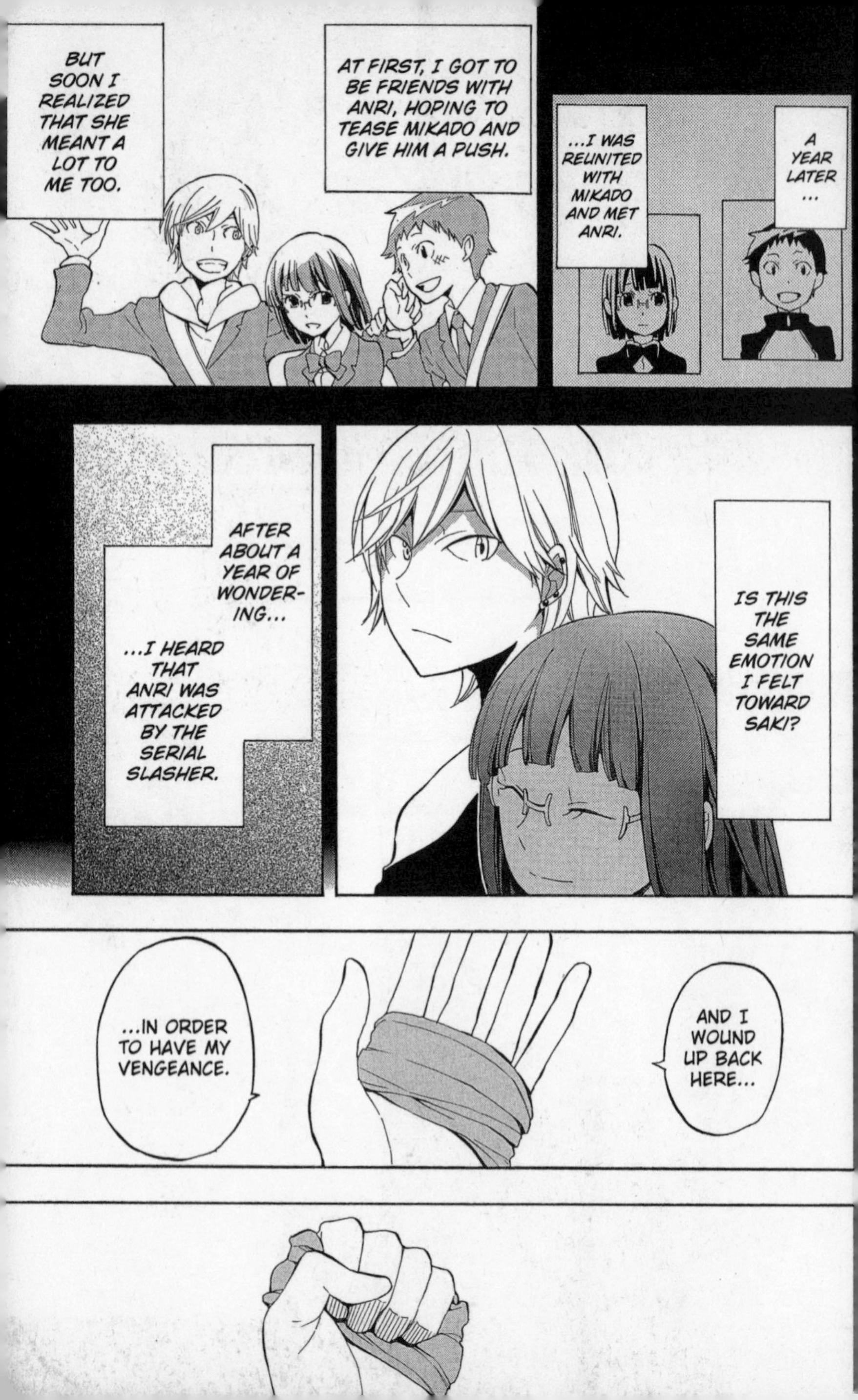
A YEAR LATER...
...I WAS REUNITED WITH MIKADO AND MET ANRI.
AT FIRST, I GOT TO BE FRIENDS WITH ANRI, HOPING TO TEASE MIKADO AND GIVE HIM A PUSH.
BUT SOON I REALIZED THAT SHE MEANT A LOT TO ME TOO.
IS THIS THE SAME EMOTION I FELT TOWARD SAKI?
AFTER ABOUT A YEAR OF WONDER-ING...
...I HEARD THAT ANRI WAS ATTACKED BY THE SERIAL SLASHER.
AND I WOUND UP BACK HERE...
...IN ORDER TO HAVE MY VENGEANCE.

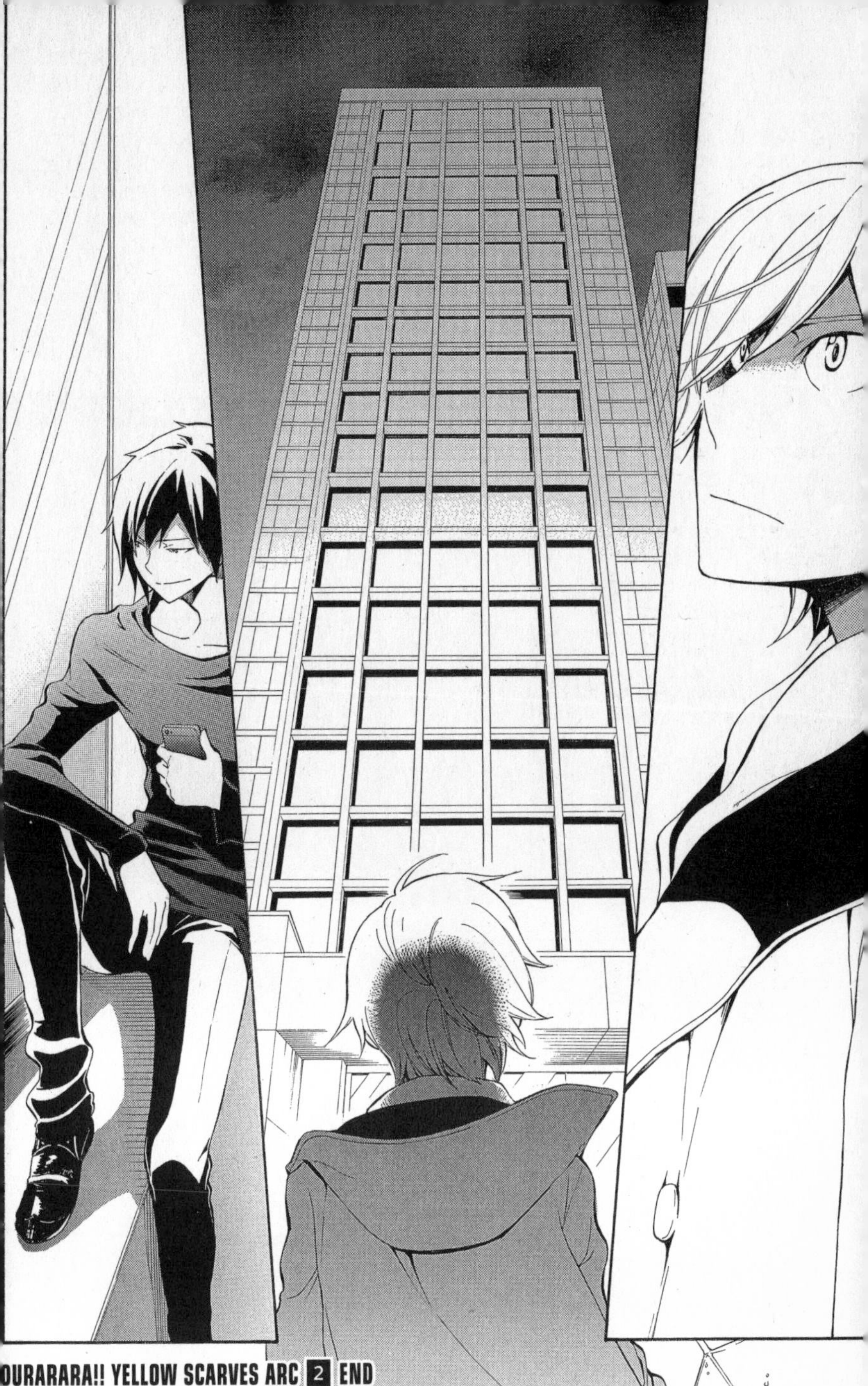

DURARARA!! YELLOW SCARVES ARC 2 END

Afterword

Every time I read a chapter of Satorigi-san's *Durarara!!*, I am filled with gratitude for her ability to complete the experience by adding expression and atmosphere to the scenes in which I didn't include such details in the text. Just as some things are easier to express in words, some things are easier to show with art, and so I learn many things about the differences between manga and prose every time I read this comic adaptation.

And with that...congratulations on the release of the second volume of *Durarara!! Yellow Scarves Arc*! .

It seems strange to congratulate someone on a story that I wrote originally, but as I've written in these afterwords before, this comic adaptation is really like a rebirth of my old work. It's like witnessing something half from me and half an entirely different story. It makes me want to celebrate it in a variety of ways.

Just as some things are born, others must come to an end. With the release of the thirteenth volume of my *Durarara!!* novels, the series is over. I'm now writing a new book called *Durarara!! SH* that features the same characters in Ikebukuro, but somewhat changed after two years. Check it out if you're interested! (Japan only)

My endless thanks go to Satorigi-san, our editor Kuma-san, the editorial department at *GFantasy*, and of course, all of you readers for your support!

Thank you so much! I'll see you next time!

Ryohgo Narita

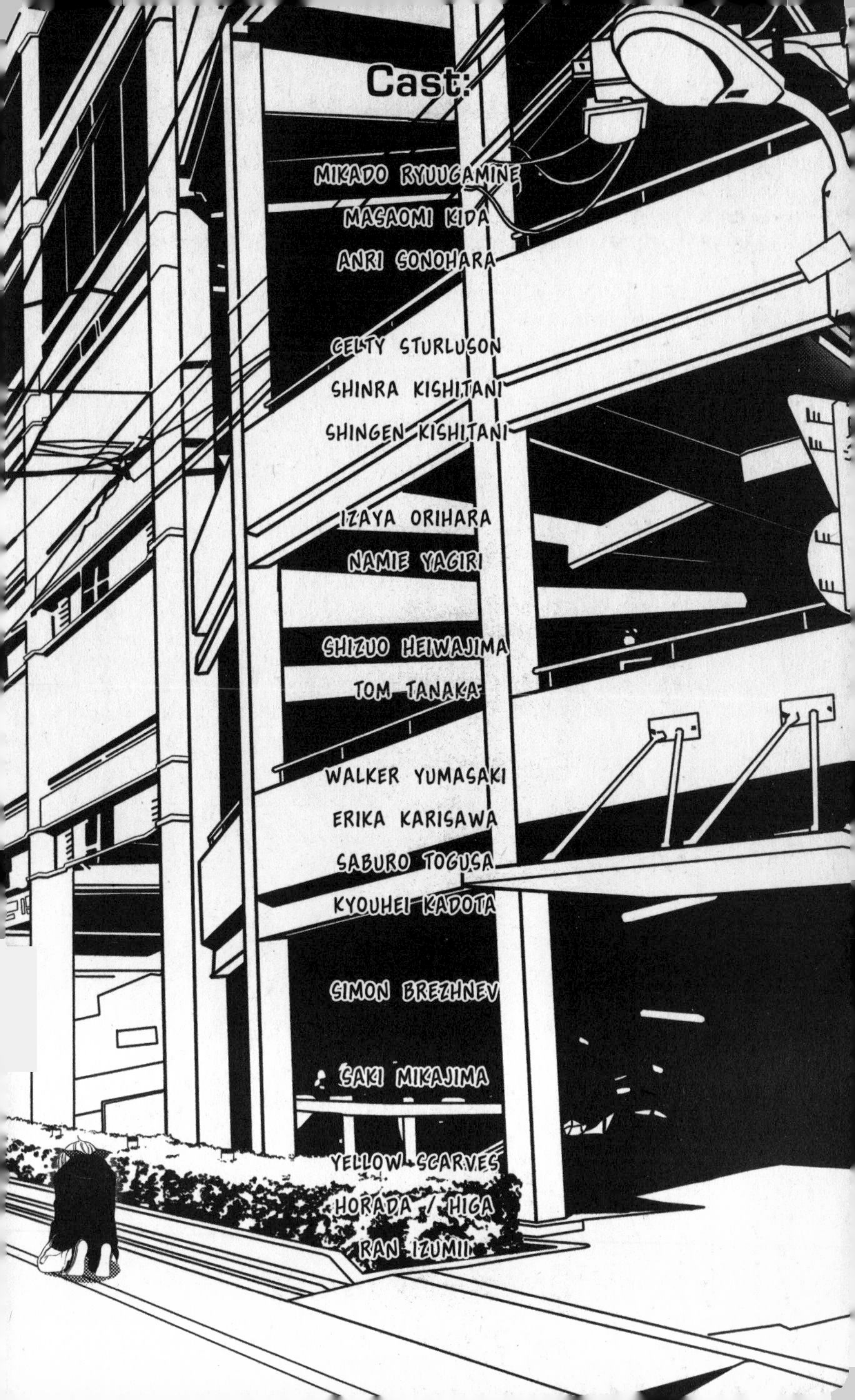
Cast:
MIKADO RYUUGAMINE
MASAOMI KIDA
ANRI SONOHARA
CELTY STURLUSON
SHINRA KISHITANI
SHINGEN KISHITANI
IZAYA ORIHARA
NAMIE YAGIRI
SHIZUO HEIWAJIMA
TOM TANAKA
WALKER YUMASAKI
ERIKA KARISAWA
SABURO TOGUSA
KYOUHEI KADOTA
SIMON BREZHNEV
SAKI MIKAJIMA
YELLOW SCARVES
HORADA / HIGA
RAN IZUMII

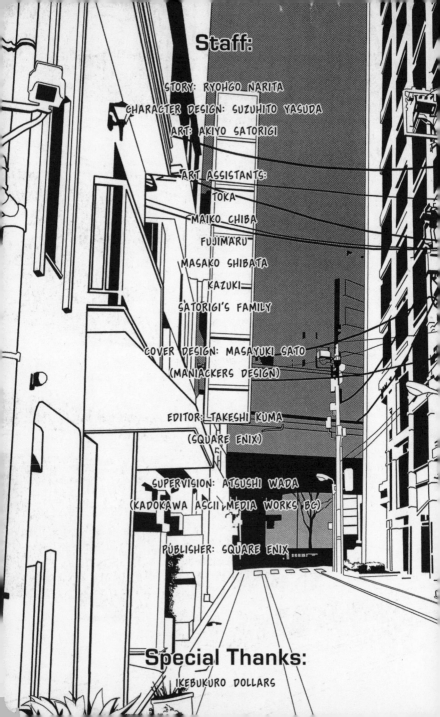

Staff:

STORY: RYOHGO NARITA

CHARACTER DESIGN: SUZUHITO YASUDA

ART: AKIYO SATORIGI

ART ASSISTANTS:

TOKA

MAIKO CHIBA

FUJIMARU

MASAKO SHIBATA

KAZUKI

SATORIGI'S FAMILY

COVER DESIGN: MASAYUKI SATO

(MANIACKERS DESIGN)

EDITOR: TAKESHI KUMA

(SQUARE ENIX)

SUPERVISION: ATSUSHI WADA

(KADOKAWA ASCII MEDIA WORKS BC)

PUBLISHER: SQUARE ENIX

Special Thanks:

IKEBUKURO DOLLARS

TRANSLATION NOTES

PAGE 17

Leanan sídhe: When Celty refers to using a leanan sídhe in her "favorite game series," she is most likely referring to the venerable *Shin Megami Tensei* RPG franchise. The games blend old-school dungeon crawling with a strategic battle system, but their most notable feature is a vast variety of demons that can be tamed and recruited to join the party. Otherworldly spirits and monsters from various mythologies around the world appear in the game, including Irish/Celtic spirits such as the dullahan, leanan sídhe, and leprechaun.

PAGE 111

"Act one": When a mangaka voluntarily ends his or her series in order to work on something different but still hopes to return to their characters someday later, they will typically end the final chapter with "The End — Act One." However, the percentage of mangaka who actually return to the series and resume the story (directly or in the form of a sequel) is actually quite low, which means that Japanese readers are trained to see the "end of act one" as synonymous with "the end, period."

PAGE 162

Toranoana and Animate: Two of the biggest otaku specialty stores in Japan, offering a wide selection of anime merchandise both popular and obscure. Animate is the largest retailer of anime, while Toranoana is more manga-centric, with a vast array of *doujinshi* (fan-created manga) for sale.

PAGE 184

Muda-Muda-Muda: A legendary battle cry from the *JoJo's Bizarre Adventure* manga and anime. Several characters in the *JoJo* universe feature rapid-fire chants when they unleash their most ferocious attacks; for example, Jotaro Kujo, the hero of Part 3 of the series, shouts "Ora-Ora-Ora-Ora!" His archenemy Dio's defensive counterpart is "Muda-Muda-Muda-Muda," which means "useless" or "pointless." These can both be seen as an extension of a trend started by Kenshiro from *Fist of the North Star* (himself based in part on kung fu action heroes like Bruce Lee) and his signature "Ata-ta-ta-ta-ta" scream.

DURARARA!!

ORRR!!

DURARARA!!
YELLOW SCARVE

Fub?

Translation: Stephen Paul

Lettering: Lys Blakeslee

This book is a work of fiction. Names, characters, places, and incidents are the product of the author's imagination or are used fictitiously. Any resemblance to actual events, locales, or persons, living or dead, is coincidental.

DURARARA!! KOKINZOKU-HEN Vol. 2
© 2014 Ryohgo Narita
© 2014 Akiyo Satorigi / SQUARE ENIX CO., LTD.
Licensed by KADOKAWA CORPORATION ASCII MEDIA WORKS
First published in Japan in 2014 by SQUARE ENIX CO., LTD.
English translation rights arranged with SQUARE ENIX CO., LTD.
and Hachette Book Group through Tuttle-Mori Agency, Inc.

Translation © 2014 by SQUARE ENIX CO., LTD.

All rights reserved. In accordance with the U.S. Copyright Act of 1976, the scanning, uploading, and electronic sharing of any part of this book without the permission of the publisher is unlawful piracy and theft of the author's intellectual property. If you would like to use material from the book (other than for review purposes), prior written permission must be obtained by contacting the publisher at permissions@hbgusa.com. Thank you for your support of the author's rights.

Yen Press
Hachette Book Group
1290 Avenue of the Americas
New York, NY 10104

www.HachetteBookGroup.com
www.YenPress.com

Yen Press is an imprint of Hachette Book Group, Inc. The Yen Press name and logo are trademarks of Hachette Book Group, Inc.

First Yen Press Edition: November 2014

ISBN: 978-0-316-33703-8

10 9 8 7 6 5 4 3 2

BVG

Printed in the United States of America